Colonial Families of York County Virginia

Volume 3

Christopher DeMarco, Ph.D.

HERITAGE BOOKS
2019

HERITAGE BOOKS

AN IMPRINT OF HERITAGE BOOKS, INC.

Books, CDs, and more—Worldwide

For our listing of thousands of titles see our website
at
www.HeritageBooks.com

Published 2019 by
HERITAGE BOOKS, INC.
Publishing Division
5810 Ruatan Street
Berwyn Heights, Md. 20740

Heritage Books by Christopher DeMarco, Ph.D.:
Colonial Families of York County, Virginia
Volumes: 1–3

International Standard Book Number
Paperbound: 978-1-68034-930-6

FOREWORD

By 1617 the Virginia colony had been divided into four Incorporations, Henricus, Charles City, James City, and Kecoughtan. By 1634, Kecoughtan had been renamed Elizabeth City, part of which, along with James City, became Charles River County, one of Virginia's eight original shires (later termed counties). Charles River County was renamed York County in 1643. Portions of York County were added to James City County in 1769 and 1852. Gloucester County was formed from the northeastern section of York County in 1651, and New Kent County was formed from the northwestern part of York County in 1654. Poquoson and Hampton, now independent cities, lie to the south of York County. When reading about York County and vicinity, one should consider all possible phonetic spellings of many names, Poquoson and Kecoughton being two good examples. Also in the records one will find parishes holding the same names as counties, but counties and parishes were run by separate groups to achieve different goals, and the boundaries of counties and parishes are rarely the same. Bell, in the introduction to his *Charles Parish, York County, Virginia History and Registers*, provides a useful discussion of the evolutions of the parishes in and near York County, e.g., Charles, York-Hampton and New Poquoson.

Yorktown, established in 1691, is the site of the famous American Revolution battle and of the subsequent British surrender in 1781. Now York County seat, Yorktown is one corner of the Historic Triangle that also includes Williamsburg and Jamestown. Yorktown, identified closely with the Revolution, was also the site of much activity and turmoil during the Civil War. We are all indebted to Bolivar Shields, clerk of the court, who removed the county records from the courthouse during the Civil War, preventing their destruction.

Volumes I and II of Colonial Families of York County, Virginia also draw on records spanning the period from the early 1600s to approximately 1783. In all three volumes, while emphasis has been placed on using published copies of original records, the views of as many other reasonable interpreters of the historical record are included to give credible possibilities of where to begin to look to strengthen the historical record. This inclusive approach carries the risk of stretching truth, but this approach also enables researchers to get a quick picture of the information and sources available on the subject. The intent here is to promote inductive thinking, giving the reader a platform of facts as well as less tested information. The less solid data become the next set of questions that need to be answered. While each reader selects hypotheses to which they can apply their skills and knowledge in an effort to uncover a progressively more factual picture to better approximate the truth associated with the events, the reader/researcher always needs to remain mindful of how close the record is to the event to judge a record validity. It is hoped that the possibilities presented here spark ideas and challenge readers and researchers to ask and answer new questions advancing our knowledge of the subject.

Christopher DeMarco, Ph.D.
F. Edward Wright

CONTENTS

Foreword iii

Source Abbreviations vii

Other Abbreviations xi

Words used in the Colonial Period xi

Legal Terms used in the Colonial Period xi

The John Baskervyle /Baskerville Family 1

The Henry Borodell Family 16

The Ambrose Cobbs / Cobb Family 22

The John Drewry Family 41

The Ralph Graves Family 54

The William & Charles Grymes Families of York Co. 66

The Edward Grymes Family of Lancaster Co. 72

The Anthony Lamb Family 75

The Gabriel Maupin Family 82

The Thomas Morgan Family 91

The John Overstreet Family 94

The Walter Patrick Family 101

The John Rogers (& John Aduston) Families 111

The Capt. William Rogers Family 127

The Rev. James Sclater Family 139

The Nicholas Sebrell Family 160

The Armiger Wade Family 167

The Thomas Wade Family of James City Co. 174

The Edward Wade Family 178

The Thomas Wade Family of York Co. 179

The John Weldon Family 187

Index 199

AB   Brown, Alexander. 1891. *The Genesis of the United States*, Vol. II. Cambridge: Riverside Press, pp. 1039-1040.

AB2   Brown, Alexander. 1886. New *Views of Early Virginia History, 1606-1619*. Liberty, VA: The Bedford Index, p. 7.

ACS   Payne, Wm. M. 1906. *Mary Stuart by Algernon C. Swinburne*. Boston: D.C. Heath & Co. Pub., p. 257.

APP   Dorman, John Frederick, C.G., F.A.S.G., 2006 (4ᵗʰ Edition). *Adventures of Purse and Person*. Baltimore: Genealogical Publishing Co., Inc.

BAC   Chapman, Blanche Adams. *Wills and Administrations of Isle of Wight County, Virginia, 1647-1800*. Baltimore, MD, USA: Genealogical Publishing Co., 2003.

BF   Fleet, Beverly. *VA Colonial Abstracts III, York County, 1646-1648*; *1648-1657*.

BLD   Bouvier, John. 1856 (6ᵗʰ Ed.). *A Law Dictionary: Adapted to the Constitution and Laws of the United States of America and of the Several States of the American Union.* (Also called *Bouvier Law Dictionary*)

BP   Vogt, John (Editor). 2004. *Bruton Parish Virginia Register, 1662-1797*. Athens, GA: New Papyrus Publishing, 2004.

BR   Barton, R. T. (Editor). 1909. *The Reports by Sir John Randoph and Edward Barradall of the General Court of Virginia, 1728-1741*, Vol. 1. Boston, MA: The Boston Book Company.

CB   Bardsley, Charles Wareing Endell. 1901. *A Dictionary of English and Welsh Surnames with Special American Instances.* London: H. Frowde.

CCC   *Charles City County, VA, Records 1737-1774*, page 51 by Benjamin B. Weisiger, III, citing original page 451; pub. by Iberian Publishing Co.

CCPR   National Society of the Colonial Dames of America in the Commonwealth of VA. 1897. *Parish Register of Christ Church,*

Middlesex County, Virginia from 1653 to 1812. Richmond, VA: Christ Church.

CD186 Family History: VA Genealogies #2, 1600s-1800s, *Genealogies of Virginia Families, Vol. II,* he Armistead Family of America and he Lamb Family of America, Broderbund Software, Inc., Banner Blue Division.

CD503 Virginia Colonial Records, 1600s-1700s, Genealogical Publishing Co., Inc. yFamily.com.

CD509 Family Archive Viewer, CD509, *North Carolina Wills, 1665-1900, Surnames E-F,* MyFamily.com, Inc.

CP I Nugent, Nell Marion. 1963 (2nd Edition). *Cavaliers and Pioneers: Abstracts of Virginia Land Patents and Grants, 1623-1666,* Vol. I. Baltimore: Genealogical Publishing Co., Inc.

CP III Nugent, Nell Marion. 1979. *Cavaliers and Pioneers, 1695-1732,* Vol. III. Baltimore: Genealogical Publishing Co., Inc.

CPR Bell, Landon C. 1996 (3rd Edition). *Charles Parish, York County, Virginia, History and Registers.* Richmond: Library of Virginia.

CVR Glover, William and Mary Newton Stanard. 1902. *The Colonial Virginia Register: A list of Governors, Councillors and Other Higher Officials, and also of Members of the House of Burgesses, and the Revolutionary Conventions of the Colony of Virginia.* Albany, NY: Joel Munsell's Sons, Publishers.

CWFN Levy, Philip & Marley R. Brown III. 2000. *Nassau Street Site Summer 1999 Excavations.* Williamsburg, VA: The Colonial Williamsburg Foundation, http://research.history.org/Files/Archaeo/MajorStudies/Nassau%20Stre et%20Ordinary.pdf

DW Dorman, John Frederick. *York County, Virginia, Deeds, Orders, Wills, Etc., 1687-1697.* Lewes, DE: Colonial Roots.

EVB Tyler, Lewis Gardiner. 1915. *Encyclopedia of Virginia Biography,* Vols. I, IV. New York, NY: Lewis Historical Publishing Co.

EVI   Greer, George Cabell. 1912. *Early Virginia Immigrants, 1623-1666.* Richmond: William C. Hill Printing Company.

GCM   *An Account of Marriage Licenses and Ordinary Licenses issued in Gloster County from Oct the 20th 1777 to Oct the 20th 1778.* [database online] Accessed via www.Rootsweb.ancestry.com.

Hening Hening, William Waller. 1823. *Statutes at Large: Laws of Virginia.* New York, NY: Printed for the Author by R. & W. & G. Bartow. Accessed via www.vagenweb.org/hening/.

HOT   Hotten, John Camden. *The Original Lists of Persons of Quality; Emigrants; Religious Exiles; Political Rebels; etc. Who went from Great Britain to the American Plantations 1600-1700.* Accessed via http://books.google.com/.

ITC   *International Library of Technology: A textboot.* 1909. Scranton, PA: International Textbook Company.

NAUK Will of John Weldon, 1675. The National Archives. Catalogue Reference: Prob/11/346, Image Reference: 1399 [database online] Crown Copyright. Original data: *Prerogative Court of Canterbury.* http://www.nationalarchives.gov.uk/

PNC   Clark, Peyton Neale. 1897. *Old King William Homes and Families: An Account of Some of the Old Homesteads and Families of King William, VA, from Its Earliest Settlement.* Louisville, KY: Jn. P. Morton & Co.

QRV   Smith, Annie L.W. 1975. *The Quit Rents of Virginia, 1704.* Baltimore: Genealogical Publishing Co., Inc.

RB   Weisiger, Benjamin B. 1987-1991. *York County, Virginia, Records, 1659-1662, 1665-1672, 1672-1676.* Lewes, DE: Colonial Roots.

RSES   Williams, John (Ed.) 1845 (6th Edition). *The Reports of Sir Edmund Saunders, Knt.: Pleadings and Cases*, Vol. 1. London: Wm. Benning & Co.

SL   Lee, Sidney. 1899. *Dictionary of National Biography*, Vol. LVIII, baldini-Wakefield. London: Smith, Elder & Co., p. 403.

VC   Harrison, Fairfax. 1919. *The Virginia Carys.* New York: The DeVinne Press.

VCA   Fleet, Beverley. 1988. *Viriginia Colonial Abstracts*. Baltimore: Genealogical Publishing Co., Inc.

VCR   Crozier, William Armstrong, (Editor). 1911. *Virginia County Records*. Hasbrouck Heights, NJ: The Genealogical Association.

VGE   Withington, Lothrop. 1980. CD503, *Virginia Gleanings in England*, Baltimore: Genealogical Publishing Co., yFamily.com.

VMHB   *Virginia Magazine of History and Biography*. Richmond: Virginia Historical Society.

VOL   Howard, J.J. & G.J. Armitage (Eds). 1869. *he Visitation of London in the Year 1568 by Robert Cook*. Reprinted in The Publications of the Harleian Society. London: Taylor & Co., Printers, p. 98.

VRMM   Chapman, Joseph Warren Chapman. 1904. *Vital Records of Marblehead Massachusetts to the End of the Year 1849, Vol. II arriages and Deaths*. Salem, MA: The Essex Institute. Newcomb & Gauss Printers, Salem, MA.

WARG   Goodman, W. A. R. 1903. *Historical Sketch of Bruton Parish Williamsburg, Virginia*. Petersburg, VA: The Franklin Press Co.

WJCM   Moens, W.J.C. 1884. *The Marriage, Baptismal, and Burial Registers, 1571 to 1874 of the Dutch Reformed Church, Austin Friars*. Lymington, Eng: King & Sons, Publishers (Private Printing), p. xviii.

WMCQ   *William & Mary College Quarterly*, Series I.

YCDB   *York County Virginia Deeds and Bonds*, 1694-1729 1763-1777. Lewes, DE: Colonial Roots

YCLRD   *York County Virginia Land Records and Deeds*, 1729-1763. Lewes, DE: Colonial Roots.

YCWI   *York County Deeds, Orders, Wills, Inventories*, 1698-1783. Lewes, DE: Colonial Roots.

OTHER ABBREVIATIONS

a. acre	accon action
ackn acknowledged	afsd aforesaid
aft after	bap. baptized
co. county	dau daughter
def(s) defendant(s)	gent gentleman, gentlemen
mon motion	pd pound (British currency)
plt(s) plaintiff(s)	pn pence
sl shilling	wit. - witness

WORDS USED IN THE COLONIAL PERIOD

Peruke ig
Shoat iglet
Whitesmith inworker and/or one who finishes iron work with a chisel and file.

LEGAL TERMS USED IN THE COLONIAL PERIOD

detinue - wrongful detention of goods

d.s.p. ecessit sine prole - died without issue

ejectione firmae - refers to a motion or matter in front of the Court

non est inventus – In law, the return of a sheriff on a writ, when the defendant is not found in his county. *Webster Revised Unabridged Dictionary* by C. & G. Merriam Co., 1913.

non est factum is a plea that the defendant signed a document without fully realizing its nature, such as signing the transfer of a property under the belief that it is a only a guarantee for a debt. Latin for t is not (his/her) deed. BusinessDictionary.com, 2007-2008.

scire facias - a judicial writ founded on some matter of record and requiring the party proceeded against to show cause why the record should not be enforced, annulled, or vacated

uxor ejus - his wife

viz., vizt. idelicet - *namely, to wit*

THE JOHN BASKERVYLE / BASKERVILLE FAMILY

English Antecedents

A. THOMAS BASKERVYLE, of Oulde Withington, Gent., Cheshire, b. 1566, baptized at the chapel at Goosetry, d. 1625, buried at Goosetry; m. 1st (N), m. 2nd Dorothy Adderly (d. 1602, bur. Goosetry), daughter of Ralph Adderly of Blackhaugh in Coton, Staffordshire. {VGE:188 citing Cheshire records}
Thomas and Dorothy (Adderly) Baskervyle were the parents of JOHN, b. 1599. {VGE:189 citing inscriptions on walls of Goosetry Chapel}

B. JOHN BASKERVYLE, of Old Withington, Cheshire, England, b. 25 Feb 1599, baptized at Goosetry, d. 13 Feb 1661/2 {VMHB:XV:58-60}, m. Magdalen Hope. Magdalen was a daughter of George Hope of Queen's Hope, County Flint, and of Dodleston, Cheshire. {VGE:189 citing tablet in Goosetry Chapel}
The arms[1] of this family are said to be: *Argent, three hurts, quartering argent, A chevron gules between three squirrels segant of the second, impaling Hope (with nine quarterings) argent, a chevron en grailed sable, between three storks sable, legged gules.* {VGE:189}
John and Magdalen (Hope) Baskervyle were the parents of GEORGE, *d.s.p.* 1649, a minor; JOHN (1), b. 1635, d. 1674-5; HENRY, will 26 Feb 1675-6, proved 19 May 1676; THOMAS, b. 1632, buried 11 Dec 1676 at Goosetry; RANDALL; LAWRENCE; REBECCA, ELIZABETH, *d.s.p.*; MAGDALENE; KATHERINE m. Thomas Hand/Hund; MARY; and ELIZABETH m. Thomas Cooper/Cowper. {VGE:188-190 citing Cheshire records and tablet in Goosetry Chapel}

First Generation in America

1. JOHN BASKERVYLE, b. 1635, d. 1674-5 intestate, m. Mary Barbar (will 12 Jul 1693, proved 25 Jun 1694), was a son of John and Magdalen (Hope) Baskervyle. {DW 1694-1697:13}
Mary Barbar was the daughter of Lt. Col. William and Mary (N) Barbar. {RB 1672-1676:169,354[254]}
John Baskervyle was ordered to be paid in Apr 1665 by Thomas Holder, who married the relict of John Davis, deceased, 800 pounds tobacco, for completing inventory. {RB 1665-1672:9}
Edward Lockey, York Parish, intending to go for England, left a will dated 15 Jun 1667 and proved 24 Feb 1667/8. To God-dau. Elizabeth Baskervyle, daughter of John Baskervyle, a foal. Isaac Collier, Jr., Mary and Anne Lockey, exs. {RB 1665-1672:171}
Adam Miles, intending for England, left a will dated 18 Jun 1667 and

---

[1] Not proven but mentioned here for those who wish to research the matter

proved 10 Apr 1668. To my son John, 400 acres at Warram. Rest of my land to my 3 daughters. To my daughter Mary Miles, a cow. Rest of estate to my wife Sarah, extx., and my 4 children. My brothers John Baskervyle and John Whisken, overseers. {RB 1665-1672:181}

Mr. Richard Walton, merchant of London, and True my wife, daughter of Elizabeth Friend, alias Lockey, natural sister of Edward Lockey, late of York River, Virginia, merchant, deceased appoint, on 10 Apr 1668, John Baskervyle, Gent., Clerk of York Co., and Robert Baldry, Gent., York Co., my attornies. {RB 1665-1672:184}

Recovered by Mr. Thomas Bushrod 500 lbs. tobacco for fees in the difference between Mrs. Letitia Barbar (Bushrod appealing), 25 Aug 1673, Mr. David Newell, having since married Letitia, [the court] ordered Newell pay John Baskervyle. {RB 1672-1676:53}

Elizabeth Lockey, York Co., left a will dated 4 Dec 1675 and proved 4 Jan 1675/6. To my grandchild Elizabeth Hansford, daughter of son William Hansford, silver tankard. All debts due me to my 2 sons, Thomas and Charles Hansford, exs. To my God daughter Elizabeth Baskervyle, a mare. {RB 1672-1676:145}

William Barbar, of Hampton Parish, York Co., left a will dated 18 Nov 1668 and proved 2 Jul 1669. To my daughter Mary Baskervyle, 100 pounds. To my granddaughter Elizabeth Baskervyle, Negro boy, 3 cows. To my granddaughter Mary Baskervyle, filly and 3 cows. To my Goddaughter Mary Dennett, a heifer and filly. To my Goddaughter Elizabeth Miles, a heifer. To my son Thomas, all my lands. My wife Mary, extx., and rest of estate to her and my son Thomas. If he has reached 19, to be joint executor. To my son in law John Baskervyle, a stud horse. {RB 1665-1672:354[254]}

The will of Mary Barbar, Hampton Parish, York Co., widow and executrix of [her] deceased husband Lt. Col. William Barbar, was dated 25 Apr 1676 and proved 30 Jun 1676. To my daughter, Mary Barbar, also to said daughter Mary Baskervyle, Black Betty, and her first child to my granddaughter Mary Baskervyle. If she dies, to her sister Magdalen Baskervyle. To my granddaughter Elizabeth Baskervyle, filly. To said grandchildren, Mary & Elizabeth, 10 pounds apiece. To my granddaughter Magdalen and Rebecca Baskervyle, 20 pounds apiece. To my grandchildren Elizabeth, Mary, John and Sarah Miles, Martha Collins, 15 pounds a piece. To my grandchild Mary Collins, 5 pounds. To my daughter Sarah Collins, 20 pounds. To my grandchildren Anne & Sarah Dennett, 15 pounds apiece. To son in law John Baskervyle, 20 pounds. To my grandchildren Mary & Elizabeth Juxon, 5 pounds a piece. To my son Thomas Barbar and Matthew [sic] his wife, Sarah Collins, my son John Baskervyle and Mary his wife, suits. Rest of estate to my son Thomas Barbar, and he and John Baskervyle, executors. {RB 1672-1676:169}

The will of Mary Baskervyle, Bruton Parish, Yorke Co., was dated 12 Jul 1693 and proved 25 Jun 1694. To my daughter Mary Batten, gown and muzzling [muslin]. To my Goddaughter Mary Batten, heiffer. To my daughter Magdaleen White, ring. To my Goddaughter, Mary White, heiffer of my cow Gentle. To my 2 daughters Rebecka and Sarah Baskervyle, 2 ewes and lambs. My Negro boy Frank to my son George Baskervyle. Rest of estate to my son, George, and my 2 daughters Rebecka and Sarah Baskervyle. My bro: Thomas Barbar, my cozen Samll. Timson and my son in law Joseph White, executors. {DW 1694-1697:13}

On 25 Jun 1694, an order for probate of the [will of Mrs. Mary Baskervyle, widow] was granted her brother Capt. Thomas Barbar, as executor along with her cozen, Mr. Samuell Timson, and Joseph White, her son. {DW 1694-1697:2}

John and Mary (Barbar) Baskervyle were the parents of: MARY m. John Batten; MAGDALEN "Mary" m. 1st Joseph White and 2nd William Jackson; ELIZABETH; REBECCA m. Timothy Pinkethman; SARAH m. Adam Miles; and GEORGE m. Eliza (N). {DW 1694-1697:13; RB 1672-1676:169}

Second Generation
2. MARY BASKERVYLE, who m. John Batten (d. 1688-1697), was a daughter of John (1) and Mary (Barbar) Baskervyle.

John Batten was a son of Ashaell (d. Sep 1666) and Ursula (N) Batten. After Ursula's death, before 29 Dec 1662; Ashaell married, before 26 Feb 1665, Anne (N). {YCWI 1711-1714:233}

An inquest on 29 Dec 1662 of the death [of Ursula Batten], found that Thomas Whaley, a neighbor of Mr. Ashaell Batten, was asked to shoot a beast for Batten, and Ursual [sic] standing too close, the bullet glanced off the horn of the beast and struck her, killing her. {RB 1659-1662:183}

Mr. Ashaell Batten brought a complaint on 26 Feb 1665 against Andrew Hill, his servant, [because Hill] offered violence to Mrs. Anne Batten, his wife, at the time [Batten] was in England. [Hill t]o serve one year after his time. {RB 1665-1672:52}

A certificate was granted on 25 Jun 1666 to Ashaell Batten for 350 acres for importing 7 persons into this Colony: Ashaell Batten, Anne Buttin [Battin?] et al. {RB 1665-1672:69}

Asheall Batten left a will dated 4 Sep 1666 and proved 12 Sep 1666. To wife Ann, 1/3 of personalty, other 2/3 to my 3 children, John, Sarah, and Constant Batten. Land to my children. Son in law John Davis, execurtor. {RB 1665-1672:115}

The deposition of Mrs. Eliz. Paulen, age 70 years or thereabouts, occurred on 28 Jul 1712. This deponent saith that Aswell Batten, of York Co., was her father-in-law who first married her own mother and afterwards married

4

another woman named Constant, by whom he had two daughters named Sarah and Constant, and who after the decease of his wife, Constant, marryed another woman named Ursula, and who had by his wife Ursula a son named John Batten. This deponent further saith not. {YCWI 1711-1714:233}

Israell Swall[ow], of York Co., age c25, was deposed on 24 Aug 1687 concerning John Batten and Matthew Miller, saying he in company with Batten and William Irish aboard the *Augine* a week after the ship came last into this colony. Batten had an account from Miller of a bill of exchange for 12 pounds protested by Mrs. Thorpe because her husband, Majr. Otho Thorpe, dyed before the bill came to her hands. Batten came to agreement with Miller [that] Batten would pay Miller to satisfaction. {DW 1687-1691:20}

On 24 Feb 1687/8, John Battin, York Co., planter, unto Samuell Timson, same, Gent. for consideration, one Negro man Sambo, formerly purchased by me of Mr. Daniel Parke. {DW 1687-1691:100}

An indenture was created on 24 May 1697 in James City Co. between Izraell Swallow and Wm. Batton, with consent of George Baskerville, his uncle Batton bound himself apprentice to Swallow to learn carpentry. {DW 1694-1697:415-416}

On 16 Feb 1704, a deed was created between Wm Batten of Bruton Parish, York Co, for £70, sold to Thomas Pinchback, of same place, a plantation & tract of land in the parish afsd on the north side of Queens Creek, being formerly the plantacon & lands of John Batten, (father of the sd William), late of this county, deceased, & now in tenure & possession of the said William as being lawful heir of the said John Batten, his father. {YCDB 1701-1708:118,119}

John and Mary (Baskervyle) Batten were the parents of MARY BATTEN and WILLIAM BATTEN.

3. MAGDALEN "MARY" BASKERVYLE, b. ca 1685, was a daughter of John (1) and Mary (Barbar) Baskervyle, m. 1st Joseph White, 2nd William Jackson.

Joseph White, will 21 Feb 1705, proved 19 Mar 1710, was a son of Henry (will proved 22 Nov 1671) and Mary (Croshaw) White (b. 1631). {RB 1659-1662:27-28,91-92; RB 1665-1672:145}

After Joseph White died, Mary (Baskervyle) White m. 2nd William Jackson (b. ca 1685, will pr. 1721), and Mary survived Wm. Jackson.

William Jackson (b. ca 1685) was also a son of William who was in turn a son of William (d. 1667) and Elizabeth (N) (b. 1635). After William died in 1667, Elizabeth married 2nd Robert Handy (d. ca. 1675). {RB 1665-1672:162}

[2]Joseph Croshaw, Poplar Neck, York Co., Gent., created an indenture

---

[2] Data pertaining to Magdalen "Mary" Baskerville as a White will be presented chronologically beginning ca. 1660 followed by data pertaining to Mary Baskerville as a Jackson that will be presented chronologically beginning ca. 1667.

on 11 Sep 1660 with Henry White, Indian Field, York Co., in view of a marriage between Henry White and Mary, daughter of Joseph Croshaw. Croshaw purchased 200 acres land next to Indian Fields from Edward Oliver. {RB 1659-1662:91-92}

Mary [Croshaw] White, age c36, deposed on 24 May 1667 concerning a sugar deal. {RB 1665-1672:145}

Henry White left a will undated but proved on 22 Dec 1671. To wife Mary, all my land and mill in Maston Parish till my son of age, then to my son Joseph White at 21. To son William White, 300 acres in New Kent Co., part of 1200 acres. To daus. Mary, Unity, and Rebecca White, each 300 acres. Maj. John West and Mr. Bryan Smith, executors. {RB 1665-1672:469[369]}

On 10 Oct 1687, Joseph White, Bruton Parish, York Co., planter, sold to Edmond Jenings, of York Co., Esqr., for 45 English money and 40 shillings, paid Magdalen my wife. Henry White, father of Joseph White, was possessed of a water mill on St. Andrew's Creek, descended to Joseph as son and heir by will dated 22 Nov 1671. {DW 1687-1691:27-28}

Joseph and William White, sons of Henry White, late dec., and Willm. Davis as marrying Mary, one of the said daughters, and Ralph Graves as marrying Unity, one of the other daughters of Henry White. They petition that Henry White by his will did bequeath 30 pounds sterling and cattle to his daughter Rebeckah White, unless she die under age and without issue, which she did. Ordered 26 Mar 1688. Exec: Colonel John West the surviving executor pay Joseph and William White, and William Davis and Ralph Graves Rebeckah's portion. {DW 1687-1691:105}

Roger Allgroe, servant to Joseph White, was adjudged on 7 Nov 1689 to be 10 years of age. {DW 1687-1691:327}

Mildred Massey, being by her natural mother, Ann Brafett, declared to be 5 years on 5 Oct last past, was bound apprentice to Joseph White until she attains 17, as per indenture of White and Brasett on 22 Mar 1693/4. {DW 1691-1694:314}

On 23 Mar 1698/9, a deed was created between Joseph White, of Bruton Parish, York Co., planter, who for £2, who sold to Thomas Crips, of same place planter, a tract of land or woodland ground containing 50 acres bounded by St. Andrews Creek, land of George Baskervyle, ye mill path, the Maine Swamp, Hamners Path & land of Jackson ... and now in the occupacon of Will White which came & descended to the said Joseph White as heir at law to Henry, his father, deceased, and now sold to the said Thomas Crips as afsd Wits: George Baskervyle, Wm Timson. Ackn 24 May 1699 by Joseph White & Magdelene his wife as to her right of dower.... {YCDB 1694-1701:188,293}

James Whaley & Joseph White, church wardens of Bruton Parish, arrested Edward Thomas for 19 lbs of tobacco due by account ... to the parish afsd and he ye defendant now failing to appear & answer ye same order is granted against Lt Col Thomas Ballard high sheriff & next court to be confirmed if he causeth not ye sd Thomas to appear and answer ye same. {YCWI 1698-1702:242}

This is to certify to whom it may concern that Joseph White hath taken up a runaway servant woman named Magdalen Browne, belonging to John Banister in Gloster Co. VA, who confessed voluntarily that she was runaway, which is at least 10 mi from the taking up from her sd masters house given under my hand this 9 Sep 1700/1699, James Whaley. {YCWI 1698-1702:372}

James Whaley and Joseph White, church wardens of Bruton Parish, on 25 Feb 1700, having summoned Elizabeth Wood to answer their information against her for fornication, and she failing to appear, ordered that the sheriff secure her for her appearance at next court to answer. On 24 Mar 1700, Elizabeth Wood who upon tryall confest the fact wherefore for want effects to pay her fine, it was ordered that the sheriff take her into custody to the whipping post and forthwith there to give her 15 lashes on her bare back laid well on. {YCWI 1698-1702:392,439}

Joseph White, being by ye sheriff returned summoned an evidence for Willm Hansford plaintiff against William Cowman defendant, is ordered to be paid for 2 days attendance at court at 40 lbs of tobacco per day with costs. George Baskervile the same. {YCWI 1698-1702:490}

Robert Beverly arresting Joseph White and Timothy Pinkithman for a debt of 4 pd 9 pence, and not further prosecuting, the suit is dismist. {YCWI 1702-1704:43}

The will of Joseph White of Bruton Parish was dated 27 Feb 1705/6. To my son, George White, that plantacion whereon George Brown does now live and other household goods now in the hands of George Brown and Eliz., his wife, to keep until my son, George, shall come to the age of 21 years or married and then to be delivered to him. Also, one gold ring which was his mother's wedding ring when he attains the age of 21 years. If he should die before that age, then to my wife, Mary White. To my daughter, Mary White, that plantacion where Edward Wigg now liveth and half the Neck of land adjoyning to the said plantacion. Also, one negro not under the age of 16 and not exceeding 26, household goods and livestock and her mother's maiden gold ring, but if she should dye before the age of 21 years or married, then to fall to my daughter Frances White. To my daughter, Frances White, the upper end of that Neck of land whereon Edward Wigg now liveth and known by the name of *Olliver Neck*, it being equally divided between the two sisters. Also, one negro not under the age of 16 and not exceeding 26 livestock and a pair of gold wier rings and if both should dye before the age of 21 years or married, then to return to my wife, Mary White. To my wife, Mary White, my manner plantacion only 1½ acres where the old Church formerly stood, not to be disposed, the land by estimacion being 500 acres, and all my negoes, cattle and household stuff, horse and mares and anything else. My wife to be my sole Extx. Ambrose Cobbs and my brother-in-law, George Baskervile, to be the overseers Proved 19 Mar 1710. {YCWI 1706-1710:70,76}

In the petition of John Hillyard, setting forth that he having intermarryed with Frances, one of the daughters of Joseph White, deceased, by which means there is become due to the petitioner a legacy expressed to be given to the said Frances, and praying order for the same against William Jackson and Mary, his wife, Executors of the said Joseph, having been summoned and failing to appear, judgment is granted him for the same and it is ordered that the said Executors deliver to the petitioner the particulars mentioned in the testator's Will to be given to the said Frances and that they pay costs *alies* execution. {YCWI 1711-1714:265}

(Refer back to footnote 1) Administration of William Jackson's estate was granted on 24 Jan 1667 to his relict, Elizabeth Jackson. {RB 1665-1672:162}

On 4 Dec 1675, the estate of William Jackson was appraised. Crop year total: 2000 lbs. tobacco Daniell Wyld took the oath of Elizabeth Handy, age about 40, the above being an account of her first husband's estate when she married Robert Handy. {RB 1672-1676:136}

The will of Elizabeth [Jackson] Handy was dated 25 Mar 1701. To grandson, William Jackson, one plantation and all ye land that belongeth to it lying upon Queens Creek; to my grandson, Philliman Jackson, one plantation & ye land that belongeth to it lying in Skimnor [Skimino?]. To my son, William Handy, my large bible. It is my will that all my personal estate be divided amongst my four grandchildren, Willm Jackson, Philliman Jackson, Eliz Jackson & Hanna Jackson, and do make my trusty friends, Willm Pinkithman & Willm Campbell, executors. Proved 24 Jul 1701. {YCWI 1698-1702:476,483}

William Jackson, legatee of Elizabeth Handy, deceased, setting forth a petition that he is arrived at age 18, and praying that Timothy Pinkethman may be admitted his guardian, hath order accordingly granted, the said Pinkethman entering into bond with good & sufficient securities.... {YCWI 1702-1704:47}

On 24 Nov 1702, Timothy Pinkethman, Nathaniel Crawley & William Taylor, of York Co., were firmly bound unto the justices of York Co for 90 pd ... the condition of this obligation is such that the afsd Timothy Pinkethman as being guardian of William Jackson, orphan of William Jackson, deceased, hath received into his care and custody the whole estate of the said orphan, if the said Timothy Pinkethman do well and truly perform the trust he hath undertaken relating to the said orphan & his estate & pay his just dues when he shall attain to age or sooner, if ye court shall (see) fit and save harmless and indemnify the said justices from all damages, then this obligation to be void.... {YCWI 1702-1704:75}

In ye suit between John Stanup, Junr., and Elizabeth, his wife, legatee of Elizabeth Handy, deceased, against William Pinkethman & Wm Cambell, executor of sd Handy, ye matter was referred ye last court to auditors is continued to next court, Wm Pinkethman and one of ye defs being sick. {YCWI 1702-1704:293}

Willm Jaxon [Jackson], on his petition, obtain'd judgment against Rebecca Pinkethman, admintrator of Timothy Pinkethman, for 30 pd being ye balance due on account of a legacy left him by Elizabeth Handy, formerly of this county, deceased, and put into ye hands of said deceased, Timothy, as guardian of said William, who is now come to age, to receive ye same & is order'd to be paid with cost. {YCWI 1705-1706:404}

The will of William Campbell, of Bruton Parish, was dated 28 May 1709 and proved 24 Nov 1709. To Margrett Wright, one good stuff gound [gown] and petticoat. To William Handy, £10. To Hannah Jackson, the daughter of William Jackson, white mare and her increase and £3. To Philliman Jackson, the son of William Jackson, all the rest of my Estate in Virginia or England. George Baskervyle to be Executor. {YCWI 1709-1711:262}

The acion upon the case between Francis Tyler, plaintiff, and William Jackson and Mary, his wife (late Mary White), Executors of Joseph White, deceased, defendants, is by consent continued until the next Court. {YCWI 1711-1714:207}

On 20 Nov 1722 a deed of gift was made by Mary Jackson of Bruton Parish, York Co., widow, for good will that I bear & divers other good considerations have given unto Robt Crawley, son of Nathaniel Crawley late of said parish deceased, all that plantation & 500 acre tract of land in the place called the Indian Field in the afsd parish, which was granted, together with 300 acres more, to Joseph White, by patent dated 20 Apr 1694, and by the will of the said Joseph dated 25 Feb 1705/6, devised in fee to me the then wife of the said Joseph during his natural life & no longer & further for the considerations afsd, I do give unto the sd Robert Crawley nine Negro slaves, *viz.*, Samson, Ben, Simon, Sambo, Jack, Kate, Sarah, Lucy & Betty, together with such increase as they shall hereafter produce forever. Also know ye that I, the said Mary Jackson, as well in consideration of the natural love & affection which I have & bear unto my loving daughter Elizabeth Jackson as for other good considerations have given unto the said Elizabeth Jackson two Negro slaves, by name, Harry & Jenny, together with the increase which they shall hereafter produce, to her forever. And further know ye that I, the said Mary Jackson, for and in consideration of the natural love & affection which I have & bear unto my loving sons Phipps Jackson & Ambrose Jackson, do give unto the said Phipps Jackson & Ambrose Jackson & their heirs forever, all my right & title which I shall may or ought to have of & in all the plantation & tract of land & premises herein above granted to Robert Crawley immediately after the decease of the said Robert in the manner following, to the said Ambrose Jackson to have the mannour house with all other the houses thereto belonging & of the said tract of land, and the said Phipps Jackson to have the other part of the said land to be laid out & divided (in case of their disagreement) by two freeholders of the county indifferently chosen by the sd Phipps & Ambrose to divide & assign the said dividends, nevertheless reserving & always saving to myself full power to dispose or sell the right I may have in reversion to the said lands after the decease of the said Robert Crawley & to such other person as I shall hereafter think fit. {YCDB 1713-1729:371}

Know all men by these presents that we, Mary Jackson, Robt Cobbs Junior, and John Harris, of the County of York, are held firmly bound into the Worshipful the Justices of the County aforesaid to the sum of Six Hundred pounds Sterling payable to the sd Justices their heirs__? Or Some of them to the which payment shall be well & Truly made We bind ourselves__? Every of us our heirs Executors & Admininstrators Joyntly & Severally firmly __? Presents Dated this 15 May 1721. {YCWI 1720-1722:43}

The Condition of the above obligation is such that if the above bounden, Mary Jackson, Executrix of the last will & Testament of the said William Jackson, deceased, do make or cause to be made a _? [good] & perfect Inventory of all & singular Goods Chattels & Credits of the said Wm Jackson, deceased, which have or shall come to the hands, possession or knowledge of the said Mary Jackson, or into the hands & possession of any other person or persons for her, the same to make exhibit or cause to be exhibited into the County Court, then this obligation to be void & of none effect to otherwise to be in full force & vertue. (Torn page)

In the name of God Amen ... In York County being Sick & weak of body_? I do make & ordain this my last will & __? Enulling by these presents all other__? And first I Commend . . . My Lord & Savior. . . .

(Margin says Jackson's Will)

__? pian Bur__?

(Page 46)

Land belonging to him & his heirs forever __? Item g__? To my son, William Jackson, Sixty pounds Current money to be payed Him at the age of Twenty one years. Item, I do give & bequeath to my daughter, Elizabeth Jackson, the Sum of Sixty pounds Current money to be payed her at the age of Eighteen years or married. Item, I Do give & Bequeath to my Son, Phips Jackson, the sum of Sixty pounds of Current money to be payed to him at the age of twenty One years. Item, I do give & Bequeath to my son, Ambrose Jackson, the Sum of Sixty pounds Current money to be payed him at the age of Twenty One years. Item, I do give to my loving wife all my Negroes Cattle Household Stuff horses & Mares And I do appoint my loving wife Mary Jackson my whole Execrx to this my last Will and Testament whereunto I Set my hand & Seal this ninth day of in the year of our Lord God 1721. William Jackson. {YCWI 1720-1722:45-46}

Magdalene "Mary" Baskervyle and Joseph White were the parents of GEORGE WHITE, b. ca. 1684; MARY WHITE; and FRANCES WHITE, m. John Hillyard. {YCWI 1706-1710:70,76; YCWI 1711-1714:265}

Magdalene "Mary" Baskervyle and William Jackson were the parents of WILLIAM JACKSON; ELIZABETH JACKSON; PHIPPS JACKSON; and AMBROSE JACKSON. {YCWI 1720-1722:43}

4. REBECCA BASKERVYLE, will 12 Mar 1707/8, proved 24 Mar 1707/8, m. Timothy Pinkethman (d. 4 Nov 1703), was a daughter of John (1) and Mary (Barbar) Baskervyle. {YCWI 1705-1706:350;YCWI 1706-1710:132}

William Pinckithman as trustee (24 Sep 1697) to the estate of John Smyth, by a letter of attorney to his brother Timothy Pinckithman, did confess judgment to John Turner. {DW 1694-1697:463}

Rebecka Pinkethman, widow & relict of Timothy Pinkethman, late of this county deceased, on her petition, hath order granted for a commission of administration of her deceased husband's estate, she having entr'd into bond with Capt. Thomas Barbar & George Baskervil, her securitys, order'd that said estate be appraised by Robt Bee et al. {YCWI 1705-1706:348}

Elizabeth Jones, assignee of York Court, hath judgment granted against George Baskervil in an action of debt for 2 pd 5 sl, due by a penal bill dated under his hand & seal & under ye hand & seal of Timothy Pinkethman, lately deceased, ye 4 Nov 1703 and is order'd forthwith to pay it to the plaintiff with cost. {YCWI 1705-1706:350}

An appraisement of ye estate completed on 31 Aug 1705, of Timothy Pinkethman, deceased. 4 old cowes, 12 young cowes, 4 heyfers, 4 bulls, 4 stears, 4 yearlings, 3 calves, 1 bay horse, 1 old gray horse, 1 young gray mare & colt, 1 bay mare, 19 old sheep & 7 lambs, 2 sowes, 7 piggs, 1 druget suit of mens cloth[e]s, old parcel of very old cloaths, 2 pairs old boots, 1 pair old shoes, etc. 3 Negro women, 2 Negro boys, 3 Negro girls. 213 pd. Presented in court 24 Sep 1705 by Rebecca Pinkethman administrator.... {YCWI 1705-1706:363}

The estate of Timothy Pinkethman, deceased, was valued at £235 pd 12 sl 3 pn, errors excepted, per Rebekah Pinkethman, admintrator, and was ordered to be recorded on 5 Aug 1706 {YCWI 1705-1706:442}

Elizabeth Jones, Francis Sharpe and Morris Jones, of the Co. of York, to the Justices of said County, in the sum of £300. Sureties to Elizabeth Jones as Administratrix of the Estate of William White, deceased, in lieu of the original Adminstrator, Timothy Pinkethman, now deceased. 2 Jul 1706. Wit: Wm. Pinkethman. {YCWI 1706-1710:second of two unnumber pages before page 1}

Rebecca Pinkethman, widow and Executrix of Timothy Pinkethman deceased, this day presented to the Court an account of her said husband's Estate, which on her request is ordered to be committed to record. {YCWI 1706-1710:3}

On 27 Nov 1706, Robt Green & Abigail (*uxor ejus*) have appointed William Coman, of York Co., their attorney, to appear at the next court held in York Co. to acknowledge the deed of sale   Wits: Hen Hales, Ambr Cobbs, Rebecca Pinkethman. Proved 24 Dec 1706. {YCDB 1701-1708:201}

The Last Will & Testament of Rebecca Pinkethman was, on 24 Mar 1707, produced by George Baskervile, one of the Executors therein named, and proved in Court by the oaths of William Taylor, Edward Nelson, and John Steward, admited to record and probate thereof granted to the Executors accordingly. {YCWI 1706-1710:125}

The will of Rebecca Pinkethman, widow of Bruton Parish, was dated 12 Mar 1707/8. To daughter, Mary Pinkethman, negro girle named Phota. To loving son, Thomas Pinkethman, negro boy named Jomoy. To daughter, Sarah Pinkethman, negro girle named Moll. To aforesaid son and daughters, negro girl named Choragio to be equallie divided amongst them, but in case my said son or daughters should lose their negro before they arrive to the age of 18, then the said negro girle to return to he or she that so lost their negro. To son-in-law William Pinkethman, one cow calf. To daughter-in-law Mary Pinkethman, £5. To goddaughter, Sarah Batten, one heifer. To godchildren beside, each of them, a cow calf. To cozen William Batten, 20 shillings to be paid him now in his necessitie. My negro woman Juda and the rest of my Estate to be sold to satisfye my debts, and what remains to be divided among my aforesaid children, Thomas, Mary and Sarah. My brother George Baskervile and brother-in-law Thomas Cripps to be Executors. Thomas Cripps to take into his care and charge my children with their Estates. Proved in Court Mar 1707/8. {YCWI 1706-1710:132}

Inventory & appraisement of the estate of Rebecca Pinkethman deceased, dated 30 Aug 1708. Among household goods, one old negro woman valued at £1:10. Total value of Estate, £6. {YCWI 1706-1710:256}

In a petition on 24 Jun 1709 of Benjamin Lillingston, setting forth that one, Timothy Pinkethman, in his lifetime, was indebted unto the petitioner in a certain sum of money and a certain quantity of tobacco, that he did by virtue of two acions obtain against Rebecca, his Administratrix, two judgments for the same, and that the said Rebecca is since dead having not duly administered the estate of the said Timothy. George Baskervyle and Thomas Cripps, Executors of the last will & testament of the said Rebecca, this day appeared by their attorney and, together with the petitioner, consented that the matters in difference should be adjusted by auditors. Henry Tyler, Richard Bland, Henry Cary and Ambrose Cobb, or any three of them, are appointed to meet on 3 Aug next, if fair, if not, the next fair day, at John Marote's [Marot's] in Williamsburgh, and audit and settle the inventory and account of the estate of the said Timothy Pinkethman, and it is ordered that they make report of their

12

proceedings to the next Court on 5 Sep 1709, the report stated the current value of Estate was £42:19:2. {YCWI 1706-1710:227,262}

Mary Pinkethman, orphan of Tim Pinkethman deceased, petitioned, on 19 Nov 1716, for liberty to chuse a guardian, and on her motion, Wm Stone is admitted her guardian, who having together with Jacob Godwin & Fran Sharp entered into bond & ackn ye same for ye said orphans estate, which bond is admitted to record. {YCWI 1716-1718:37}

On 19 Nov 1716, Wm Stone, Jacob Godwin & Francis Sharp, of York Co., are firmly bound unto the justices of York Co. for 60 pd ... the condition of this obligation is such that whereas ye afsd Wm Stone became guardian of Mary Pinkethman, orphan of Tim Pinkethman, deceased, and hath received into his care & custody ye whole estate of said orphan, if the said Wm Stone do well & truly perform ye trust he hath undertaken relating to sd orphan & her estate & pay her full dues when she attains to lawful age, and shall save harmless & indemnify the said justices from all damages that shall or may accrue concerning said estate, then this obligation to be void.... {YCWI 1716-1718:46}

On 21 Mar 1719/20, Thomas Cripps, on his petition, is admitted guardian to Sarah Pinkethman, orphan of Timothy Pinkethman, deceased, he [Cripps] having together with Giles Moody & John Davis, his securitys, entered into & acknowledge their bond for that purpose, which bond is admitted to record. Ordered that the said petitioner take care of the said orphan & her estate. {YCWI 1718-1720:564}

On 11 Mar 1720, the petition of Thomas Crips, guardian of Sarah Pinkethman, orphan of Thomas Pinkethman deceased, setting forth that the estate of the said orphan being in the hands of Wm Bigges and praying that the estate may be committed to the petitioners care. It is thereupon ordered that the said Wm Bigges & Richard King deliver the said orphan's estate in their hands to the petitioner, and the sd Bigges, refunding to the said King all such costs as [have occurred] in obtaining the said estate from the said Bigges. {YCWI 1720-1722:25}

Rebecca Baskervyle and Timothy Pinkethman were the parents of MARY PINKETHMAN; THOMAS PINKETHMAN; and SARAH PINKETHMAN.

5. GEORGE BASKERVYLE, who m. Eliza (N), was a son of John (1) and Mary (Barbar) Baskervile. {YCWI 1716-1718:92}

On 19 Nov 1702, Henry Cross, together with William Timson & George Baskervile, securities, did jointly and severally confess judgment before Captain Thomas Barber & Captain Baldwin Mathews, justices, to Henry Tyler, trustee to the estate of Cope Doyley, late of this county, deceased, for payment of 19 pd with cost and stay of execution until 10 Jan 1703. {YCWI 1702-1704:52}

Whereas it was formerly ordered that the Sheriff should take and in safe custody keep the body of Barbara Hutton up till she should give bond with good and sufficient security to appear at this Court to answer the informacion of John Wythe, Church Warden of York Parish, for fornicacion, and said order being by George Baskervill [?] execution, and she not appearing, it is therefore ordered that unless the said George cause the said Barbara personally to appear at the next Court to answer the said informacion, the judgment shall be awarded against the said George for her fine, which the Law prescribes for the sin of fornicacion. {YCWI 1706-1710:66}

On 25 Aug 1707, in the *ejectione firmae* brought by Abel Dun, plaintiff, against Arthur Laws, defendant, George Baskervyle, Under Sheriff of this County, this day made oath in Court that he served Nicholas Sebrell, the tenant in possession of the lands in question, with a copy of the conditional order in this cause. And the said Nicholas Sebrell comes by Henry Holdcraft, his Attorney, and prayed to be admitted defendant in the room of Arthur Laws, and he is admitted accordingly having ordered into rule to come to tryal of these till the next Court. {YCWI 1706-1710:84}

Elizabeth Moody, William Barbar Gent., and George Baskervyle, all of the Co. of York, to the Queen in the sum of 10,000 lbs. of tobacco, to be Sureties for Elizabeth Moody for her lycense to keep an ordinary at her dwelling house in York Town. 25 Jan 1708. {YCWI 1706-1710:192}

Frances Wilkinson, wife of Thomas Wilkinson, gave power of attorney to friend George Baskervyle, my lawfull Attorney in all cases and acion whatsoever. 22 Mar 1707/8. Wits: Letitia Armstrong and E. Foulkes. {YCWI 1706-1710:132}

The acion upon the case between William Randolph, plaintiff, and George Baskervile, defendant, is dismist, the plaintiff not prosecuting. {YCWI 1709-1711:83}

George Baskervile preferred [proffered] a claim for taking up a runaway negro man belonging to Richard Richardson, of New Kent Co., and it appearing by a Certificate that the said negro was apprehended more than 5 miles from his Master's, and the said Baskervile having made oath that he never has received any satisfaction thereof, it is ordered to be transmitted to the Assembly for allowance. {YCWI 1709-1711:115}

John Gibbons and George Baskervile, having taken the aforementioned oaths to her Majesty and test, were sworn Under-Sheriffs for this County. {YCWI 1709-1711:204}

On 29 Nov 1714, George Baskervyle, of Bruton Parish York Co, for 5 shillings, leased to Ralph Graves of same place, a 350 acre tract of land in Bruton Parish with a dwelling thereon, being the tract of land formerly of John Baskervyle, father to the said George, by him purchased of John Horsington, to whom the 350 acres of land was granted by patent dated 18 Mar 1662, bounded by 300 acres part of the parish formerly called Marston Parish, the Main Swamp, St. Andrews Creek, land of Thomas Pinkethman & the Rockahock Path, the first mentioned 50 acres, the residue on the Main Bridge of St. Andrews Creek bounded by the said Horsington for the term of one year, paying the yearly rent of one grain of Indian corn, if demanded. Ackn'd 20 Dec 1714. {YCDB 1713-1729:39}

On 24 Apr 1716, George Baskervyle, of Charles Parish, York Co, for £30, released unto Wm Wise Junr, of same place, a 100 acre tract of land in Charles Parish. Ackn 21 May 1716 by Geo Baskervyle & at the same time appeared Eliza, wife of the said George, who being first privately examined, relinquished her right of dower.... {YCDB 1713-1729:116}

On 19 Nov 1716, in the action of debt between Thomas Roberts gent, late sheriff of York Co, plaintiff, and George Baskervyle, defendant, for 1000 pd due by bond under ye defendant's hand dated 3 Jun 1713 ye matters in difference between both parties having been refer'd to ye arbitration of Simon Hollier, Wm Row & Richd Slater, on ye plaintiff's motion, judgment is granted him against ye defendant for 8120 3/4 lbs of tobacco & ye sum of 4 pd 5 sl 11 pn according to ye specialty of said arbitrators award, ordered that ye defendant pay ye afsd sums to plaintiff with costs. {YCWI 1716-1718:37}

Geo Baskervyle acknowledged his deeds of lease & release of land to Wm Wise Junr, also at ye same time appeared Eliza, wife of said George, [who] voluntarily relinquished her right of dower in said land.... {YCWI 1716-1718:92}

George and Eliza (N) Baskervyle were the parents of <u>JOHN</u>, <u>HUGH</u>, and <u>NORVIL (NOWEL)</u>.

Third Generation

6. JOHN BASKERVYLE was a son of George (5) and Eliza (N) Baskervyle.

On 17 Mar 1742, John Lidderdale of the City of Williamsburg, merchant, and Elizabeth, his wife, for 5 shillings, leased to John Baskervile, bricklayer, a tract of land in Bruton Parish on both sides of the main road leading from the City of Williamsburg to Queen Mary's Port adjacent Matthews Schoolhouse, land late of Mann Page esqr & John Hubard deceased, a marsh on Queens Creek, now in the tenure of John Custis esqr and formerly granted by patent to Mary Whaley, widow, and land late of Elizabeth Bray, widow, containing the high land Ackn 21 Mar 1742. {YCLRD 1741-1754:44,46,50,60}

John Baskervile, of James City Co., his securities, two lots or acres of ground on the north side of Nicholson Street in the City of Williamsburgh whereon he now dwells, also his shop on Main Street with the ground and four slaves, Judith with Adam & Eve, her children, & Jo, a mulatto boy, with their increase, during the term of 500 years paying the yearly rent of one ear of Indian corn upon the Feast of St. John the Baptist if demanded, whereas the said Henry Weatherburn, Mark Cosby & John Baskervile have, at the request of said

Andrew Anderson, become bound for him as securities unto Thomas Creas, of the College of William & Mary, gardener, for the payment of £250 with interest before 21 Jun 1745. 21 Jan 1744. {YCLRD 1741-1754:113}

On 15 Nov 1751, an Indenture Tripartite [was formed among] Andrew Anderson, of the City of Williamsburgh, peruke maker, and Mary, his wife, of the first part, Henry Wetherburne and Mark Cosby, of same place, and John Baskervyle, formerly of James City Co, but now of [blank] county, of the second part, and Nathaniel Walthoe, of same city, esqr, of the third part. Whereas the said Andrew Anderson stands seized in two lots or acres of ground on the north side of Nicholson Street in the City of Williamsburgh (Nos. 272 & 273), and whereas the said Andrew Anderson and Mary his wife, by indenture of mortgage dated 25 Jun 1744, did sell unto the said Henry Wetherburne, Mark Cosby and John Baskervyle the said two lots of ground during the term of 500 years, and whereas the said Andrew Anderson hath erected and built on part of the said lotts one messuage or dwelling house, which he is willing and desirous to sell and to apply the money arising by the sale towards discharging a bond, now this indenture witnesseth that the said Andrew Anderson and Mary, his wife, with the consent of the said Henry Wetherburne, Mark Cosby & John Baskervyle, for £107.10, sold to the said Nathaniel Walthoe a parcel of ground on the north side of Nicholson Street in the City of Williamsburgh, adjacent Mrs. Lydia Char[l]ton. {YCLRD 1741-1754:457,459}

7. HUGH BASKERVYLE was a son of George (5) and Eliza (N) Baskervyle.

Hugh Baskerwyle et al. witnessed the will of David Layton, of Bruton Parish, York Co., on 3 Apr 1740 that was later proved 19 Dec 1743. {YCWI 1740-1743:251}

Hugh Baskervyle, of Bruton Parish, York Co., left a will dated 31 Dec 1747 stipulating that all household goods, cattle, hoggs and ... salted meat ... be sold. I give to my sister Sarah Baskervyle my land and a Negro woman Bess and all the money that my goods and chattels are sold for after my debts and funeral charges are paid. If my said sister should die without heirs, my will is that George Baskervyle, son of John Baskervyle, shall have and enjoy the afsd estate. My will is that the plantation be rented out and the income to be paid unto my sister afsd. My sister may have and enjoy all the money that my crop of tobacco sells for and all the debts now due to me. I likewise give unto my sister Sarah Baskerwyle my riding horse. I appoint Sarah Baskervile, Pinkethman Eaton & Fleming Bates executors. Proved 21 Mar 1747. Sarah Baskervyle, executrix, and Fleming Bates, executor (a Quaker), were granted a certificate for obtaining a probate, and they, together with Matthew Shields & William Stanup, their securities, acknowledged a bond. {YCWI 1745-1759:85}

The inventory & appraisement of the estate of Hugh Baskervyle, deceased, was recorded 16 May 1748. Seven shoats, 2 sows, a horse, salted pork, corn, pot of hog's lard, case of draws, 2 beds, bolsters, rugs, cords etc. totaled £36 pd 9 sl 4 pn, errors excepted. 12 Apr 1748. Matt Moody, Fips Jackson, Ambrose Jackson. {YCWI 1745-1759:98}

In obedience to a court order, Pen Eaton, Fips Jackson & Ambrose Jackson settled the estate of Hugh Baskerfield, deceased. Paid for 1 coffin, digging a grave, sheet to bury the corps[e], cash let Henry Bates have to go for a doctor, paid Thomas Brodrik, Sarah Rhodes, Alice Bruce, Doctor Gilmer, Elizabeth Macarty, Mr. Graves' estate, Doctor McKenzie, John Blair esqr, Mr. Hornsby, Mr. Holt, Mr. Stanup, Henry Bates for crying[3]. £51 pd 1 sl 7 1/4 pn. Recorded 18 Jun 1750. {YCWI 1745-1759:176}

On 12 Jan 1752, John Carter, of the City of Williamsburgh, ordinary keeper, and Hannah, his wife, for £5, sold to William Prentis of same city, gent., a 150 acre tract of land in Bruton Parish bounded by [the late?] Hugh Baskervyle, Pinkethman Eaton, the land that was Henry Hacker's & James Bates's. Ackn 20 Jan 1752. {YCLRD 1741-1754:466}

8. NOWEL/NORVILE BASKERVYLE

[On 19 Nov 1744, the Court dismissed] the action of trespass brought by John Parker against Nowel Baskervyle. {YCWI 1743-1746:318}

[On 19 May 1746, the Court dismissed] the case between John Coke, William Parks & Thos Vobe, executors of John Parker, deceased, plaintiffs against Norvile Baskervyle, defendant, for want of prosecution, the writ not being served. {YCWI 1743-1746:432}

THE HENRY BORODELL[4] FAMILY

1. HENRY BORODELL m. 1st Elizabeth (N) (d. 15 Mar 1717) and m. 2nd Judith (N) Hynton. {CPR:204; YCWI 1720-1722:17}

Thomas Townzend (d. 27 Sep 1711) was a son of Susanna and a servant to Henry Borradell. {CPR:250}

Elizabeth Varnum, widow, Henry Hayward, Junr., and Henry Burrowdill, all of the Co. of York, to the Justices of said County, in the sum of £100 as surety for Elizabeth Varnum as Adminstratrix of the whole Estate of Lewis Varnum, dec'd.... 24 Nov 1708. {YCWI 1706-1710:178,180}

In the petition of James Hill, Adminstrator of the Estate of Thomas Taylor, deceased, for part of the decedent's Estate in the hands of Henry

---

[3] Crier used in the sense of announcer or publicizer.
[4] Given the phonetic spelling of the time, the name appears in many variations, all of which were retained as written in the original records.

Borrowdill, the appraisers appointed having returned an appraisement of the said goods, and Henry Borrowdill having also made oath to the inventory, at the said Hill's mocion, the said appraisement is admitted to record. {YCWI 1706-1710:207}

Henry Borrowdill hath judgment granted him for £2:3:9 against James Hill, Administrator of the Estate of Thomas Taylor, deceased, for funeral expenses, he having proved his account by his oath and ordered that the said Hill pay the same *alies* execution. {YCWI 1706-1710:208,215}

Simon Stacy, planter, and Thomas Burnham, planter, both of the Parish of Charles in the Co. of York, to Henry Heyward the Younger, of the aforesaid Parish, in the sum of 6,000 lbs. of every way good, sweetscented, merchandizable tobacco and good cask to contain the same to be paid to the said Heyward or to Henry Borridell.... 20 Aug 1711. The condition of this obligacion is such that if the above bounden Simon or Thomas ... shall from time to time and at all times hereafter well and truly save and keep harmless and indemnifyed the above named Henry Heyward and Henry Borridell ... from all matter of suits ... which may arise by reason of their the said Heyward and Borridell being bound together with Elizabeth Vernam, widow, Administratrix of the goods and chattles of Lewis Vernam, her late husband, for her duly and truly administering the Estate of the said Lewis according to Law, then this obligacion to be void.... {YCWI 1709-1711:105,108}

In the acion upon the case between William Bond, plaintiff, and Henry Borrodall, defendant, for £12:15:0 by account, the defendant being called and failing to appear and no security returned for him, judgment is granted the plaintiff for the said sum with costs against the said defendant and Thomas Roberts, Sheriff, unless the defendant appears at the next Court and answers the plaintiff's action. {YCWI 1711-1714:221}

Henry B[o]rradall having been presented by ye grand jury for stopping of publick road [blocking the road] in Charles Parish ye court upon hearing his defence & ye law relating thereto do fine & [?] him 10 sl to ye church wardens of said parish to be paid at their next levy for ye use of said parish otherwise by distress, and it is further ordered that ye said Borradall immediately remove & take away ye fence stopping ye said road. {YCWI 1716-1718:23}

In settling the estate of John Wythe, deceased, sums were paid to ... Henry Borradall et al.... {YCWI 1716-1718:32}

On 17 Nov 1716, in ye case between Anne Phillips, executor & plaintiff, and Henry Borradall, for 1091 lbs of tobacco due by account, ye defendant failing to appear, on ye plaintiff's motion, an attachment was granted her against defendant's estate for sum sued for & costs returnable to next court for judgment. {YCWI 1716-1718:42}

Upon ye petition of Henry Borradall, setting forth ye inconveniency of having a publick road through his corn field & praying that he may have liberty to turn ye said road about a hundred yards farther into ye old field where it will be equally as good & convenient as ye present road, the court ordered that ye surveyor of ye highways in that precinct go & view said road he proposed to make a report to next court. {YCWI 1716-1718:59}

Benjamin Clifton, an evidence for Armiger Parsons & Eliza, his wife, against William Wise, having attended 4 days on the said suit, the court ordered that the said Armiger Parsons pay him 160 lbs of tobacco for the same with costs.... Henry Borrodale, the same, only 160 lbs for 4 days. {YCWI 1718-1720:667}

In Apr 1720, the action upon the Case between Henry Borrodale & Judith his wife, late Judith Hynton, on behalf of the legatees of Mary Moory, deceased, and Wm Tucker, Executor etc., of John Merry, deceased, who was Executor. {YCWI 1720-1722:17}

An Inventory of ye estate of Jane Culley decd....
To he ... sold to Henry Barradale - £2.10.0 ... Barradale for Schooling - £0.15.0 ... (all the rest of the names have been obliterated.)
... Court dated Mar 19 1721 we ye Subscribers.... {YCWI 1720-1722:129}

The suit in Chancery between ... Barradale and Judith his wife, Complaintants, and John Merry Sur ... Merry, deceased, is dismist. {YCWI 1720-1722:134}

The Suit of Chancery depending between Henry Borrodale and Judith, his Wife, Complaintants, and William Tucker, Executor of Thomas Merry, respondent, is dismist. {YCWI 1722-1725:253}

In obedience to a court order dated 16 May 1743, the subscribers settled an account of the estate of John Adduston Rogers, deceased. Paid ... Judith Burrodale et al. 42 pd 2 sl 5 pn. Balance due the estate 11 pd 7 sl 11 pn. 18 May 1743. Ishmael Moody et al.... Recorded 20 Jun 1743. {YCWI 1740-1743:198}

Henry and Elizabeth (N) Borodell were the parents of SARAH, b. 6 Jan 17[03]; HENRY, b. 3 Apr [1708], d. 31 Aug 1710; MARY, b. 1 Jan 1710, d. 27 Apr 1720; and ANN, b. 24 Dec 1713, d. 3 Mar 1717. {CPR}

Henry and Judith (N) were the parents of THOMAS, b. 1 Oct, bapt. 14 Dec 1720 {CPR:53,204} and HENRY. {YCWI 1740-1743:149}

Second Generation

2. HENRY BORODELL was a son of Henry (1) and Judith (N); was b. ca. 1720; d. bef. 18 Jul 1743; and m. Elizabeth (Tenham) Burt, relict of Moody Burt (d. ca. 1734). Elizabeth Tenham was the dau. of John Tenham (will 9 Aug 1735). {YCWI 1732-1737:240}

The court ordered that John Goodwin, Junr., be appointed constable in the room of Moody Burt, and that he be sworn accordingly. {YCWI 1732-1737:176}

The will of John Tenham, of Yorkhampton Parish, York Co., was written on 9 Aug 1735. To my daughter, Anne Wright, one cow, one 3 year old [horse], and one yearling. To my daughter, Elizabeth Burt, one servant boy named Francis Luck, she paying 40 shillings a year toward the payment of his estate, except the last year which is to be emitted for the payment of his freedom dues. To my son, John, and my daughter, Rebecca, all my crop to be divided between them. My will is that after my debts are paid all the rest of my estate be divided among all my children. I appoint my son John Tenham executor.... {YCWI 1732-1737:240}

In court held on 15 Dec 1735, Elizabeth Burt, the widow and relict of Moody Burt, deceased, made oath that the said deceased departed this life without making any will and on her motion and giving bond and security, the court ordered that a certificate be granted her for obtaining a Letter of Administration. {YCWI 1732-1737:242}

In obedience to a court order dated 15 Dec 1735, John [W]Right, Thomas Powell & John Goodwin met at the house of Moody Burt, deceased, and appraised so much of the estate as was brought before us by Elizabeth Burt, his relict-- Negroes: man named Tom, boy named Will, girl named Phillis, girl named Jude. 12 cows & stears, 6 young cattle, 4 calves, 2 draught stears, 2 yokes, 18 head of sheep, a parcel of hogs & piggs, 1 horse, 2 mares, a colt, 6 cows, a parcel of tools, etc. 163 pd 17 sl 5 1/2 pn.... Recorded 19 Jan 1735.... {YCWI 1732-1737:242,258}

On 15 Jul 1739, the action of trespass, assault & battery brought by James Southerland against Henry Borrodell, Thomas Loyd, James Black and John Tenham, is dismist neither party appearing. {YCWI 1737-1740:510}

On the motion of Henry Borrodell, an evidence for Francis Moss at the suit of Edward Moss, the court ordered that the said Francis pay him for 4 days' attendance. {YCWI 1737-1740:511}

In the action of trespass between John Ballard, merchant & plaintiff, and John Dailey, defendant, the defendant not appearing, it's considered by the court that the plaintiff recover against the defendant and Henry Borrodell, his security, 20 pd unless the defendant shall appear & plead at the next court. {YCWI 1737-1740:530}

Upon the prayer of Elizabeth Burrodale, widow, and her making oath on 18 Jul 1743 that Henry Burrodale, deceased, departed this life without making any will, and giving bond and security, the court ordered that a certificate be granted her for obtaining a Letter of Administration.... The court ordered that Isaac Collier, Edward Potter, Wm Moss & Edward Baptist appraise the estate of Henry Burrodale, deceased. {YCWI 1740-1743:207,231}

Upon the petition of Elizabeth Burrodell, the court ordered that Samuel Reade, John Ballard, Ishmael Moody & Matthew Hubard, Gent., meet & settle an account of the estate of Moody Burt, deceased, and divide the same. {YCWI 1740-1743:233}

In obedience to a court order on 21 Nov 1743, the subscribers settled an account of the estate of Moody Burt, deceased, and divided the same. Paid the widow her 1/3 part of the personal estate, paid the children of said deceased for their parts, John Burt, Wm Burt, Matthew Burt, Philip Burt, Moody Burt. Negroes: Tom, Will, Phillis, Judy (Judith), Cazar. 206 pd 8 sl 9 1/2 pn. Elizabeth Borrodale late widow of Moody Burt, deceased.... Recorded 19 Mar 1743. {YCWI 1743-1746:271}

In a court session held 16 Jul 1744, a power of attorney from Samuel Palmer and others to Elizabeth Banadall, of the City of Williamsburgh, was proved by the oath of Robert Robinson and ordered to be certified. {YCWI 1743-1746:295}

Pursuant to a court order dated 21 Sep 1747, Samuel Reade, Edward Moss & William Allen settled the estate of Henry Burradell, deceased. Negro man named Jimmy. Paid cash to Doctor John Payras, Thos Brewer, Walter Charles, John Harris, Ishmael Moody, James Bird, John Trotter, Ann Bond, John Tenham, Thos Avery, John Bond, Capt. John Ballard, Robt Ranson, John Chapman, John Allman, Richd Hurst, Wm Dudley, bond to Thos Reynolds, Mr. Ambler, Rev. John Camm, Thos & Wm Nelson, orphans of Moody Burt. Balance received for account from Haswell & Hung, Honorable Philip Lightfoot esqr, Richard Ambler esqr. 192 pd 6 sl 5 3/4 pn.... Recorded 16 Nov 1747. {YCWI 1745-1759:75}

Henry and Elizabeth (Tenham) Borodell were probably the parents of MATTHEW and possibly HENRY. {YCLRD 1741-1754:384}

3. MATTHEW BORODELL, b. ca. 1738, was probably a son of Henry (2) and Elizabeth (Tenham) Borodell.

The court ordered that the church wardens of Yorkhampton Parish, or one of them, bind out Matthew Burradell to some handy craft trade until he comes to age 21. {YCWI 1740-1743:149}

On 17 Sep 1750, Henry Burradall, of York Co., doth vollentarily bind himself unto Matthew Burradell, of York Co, for 3 ½ years as an apprentice to learn the trade or mistery of a house carpenter.... {YCLRD 1741-1754:384}

OTHERS NAMED BORODELL

BLUMFIELD BURRADELL, possibly son of Edward and Elizabeth, both described in the following paragraphs.

In a court held 19 Nov 1744, power of atty from Blumfield Burradell to Wm Prentis was proved by the oath of John Clark, and it was ordered that the same be certify'd. {YCWI 1743-1746:317}

EDWARD BARRADELL, GENT., m. Elizabeth (N).

Robert Beverley, esqr., was granted 4254 acres N.L. (new land) in King & Queen and Caroline Counties on 24 Feb 1730 for 17 pounds, 15 shillings and for the importation of 14 persons: Robert Rose, Jerome Armore, Mungo

Roy, Edward Barradell, Adam Reid, James Reid, John Wilcox, Alexander Parker, Pittman Scandutt (or Scandrett), John McCollock, John Froman, John Cordell, Mar Weeks, and Thomas Parker. {CP III, citing Patent Book 14:151}

Ordered that all matters in difference between John Hansford and John Moore touching the estate of Matthew Hansford, deceased, be refer'd to Wm Robertson and Edwd Barradell, gent. and award is to be made the judgment of the court by consent of both parties. {YCWI 1732-1737:291}

John Hansford, plaintiff, against John Moore and Elizabeth, his wife, administrator and defendants of Matthew Hansford, deceased, by consent of both parties, all matters in difference between them touching the estate of Matthew Hansford, deceased, was refer'd to Wm Robertson and Edward Barradell gent. whose award was to be the judgment of this court, and they having stated and settled an account of the same, do report as followeth, we award that the defendant pay to the plaintiff 12 pd 11 sl 7 pn 3 farthings in full for the balance of the estate of Matthew Hansford, deceased, in the hands of the defendant, and that the plaintiff pay to the defendant 185 lbs of tobacco for the costs of this judgment law. The court ordered that judgment be enter'd for the plaintiff and that he recover against the defendant the aforesaid sum, and that the plaintiff pay to the defendant 185 lbs of tobacco. {YCWI 1732-1737:323}

On 1 Dec 1740, Edward Barradall, of the City of Williamsburgh esqr., for £110, sold to William Keith, of same place, a 100 acre parcel of land in Yorkhampton Parish, York Co, lately purchased by the said Edward Barradall of Benjamin Carrson, esqr, on 13 Jun 1739, and also an 18 acre parcel of land contiguous to the aforesaid parcel lately purchased by said Edward Barradall of said William Keith & Anna, his wife, on 14 Mar 1737.... Wits: Isabella Cocke, Elizabeth Barradall, Jno Baskewyle, Jno Kendall. Ackn 16 Mar 1740/1. {YCLRD 1729-1740:633}

SARAH BARRADELL

On 28 Jul 1743 a Deed of Mortgage was agreed. Hugh Orr, of the City of Williamsburg, blacksmith, in consideration of the bond with Benjamin Waller, sold to Benjamin Waller, of same city, gent, a ½ acre lot of ground on the south side of Duke of Gloucester Street in the City of Williamsburg (No. 15) ... whereas the said Benjamin Waller, together with the said Hugh Orr, at special request, did for the proper debt of the said Hugh Orr, by one obligation dated this date, did become jointly & severally bound unto Sarah Barradell, Blumfield Barradell & William Prentis, executors of the will of Edward Barradell, esqr., deceased, for £200, for the payment of £100 on 28 Jul next ensuing ... provided that if the said Hugh Orr shall cause the said Benjamin Waller on 28 Jul next ensuing to be cleared and absolutely acquitted and discharged from the bond then these presents to be void.... {YCLRD 1741-1754:89}

THE AMBROSE COBBS / COBB FAMILY

First Generation

1. AMBROSE COBBS, b. ca. 1600, m. Ann (N).

Ambrose Cobbs received 350 acres on the Appamattuck River, adjacent the land of Robert Baugh and Mr. Abraham Wood, on 25 Jul 1639, for the transportation of seven persons: himself, his wife Ann, his son Robert, his daughter Margarett, Richard Barker, Hugh Barker, and Thomas Harding. {CP I:111}

Ambrose and Ann (N) Cobbs were the parents of ROBERT and MARGARETT. {CP I:111}

Second Generation

2. ROBERT COBBS, b. 1627 England, d. 21 Dec 1682, m. Elizabeth (N) (d. 1684) {WARG:135}, was a son of Ambrose (1) and Ann (N) Cobbs.

Robert Cobbs, guardian of Thomas Bates, son in law of Robert Wilkinson, deceased, agreed on 13 Nov 1660 to keep Bates until he reaches 21 years of age. {RB 1659-1662:94}

Robert Cobbs, age c34, was deposed on 27 Aug 1661 concerning a broll [brawl] at the home of deponent. {RB 1659-1662:127}

Robert Cobbs witnessed the probate of the will of John Margaretts on 24 Jan 1661. The will names wife Anne, daughter Anne, and Thomas Bromfield, guardian to daughter Anne. {VCR:Vol IX}

An examination of the accounts of Mr. Robert Cobbs, relating to Sarah Wilkinson, orphan, was reported on 12 Apr 1669. The court ordered that Peter Glanister, who married said orphan, give bond and receive estate. {RB 1665-1672:340[240]}

Robert Cobbs was one of the founders of the Bruton Parish Church in Williamsburg. The first entry to the Parish Vestry Book on 18 Apr 1674 gives the names of those who attended the initial meeting: "The Honourable Coll. Danl. Parke, Mr. Rowland Jones, Minister, Mr. John Page, Mr. James Besouth, Mr. Robert Cobb and Mr. Bray,--Capt. Chesley, and Mr. Aylette, Church Warders. Mr. John Owens, Sidesman."[5] {WARG:12}

On 14 Nov 1678, Robert Cobb was one of the subscribers who pledged

---

[5] The Parke family was associated with the Cobbs, Graves, and Weldon families in this volume. Col. Daniel Parke (d. 1677) was the father of Daniel Parke who appears in the York records in 1687 when he was about age 18. They were ancestors of Martha Dandridge's first husband, Daniel Parke Custis. Rowland Jones, the first minister of Bruton Parish Church, was the great-grandfather of Martha Dandridge Custis Washington.

to build "A Brick Church, on ye Middle Plantation[6], for ye said Parish...."
{WARG:14}
    In his will dated 11 Aug 1677, Daniel Parke Esq, of London and
Virginia, named Robert Cobb and James Bray executors in trust for Virginia.
{CD503:164}
    Robert Cobbs and (N) were the parents of EDMUND m. Frances (N);
AMBROSE; ROBERT; OTHO, b. ca. 1670; and MARY, m. William Kerle.

3. THOMAS COBBS, d. 1702 *d.s.p.*, prob. nephew of Ambrose (1) Cobbs.
    Peter Glenister, Middletown Parish York Co., planter, with consent of
his wife, Sarah Glenister, sold land at Queens Creek Middletown Parish, which
was a former plantation of Robert Wilkinson and Richard Thorpe's land, to
Thomas Cobbs, of Marston Parish, on 24 Mar 1670. {RB 1665-1672:438[338]}
    Thomas Cobbs, of Bruton Parish York Co., left a will dated 8 Dec 1702.
To my couzin William (10) Cobbs my house & land whereon I now live & one
cow called Cherry & also 10 pd which he is now indebted to me and if he dyes
without heirs then my house and land to go to Thomas Cobbs (12). To Isaac
Scot one black mare running now in Powhaten as also one salune cote lin'd with
serge. To Alice Newman two cows. To Robert Cobbs (11) sone of Ambrose (7)
Cobb one 2 year old heifer. All ye remaining portions of my estate to my
couzins Ambrose Cobbs, Robert Cobbs, Otho Cobbs & Robert Kenle[7]. I
appoint my couzens Ambrose Cobbs & Otho Cobbs executors. Wit: Mary Fips,
John Revere, Mary Pickman (Rickman?) [Pinkethman?]. Proved 24 Feb
1702[/3]. {YCWI 1702-1704:78,84}
    An inventory & appraisement of the estate of Thomas Cobbs, deceased,
was taken 1 Mar 1702. The estate included 10 steers, 1 bull, 3 cowes, 2 heiffers,
4 yearlings, 1 mare, 2 bay horses, 2 grey horse colts, 13 shoates, 10 hoggs, 3
sowes, 10 small piggs, 2 feather beds, bolters, pillows, blankets, ruggs, curtains,
vallins [valences], bed tick[ing], sheets, 4 pillobers, 4 dowles shirts, 9
neckleather, 4 capps, 12 handkerchiefs, 2 coates, 1 pr leather breechers, 4 pr
dimothy breeches, 2 pr old worsted hose, etc. Negroes: man called Knap, a new
woman. 180 pd 1 sl 10 1/4 pn. Ambrose Cobbs & Otho Cobbs executors. In
pursuant to an order of court dated 24 --- 1702, Wm Pinkethman et al. appraised
the estate.... {YCWI 1702-1704:107}

4. AMBROSE COBBS, b. ca. 1640s, d. 1683 {WARG:135}, m. Mary (N). After
Ambrose's death, Mary (N) m. 2nd George Glascock (d. 1689) {WARG:136}, and
3rd William Taylor.
    George Glascock, being possessed on 24 Jun 1687 with the estate of

---

[6] By the turn of the 17th century, this was the town Williamburgh.
[7] See Margaret (10) Cobbs, who by her husband William Kirle, had a son Robert.

William Cobbs, orphant of Ambross Cobbs, by intermarrying with the dec's relict. Finding Glascock hath much imbesled the estate, at Court 24 Jan 1687/8, the Sherriff summoned Glascock. The Sheriff ordered Glascock into custody until he gives bond with sufficient securytie. {DW 1687-1691:153}

The order of last court for summoning Col Edmund Jennings to this court, which is being held on 24 Feb 1701, to answer the complaint of William Cobb, orphan of Ambrose Cobb, for that part of his deceased father's estate due to him out of the hands of the sd Col Jennings, his trustee, for the same is referred to next court and it is further ordered that the clerk give notice thereof to the sd Col Jennings. {YCWI 1698-1702:539}

On 24 May 1701, the Court ordered that the clerk signifie to Col Edmund Jennings that ye estate put into his hands [by] Glascock, as marrying with the relict of Ambrose Cobb, deceased, belongs to ye orphan of said Ambrose, and that he would send an account of the just sum thereof next court, may order it to whom it belongs. {YCWI 1698-1702:565}

The Court ordered that William Taylor, [who] married the widow of George Glascock, be summoned to next court to given an account of the rents of the plantation belonging to Glascock. {YCWI 1698-1702:565}

... I [Edward Jennings] am also further compelled to acquaint you that I have also received notice from the clerk that William Cobb, orphan of Ambrose, hath entered a plaint against me, I do not remember I was ever conce[?] my estate except the former [Ambrose's] and George Glascock's estate, with which I entrusted by the court to receive bills in my name, which amounted to about 4000 lbs tobacco, if that related to Cobb, and the court please to direct me to pay it to him.... I'm necessitated to pass to Rappahannock having been appointed [?] which will occassion my stay there.... 20 Mar 1701/2. {YCWI 1702-1704:9}

In obedience to a court order dated 24 Jul 1702, Henry Tyler, Wm Pinkethman & Joseph White met at the house of John Bently in Williamsburgh and appraised that estate of Ambrose Cobbs, deceased, which was unappraised in the first appraisement. The second appraisement comprised 3 steers, 6 cows, 3 heifers, 4 yearlings, 1 bull, 1 cow calf, 3 mares, 2 colts, 11 heads of hogs, 1 small drane cup, 1 pewter tankard, 1 old spade, 520 lbs of tobacco. The current appraisement of 49 pd 7 sl added to the former appraisement of 21 pd 9 sl 9 pn made a total appraisement of 65 pd 16 sl 9 pn.[8] {YCWI 1702-1704:46}

Ambrose and Mary (N) Cobbs were the parents of <u>WILLIAM</u> and ROBERT.

5. SAMUEL COBB entered Virginia ca. 1661.

---

[8] The sum doesn't make sense, but these are the numbers in the original records.

On 26 Aug 1661, William Whitaker was granted a certificate for 450 acres due for the importation of 9 persons into the colony: William Winter, Samuel Cobb, Lemuel Morris, William Hopkins, Peter Shepheard, Joseph Cooper, John Kinchley, William Macklin, and Henry Burt. {RB 1659-1662:126}

Third Generation

6. EDMUND COBBS, b. ca. 1650s, will 2 Mar 1690/1, d. 1692 {WARG:136}, will proved 24 Aug 1693, m. Frances (N), was a son of Robert (2) and Elizabeth (N) Cobbs. Edmund and Frances (N) appear to have had no children.

Frances was m. 1st to (N) Pierce and was the mother of Matthew Pierce. After Edmund's death, Frances m. 3rd John Steward by Jun 1695. {DW 1694-1697:171}

Edmund Cobbs, Co. of York, Parish of Bruton, left a will dated 2 Mar 1690/1, presented in Court 24 Aug 1693. Unto brother Ambrose Cobbs, a Negro boy, Guy, also goald ring of my father's. Unto brother Robert Cobbs, Negro boy, Dick. Unto son in law Matthew Pierce, my youngest Negro boy, Tom. All the rest of my estate to my wife Frances Cobbs, executrix, she to pay my brother Otho, when 21, his portion of my deceased father's estate. Unto my coz: Elizabeth Kerle which lives with me, maintenance until 16. After decease of my wife, to my 3 brothers Ambrose, Robert and Otho Cobbs and my son in law Matthew Pierce. {DW 1691-1694:243-244}

Mrs. Frances Cobbs made a deed of guift on 26 Mar 1694 of 2 Negro girls, mon[e]y, and sheep to her son Mathew Peirce. {DW 1691-1694:314}

Mrs. Frances Steward, late widow of Edmund Cobb, and now wife of John Steward, sets forth on 24 Jun 1695 to protect the bequests of Cobb's will, John Steward giving security for same. {DW 1694-1697:171}

7. AMBROSE COBBS, b. ca. 1660s, d. 1719 {WARG:140}, was a son of Robert (2) and Elizabeth (N) Cobbs.

Ambrose Cobbs was executor, with Elliner Yates, wife of the deceased, of the will of Thomas Yates, dated 7 Mar 1693/4, proved 2 Apr 1694. To son Peter Yates, 250 acres in New Kent Co. and horse and mare. To daughter Elizabeth Yates, mare and colt. To wife Elliner Yates, rest of plantation and personal estate. {DW 1691-1694:334}

Ordered on motion of John Bentley & Margrett, his wife, adminr of ye estate of Christopher Penston, deceased, against Ambrose Cobb, Thomas Cobb, Mathew? Crawley, Joseph Sherinton? to meet at ye home of said administrator & appraise said deceased's estate. {YCWI 1698-1702:68}

On motion of Nathaniel & Robert Crawley, ye sons & admininstrators of their deceased father's, Robt Crawley's, estate, it is ordered that James Whaley, Ambrose Cobb, John Steward & Robert Bee appraise the said deceased's estate. {YCWI 1698-1702:69}

19 Nov 1702. John Bently, together with Ambrose Cobb & John Bates securities, did jointly & severally confess judgment before Capt Thomas Barber & Capt Baldwin Mathews, justices, to Henry Tyler, trustee to ye estate of Cope Doyley, late of this Co., deceased, for payment of 9 pd with cost & stay of execution until 10 Jan 1703. {YCWI 1702-1704:49}

Henry Cary, together with Ambrose Cobb & George Baskervile, securities, did jointly and severally confess judgment before Capt Thomas Barber & Capt Baldwin Mathews, justices to Henry Tyler trustee to the estate of Cope Doyley, late of this Co., deceased, for payment of 4 pd with cost & stay of execution until 10 Jan 1703. {YCWI 1702-1704:52}

Ambrose Cobbs and Nat Crawley witnessed the appraisal of the estate of Edward Randolph, the estate consisting of 18 lbs of reasons [raisins], 10 lbs of currants, a quarter of a lb of cinnamon, a quarter of a lb of cloves, a quarter of mace, a quarter of nutmeg, 3 oz of silk, 1 pr of shoe buckles, 1 lot of shirt buttons, 1 ivory headed cane, 2 pr slippers, 1 pr of spectacles. 6 pd 10 sl 1 1/2 penny ... recorded 24 May 1704. {YCWI 1702-1704:192}

Ambrose Cobs hath judgment granted against ye estate of Thomas Cobs, deceased, for 5 pd and is ordered to be payd with cost. {YCWI 1702-1704:205}

Ambrose Cobbs owned 163 acres of land in York Co. {QRV:19}

At York Co. court on 24 May 1707, a Grand Jury of 19 freeholders was formed: viz. Wm. Davis, Ralph Hubbard, Thomas Feare Junr., Ambo. Cobb, Richd. Kendall, Robt. Jaxon, Robt. Peters, Charles Collyer, Thomas Whitby, Wm. Lee, Thomas Chessman Junr., Hen. Hayward Senr., Hen. Hayward Junr., John Tomer, John Adduston Rogers, Wm. Sheldon, John Moss, Willm. Allen and Charles [no last name].... {YCWI 1706-1710:62}

William Pinkethman this day presented his commission from the Hon. Alexander Spottswood Esq, her Majesty's Lt. Govr. of this Colony, to be Sheriff of this County, and he together with Ambrose Cobbs and Henry Holdcraft, his securitys, entered into bond to the Queen in the sum of £1,000 for the due performance of his office and ... was admitted to record. {YCWI 1711-1714:154}

John Clayton & Hugh Norvell, feofees or trustees for the land appropriated for the building & erecting the City of Williamsburgh, for 5 shillings, lett a farm unto Ambrose Cobbs of York Co, two lotts of ground in the sd City of Williamsburgh, designed in the plan of the said city by the figures 43 & 44 ... for the term of one year, paying the yearly rent of one grain of Indian corn on 10 Oct, if demanded.... Ackn 16 Jun 1718.... {YCDB 1713-1729:243}

On 14 Feb 1718, Ambrose Cobbs and Robert Cobbs Junr witnessed the sale of a ½ acre lot of ground in the City of Williamsburgh denoted in the plan of the said city by the figure 337, from David Cuningham of York Co., for £10, sold to John Blair of the City of Williamsburgh.... {YCDB 1713-1729:270}

Ambrose and Elizabeth (N) Cobbs were the parents of FRANCES;

ROBERT; THOMAS; JOHN; EDMUND; and AMBROSE.

8. ROBERT COBBS, b. ca. 1660s, will 10 Dec 1725, proved 21 Feb 1725/6, was a son of Robert (2) and Elizabeth (N) Cobbs. Robert m. 1st Rebecca Pinktheman (d. ca 1715) and 2nd Elizabeth Allen. After Robert's death in 1725, Elizabeth m. Samuel Weldon of James City Co. {CD503:125}

Rebecca Pinkethman was a daughter of William and Rebecca (N) Pinkethman. {YCWI 1711-1714:231-232}

Elizabeth Allen was the daughter of Daniel Allen. {CD503:125}

On 24 Feb 1696, Matthew Jeffreys, of James City Parish James City Co., planter, for £25, sold to Robert Cobbs of Bruton Parish, York Co., planter, one tract or plantation of ground, containing 50 acres in Bruton Parish at ye head of Queens Creek, bounded by ye Old Mill, Silvester Tatnum's Field, and the Mill Swamp, as appears by one deed (of) conveyance dated 25 Jan 1652 of the said land from Thomas & Maurise Prise unto Stephen Royston.... Whereof Matthew Jeffreys doth hereby convey the same to the said Robert Cobbs forever.... Wit: Tho Cobbs, John Frayser.... {YCDB 1694-1701:126}

Robert Cobbs owned 100 acres of land in York Co. {QRV:19}

On 24 Mar 1704, Robert Cobbs & Rebecca his wife, providing evidence for plaintiff in a trial, hath order granted for 5 days attendance at court. {YCWI 1705-1706:320}

In the petition of Ralph Graves, setting forth that William Eaton and Sarah, his wife, and Rebecca Pinkethman (alias Cobbs), Executors of the last Will & Testament of William Pinkethman, deceased, refuse to pay and deliver the several legacys in the decedent's will expressed to be given to Mary [Graves], the petitioner's wife, therefore, the Court ordered that the Sheriff summon the said Executors to appear at the next Court to show cause as to why they do not perform the will of the decedent. {YCWI 1711-1714:247}

The acion upon the case between William Eaton and Sarah, his wife, and Rebecca Cobbs, the wife of Robert Cobbs, Executors of William Pinkethman, deceased, plaintiffs, and George Baskervile and Thomas Cripps, Executors of Rebecca Pinkethman, widow, deceased, defendants, is continued until the next Court on the defendant's mocion for them to produce their discount. {YCWI 1711-1714:269}

In the petition of Philloman Jackson on 21 Sep 1713 against William Eaton and Sarah, his wife, and Rebecca, the wife of Robert Cobbs, Executors of William Pinkethman, who was Executor of Eliz. Handy, for his share or part of her Estate given by Will, the court ordered that the Sheriff summon the Executors of the said Pinkethman to appear and answer the said petition at the next Court. {YCWI 1711-1714:275}

Robt Cobbs, of Bruton Parish, York Co., planter, for 5 shillings, lett a farm unto Mathew Pierce, of same place, planter, a 45 acre tract of land being part of a tract of land whereon the said Robt now dwells in the afsd parish & is separated therefrom by the following bounds, n side of the Widdow Gibson's Spring Bridge, the dividing line between Major Jno Holloway & the said Pierce, near Major Custis's Mill Swamp, the Main Runn, said Pierce's Spring Bridge & the said Cobbs ... during the term of one year paying the rent of one grain of Indian corn at the feast of Christmas next if demanded ... Ackn 19 Jun 1721.... {YCDB 1713-1729:365}

On 17 May 1721, Robt Cobbs, of Bruton Parish, York Co., planter, for £45, released unto Mathew Pierce [whose guardian was Edmund, brother of Robt Cobbs], of same place, planter, a 45 acre tract of land ... 19 Jun 1721.... {YCDB 1713-1729:366}

The will of Robert Cobbs, of the County of York & Parish of Bruton, was presented to the Court on 10 Dec 1725. To Daughter Elizabeth Cobbs, one good feather bed and all furniture, £10, and One Negro Girl named Sary at age 21 or day of marriage. To my Daughter Rebecca Cobbs, one good feather bed and all furniture, £10, and one Negro Girl named Rachael at age 21 or day of marriage. To Daughter Sarah Cobbs, £25, one Negro Girl named Bess and one Negro Girl named Susan at age 21or day of marriage. To Daughter Martha Cobbs, one Good feather bed and furniture, Negro wench named Sary at age 21 or day of marriage. To Daughter Sarah Cobbs, my land & Planta[*tio*]n whereon I now dwell and to male heirs and if she should die without such heir then same to her Sister Martha Cobbs and to the male heirs. Rest of Estate to Wife Elizabeth Cobbs and after her decease to be equally divided between Daughters Sarah & Martha Cobbs. Wife Elizabeth Cobbs and her father, Daniel Allen, Executors.... At a Court held for York County 21 Feb 1725, this Will & Testament of Robert Cobbs, deceased, was presented by Elizabeth Cobbs & Daniel Allen, the Executors, who made Oath to it and being proved by the Oaths of all the Witnesses thereto is admitted to record ... Elizabeth Cobbs, Daniel Allen, Mat Peirce, and Saml. Cobbs of the County of York are held and firmly bound in the Sum of £1000 pounds.... Elizabeth Bobbs [Cobbs] & Daniel Allen [missing] ... [*missing*] into the hands his death which at any time after shall Come to the hands & Possession of Elizabeth Cobbs etc., the said Executors, or into the hands & Possession of any other person or persons for them and further Do make a true & Just Account of their Actings & Doings therein when required by the said Court and also pay and deliver all the legacys contained and Specified in the said testament as far as the said Goods, Chattles, and Credits will thereunto Extend according to the Value thereof.... {YCWI 1725-1727:374-375}

Robert and Rebecca (Pinkethman) Cobbs were the parents of ELIZABETH (d. 1710); LYDIA (d. 1712); (N) (d. 1713) {WARG:139}; ELIZABETH. {BR:B368}; and REBECCA. {YCWI 1725-1727:374-375}

Robert and Elizabeth (Allen) Cobbs were the parents of SARAH and MARTHA. {BR:B369}

Sarah m. Robert Jones Junr., of Sussex Co., Virginia. They emigrated to North Carolina where he became Attorney General. Martha m. Dudley Richardson. {BR:B367}

9. OTHO COBBS, b. ca. 1670, d. 1705 *d.s.p.*, m. Mary (N). Otho was a son of Robert (2) and Elizabeth (N) Cobb.

Otho Cobb petitioned, and it was so ordered on 13 Feb 1692/3, that Mrs. Frances Cobb, widow of Mr. Edmund Cobb, be summoned to prove her husband's will. Otho alleging that his estate, left him by his deceased father, Mr. Robert Cobb, is in Frances' hands as relict, notwithstanding he is 21. {DW 1691-1694:199}

On 19 Nov 1702 George Hughes, together with Mungo Ingles & Otho Cobb, securities, did jointly and severally confess judgment before Capt Thomas Barber & Capt Baldwin Mathews, justices, to Henry Tyler, trustee to the estate of Cope Doyley, late of this Co., deceased, for payment of 2 pd 7 sl 6 pn with cost and stay of execution untill 10 Jan 1703. {YCWI 1702-1704:56}

10. MARGARET COBBS, d. 1687, m. William Kerle {WARG:135}, was a daughter of Robert (2) and Elizabeth (N) Cobbs.

After Margaret's death in 1687, William m. 2nd Eleanor (N).

The Parish Registry shows that James, son of William Cobbs, d. 1696. The mother of James is not mentioned. {WARG:137}

William Kirle left a will in Isle of Wight Co., Virginia, dated 24 Dec 1719, registered 28 Nov 1720. Leg. eldest son William Kirle, the son of Margaret Cobb, daughter of Robert and Elizabeth Cobb; to my son Robert Kirle, the son of Margaret Cobb, daughter of Robert and Elizabeth Cobb; wife Ellinor; my ... to wit., George, William and Joseph, the sons of ... when their mother Elianor marries again; my son William Kirle, the son of Elioner Kirle. Wife, Executrix. Wits: John Murphrey et al. {BAC:83, citing W&A,Vol. II(Great Book 1719-1729):58)}

Margaret Cobb and William Kerle were the parents of WILLIAM KERLE and ROBERT KERLE.

11. WILLIAM COBB, b. ca. 1680, d. by 9 Oct 1705, m. Mary (N), was a son of Ambrose (4) and Mary (N) Cobb.

On 20 Sep 1702, in the difference between William Cobb, son of Ambrose Cobb, deceased, plaintiff, and Col Edmund Jenings, defendant, wherein the plaintiff requires of the defendant what part of his said decendant's father's estate was and is in the defendant's hands as trustee to the same & sold at a public outcry on 13 Oct 1690, as by a list of debts now produced in court amounting to 4,500 lbs of tobacco against which the defendant, having exhibited his discourse of clerks and sheriff fees at the said outcry amounting to 405 lbs of tobacco being by the court deducted & allowed from the debt afsd there [?], to balance due to the plt of 4,100 lbs of tobacco which the def is ordered to pay to the plaintiff, in Bruton Parish, with cost. {YCWI 1702-1704:43}

William Cobbs owned 50 acres of land in York Co. {QRV:19}

On 9 Oct 1705 Mary Cobbs, Ambross Cobbs & Thomas Wade, planters, of York Co., Virginia, were firmly bound unto ye justices for 100 pd ... the condition of this obligation was such that whereas the afsd Mary Cobbs, on her petition, obtain'd order for a commission of administration of ye whole estate of Willm Cobbs, her deceased husband, whereby she is fully impower'd to take ye same into her care & custody, if ye said Mary Cobbs do present unto said justices a true & perfect inventory of sd estate, and also pay & satisfie all such debts as remain due & owing from said estate, and also do bring a just & true account of the surplusage or remainder to ye justices for the use of those to whom of right it shall belong, and save harmless & indemnifie the said justices from all damages that shall or may accrue, then this obligation to be void.... {YCWI 1705-1706:371}

On 9 Oct 1705, Mary Cobbs, widow & relict of Willm Cobbs, late of this Co., deceased, on her petition, obt'd order for a commission of administration of said deceased's estate & enter'd into bond. {YCWI 1705-1706:371}

Mary Cobbs, relict of William Cobbs, late decd of Bruton Parish, York Co, produced an inventory of his estate as follows: 2 cows, 3 heyfers, 2 bulls, 1 old horse, 1 young mare, 1 mans saddle & snaffle bridle, 1 old side saddle & bridle, 1 feather bed, 1 flock bed, bolster, pillows, sheets, blankets, rugs, bedsteads, cord & matt, 2 trunks, 2 chests with locks & keys, 2 boxes, 2 tables, 1 wooden cradle, 2 looking glasses, 2 old guns, 1 sword & belt, 1 pr old boots, 1 razor & sickle, etc. 29 pd 17 sl 1 pn. Debts owing out of Willm Cobs's estate: John Wade, Thomas Wade, Barrantine Howells, John [blank], Robt Bell, Robt Cobbs, John Loynes, Dr. Wray, Henry Fleman, Francis Rodes, Henry Tyler. [No total] Debts owed to Willm Cobbs: Widow Pinkethman, Wm Pinkethman, Thomas Hicks, [No total]. Presented & recorded in court by Mary Cobbs, widow, on 25 Mar 1706. {YCWI 1705-1706:401}

William m. Mary (N) Cobb and they were the parents of SAMUEL, b. 1695, d. 1757.

Fourth Generation

12. ROBERT COBBS was b. 1690s, d. 1725 {WARG:140}, m. (N) Vinckler, and was a son of Ambrose (7) and Elizabeth (N) Cobbs.

Abraham Vinckler bought land in Virginia in 1667 {RB 1665-1672:136}

In the Bruton Parish records on 14 Nov 1678, Abraham Vinckler witnessed the vestry's purchase of the glebe land and the financial sponsorship of the brick church. {WARG:14}

On 31 Apr 1679, Abraham was naturalized in Virginia. {Hening II:447}

"Mrs. Lydia Vinckler, widow" died in Bruton Parish in 1701.
{WARG:137}
The wife of Robert Cobbs was probably a daughter of Abraham and Lydia (N) Vinckler.
Another Abraham Vinckler [Jr?] was naturalized in Virginia on 4 Oct 1705 {Hening:III:479}.
The Will of Abraham Martin, of Bruton Parish, was presented in court. To my son, William Martin, one gold ring, one silver snuff box, two silver buckles and a set of silver buttons. To my daughter, Jean Martin, one gold ring, one silver thimble and one pair of shoe buckles. To my cozen, Eliz. Stanton, all my wife's cloeth. To my aforesaid son and daughter after my debts are paid, all the rest of my Estate to be equally divided between them. My cozen Eliz. Stanton to be Executrix. Dated 10 Feb 1710. Further, I do give my aforesaid son, William, unto Robert Cobbs, the son of Ambrose Cobbs, to have him till he comes of age of 21 years. Wits: Ambrose Cobbs et al. Proved 18 Jun 1711.
{YCWI 1709-1711:95}
Samuel Hyde, Robt. Cobbs, and Saml. Cobbs presented a Bond in York County Court on 20 Sep 1725, the Condition of this Obligation is Such that whereas the above bounden Samuel Hyde ... became Guardian of Martha Moody and hath received into his Care & Custody the whole Estate of the said Orphan.... {YCWI 1722-1725:360}
Robert and (N) Cobbs were the parents of VINKLER and JOHN.

13. THOMAS COBBS, d. 1748-50, will 15 Jun 1736, proved 17 Sep 1750, m. Mary Shield, was a son of Ambrose (7) and Elizabeth (N) Cobbs.
Thomas Cobbs was present at Court held for York County Jul 18th 1726.... {YCWI 1725-1727:396}
Upon the motion of William Robertson gent, it was ordered that Hannah Shields's ordinary licence be renewed for the ensuing year upon her entering into bond with James Shields and Thomas Cobbs, her securities. {YCWI 1732-1737:175}
... Edwd Barradell and Thos Cobbs, church wardens of Bruton Parish....
{YCWI 1737-1740:385}
Daniel Moore, Samuel Reade, John Ballard, John Goodwin, Thomas Cobbs, James Barbar, Ellyson Armistead & Arthur Dickeson gent were recommended to the Governor as persons fit to be added to the commission of the peace for this county in the room of Robert Armistead, given that Samuel Timson, Richard Ambler, Anthony Robinson, Edward Tabb, John Harmer & Walter King gent ... have refused to serve & act as justices of the peace. {YCWI 1737-1740:407}
The Court ordered that the following persons take the lists of titheables for this year in the precincts of this co: Francis Howard in the upper & Daniel Moore in the lower precinct of Charles Parish; Arthur Dickeson in the upper and William Lightfoot in the lower precinct of Yorkhampton Parish; Thomas Cobbs

in that pt/o Bruton Parish which lies in this county. {YCWI 1737-1740:425}

Samuel Jordan petitioned to have the estate of James Bates, deceased, divided. It was order'd that James Barbar, Ralph Graves, Thomas Cobbs & Robert Crawley meet & divide the slaves into four parts and that 1/4 part thereof be delivered to Sarah Bates, widow, 1/4 part to Hannah Bates, now Hannah Jordan, and the remainder to James Bates as his part, and the part of Mary Bates, deceased, and that the personal estate be divided into three parts between the afsd Sarah, Hannah & James. {YCWI 1737-1740:433}

In Court held 21 Aug 1738, Thomas Cobbs gent took the usual oaths of justice of the peace in Chancery and took his place on the bench. {YCWI 1737-1740:438}

Samuel Reade, Robert Shields, Daniel Moore, Anthony Robinson, Thomas Cobbs, inspectors; Ellyson Armistead, Mattw Moody, Francis Moss, sheriffs; and James Gemmill, Edward Moss, Edward Potter, Wm Robinson, constables, were sworn for amending the staple of tobacco & for preventing fraud of his Majesty's customs. The constables were likewise sworn for the better preservation of the herd of deer and preventing unlawful hunting. 19 Feb 1738. {YCWI 1737-1740:470}

On 20 Aug 1739, the Court order'd that Anthony Robinson, Danl More, Gerald Roberts Junr & Thomas Hawkins be recommended to the Governor as persons fit & capable to execute the office of inspectors at Roe's Warehouse in this Co.; Saml Reade, Robt Shields, Edmd Smith & John Goodwin Junr gent, at York; and Thomas Cobbs & Arthur Dickeson gent, at the Capitol Landing Warehouse. {YCWI 1737-1740:517; YCWI 1740-1743:57}

On 21 Jul 1740, the Court order'd that John Custis esqr, John Blair, George Gilmer & Thos Cobbs gent do [make an] agree[ment] with some workmen to rebuild the bridge at the Capitol Landing at the charge of this County. {YCWI 1737-1740:618}

Thomas Cobbs gent took the usual oaths of Government and was sworn a coroner for this county on 18 Jul 1743. {YCWI 1740-1743:203}

John Grame, of the College of William & Mary, professor of mathematicks, executor of the will of Alexander Kerr late of the City of Williamsburgh gent decd, for £100, sold to Thomas Cobbs, of York Co gent, a 100 acre tract of land on 18 Jul 1738 ... whereas Alexander Kerr in his lifetime was seized in 100 acres of land upon Queens Creek above the Capitol Landing called *Hicks'* which he purch of Sir John Randolph knight decd, and being so seized made his will dated 15 Oct 1738 and proved 2 Nov 1738, in which he did desire that all his lands and other goods & chattels be sold by his executor.... {YCLRD 1741-1754:61}

On 20 Aug 1744, a commission of the peace was assembled to carry out the order, dated 14 Jun last past, under the hand of the Honble Wm Gooch esqr, Lt Governor and Commander in Chief of Virginia, which appointed Thomas Nelson, John Blair, Edward Digges, John Buckner, Francis Howard,

Edmd Smith, Wm Nelson Junr, George Gilmer, Daniel Moore, Saml Reade, John Ballard, John Goodwin, Thomas Cobbs, Ellyson Armistead, Arthur Dickeson, Anthony Robinson, Edward Tabb, Merrit Moody, Nathaniel Bacon Burwell & Matthew Pierce gent as justices of the peace for this county. {YCWI 1743-1746:300}

Matthew Moody of York Co and Ann (Anne), his wife, on 24 Apr 1740, for £10, sold to Thomas Cobbs, of York Co., 1 acre of land adjacent John Coke & the main road leading to the Capitol Landing.... Ackn 18 Jun 1750. {YCLRD 1741-1754:370}

Thos Cobbs, John Coulthard, Mary Cobbs, and Rebecca Coulthard witnessed the will of John Crawley, of Bruton Parish York Co., dated 12 Apr 1748.... {YCWI 1745-1759:107}

The will of Thomas Cobbs, of York Co., was written on 15 Jun 1736[9] and proved 17 Sep 1750. To my three sons Ambrose, Thomas and Matthew Cobbs, one tract of land in Henrico County lately purch of Henry Cary. To my son Ambrose, 50 pd. To my son Thomas Cobbs, 50 pd. To my son Matthew Cobbs, 50 pd. To my dau Hannah Cobbs, 50 pd to be paid her at lawful age or marriage. In case any of my children should dye before lawful age, the money belonging to such child to be divided between the survivors. To my wife, Mary Cobbs, the plantation I now live on, my Negroes and all the rest of my estate she paying my debts and the afsd legacies and giving up her right of dower to the land in Henrico Co. I appoint my wife Mary Cobbs as executrix. Wits: Benj Eggleston, Edmund Cobbs, James Shields.... {YCWI 1745-1759:190}

Mat Pierce, William Graves & Ambrose Jackson appraised the estate of Thomas Cobbs, deceased. The estate comprised 1 bed & furniture, a parcel of feathers, 5 Negro rugs, 4 chests, 1 shoemaker's bench & tools, 1 warming pan, 1 old bedstead, 9 broad hoes, 1 spinning wheel, 3 pair cards, etc., and Negroes: Peter a man, Stafford a man, Sue a woman, Sarah a woman, Bess a woman, Bess a girl, Peter a boy, George a boy, Cate a girl, & Jack Ashbe a servant man. 409 pd 16 sl 1 pn ... recorded 19 Nov 1750. {YCWI 1745-1759:192}

On 21 Dec 1758, Mary Cobbs, of York Co., widow, for £80, sold to Peter Powell, of the City of Williamsburgh, chairmaker, a 120 acre tract of land in Bruton Parish on the south side of Queens Creek that was devised to the said Mary Cobbs by the will of her late husband Thomas Cobbs, deceased ... the said Peter Powell will suffer and permit the said Mary Cobbs, and the servants & slaves properly belonging to her, to dwell and remain in the house and on the plantation upon the said land during her life.... Proved ... 21 May 1759.... {YCLRD 1755-1763:183}

James Anderson, of the City of Williamsburg, blacksmith, and Hannah,

---

[9] Thomas and Mary Cobbs who witnessed the will of John Crawley are both alive in 1748.

his wife, on 15 Apr 1774, for £240, sold to Benjamin Powell, of same city, all that 120 acre tract of land in Bruton Parish on the s side of Queens Creek bounded according to the known ancient & legal bounds thereof which said tract of land ... [*pg torn*] ... to Mary Cobbs by the will of her late husband Thomas Cobbs, deceased, as by the said will proved & recorded in the Co. Court of York & afterwards sold by the said Mary Cobbs to Peter Powell by indenture dated 21 Dec 1758 & by the sd Peter Powell sold to the sd James Anderson by two several indentures dated 7 Jul 1766 & 15 Oct 1772.... {YCDB 1763-1769:391}

The will of Mary Cobbs, of Parish of Bruton, York Co., was written 13 Mar 1773 and proved 20 Jul 1778. To granddaughter, Mary Powell one negro girl named Peg. To granddaughter Hannah Burfoot, four negroes to wit, Fanny, Jamy, Pat and Billy and their increase. Her mother Mary Burfoot (?) should have the use of said four negroes until the said Hannah Burfoot should arrive to the age of 21 or married, and then her mother should have her choice of two. Also mentioned were Martha Cobbs, daughter of Ambrose Cobbs; Sally Cobbs Hulett and Armistant Hulett, daughter & son of my daughter, Hannah Hulett. Remainder of negroes to wit. Betty, Sukey, Joe, Nanny, Billy, Pompey and Molly Roberts should be hired out by my executors for the most money that can be got and the money arising there from to be used toward the maintaining my daughter Sarah Valentine during her natural life and at her death to be divided between my said daughter Sarah Valentine's children and if she dies without issue then they are to be divided between my daughter Elizabeth Powell's children and Hannah Burfoot. Executors: Mr. John Tazewell and James Shields. Wits: Peter Powell, Pennel Penny, Henry Bolton... Benjamin Valentine was security for James Shields, to whom Probate was granted. {YCWI 1771-1783:400}

Thomas and Mary (Shield) Cobbs were the parents of <u>THOMAS</u>; <u>AMBROSE</u>; MATTHEW; and HANNAH.

14. JOHN COBBS was a son of Ambrose (7) and Elizabeth (N) Cobbs.

Vinkler Cobbs & John Cobbs, executors of the will of Robert Cobbs Senr, late of York Co., deceased, for 5 shillings, leased unto Matthew Pierce of York Co gent, the plantation & all the land thereunto belonging which was the plantation & land of the said Robert Cobbs at the time of his decease & by his said testament ordered to be sold, the same containing 55 acres bounded by the Mill Dam of John Custis esqr, the widow Gibbons Spring Bridge & the line dividing this land from a dividend which the said Pierce purch of the said Cobbs in his lifetime ...during the term of one year paying the rent of one pepper corn at the feast of Christmas next if demanded.... Ackn 15 Jan 1727.... {YCDB 1713-1729:478}

Richard Ambler esqr & John Richards, clk, the executors, presented the will of James Thompson, deceased, and the will was proved by the oaths of Robert Bowis and John Cobbs, the witnesses, and is admitted to record on 19

Feb 1732, and the executors acknowledge their bond & a certificate is granted them for obtaining a probate. {YCWI 1732-1737:12}

In the suit on the petition brought by Edward Jaquelin gent on 16 Feb 1735 against John Cobbs and James Shields, the defendants, confess'd judgment, it is therefore considered that judgment be enter'd for the petitioner, and that he recover against the defendants 3 pd 10 sl and his costs.... {YCWI 1732-1737:266}

15. EDMUND COBBS, d. 1755-1759, will 30 Nov 1759, will probated 17 Dec 1759, was a son of Ambrose (7) and Elizabeth (N) Cobbs.

Edmund Cobbs, Ralph Graves et al. witnessed the sale, by John Daniel of Bruton Parish. York Co., on 26 Jun 1724, for 5 shillings, a farm letten unto William Stone, of same place, a 100 acre tract of land in the afsd parish, it being the land that John Daniel, the grandfather of the said John Daniel, bought of William Gantlett as per his deed dated 8 Dec 1665, bounded by the run of Reedy Swamp, the Lower Landing, Pinkethman Eaton & the said Daniel ... for the term of one year paying the yearly (rent) on 10 Nov one ear of Indian corn if demanded.... {YCDB 1713-1729:422}

On 17 Sep 1739, Arthur Dickeson, John Goodwin & Ellyson Armistead gent captains; Mattw Peirce & James Shields, lieutenants; David Layton, cornet; & Edmond Cobbs, ensign, took the oaths of government and subscribe the test. {YCWI 1737-1740:520}

The court ordered that the accounts of Edward Bowcock, administrator to the estate of Elizabeth Barber, he reviewed and the cash paid to Edmund Cobbs et al.... Recorded 16 Dec 1754. {YCWI 1745-1759:339}

The estate of Edmund Cobbs, deceased, was appraised, presented in Court on 30 Nov 1759, and recorded on 17 Dec 1759. The estate comprised 1 grey mare, 1 gun, 1 chest & lumber, 3 boxes with lumber, 1 saddle & bridle. 10 pd 2 sl 6 pn. {YCWI 1745-1759:530}

16. SAMUEL COBBS, b. ca 1695, d. 1757, was a son of William (11) and Mary (Shield) Cobbs. Samuel m. in 1717 Edith Marot, dau. of Jean Marot. {EVB I:213}

John Clayton & Hugh Norvel, feofees or trustees, for the land appropriated for the building & erecting the City of Wmsburgh, for 5 shillings, lett a farm unto Samuel Cobbs, of York Co., two lotts of ground in the said City of Wmsburgh designed in the plot of the said city by the figures 161 & 162 ... for one year paying the yearly rent of one grain of Indian corn on 10 Oct if demanded.... Ackn 18 Feb 1716 & admitted to record.... {YCWI 1713-1729:149}

Samuel Cobbs & Edith, his wife, of York Co., for 5 shillings, leased unto Samuel Boush Junr, of Norfolk Co., two lotts of land in the City of Williamsburgh adjacent the Main Street, Palace Street & the Market Place, the same being taken up by the sd Cobbs & ackn by the feofees for the said city as per deed dated 5 Feb 1716 ... for the term of one year paying the yearly rent of one pepercorn at the feast of St. John the Baptist if demanded.... Ackn 20 Jul 1719 & admitted to record. {YCDB 1713-1729:297}

William Robertson & Samuel Cobbs, of York Co gentlemen, surviving executors of the will of David Cuningham, late of said county, barber, deceased, for £75, released to George Newton, of Norfolk Co. gent, all that lott of land in the City of Williamsburgh near the Capitol in York Co. designed in the plot of the said city by the figure 280.... Ackn 20 Feb 1720 & admitted to record.... {YCDB 1713-1729:349}

Samuel Cobbs, of the City of Wmsburgh, merchant, for £22:10, released unto Christopher Degraffenried, of same city, dancing master, one lot of ground in the said City of Williamsburgh, designed in the plan of the said city by the figure 235 with all houses thereon.... 15 Jul 1723 & admitted to record.... {YCDB 1713-1729:399}

Samuel Cobbs, of the City of Williamsburgh, York Co., merchant & Edith his wife, on 17 Dec 1728, for £8, sold to Martha Drewit, of same county, widow, all that lot or parcell of land being at Queen Mary's Port designed in the plott of the said Port by the figure 7, now in the occupation of the said Martha Drewit & adjacent to the back part of a lott late of Jonathan Deuit, now in the possession of the sd Martha Dreuit called *The Swan* ... which said lot & premises by indentures of lease & release dated 7 & 8 Oct 1704, were by the feofees or trustees for the land appropriated for the building & erecting the City of Williamsburgh, granted to Francis Sharp, of York Co., & by the said Sharp conveyed to the said Samuel Cobbs & his heirs.... Wits: Matt Pierce et al. Ackn 17 Mar 1728 ... & the said Edith being privately examined relinquished her right of dower.... {YCDB 1713-1729:512}

Samuel Cobbs, of Amelia Co., and William Prentis, of the City of Williamsburg gent, executors of the will of Lewis Holland, late of York Co. gent, deceased, on 20 Sep 1736, for £18, sold to John Harmer & Walter King, of the City of Williamsburg, five lotts of land at Queen Mary's Port adjacent lotts late belonging to John Davis (Nos. 13, 14, 64, 65 & 68), which were granted to the said Lewis Holland by the trustees for the City of Williamsburg by deeds of lease and released dated 18 & 19 Jul 1720 ... "to be sold and the monies arising from the sale I give to my three sisters." {YCLRD 1729-1740:429}

In 1736, Col. Samuel Cobbs, clerk of Amelia Co., collected fees of 779 lbs of tobacco from 9 residents, including 61 lbs of tobacco from John Cobbs. {VCA:III:394}

Samuel Cobbs represented Amelia Co. in the Virginia House of Burgesses from 1742-1747 and from 1748-1749. {EVB I:213}

On 15 Aug 1743, the court ordered that Samuel Cobbs, of Amelia Co., guardian of Alexander Walker, an infant under his care, be summoned to appear and render an account of the said orphan's estate at the next court. {YCWI 1740-1743:213}

Samuel Cobbs, of Amelia Co. gent, and Edith, his wife, and James Shields, of the City of Williamsburgh, ordinary keeper, and Anne, his wife, on 4 May 1745, for £50, sold to John Harmer, of the City of Williamsburgh gent, part of a lott of ground in the City of Williamsburg (No. 56) in breadth 52' which did formerly belong to John Marott and the other part being 30' in breadth ... bounded by Duke of Gloucester Street, lott of Henry Weatherburne now in possession of Thomas Penenan & Nicholson Street.... {YCLRD 1741-1754:130,132}

John Harmer, of the City of Williamsburgh, merchant, on 17 Nov 1746, for £215, sold to Walter King, of same place, merchant, a messuage and lot of ground in the City of Williamsburgh (No. 52) which was ... then letten for lodgings to William Randolph esqr.... {1741-1754:181}

Samuel and Edith (Marot) Cobbs were the parents of SAMUEL JR; EDITH MAROT; JOHN CATLIN; ANNE; SARAH; THEODOCIA; JUDITH; and MARY. {WMCQ 1:19:51-56}

Fifth Generation

17. VINKLER COBBS was a son of Robert (12) and (N) Vinckler Cobbs.

12 Jan 1727. Vinkler Cobbs & John Cobbs, executors of the will of Robert Cobbs Senr, late of York Co., deceased, for 5 shillings, leased unto Matthew Pierce, of York Co. gent, the plantation & all the land thereunto belonging which was the plantation & land of the said Robert Cobbs at the time of his decease & by his said testament ordered to be sold the same containing 55 acres bounded by the Mill Dam of John Custis esqr, the widow Gibbons' Spring Bridge & the line dividing this land from a dividend which the sd Pierce purch of the sd Cobbs in his lifetime ... during the term of one year paying the rent of one peppercorn at the feast of Christmas next if demanded.... {YCDB 1713-1729:478}

Vinkler Cobbs & John Cobbs, executors of the will of Robert Cobbs Senr, late of York Co., deceased, on 13 Jan 1727, for £35, released unto Matthew Pierce, of York Co. gent, a plantation & 55 acre tract of land ... [same as above].... Wits: Thos Dickson, Wil Toplis, Peter Candray.... {YCDB 1713-1729:479}

On 7 Nov 1734 "Robt. Spears of Henrico, cooper, to Vinckler Cobb (carpenter)." {WMCQ 1:21:55, citing Hanover County, Small Book, 1734-1735}

18. THOMAS COBBS, was a son of Thomas (13) and Mary (Shield) Cobbs.

Thomas Cobbs, of the City of Williamsburgh, carpenter and joiner, on 18 May 1761, for £200, sold to John Bell, of same city, white smith[10], a

---

[10] ....the blacksmith and the whitesmith, the former working with the forge and hammer and the latter with the chisel and file, the material being wrought iron.... {ITC:44} Merriam-Webster dictionary gives tinworker as the primary definition.

messuage in the City of Williamsburgh, adjacent the lot of John Coke, and now in the possession of the said Thomas Cobbs, 65' at front and 92' at the back ... and enjoy the privilege of drawing water out of the well on the end of the lott adjacent the afsd premises and now in the occupation of Thomas Stroud, the well being sunk by the said Thomas Cobbs and intended to be in common among all his tenants and shall require the said Bell bearing an equal part of the charges in keeping the said well in repair.... {YCLRD 1755-1763:345}

William Pearson and Magdalen, his wife, of Bruton Parish, York Co., tanner, for £100, sold to Thomas Cobb of the City of Williamsburgh, joiner, a parcel of land bounded by the Capitol Landing Road, said Pearson & Benjamin Waller esqr, in the City of Williamsburgh, also the dwelling house and kitchen there on.... Ackn 17 May 1762.... {YCLRD 1755-1763:435}

William Pearson of the City of Williamsburg, on 16 Sep 1765, for £100, sold to Thomas Cobbs, of the same city, a parcel of ground in the City of Williamsburg in Bruton Parish bounded by the nw corner of Lot No. 5 belonging to Benjamin Waller esqr, the road leading from Queen Mary's Port & Lot No. 14, which said lot is denoted in the plan thereof by the figure 6 & is part of a larger tract of land which Benjamin Waller purchased of Mann Page esqr ... provided that the said William Pearson's wife or any other person shall claim any part thereof of the house or lot that the said William Pearson shall pay to Thomas Cobbs the sum of £150.... {YCLRD 1763-1769:146,148}

Thomas Cobbs, of the City of Williamsburg, for £50:15:5 3 farthings, sold to Thomas Hornsby, of the said city, two Negro slaves, *viz.* Jack & Mary ... provided that if the said Thomas Cobbs shall well & truly pay to the said Thomas Hornsby the sum of £50:15:5 3 farthings on or before 1 Jan next with lawful interest for & in redemption of the above bargained slaves then this bill of sale to be void.... Ackn 21 Oct 1765 & recorded.... {YCLRD 1763-1769:177}

Thomas Cobbs, of the City of Williamsburg, carpenter, of the one part, & John Ferguson, of York Co., of the other part, whereas the said John, at the request of the said Thomas, hath become bound with him in a bond as his security to Tarpley Thompson & company for the payment of £51:7:6, & the said Thomas is also indebted to the said John in the sum of £30 for money advanced for him, now this indenture wit that for securing the sd sum of £51:7:6. Ackn 16 Mar 1767 & recorded.... {YCLRD 1763-1769:256}

The Will of Thomas Cobbs, of York Co., parish of Bruton, was presented. All estate to be sold, and after debts paid, money to be divided between Mrs. Elizabeth Davis and her three children, viz. Anne, Thomas and Mary Davis. Mrs. Elizabeth Davis to have the benefit of a lease of land from Mr. Tips Jackson, she paying the annual rent. Execs: friends Philip Bullifant and Elizabeth Davis. 18 Jan 1771.... {YCWI 1771-1783:208}

The estate of Thomas Cobbs, deceased was inventoried and appraised to be valued at £218.18.4 ½. Returned 21 Nov 1774. {YCWI 1771-1783:245}

On 21 Feb 1774 the subscribers of York Court met, ordered, and allotted the widow of Thomas Cobbs her third part of the slaves belonging to the said estate. Slaves: Jack, Charles, Pompey, Mary, Jack, ...? 12 Jul 1777. {YCWI 1771-1783:371}

Mrs. Elizabeth Cobbs, administrator of Lewis Davis's estate. Payments: £5.5.3. By order of York Court 21 Feb 1774 the accounts of Elizabeth Cobbs, admistratrix of Lewis Davis, were examined and a balance of £2.5.4 was due to the estate. 23 Jul 1777 ... William Eaton, James Sheilds, Saml. Timson.... {YCWI 1771-1783:371}

19. AMBROSE COBBS, m. Martha (N), was a son of Thomas (13) and Mary (Shield) Cobbs.

On 29 Jan 1754, Ambrose Cobbs of York Co., for £150, sold to Lawson Burfoot, of York Co., a 100 acre tract of land adjacent Col. Custis & Keith, Queen's Creek & the Great Quarter Gut.... Wits: Thomas Burfoot, Charles Thomson, Judith Barfoot. Ackn 18 Mar 1754. {YCLRD 1741-1754:592}

Martha Cobbs, wife of Ambrose Cobbs, on 12 Apr 1756, for the consideration within mentioned and also 5 shillings, sold to Lawson Burfoot all my right of dower which I may have after the death of my husband in case I should survive him to 100 acres of land conveyed unto the said Lawson Burfoot by the within indenture.... Wits: William Graves, Fips Jackson. At a court held 21 Jun 1756 the release and the certificate of the execution now on the motion of Lawson Burfoot ordered to be recorded.... {YCLRD 1755-1763:58}

10 Jun 1773. Deed. Between John Ferguson, of the City of Williamsburg, merchant, and Elizabeth, his wife, of the one part, and John Tazewell, of same place, attorney at law, of the other part, whereas by decree of the Co. Court of York dated 19 Nov 1768 made in a suit in Chancery there depending between John Carter & others plaintiffs & the said John Ferguson, executor of the will of Lawson Burfoot, deceased, and others defendants, it was ... ordered that the said John Ferguson should sell at public auction all that 100 acre tract of land in Bruton Parish being the land in the plaintiff's bill mentioned & convey the same to the purchasers, and whereas the said John Ferguson in pursuance of the decree exposed the said land for sale at public auction & became himself the purchaser thereof for the sum of £111:10, he being the highest bidder for the same and hath now sold the said land to the said John Tazewell, for £300, now this indenture wit that, for £300, the said John Ferguson & Elizabeth, his wife, have sold unto the said John Tazewell all that 100 acre tract of land bounded by the Governor's land, land of Benjamin Powell, part of Queens Creek, the lands of Peter Powell & the lands of the late Colonel Custis being the land formerly sold to Thomas Cobbs by John Grome executor of the will of Alexander Kerr, deceased, by indenture dated 10 Jul 1743 & which

at the death of the said Thomas Cobbs descended to his son & heir Ambrose Cobbs, the same having been purchased by the said Thomas Cobbs after the making of the will & not mentioned therein & was afterwards sold & conveyed by the said Ambrose Cobbs to the said Lawson Burfoot by indenture dated 29 Jan 1754 & decreed to be sold as afsd ... except only the dower of Mary Burfoot widow of the said Lawson Burfoot, deceased, therein.... {YCLRD 1769-1777:343}

Sixth Generation
20. SAMUEL COBBS, Jr. was a son of Samuel (16) and Edith (Marot) Cobbs. Samuel Jr. m. Elizabeth (Munford) Cobbs. {WMCQ 1:19:51-56}
On 14 Nov 1761, Samuel Cobbs of the City of Williamsburgh gent, for £110, sold to James Sheilds of same city gent, two ½ acre lots of land ... [*pg torn*] ... Nos. 274 & 275, which were devised to the said Samuel Cobbs by the will of his mother Edith Cobbs (recorded in Amelia Co).... {YCLRD 1755-1763:380}
Samuel Jr. and Elizabeth (Munford) Cobbs were the parents of ROBERT, JANE, and JUDITH. {WMCQ 1:19:51-56}

OTHERS NAMED COBBS

JAMES COBBS
Thomas Sessions set forth a petition on 24 Nov 1699 that whereas one James Cobbs was late an inhabitant in the petitioners house and there dyed considerably in his debt without will who praying order that administration as greatest creditor to said deceased ... [pg torn] ... ordered that he take ye same into his ... [pg torn] ... a just & true account thereof ... [pg torn] ... be accordingly confirmed to him ... [pg torn] ... credits within 9 months. {YCWI 1698-1702:231}

JOSEPH COBB
Joseph Cobb, Isle of Wight Co., Virginia, transported his wife Elizabeth, son Joseph Jr, son Benjamin and daughter Elizabeth to Virginia in 1637. {EVI:71}
On 1 Sep 1643, Joseph Cobb received 400 acres of land in Isle of Wight Co., Virginia, due by patent dated 4 Aug 1637. {CP I:146}

JOSEPH COBBS
On 24 Aug [1698], Eliz Webb's deed of gift to Thomas, Willm, Richard, John & Joseph Cobbs & Willm Webb, her six children, was acknowledged in court by Robert Bee in said deed mentioned by vertue of her letter of atty from said Eliz Webb being first proved in court and both ordered to record. {YCWI 1698-1702:79}

REBECCA COBBS

On 9 Nov 1723, Rebecca Cobbs et al. witnessed the last will and
testament of Joseph Walker Esq., of York County in Virginia. {YCWI 1722-
1725:244}

SARAH COBBS
On 15 Mar 1735, in the action of debt between Sarah Cobbs, widow,
plaintiff, and Wm Prentis gent, admininstrator of Charles Stagg, deceased,
defendant, the defendant confess'd judgment, it is considered by the court that
judgment be enter'd for the plaintiff and that she recover against the defendant 43
pd 4 sl 6 pn & costs. {YCWI 1732-1737:274}

WINFIELD COBB
A Certificate was granted unto Madam Jane Parke (wife and atty of
Daniell Parke esqr) on her motion for ye importation of 70 persons into this
colony, *viz.*, Winfeild Cobb et al.... {YCWI 1702-1704:137}

THE JOHN DREWRY FAMILY

1. JOHN DREWRY d. by 10 Apr 1667.
On 10 Apr 1667, an account of cattle belonging to the orphans of John
Drury, deceased, was made: To John Drury: cow and calf. To Mary Drury:
cow and heifer. To Robert Drury: 2 cows and heifer. To Rachell Drury: 2
cows, heifer and calf. {RB 1665-1672:129}
John was father of JOHN; MARY; ROBERT; RACHELL.

Second Generation
2. JOHN DREWRY, d. bef. 16 Jul 1716, son of John (1) Drewry, m. Deborah
(N).
On 24 Oct 1702, Anthony Watts surveyor of the highways for the upper
precinque of Charles Parish having made information to this court that divers
persons notwithstanding they have been warned to meet him in order for
clearing the roads within his precinque refused to performe the same, *viz.*, John
Drewry Senr., John Drewry Junr., William Drewry, John Muckendry et al.
ordered that the sherriff summon them to the next court to show cause why they
misperformed their duty. {YCWI 1702-1704:48}
On 24 May 1703, John Drewry his deed of sale dated 26 Apr last past
for two parcels of land containing 100 acres, one of which parcells in Charles
Parish on the s side of Charles River, and the other over Horse Brooke, together
with ye bond for performance of covenants which lease from Enos Muckentosh
was by him ackn & committed to record. {YCWI 1702-04:113}
On 2 Dec 1707, a Bond was created. Daniell Mackentosh, of York Co.,

planter, do hereby acknowledge myself to owe & stand indebted unto John Drewry (Drury) of the afsd Co., wheelwright, for £100 ... the condition of this obligation is such that if the afsd Daniell Mackentosh shall save harmless & forever defend & disclaime all right & tytle that in him or his heirs lyes that he hath unto 50 acres of land that lyes on Hornebrooke which the afsd John Drewry bought of Enus Mackentosh & likewise 50 acres of land which the afsd Drewry purch of the afsd Enus which lyes on Charles River & that the said Drurey shall peaceably & quietly enjoy all bargains, grants, conveyances, contracts that he has had from my brother, Enus Mackentosh, and the said Daniell doth further oblige himself to withdraw all accons or suits by him brought against the said Drewrey or any other person for him that then this obligation to be void.... Wit: Richard Willett, Thomas Slater, Sarah Slater. Acknowledged in Jan Court 1707 by Henry Clark, attorney of Daniell Mackentosh, and admitted to record. {YCDB 1701-1708:267}

The action of detinue between Debach(?) [Deborah] Drewry, plaintiff, and John Drewry, defendant, on defendant's motion, time is given him to consider ye plaintiff's replication untill next court by consent of both partys. Lawrence Smith & James Burwell, gentlemen, are appointed to settle all matters in difference between plaintiff & defendant before next court. {YCWI 1716-1718:6}

On 16 Jul 1716, Deborah Drewry, administrator of Jno Drewry, deceased, presented an account of ye estate, and it was admitted to record. {YCWI 1716-1718:13}

From the estate of Jno Drewry, deceased, sums were paid to Phil Lightfoot, churchwardens of Charles Parish, James Sclater, Wm Gordon, Robt Phillipson, Mr. Clayton for Mr. Perry, Henry Hayward, Mrs. Martha Hill, Peter Manson, and Jacob Lohman. Sums due to estate from rent, Jno Welsh, Ambr Singleton, goods & Negroes. 142 pd 6 sl 2 1/4 pn., errors excepted, 16 Jul 1716, Deborah Drewry. {YCWI 1716-1718:20}

On 18 Mar 1716/17, in the petition of Wm Tavernor against Deborah Drewry, administrator of Jno Drewry, deceased, for 1/8 part of deceased's estate belonging to him (in right of his wife as daughter of said Jno Drewry, deceased), it was ordered that ye sheriff summon said Deborah Drewry to appear & answer said petition at next court. {YCWI 1716-1718:93}

In ye case between Phi Lightfoot, plaintiff, and Deb Drewry, defendant, for 272 lbs of tobacco due by account ye defendant having had time given her to plead & being now called failing to do ye same, on plaintiff's motion, ye judgment of last court against said defendant & Saml Drewry, her security, is confirmed & ordered that they pay ye afsd sum to plaintiff with costs. {YCWI 1716-1718:138}

In the case between Charles Chiswell, plaintiff, and Deborah Drewry, administrator of the estate of John Drewry, deceased, defendant, the court upon hearing the evidence and plaintiff's oath are of opinion that the plaintiff recover against the deceased's estate in the defendant's hands 1,080 lbs of tobacco & costs.

{YCWI 1716-1718:218}

John and Deborah were the parents of JOHN, b. 24 Jul 1673; ELIZABETH, b. 17 Jul 1677; ROBERT, b. 22 Oct 1679; THOMAS, b. 12 Sep 1684; MARY, b. 14 Oct 1688; SAMUEL, b. 28 Feb 1690; JAMES, b. 28 Dec 1693. {CPR}

3. ROBERT DREWRY, son of John (1) Drewry (d. 1694), m. Jane (N).
Robert and Jane (N) Drewry were parents of ROBERT, b. 18 Nov 1683; JOHN, "son of Robert, deceased, d. 13 Nov 1694." {CPR}

Third Generation

4. JOHN DREWRY, b. 24 Jul 1673, d. 1727, m. Mary (N), was a son of John (2) and Deborah (N) Drewry.

On 25 Jan 1699, Henry Jenkins & Daniell Jenkins, executors of Capt Henry Jenkins, arrested John Drewry Junr in an action of debt for 256 lbs of tobacco and not further prosecuting the suite is dismist. {YCWI 1698-1702:263}

On 17 Dec 1711, John Drewery Senr., in open Court, presented and acknowledged his Deed of Gift of land lying in this County to his son, John Drewery, and at his mocion it is admitted to record. {YCWI 1710-1711:152}

In the action of Trespass between Elizabeth Taylor, plaintiff, and John Drewry Junr., defendant, for that the said John on 12 Jul 1712 in the Parish of Charles did, with force and armes, [in] the close [the area leading to the house] of the said Elizabeth, break her fences then there standing did throw down and her grass then and there growing (to the value of £5) with diverse horses, cattle and hoggs did eat up and destroy and other harmes to the said Elizabeth did do to the great damage ... to the value of £10. The defendant having pleaded not guilty, it is therefore ordered that the Surveyor of this County with an able Jury of the antient freeholders of the vicinage ... go upon the land in difference on 11 Dec next if fair, if not the next fair day, and survey and lay out the same according to the most antient known and reputed bounds thereof, having regard to all patents and evidences that shall be produced by plaintiff or defendant, and if they find the defendant a trespasser, they are to value the damage and make report of their proceedings to the next Court. {YCWI 1711-1714:198}

21 Mar 1719/20. On the petition of John Muckendre praying to have a guardian appointed him, it was ordered that John Drewry be guardian to the petitioner and that he, the said Drewry, take care of the said orphan & his estate. {YCWI 1718-1720:566}

John Drewry came into Court and made Oath that John Drewry departed this life without making any Will so far as he knows and believes and he, having together with William Watkins and Griggs Moore, his Securities, entered into bond for his Just & Faithfull Administrators of the said Drewrey's Estate, which bond being acknowedged is admitted to record. On his motion,

44

Certificate is granted him for obtaining Letters of Admininistration on the said Estate in due form ... Know All Men By These Presents that Wee John Drewry, William Watkins & Griggs Moore, of the County of York, are held and firmly bound unto Lawrence Smith, Archibald Blair, Thomas Nelson, Graves Pack, William Stark, Edward Tabb, etc., Gentlemen Justices of the County aforesaid, in the Sum of Two Hundred pounds Sterling to which payment ... Wee bind our Selves and every of us our and every of our heirs Executors and Administrators Jointly and Severally firmly.... 20 Nov 1727. {YCWI 1725-1727:489-491}

In Pursuance to an Order of York County dated 20 Nov 1727, we the Subscribers being first Sworn before Capt. Edward Tabb did Value the Estate of John Drewry, deceased, as follows, *vizt*.: 6 Hogs, 1 Bed & Furniture, an old Chest & Some books, 5 head of Cattle & I Steer hide £ 5.4, 8 milk trays, 5 chairs 24 bushels of Tobacco @ 4s. Total: £21.3.7. Robert Sheild, Justinian Love, Jones Irwin. {YCWI 1725-1727:498}

John and Mary were parents of JOHN, b. 1 Mar 1695; THOMAS, b. 18 Sep [1698]; MARY, b. 17 Feb 1700; ELIZABETH, b. 23 Oct 17[03]; SARAH, b. 23 Feb 1705; CATHERINE, b. 14 May 170[9]. {CPR}

5. ROBERT DREWRY, b. 22 Oct 1679, d. 25 Mar 1744 {CPR}, son of John (2) and Deborah (N) Drewry, m. Elinor (N) (d. 2 Dec 1748 {CPR} Freeman, widow of Henry Freeman.

21 Sep 1741. In the Suit in Chancery brought by Mattw Freeman agt Robert Drewry and Ellinor his wife executrix of Henry Freeman decd, the parties having agreed the suit is dismissed. {YCWI 1740-1743:57}

18 Jun 1744. Upon the prayer of Ellinor Drewry the widow & relict of Robert Drewry decd and her making oath that the said decd departed this life without making any will and giving bond & security, ordered that a cert be granted her for obtaining a Letter of Administration. {YCWI 1743-1746:284}

In obedience of a court order dated 18 Jun 1744, the subscribers being first sworn before Daniel Moore, gent justice of the peace, appraised the estate of Robert Drewry, deceased, and made inventory thereof: 5 cows, 7 calves, 5 stears, 1 cow, 2 heiffers, 1 bull, etc. 60 pd 2 sl 10 pn. Gerd Roberts, Thos Presson, John Hay.... {YCWI 1743-1746:297}

Elinor Drewry, widow, d. 2 Dec 1748. {CPR}

Robert and Elinor were parents of ELIZABETH, b. 30 Jun, bapt. 1 Aug 1725; WILLIAM, b. 7 Apr, bapt. 15 May 1727; MORGAN, b. 1 Jul, bapt. 10 Aug 1729; DEBORAH, b. 19 Dec, bapt. 23 Jan 1731; MARY, b. 9 Dec 1733; SARAH, b. 13 Dec, bapt. 12 Feb 1737. {CPR}

SPECIAL NOTE: Robert (5) Drewry was b. 1679, and Robert (9) Drewry was b. 1683. Due to incomplete information, although the following women, Ann,

Elizabeth, and Agnis, married a Robert Drewry, it is not yet possible to
determine which woman married which Robert. Further study will determine
what of the following information should be placed under Robert (5) or under
Robert (9).

Robert and Ann were parents of HENRY, b. 28 Sep 17[03]. {CPR}
Robert and Elizabeth were parents of ELIZABETH, b. 20 Mar 1706.
{CPR}

Robert and Agnis (d. 11 Feb 1723) {CPR} were parents of MARY, b. 26
Oct 1710, d. 23 Sep 1732; HOPE, b. 5 Aug 1714; JAMES, b. 12 Jun, bapt. 9 Jul
1721; ROBERT, b. 1 Sep, bapt. 6 Oct 1723. {CPR}

6. THOMAS DREWRY, b. 12 Sep 1684, was a son of John (2) and Deborah (N)
Drewry.

In the *scire facias* brought by Robt Havewell, plaintiff, against Thomas
Drewry, defendant, for renewing a judgment of this court for 100 lbs of tobacco
& costs of suit amounting to 415 lbs of tobacco more the defendant having been
summoned to show cause (if any he have) why the said judgment ought not to
be renewed & he failing to appear on the plaintiff's motion ordered that
Execution go against the defendant for the afsd 515 lbs of tobacco together with
present costs. {YCWI 1716-1718:524}

Nicholas Worley, on his petition, having liberty made Choice of
Thomas Drury for his Guardian, who having together with Robert Sheild &
Plany Ward, his Securitys, entered into bond for that purpose ... which was
accordingly admitted and ordered that he take care of the said orphan and his
Estate. {YCWI 1725-1727:489}

Know All Men By These Presents that Wee, Thomas Drewry, Robert
Sheilds & Plany Ward, of the County of York, are held and firmly bound unto
Lawrence Smith, Archibald Blair, Thomas Nelson, William Stark, Edward Tabb,
etc., Gent Justices of the County, in the Sum of One Hundred pounds Sterling to
which payment well & Truly be made to the said Justices their heirs or
Sucessors or Some of them.... 20 Nov 1727.... {YCWI 1725-1727:492}

On 14 Jun 1735 Francis Hayward, of Charles Parish, for 5 shillings,
quit claim unto Thomas Drury, of same parish, during the term of said Thomas
Drury's life a 1 acre parcel of land in Charles Parish adjacent Joseph Hopkins &
Mill Swamp. {YCLRD 1729-1740:372}

19 May 1735. Bash a Negro boy belonging to Thomas Drury adjudged
to be 11 years of age. {YCWI 1732-1737:190}

17 Sep 1739. Moll a Negro girl belonging to Thos Drewry adjudged to
be 12 years of age. {YCWI 1737-1740:517}

7. MARY DREWRY, b. 14 Oct 1688, daughter of John (2) and Deborah (N)
Drewry, m. 1st William Tavernor [See Tavernor Family, this volume] and 2nd

Edward Tabb.

On 18 Mar 1716, in the petition of Wm Tavernor against Deborah Drewry, adminstrator of Jno Drewry, deceased, for 1/8 part of deceased's estate belonging to him (in right of his wife as daughter of said Jno Drewry, deceased), it was ordered that ye sheriff summon said Deborah Drewry to appear & answer said petition at next court. {YCWI 1716-1718:93}

On 31 Jan 1752 Mary Tavernor, relict of William Tavernor of York Co., deceased, for 5 shillings, sold to Thomas Roberts, of York Co., three Negro slaves Jimmy, Patty & Rachel, likewise a feather bed & furniture reserving the use of the said slaves and bed to herself during her life in trust that the said Thomas Roberts shall after the determination of the natural life of said Mary Tavernor dispose of all the premises to her loving brother Samuel Drewry. Wits: Samuel Drewry, Margaret Drewry, John Mills. Proved 15 Jun 1752 by Samuel & Margaret Drewry (Memorandum: Benjamin Waller gent, in behalf of Edward Tabb, who hath intermarried with the said Mary Tavernor, objected to the proof of said deed as being made without his privily[11] and against his consent.) {YCLRD 1741-1754:487}

8. SAMUEL DREWRY, b. 28 Feb 1690, was a son of John (2) and Deborah (N) Drewry.

In the case between Charles Chiswell, plaintiff, and Deborah Drewry, administratrix of John Drewry, deceased, defendant, for 117 lbs of tobacco, the defendant failing to appear, judgment is granted the plaintiff for said sum & costs against defendant and Saml Drewry, her security, unless the defendant appears at next court and answers the plaintiff's action. {YCWI 1716-1718:185}

Judgment being this day passed unto Benjamin Clifton against Henry Hayward gent, sheriff, for 10 pd & costs by means of the nonappearance of Saml Drewry at the said Clifton's suit on the said sheriff's motion, an attachment is granted him against the said Drewry's estate for the afsd sum & costs returnable to next court for judgment. {YCWI 1716-1718:392}

The action of trespass, assault & battery between Benjamin Clifton, plaintiff, and Samuell Drewry (Druery), defendant, the defendant appeared, and the plaintiff's attorney being sick, on his motion, the suit is continued. {YCWI 1718-1720:395}

In the action of trespass, assault & battery between Benja Clifton, plaintiff, and Saml Drewry, defendant, for 10 pd damage by means of the defendant's assault & beating the plaintiff, issue being joyned a jury, *viz.*: James Parsons, Thos Hawkins et al. were impannelled & sworn & they having heard the evidence returned their verdict, we find for the plaintiff & damage 3 pd

---

[11] Privily refers to interested connection with a legal case. As the attorney, Waller was stating that he should have been consulted.

which verdict at the plaintiff's motion is recorded & it is considered that the plaintiff recover against the defendant his damages by the jurors in manner afsd assessed with costs. {YCWI 1716-1718:437}

9. ROBERT DREWRY, b. 1683, was a son of Robert (3) and Jane (N) Drewry. See note under Robert (5) Drewry for explanation.

Fourth Generation

10. JOHN DREWRY, b. 1 Mar 1695, m. Sarah (N), was a son of John (4) and Mary (N) Drewry. [12]

13 Jul 1730. Deed of Lease. John Drewry, of Charles Parish, York Co., and Sarah, his wife, for 5 shillings, leased to Edward Tabb of same parish ... [pg torn] 100 acres of land adjacent Edmund Hudson, deceased, Enos [?] which land was granted unto Morris Price by patent 28 Jan 1672/3 and was by said Morris Price assigned unto John Drewry, the grandfather of the afsd John Drewry on 9 Apr 1675, the other 38 acre tract of land which the said John Drewry, the grandfather, bought in a 50 acre tract of Enos McKentock 26 Apr 1703, and the remaining the said John Drewry hath sold unto Thomas Presson in Charles Parish [pg torn]. {YCLRD 1729-1740:45}

14 Jul 1730. Deed of Release. John Drewry, of Charles Parish, York Co., and Sarah, his wife, for £75, released unto Edward Tabb, gent of same parish, [pg torn] a tract of land [same as above]. {YCLRD 1729-1740:47}

Jul 1730. Deed of Lease & Release. John Drewry, of Charles Parish, York Co., and Sarah, his wife, for 5 shillings, leased to Thomas Presson, of same parish, two tracts of land in Charles Parish, the one 12 acres adjacent Hayward mill and Calthorp Hays, and the remaining part of a 57 acre tract of land which John Drewry, grandfather of said John Drewry, bought of Enos McKintoch [pg torn] for the term of 1 year, paying one ear of Indian corn on the last day of said term. {YCLRD 1729-1740:51,53,55}

OTHERS NAMED DREWRY

AGNES DROWRY

In ye Suit ... Parsons and Eliza, his wife, Complaintants, and John Hay ... respondr ye Auditors report is admitted to record on ... defendant's discount, It is adjudged and decreed that ye plaintiff's ... Costs als Exo Agnes Drowry ... John Hay at ye suit of Armiger Parsons and Eliza, his wife ...

---

[12] Grandfather, John (2), owned the land first. After his death in 1716, the land passed to his eldest son, John (4), who died in 1727. When John (4) died, the land passed to his eldest son, John (9).

days orderd that ye said Hay pay her eight. . . . . with costs als Exo.... [portions of original record missing]. {YCWI 1720-1722:169}

ANN DREWRY

The Will of Sarah Rogers, of Charles Parish in York Co., Whole estate to be equally divided amongst my children and grandchildren, namely Martha Patrick, John Rogers, Anne Drewry, Mildred Patrick, William Rogers and my two grandsons, William Addirston Rogers and John Rogers, sons of my late son Adderston Rogers, deceased, which two grandsons I give one equal part with my said children to be equally divided between them, but if either of them should die without issue, then to the surviving one, but if both should die, then to be divided amongst my said children. Granddaughter, Patsy Patrick, should have one heifer. Negro woman Bess shall go to either of my children that she chooses. The others, namely Tom, Phill, Hannah, Harry with the above said Bess to be equally divided as above. Execs: Curtis Patrick and John Rogers. 8 Feb 1778. Wits: Thos. Pescud, Giles Morris. Proved 20 May 1778. {YCWI 1772-1783:399}

JAMES DREWRY

On 19 Jan 1756, Reuben Lilburn, son of John Lilburn, hath put himself apprentice to James Drewry to learn the art and mystery of a taylor during the term of 5 years 2 months.... 19 Jan 1756 acknowledged by the parties.... {YCLRD 1755-1763:45}

On 17 Aug 1771, deed poll. George Bradley, of York Co., for £20, sold to Clausel Clausel, of Elizabeth City Co., acknowledge a small schooner called *The Betsey* with all her rigging, sails, tacle & apparel.... Wits: James Drewry, Mary Drewry. Proved 16 Mar 1772 & recorded. {YCDB 1763-1769:213}

JOHN DREWRY

Matthew Collins, having on 24 Nov 1697, by the last fleet, departed this Collony for ould England, and leaving an estate in diverse goods in custody of his wife Judeth, since deceased, it was ordered her sonn in law, John Drewry, take into his care the said estate. {DW 1694-1697:473}

On 24 Mar 1698, John Drewry, trustee to ye estate of Mathew Collins, arresting Charles Allin in an action of debt, he not appearing, order is granted against Capt Thomas Barbar, high sheriff, and next court to be confirmed if he causeth not ye sd Allin to appear & answer ye same. {YCWI 1698-1702:10}

JOHN DREWRY

In the suit brought to this Court by John Cox, plaintiff, against John Fergason, defendant, in an *Ejectione firmae*, Wm. Gordon, Sub Sheriff, this day making oath that he deliverd a copy of the declaracion to John Drury, tenant in possession of the land in question. It is therefore ordered that unless the said tenant appeare at the next Court and confess lease entry and ouster, judgment shall go by default and he honsled[?] of possession. {YCWI 1706-1710:65}

JOHN DREWRY
On 25 Jan 1708, John Drury, being presented by the Grand Jury for topping, succouring, and tending seconds[13], appeared and made oath that he never tended any within the intent of the Law, and is therefore discharged. {YCWI 1708-1710:187}

JOHN DREWERY
In the action upon the case between William Gordon, late Sub-Sheriff of York Co., plaintiff, and John Drewery and John Chisman, Churchwardens of Charles Parish, defendants, for 240 lbs. of tobacco due upon account for quit rents of the gleab land, judgment is granted to the plaintiff for the tobacco, and it is ordered that the defendants pay the same to the plaintiff with costs alies execution. {YCWI 1711-1714:273}

JOHN DRURY
At the sale of the real estate of Mary Barnes, John Drury purchased the following: pewter, 1 rug, 1 cart & wheels, 2 heifers, pr of stylyard, 2 wedges, 1 kettle, old pewter, 1 chest, 1 bottle, 2 chests, 1 iron pot. Ordered to be recorded 17 Feb 1755. {YCWI 1745-1759:341}

JOHN DRURY, d. ca. 1779.
Appraisal of the estate of John Drury. Total: £77.15. John Gremtew, John Lamb, P. Moody. Returned 21 Jun 1779. {YCWI 1772-1783:431}

PETER DRURY, JAMES DREWRY, KATHERINE DREWRY
James Drewry, Peter Drewry, and Katherine Drewry were the witnesses to the 21 May 1753 proving of the will of Robert Sheild. None of the Drewrys was mentioned in the body of the will. Robert Sheild, of Charles Parish, York Co., willed that his property be divided amongst his five children, Ann Howard, Robert Sheild, John Sheild, Mary Kerby & Sarah Sclater. {YCWI 1745-1759:292}
Appraisement of the estate of Peter Drewry, deceased. Total: £6.18.3. Appraised by Harwood Burt, John Tabb, William Moss Junr. Returned 17 Aug 1767. {YCWI 1760-1771:358}
By court order on 15 Jun 1767 settlement of the estate of Peter Drury,

---

[13] See Hening 1:399 (Mar 1655-1656), 4:507-509, and 5:438-439 for Virginia's laws regarding tobacco laws and the illegal practice of tending seconds.

deceased. Payments £--.15.1. Balance due to the estate £4.3.8. Examined by Thomas Chisman, John Tenkam, Thomas Pescud. Returned 19 Sep 1768. {YCWI 1760-1771:429}
    Division of the estate of Peter Drewry, deceased, into three equal parts. Balance: £4.3.8. The widow's part being 1/3—£8.1.2, the two children's part being 2/3—£6.2.5. John Chisman, William Moss Junr. {YCWI 1772-1783:41}

RICHARD DREWRY
    On 24 May 1705, Richard Drewry, being by ye sherriff returned summoned an evidence for John Bates, plaintiff against Thomas Stear, defendant, in a case of damage is ordered to be payd 160 lbs of tobacco for 4 days' attendance at court with cost. Catherine Lewis ye like. Charles Tyler ye like. Barrintine Howels ye like allowance for 1 day. {YCWI 1705-1706:329}

RICHARD DREWRY, JAMES DREWRY, JOHN DREWRY
    Richard Drewry, James Drewry, and John Drewry owed sums to the estate of Samuel Reade, deceased, taken 8 Jan 1759 and ordered to be recorded 19 Mar 1759. {YCWI 1745-1759:509}

ROBERT DREWRY, probably son of James (2) or Robert (3).
    In the acion of trespass between James Faison, plf. and Robert Drewry, deft. for £20 damage by means of the deft. with force and armes the close of the said James at the Parish of Charles breaking and entring and his trees of the value of £10 there lately growing cuting down and also the soil of five acres of land of the said James breaking up and subverting, the said Robert by Samuel Seldon, his Attorney, comes and...saith that he is not guilty of coming with force and armes, and as to the residue of the trespass, he saith... that the plf. by his certain deed in writing under his hand and seal dated the 10th day of Oct 1702, for the consideration of 4,463 lbs. of sweet scented tobacco and cask...did bargain, agree, set and to farm lett all his lands with the appurtenances in Charles Parish... from the date thereof for and during the term and time of 6 years unto one Thomas Roberts of the same parish, by which said writing the said James, the plf., did for himself, his heirs, Extrs. and Admrs. covenant, promise and agree to and with the said Thomas Roberts, his Extrs., Admrs. and Assigns, that what new plantation the said Thomas, his heirs or assigns... should seat or cause to be seated upon any part of the land aforesaid, he the said Thomas Roberts, should enjoy the rents of them 5 years after they become due, notwithstanding the expiration of the said 6 years, and... that the five years after the rent of the new plantation became due are not yet expired, and... and the said Thomas into the lands and tenements aforesaid entred and was thereof possessed and so being thereof possessed, afterwards by parol lett a certain part thereof unto said Robert, the deft., to make and seat a new plantation thereon for

and in consideration of the yearly rent of 300 lbs. of tobacco and cask, and further in fact saith that by virtue thereof he entred into the parcell of land to him let as aforesaid ...and on the 20th day of Sep in 1708, did cut down severall trees, plant fruit trees, break up the soil and build an house and so seated a new plantation as was lawfull for him to do. The plf. replys and saith... that he did make such Deed in writing under his hand and seal to the said Thomas Roberts... but that the said deft. did not seat a new plantation according to the true intent and meaning of the said Deed and this he prays may be enquired of by the Country, and the deft. also. Therefore, a jury by name Peter Goodwin, Wm. Wise, Thos. Bournham, Wm. Allen, Edward Powers, Mathew Peirce, Joseph Mountfort, Simon Stacy, Francis Sharp, Nathaniel Crawley, Nathaniel Hooke and Robert Snead were impannelled and sworn to try the issue joyned, who after hearing the evidence and receiving their charge went out and soon after came against into Court and returned their verdict: Wee find for the deft. Which at the deft.'s mocion, is recorded and ordered that the suit be dismist with costs. {YCWI 1706-1708:229}

ROBERT DREWRY, of Warwick Co., will written 21 Feb 1772, proved 20 May 1782, m. Mary (N).

On 13 Mar 1755 William Green, of the City of Williamsburgh, merchant, and Sarah, his wife, late Sarah Packe, widow, for £5, sold to Robert Drurey, of Warwick Co., planter, a 50 acre tract of land in Yorkhampton Parish bounded by Robert Roberts, deceased, William Moody, Wells Dunford, deceased, and Edmond Searburgh, deceased, which was sold to the said Sarah, then Sarah Packe, by David Brooke. 23 Oct 1747. {YCLRD 1755-1763: 31}

Martha Freeman, wife of Joseph Freeman, and Elizabeth Haley, spinster, both of the Co. and Town of York, being first sworn deposeth that they were present with Elizabeth Peters at the house of the Honble William Nelson esqr when the said Elizabeth departed this life on 23 Oct 1758 in the morning, that about half an hour before her death her sister, Mary Drewry, wife of Robert Drewry, was by her desire, called into the room where the said Elizabeth Peters lay and the said Elizabeth then desired her sister, after shaking hands with her and taking leave, to take all she was possessed of or had in the world calling her her dear sister for that it was all hers. Sworn before John Norton 26 Oct 1758. At a court held 16 Jul 1759, this writing purporting the nuncupative will of Elizabeth Peters, deceased, was proved by the oath of Mary Haley, one of the witnesses and on the motion of Robert Drewry ordered to be recorded. {YCWI 1745-1759:518}

Will of Robert Drewry, Warwick Co.: Nathaniel Burwell, of Carter's Grove in James City Co., to dispose of my sorrel horse and 12 barrels of corn due to me from Mr. Nathaniel Nelson for the best price. I give the money arising from the sale of the said horse and corn to my daughter Martha Drewry.

To daughters, Ann Hubard, Mary Hill, and Elizabeth Maston, 1 shilling. All the rest of my estate to my wife, Mary Drewry. After her death, I give my land to my son, Robert Drewry. In case he has no heirs, I then give my land to my son, Thomas Drewry. After my wife's death, the rest of my estate to be equally divided between my children, Thomas, Robert and Martha Drewry and my grandson, Robert Nicholson Drewry. It is my desire that my sons, Thomas and Robert Drewry, take care of my grandson, Robert Nicholson Drewry, put him to school, and afterwards have him bound out to a good trade. 21 Feb 1772. Wits: Richard Wynne, Richard Noblin and Lucy Noblin. Proved 20 May 1782. {YCWI 1772-1783:505}

Appraisal of the estate of Robert Drewry, deceased. Total: £17.9.6. Appraised by John Cosby, John Chapman. Returned 15 Jul 1782. {YCWI 1772-1783:523}

Robert was father of MARTHA; ANN, m. (N) Hubard; MARY, m. (N) Hill; ELIZABETH, m. (N) Maston; THOMAS; ROBERT; (N), father of Robert Nicholson Drewry.

SAMUEL DREWRY, will 6 Aug 1768, proved 19 Dec 1768, m. Mary (N).

Will of Samuel Drewry, of York Co., Charles Parish. To wife Mary, all my estate. To sons William and Henry Drewry, negro man, Charles. To son William Drewry, a feather bed and furniture. To son Henry Drewry, a feather bed and furniture. To daughter Elizabeth Write, my chest of drawers. To son Daniel Drewry, a bed and furniture. Rest of estate to wife & Executrix, Mary. 6 Aug 1768.... Proved 19 Dec 1768. Probate granted to Mary Drewry with said Thomas Pescud and Peter Robinson her securities. {YCWI 1760-1771:435}

By court order 19 Dec 1768. The appraisement of the slaves and personal estate of Samuel Drewry Includes negro, Charles. Total: £26.17.4. Appraised by John Patrick, William Robinson, Thomas Hunt. Returned 20 Feb 1769. {YCWI 1760-1771:437}

Samuel and Mary (N) Drewry were parents of DANIEL, b. 30 Sep, bapt. 23 Dec 1739. {CPR}

Samuel was father of WILLIAM; HENRY; ELIZABETH, b. 31 Dec, bapt. 27 Jan 1733 {CPR}, m. (N) Write; DANIEL, b. 1739. {YCWI 1760-1771:435}

SAMUEL DREWRY, Junr., will 22 Dec 1766, will proved 19 Jan 1767, m. Mary (N).

Will of Samuel Drewry junr ... [obliterated] ... To wife, Mary Drewry, side saddle and bridle. To son, £7, and to daughter, Dianna, £3, for their education. Whole estate to be kept together till my son, John, arrives to age 21 or married, or until my wife marries again. 22 Dec 1766. Wits: Hinde Russell, Thomas Roberts, Thomas Russell junr. Proved 19 Jan 1767. Mary Drewry, executrix, granted probate with James Drewry and Gardan Jegitts, her securities.

53

{YCWI 1760-1771:297}
By court order 19 Jan 1767. Appraisement of the estate of Samuel Drewry, deceased, Includes negroes [names obliterated] ... Total: £45.9.0. Appraised by Richd. Selater, Samuel Presson, Thomas Tomer. Returned 16 Mar 1767. {YCWI 1760-1771:322}
Samuel was father of JOHN; DIANNA.
Samuel and Mary (N) Drewry were the parents of DIANA, b. 20 Mar, bapt. 15 Apr 1764.

THOMAS DREWRY, JUNR.
The suit in Chancery between Thos Drewry Junr & Saml Hyde is dismist. {YCWI 1732-1737:45}

WILLIAM DREWRY, will 1723, proved 18 Jul 1726, m. Sarah (N).
In the acion of debt between Edward Moss, plaintiff, and Wm. Drury, defendant, Wm. Gordon, Sub Sherrif, having returned a retraxit [retraction?] and neither party appearing, is dismist. {YCWI 1706-1710:131}
Edmund Sweney, Robt Shield Junr, Benjamin Clifton & William Drewry are appointed to appraise the estate of James Bennet, deceased. {YCWI 1716-1718:586}
The last Will & testament of William Drury, deceased, was presented in Court by Sarah Drury, the Executrix, who made Oath to it and being proved by the Oaths of all the Witnesses thereto is admitted to record and on the said Executrix motion Certificate is granted her for obtaining a probate thereof in due form. Lawr. Smith, (on margin Baptists Appr.) [fragments viewable are:] £21.11 4 ½. Elizabeth Baptist, deceased, are presented admitted to record ... {YCWI 1725-1727:400}
Will of William Drewry, of Charles Parish, York County. To Wife, Sarah Drury, my personal Estate to her and at her disposal paying such small legacys as shall hereafter mentioned. To Brother Samuel Drury, one Suit of Cloaths that is a Coat of duroys britches & Jacket of Sarge a black pair of Worsted Stockings and a Castor hat. Imprimis to my God Son, William Drury, the Son of John Drewry Senr., one heifer, one Yew [ewe] & Lamb and their Increase. To John Drury, the Son of Edward Drury, deceased, one heifer, one Yew [ewe] and lamb with their Increase. To God Son, Francis Hayward, the Son of William Hayward, deceased, one heifer, one yew [ewe] and also a lamb. To Wife, Sarah Drewry, my Negro fellow, Tom, during her life and at her decease for the said negro, Tom, to be set free. To Wife Sarah Drury, my Negro Peter during her life and at her decease to Samuel Drury the Son of Thomas Drury.... Wits: John White, Samuel Spar, Augian Miles. 18 Jul 1726.... {YCWI 1725-1727:399-400}
I, the Subscriber, being first Sworn to give a true Inventory of my

deceased Husband's, William Drewry's, Estate have accordingly done: Cash
£1.10, 2 Negro Men, 2 feather beds & Furniture, 22 lbs feathers, 3 Chests & a
trunk, 2 Tables, 8 Chairs, 11 pewter dishes, 11 pewter plates, 2 Do.
tankards, 23 Spoones, 1 Spice mortar & pestle, 2 candlesticks, 2 Glasses, a pepper box &
Grater, 3 Salts, a Chamber pot ... gun & Sword; 2 Suits of Cloaths, 3 Jacketts &
Britches ... 17 hogs, 1 young horse bridle and Saddle, 21 head of cattle, 12
Steers, 1 looking Glass, 1 tin saucepan, 1 Spinning Wheel, a Meal Sifter, a
Cutting knife, 1 Cart & Wheels, Some Carpenter's tools. Sarah Drewry. 15
Aug 1726.... {YCWI 1725-1727:407}

The RALPH GRAVES FAMILY

1. RALPH GRAVES, will 25 May 1667, proved 24 Jul 1667, m. Rachel Wright,
daughter of Edward Wright. {RB 1665-1672:152}
    Deed of gift. 23 Dec 1654. Joseph Croshaw, out of natural affection,
gives "Ralph Graves and Rachaell Graves, the espoused of the said Ralph,"
1000 acres in the County of New Kent on the South side of the Mattaponie,
adjacent East on land of Capt. John West on the Creek dividing the land of Leiut
[sic] Palmer, North by Mattapony River and marshes of the same ... recorded 24
Apr 1656. {VCA:III:128}
    The estate of Mr. Henry Lee, deceased ... includes payments made
to ... Ralph Graves for Whitelymeing[14] the house, 400 lbs. tobacco ... recorded
26 Oct 1657. {VCA:III:141}
    On 27 Jul 1660, Mr. Ralph Graves, planter in VA, at present in London,
requested John Daniel, Notary & Tabellion[15] Public, dwelling in London ... to
require Mr. Robert Lewellin, merchant in London, to receive and pay original
bill of exchange.... {RB 1659-1662:69}
    John Wells, age c22, was deposed on 25 Jan 1661 concerning his
mistress' Rachaell Graves's fever. {RB 1659-1662:145}
    John Wells and Katherine Wells, servants of Ralph Graves, are
presented to the court for fornication by the Minister & Churchwardens of
Marston Parish and are to be summoned to next court. {RB 1659-1662:161}
    Maj. Joseph Croshaw was granted a certificate on 25 Aug 1662 for

[14] Whitelymeing refers to coating a building with lime to help protect it
[15] "Tabellio. An officer among the Romans who reduced to writing and into proper form,
agreements, contracts, wills, and other instruments, and witnessed their execution. The
term tabellio is derived from the Latin tabula, seu tabella, which in this sense, signified
those tables or plates covered with wax which were then used instead of paper....
Tabelliones ... had jurisdiction in some cases, and from their judgments there were no
appeals. Notaries were then the clerks or aiders of the tabelliones." {BLD}

1200 acres due for the importation of 24 persons: Ralph Graves et al.... {RB 1659-1662:169}

    Ralph and Rachel Graves witnessed a transaction of Sir William Berkeley, Knt., Governor and Captain General of VA. On 25 Jun 1666, a grant made to Henry White of 100 acres was found to escheat[16] to His Majesty. {RB 1665-1672:73}

    On 25 Jan 1666, a certificate was granted to Mr. Ralph Graves for 1500 acres due for the importation of 30 persons into the Colony: [names in original omitted here]. {RB 1665-1672:123}

    The will of Ralph Graves was dated 25 May 1667 and proved 24 Jul 1667. To wife for life, land I live on, Indian Field, then to my son Ralph. My seat of 1000 acres in Mattapony to be divided as follows: To youngest son William, 300 acres. To dau. Anne Graves, 250 acres. To younger daughter Mary Graves, 250 acres. Other 200 acres to my nephew, William Grancher. Capt. Richard Croshaw and my wife, Rachell, executors. Probate granted to Mrs. Rachel Graves. {RB 1665-1672:147,150}

    Edward [W]Right left a will dated 25 Feb 1659 and proved 24 Jul 1667. To son John [W]Right, my land, and if he die under age, to my other children. To grandson William Graves, cow and calf. If wife marries, children to have cattle equally. {RB 1665-1672:152}

    On 26 Jul 1669, Mr. Daniel Wyld and Mr. Phillipp Chesley were requested to divide estate of Mr. Ralph Graves, deceased, between Richard Barnes, who married the relict, and Ralph and William Graves his sons, the rest to be delivered to Mr. Henry White, guardian. {RB 1665-1672:351[251]}

    Mr. William Hartwell produced security having married (26 Apr 1675) the relict of Richard Barnes, deceased, late guardian to William Graves, orphan. {RB 1672-1676:109}

    Ralph and Rachel (Wright) Graves were the parents of <u>RALPH</u>, b. 1653-55; WILLIAM; ANN; and MARY.

    Rachel m. 2nd bef. 26 Jul 1669 Richard Barnes, and m. 3rd on 26 Apr 1675 William Hartwell.

2. WILLIAM GRAVES, d. bef. 10 Apr 1668, was brother of Ralph (1) Graves.

    William Graves was granted 80 acres in Yorke Co. on 3 Oct 1655 ... bounded on the w. side with a swamp dividing this and land of Tho. Pencherman [Pinktheman][17], n. upon land of Wm. Gauntlet, e. upon Skimenoe and s. upon his own land ... for the transportation of Bryon Coxon and Ellis Wheatley. {CP

---

[16] Escheat refers to a parcel of land reverting to the government, in this case, because it was unused.

[17] After viewing the land records of Graves, Gantlett, and Pinkethman the authors conclude that this is one of the many variations of the spellings of Pinkethman.

56

Mrs. Rachel Graves, executrix of Mr. Ralph Graves. On 10 Apr 1668, on behalf of her son, Ralph Graves, as nearest of kin to Anne, daughter of William Graves, deceased, claims the estate bequeathed to Anne, descending to said Ralph as heir of said Anne. {RB 1665-1672:178}

William was the father of ANNE.

Second Generation

3. RALPH GRAVES, b. 1653-1655, d. 1693-1695, m. Unity White (d. by 26 Dec 1698) {YCWI 1698-1702:97}, daughter of Henry and Mary (Croshaw) White. Unity (White) Graves m. 2nd Thomas Crips. {DW 1694-1697:143; RB 1659-1662:91-2}

Ralph Graves, son of Ralph Graves, deceased, declared on 13 Apr 1672 being 17 [years of age] and is ordered the benefit of his labor. {RB 1672-1676:11}

Having attained 21 [years of age] by 24 Jul 1674, Ralph Graves was ordered possessed of his estate by his guardian. {RB 1672-1676:76}

The court ordered on 10 Sep 1674 that Ralph Graves, having attained 21 [years of age], be possessed of his estate in the hands of Thomas Taylor who married the relict of Henry Whitehead[18], deceased, his former guardian, in hands of Richard Barnes, his father in law. {RB 1672-1676:85}

Maj. John West, an executor of Mr. Henry White, deceased, in his difference with Thomas Taylor, who married on 24 Jun 1672 the decedent's relict, liberty [was] granted to produce evidence. {RB 1672-1676:17}

Anthony Dawson, imported in the *George*, Capt. Thomas Grantham, Commander, a servant to Ralph Graves, was adjudged on 25 Jan 1674/5 to be 14 years of age [and ordered] to serve to 24 [years of age]. {RB 1672-1676:93}

Joseph White and William White, sons of Henry White, late deceased, and Willm. Davis as marryeing Mary, one of the said daughters, and Ralph Graves as marrying Unity, one other daughter of Henry White. They petition that Henry White by his will did bequeath 30 pounds sterling and cattle to his daughter Rebeckah White, unless she die under age and without issue, which she did. Ordered 26 Mar 1688. Exs: Colonel John West the surviving executor, pay Joseph and Willm. White, and William Davis and Ralph Graves, Rebeckah's portion. {DW 1687-1691:105}

John Keen, Parish of Bruton, Co. of Yorke, left a will dated 7 Jan 1692/3 and proved 24 Aug 1693. Unto my eldest daughter, Elizabeth Jackson, wife of Richard Jackson ... executrix, Mr. Ralph Graves ... my son in law Richd Jackson, overseer.... {DW 1691-1694:245-246}

On 13 Apr 1695, in an action of debt, John Lyall arrested Thomas Crips, as marrying Unity Graves, administratrix of Ralph Graves. {DW 1694-1697:143}

---

[18] Compare this passage with the next to see an example showing White, not Whitehead.

On 26 Sep 1698, James Ming[e] hath judgment granted against Thomas Cripps, executor of Unity, his late wife, deceased, which said Unity was relict & administrator of Ralph Graves, deceased, in an action for 500 lbs of tobacco which ye defendant is ordered to pay with costs. {YCWI 1698-1702:97}

William Jackson is appointed Constable in the upper precincts of Bruton Parish in the room of Ralph Graves and ordered upon receipt hereof that the said Jackson repair to some Justice in the Co. and take the usual oath. {YCWI 1711-1714:228}

Ralph and Unity (White) Graves were the parents of RALPH; WILLIAM; and MARY, who m. Richard Easter.

Third Generation

4. RALPH GRAVES, b. ca 1680s, will 11 Feb 1748, proved 15 May 1749, m. 1st Mary (N) and 2nd Elizabeth (Valentine) (will 23 Aug 1760, pr. May 1761). Ralph (4) was a son of Ralph (3) and Unity (White) Graves,

Ralph Graves being by ye sheriff returned summoned an evidence for Rebecca Burleigh, plaintiff, against Joseph White & Thomas Crips in an action of detinue is ordered to be paid 160 lbs of tobacco for 4 days attendance at court with cost.... {YCWI 1702-1704:170}

On 1 Mar 1710/11, a Deed of Lease was agreed. Ralph Graves of Bruton Parish, York Co., for divers good causes consideracons hath farm let to Richard Easter, of same place, planter, and his wife, Mary Easter, one plantacon & tract of land in the Indian Field in Bruton Parish adjacent the Old Church, the Old Road, Spring Bridge of Cripps & formerly Tibbs, Col Jenings & Mr. White deceased, during the life of my loving sister Mary Easter.... {YCDB 1709-1713:367; YCWI 1709-1711:81}

On the petition of John Daniell, Constable of the Upper Precincts of Bruton Parish, he is discharged from the said office, and Ralph Graves is appointed in his stead, and it is ordered that ... he repair to some Justice in the County and take the usual oath. {YCWI 1709-1711:106}

On 27 Jun 1712, Edmund Jenings, esqr of Bruton Parish York Co, for 5 shillings, leased to Ralph Graves, of same place, a plantation & 825 acres of land in Charles Parish being part of a tract of land called *Boar Quarter* adjacent Boar Quarter Creek, Jno Lyall, the Tobacco Swamp & Pocoson River, including Batchelor's Island, Tobacco Swamp & Tobacco Ridge & part of the marsh on the [northeast] side of the said tract, as by the courses mentioned in the survey dated 25 Apr last past performed by Maj Wm Buckner, Surveyor General ... for the term of one year.... 15 Sep 1712. {YCDB 1709-1713:400,401,403}

On 29 Nov 1714, George Baskervyle of Bruton Parish, York Co., for 5 shillings, leased to Ralph Graves, of same place, a 350 acre tract of land in Bruton Parish with a dwelling thereon being the tract of land formerly of Jno Baskervyle, father to the said George, by him purchased of Jno Horsington to whom the 350 acres of land was granted by patent dated 18 Mar 1662, bounded by 300 acres part of the parish formerly called Marston Parish, the Main Swamp, St. Andrews Cr, land of Thomas Pinkethman & the Rockahock Path, the first mentioned 50 acres the residue on the Main Bridge of St. Andrews Creek bounded by the said Horsington ... for the term of one year.... {YCDB 1713-1729:39}

On 18 Dec 1714, Jno Hillyard, of St. Johns Parish, King William Co., VA, became firmly bound unto Ralph Graves of Bruton Parish, York Co., for £100 ... the condition of this obligation is such that whereas the afsd Jno Hillyard & Frances, his wife, daughter & devisee of Joseph White, late of York Co. deceased, have sold to the said Ralph Graves a 130 acre dividend of land by deeds of lease & release.... {YCDB 1713-1729:48}

On 17 Feb 1714, a deed was transferred from Ralph Graves, of Bruton Parish, York Co., for £80, to William Jones, of same place, a 120 acre tract of land lying in the Indian Field in the parish afsd & is part of a greater tract of land belonging to the said Graves & bounded by Major Custis, the Old School House, Flax Hole Swamp, Capt Archer, Archer's Road & Wm Davis.... Ackn 16 May 1715 by Ralph Graves & at the same time appeared Mary, wife of the said Ralph, who being first privately examined relinquished her right of dower. {YCDB 1713-1729:73}

On 15 Sep 1715, Wm Jones, of Bruton Parish, York Co., planter, for £56, released to Wm Davis, of same place, planter, a 56 acre parcel of land purchased by the said Wm Jones of Ralph Graves of same parish ... being part of a greater tract formerly belonging to Ralph Graves, father of the said Ralph Graves, formerly of York Co., deceased.... {YCDB 1713-1729:85}

Ralph Graves was appointed Surveyor of the roads in the upper precinct in Bruton parish and the ferry road to Baldwin Mathews' plant[ati]on, ordered that he keep ye roads & bridges in the said precinct in repair accordingly. {YCWI 1722-1725:301}

The will of Ralph Graves, of Bruton Parish, York Co., was written 11 Feb 1748 and proved 15 May 1749. To son William Graves, that now mansion house and plantation I live upon which I purchased of Baskervyle. To my son Henry Graves, all the land I have at Skiminoe which was formerly my uncle William Graves'. To my son Richard Graves, that part of land on Chickahominy River in James City Co which I purch of Brown, Nance & Pond, I mean that upper part of the whole land where Nance did dwell & in 1744 did make a dividing line in presence of James Nance, Thomas Hilliard, William Hilliard, Ralph Graves Junr, Christopher Bonfield et al. To my son, Richard Crosher Graves, that lower part of the said land in James City Co. which is called the Indian Field wherein is contained the late dwelling house of Brown and the land I bought of Nance adjacent Thomas Hilliard, the line mentioned in the afsd devise to my son Richard Graves to be the division between my son, Richard, and my son, Richard Crosher. To my wife Elizabeth Graves, the use of my mansion house jointly with my son, William Graves, and her thirds on the said plantation during her life and nowhere else, but in case my wife and son cannot agree to dwell together, then my son, William, to have free liberty to build on any part of the plantation a dwelling house. My Negroes and personal estate may be divided after my debts are paid between my wife Elizabeth Graves and my son William Graves, Richard, Richard Crosher and my daughter, Unity Hilliard. Whereas I have given my daughter, Unity Hilliard, two Negro girls named Pegg & Betty, which I value at 45 pd, it is my desire that the value of these Negroes may be taken out of her part of my other Negroes. My executors and trustees to make division of the Negroes and personal estate between my wife and children. My daughter, Elizabeth Stone, may have and enjoy the two Negro girls I gave her at her marriage and their increase. To my daughter, Elizabeth Stone, 1 shilling. I appoint my wife, Elizabeth, and my sons, William, Henry & Richard, executors, and earnestly requesting of my well beloved friends John Blair esqr, Benjamin Waller & Fleming Bates to be my trustees to see my will performed that my children may not be wronged to the true intent and meaning of this my will.... {YCWI 1745-1759:147}

In obedience to an order of court dated 15 May, Pin Eaton, Fips Jackson & Ambrose Jackson appraised the estate of Ralph Graves, deceased. Negroes: Sampson a man, Jemmy a man, John a man, Sam a man, Old Lucy a woman, Judith a woman, Young Lucy a woman, Short Pegg a woman and her child Isham, two old Negroes a man & woman, Oxford a man, Hannah a woman, Moll a woman, Dinah a girl, Peter a boy, Jane a girl. 29 cows & calves, 6 steers, 2 steers, 3 bulls, 13 yearlings, etc ... 591 pd 5 pn.... {YCWI 1745-1759:152}

Pursuant to an order of court dated 18 Sep 1749, Pen Eaton, Fips Jackson & Ambrose Jackson divided the Negroes & stock part of the estate of Ralph Graves, deceased, between his wife and five of his children. The widow, William Graves, Henry Graves, Richard Graves, Richard Crosher Graves, William Hilliard & Unity, his wife, daughter to the decesased. 92 pd 18 sl 6 pn each ... recorded 18 Jun 1750.... {YCWI 1745-1759:178}

The will of Elizabeth Graves, York Co., was written 23 Aug 1760 and proved May 1761. To son William Graves, £10. To son Richard Graves, £10. To daughter Elizabeth Stone, £15. To son Henry Graves, large trunk. To son Richard Crosher Graves, young heifer. To granddaughter Mary Graves, a young heifer and small flowered trunk. To granddaughter Frances Stone, small black trunk. To granddaughter Susannah Graves, small red trunk and box iron. Son William Graves may keep my three negroes, Lucy, Hannah and Oxford, at the appraisement if he thinks proper, if not then they are to be sold. Overplus to be divided amongst my four children, William Graves, Richard Graves, Elizabeth Stone and Richard Crosher Graves. Executor: William Graves.... [remainder

60

missing].... {YCWI 1760-1771:59}

Ralph and Elizabeth (Valentine) Graves were the parents of WILLIAM; HENRY, m. Sarah (N); RICHARD m. Dionysia; RALPH, JR.; RICHARD CROSHAW[19]; UNITY, m. William Hilliard; and ELIZABETH, m. (N) Stone.

Fourth Generation

5. WILLIAM GRAVES, son of Ralph (4) and Elizabeth (Valentine) Graves.

In obedience to an order of court, Fips Jackson, William Graves & Ambrose Jackson appraised the estate of Elizabeth Barbar, deceased: 1 sow & piggs, 4 hoggs, 4 cows & calves, 4 steers, 6 butter pots, 1 copper kettle, 1 brass kettle, 1 small still, etc. Negroes: London a man, Jenny, Jammy, Daniel, Robin, Sarah, Will a boy, David, Jack, Bob, Hannah. 411 pd 11 sl 9 pn. ... recorded 18 Jun 1750. {YCWI 1745-1759:181}

On 17 Nov 1761, Sarah Stanhope and Elizabeth Davis, of Bruton Parish, York Co., for £14, sold to William Stanhope, the younger, of Yorkhampton Parish, York Co., a 20 acre parcel of land in Bruton Parish adjacent William Graves.... Wit: Henry Graves et al. {YCLRD 1755-1763:469}

On 15 Jun 1765, William Eaton & Mary, his wife, of Blisland Parish, New Kent Co., and Mary Eaton, widow of Penkethman Eaton, late of York Co., deceased, for £260, sold to Benjamin Eggleton, of York Co., all that tract of land on the n side of the Mill Swamp (excepting a small parcel which the sd William Eaton sold to William Holt) containing 180 acres bounded by the Main Road which leads from Horsington Swamp to Williamsburg near the fence of William Graves, the line of Col. George Washington, William Eaton & Fleming Bates ... all the estate, right, title, claim & demand whatsoever of the said William Eaton, Mary his wife & Mary his mother.... Wits: James Sheilds, William Sanders, Penkn Eaton. Ackn 17 Jun 1765 by William Eaton & Mary his wife she having been first privily examined & recorded. {YCDB 1763-1769:99}

On 6 Oct 1772, Ambrose Jackson Easterd, of Hanover Co., for £140, sold to William Graves, of York Co., gent, a 250 acre tract of land in Bruton Parish bounded by the lands of Landon Carter esqr & Ambrose Jackson, deceased, son of Fips Jackson, deceased ... Ackn 19 Oct 1772.... {YCWI 1771-1783:264}

By order of the court, cash received of William Graves— £17.8.0. to help settle the estate of John Warrington, deceased ... Returned 16 Dec 1771. {YCWI 1771-1783:51}

To John Blair, John Dixon & Joseph Hornsby gent greeting, whereas

---

[19] One of his grandmothers was Mary Croshaw. See Ralph (3) Graves for references. In the records, although Croshaw is spelled many ways in the records, the variant Crowsher is found more times than Crozier or Croz., its abbreviation.

William Eaton & Mary, his wife, by their indenture of sale have sold unto William Graves the fee simple estate of 300 acre of land in Bruton Parish ... 1 Nov 1774. {YCWI 1771-1783:457}

On 17 Nov 1773, William Graves of York Co did hereby make over all right, title, interest & demand to the within indenture to Samuel Timson excepting to (*sic*) Negroes mentioned in the said deed to me by William Jackson.... Ackn 21 Aug 1775 & recorded.... The deed mentioned in this assignment recorded in folio 99. {YCWI 1771-1783:491}

19 Aug 1775. Philip Burt & Anne, his wife, of York Co., for £6, sold to William Graves of Co. afsd, a 3 acre parcel of land taken off my tract as I purchase of William Holt formerly belonging to Edward Bowcock on the east side of the Main Road that leads from the Horsington Swamp to Capahosick Ferry.... Ackn 18 Dec 1775. {YCWI 1771-1783:498}

The will of William Graves, of Bruton Parish, York Co., was written on 19 Aug 1781 and proved 17 Jun 1782. To son Ralph Graves, the tract of land I now live on and part of the tract I purchased of Mr. Willis lying on the right hand side of the road leading to Copp ... rick Ferry down to the head of a branch nearly opposite to where Mr. Eaton formerly lived.... Also the following Negroes: Old Will, Carpenter Bob, Frank(?), Alice, Sam, Sera, Harry, Gaby, and Reubin; also 1½ dozen black walnut chairs, and other furniture, cows, horse, 20 head of sheep, 4 breeding sows, 50 barrels of corn, 6 work steers, furniture, [and other items]. To son John Graves, the tract I purchased of John C. Cocke lying in the county of James City with the mill and all the implements there unto belonging to it. Also the following negroes: Old Will, Great Peter, Moll, Stephen, Little Bob, Cate, Grump, Tom, Jossey, all the stock of cattle that is now on the said plantation, work horse, other stock and furniture. To son, Henry Brown Graves, my tract I purchased of Wm. Eaton. Also a small part of that tract I purchased of Mr. Willis at the head of the branch adjacent my son Ralph's land opposite as before mentioned; also a small piece of land I purchased of Mr. Willis and Wm. Nelson that lies on the right hand of side of the road leading to the Bates Mill and joining the land I purchased of Mr. Easton; also the following negroes, vizt.: Old Frank, Andrew, John, Toney, Moses, Nell, Rachel, Fanny; 15 head of cattle, 10 young cattle, other stock and furniture, and crops. To daughter, Mary Winfrey, the tract I purchased of Mr. Joseph Hornsby, the negro called Little Peter, 10 head of cattle, 5 young cattle and other stock and furniture including all furniture at my plantation in James City, double riding chair and harness and horse called Buck, a filley colt. To granddaughter, Elizabeth Wimfrey, a negro girl named Jenny. To daughter, Susanna Power, 2 negroes Ned and Roger. I have given her £120 in cash. I also give her 2 head of cattle and other stock. To granddaughter, Sally Powers, a negro girl named Ann. To daughter, Sally Graves, part of the tract I purchased of Mr. Willis and Mr.

Nelson on the left hand side leading from Horrinton Swamp to Bates Mill called Hackers and the following, Marget, Jemmy, Judith, Isaac, Hancock and Temp and 15 head of cattle. Rest of estate to be sold and residue to be divided between Susanna Powers and Sally Graves. All the negroes that have gone to the enemy should return home except Lucy. They may be sold and the money equally divided amongst the whole of my children. Executors: son Ralph Graves, my bro. Richard Crosher Graves, and Mrs. Joseph Hornsby. {YCWI 1771-1783:531}

William and (N) Graves were the parents of WILLIAM; RALPH; JOHN; HENRY BROWN; MARY, m. (N) Winfrey; SUSANNAH, m. (N) Powers; and SALLY.

Mary m. (N) Winfrey and they had a daughter, ELIZABETH WINFREY. Susannah m. (N) Powers, and they had a daughter, SALLY POWERS.

6. HENRY GRAVES was a son of Ralph (4) and Elizabeth (Valentine) Graves.

On 3 May 1763, Henry Graves of [*pg torn*] and Sarah, his wife, for £1420, sold to Richard Graves, of York Co., planter, a 250 acre tract of land in Bruton Parish on Broadneck Creek whereon Humphrey Jones, deceased, lately lived and also that other 200 acre tract of land in the same parish bounded by Fleming Bates & William Ratcliff, which said tracts of land were devised by the said Humphrey Jones to Ralph Graves, father of the said Henry, and by the said [?] the same were devised to the said Henry.... Ackn 29 Jun 1765.... {YCLRD 1755-1763:513}

... Henry Graves and Sarah, his wife, on 23 Apr instant, sold unto Richard Graves 450 acres of land in Bruton Parish, and whereas the said Sarah cannot conveniently travel to our court to make acknowledgment of the conveyance, therefore we give unto you power to receive the acknowledgment which the said Sarah shall be willing to make before you, and we command that you personally go to the said Sarah and receive her acknowledgment and examine her privately and apart from her husband.... By virtue of the commission hereunto annexed at St. Peter's Parish, James.... {YCLRD 1755-1763: 516}

The will of Henry Graves, of Bruton Parish, York Co., was written 16 May 1758 and proved 19 Jun 1758. My debts of every sort to be fully paid. To my mother, 15 pd. To my brother William Graves, all my tract of land I now live on his paying to the rest of my legatees 50 pd at the expiration of 3 years. To my brother Richard Crosher Graves, 5 head of cattle his choice of my stock. To my godchild, Mary Graves, my Negro boy Jack. To John Watts, all my wearing cloaths. My executors shall sell my two Negroes, Sampson & Isom, and all the residue of my estate may be divided amongst my brother, Richard Graves, Richard Crosher Graves & Elizabeth Stone. I appoint my brothers

63

William Graves, Richard Graves & Richard Crosher Graves as executors ...
Robert Carter Nicholas gent, their security.... {YCWI 1745-1759:484}

7. RICHARD GRAVES was a son of Ralph (4) and Elizabeth (Valentine)
Graves.
On 25 May 1763, Richard Graves, of York Co., planter, and Dionysia,
his wife, for £410, sold to Joseph Hornsby, of the City of Williamsburgh,
merchant, a 200 acre parcel of land in Bruton Parish bounded by Fleming Bates
& William Ratcliff, which said tract of land was sold unto the said Richard
Graves by Henry Graves and Sarah, his wife, 3 May instant.... {YCLRD 1755-
1763:517,520}
On 1 Nov 1766, Richard Graves of James City Co., planter, and
Dyonisia, his wife, for £800, sold to the Honourable Robert Carter, of the City
of Williamsburg, all that 250 acre tract of land in Bruton Parish on Broad Neck
Creek whereon Humphry Jones, deceased, lately lived which said tract of land
was sold & conveyed to the said Richard Graves by Henry Graves & Sarah, his
wife, by indenture dated 3 May 1763.... Wit: William Graves, et al.... Proved
17 Nov 1766.... {YCDB 1763-1769:212,214}
On 12 Sep 1772, Benjamin Valentine, of York Co., for £125:17, sold to
Richard Crosher Graves, of New Kent Co., a 200 acre tract of land whereon the
said Benjamin now lives in Bruton Parish bounded according to the known
ancient & lawful bounds thereof & also one Negro man slave named Will ...,
provided & upon this condition that if the said Benjamin Valentine shall well &
truly pay unto the said Richard Crosher Graves the full & just sum of £125:17
with lawful interest on or before 1 Apr 1773 then these presents & everything
therein contained shall become void.... Wits: Stanhope Vaughan, James
Vaughan, Anne Vaughan. Ackn 15 Feb 1773.... {YCDB 1769-1777:284}

8. RALPH GRAVES JR., son of Ralph (4) and Elizabeth (Valentine) Graves.
On 7 Nov 1774, a deed was created among ... William Eaton, of
Bruton Parish, York Co., and Mary, his wife, and William Graves, of Co., afsd
of the second part, and Joseph Hornsby, of the City of Williamsburg, merchant,
of the third part, witness that, for £400, by the said William Graves to the said
William Eaton & Joseph Hornsby in hand paid they the said William Eaton &
Mary, his wife, have sold unto the said William Graves all that tract of land
devised to the said William Eaton by the will of his father containing 300
acres.... Wits: Edmund Parke, Ralph Graves, May Eaton, Elizabeth Eaton....
{YCDB 1769-1777:453}

9. RICHARD CROSHAW GRAVES, son of Ralph (4) and Elizabeth
(Valentine) Graves.
The will of Joseph Valentine parish of Bruton, York Co was written on

30 Nov 1771 and proved on 16 Dec 1771. To son John Valentine all my tract of land in New Kent Co. with all the stock and the following negroes: Bob, Kate, Milla, David, Bob and Dorcus. To dau. Elizabeth Graves, wife of Mr. Richrd Crz(?) Graves the following negroes: Peter and Lucy with her children which is now in the possession of the said Graves; also £50.... And in case son Joseph dies before age 21 then plantation and negroes to be divided between Elizabeth Graves, wife of Richd. Crz. Graves, Benjamin Valentine and Anne Vaughan, wife of Stanup Vaughan.... Residue of estate to be sold, paying to Mr. Richard Croz. Graves £50, and remainder divided between wife Mary and son Joseph. Execs. Mr. Richard Cro. Graves and Mr. Stanup Vaughan.... Probate granted to Richard Croshaw Graves and Stanup Vaughan with William Graves, Benjamin Valentine and Henry Street their securities. {YCWI 1771-1783:48}

The estate of Joseph Valentine decd. to Richard Cro: Graves (exec.) Payments: 396.4.5 ½. Balance of 78.3.1 ½. To Mary Timson by Mr. Valentine's will 34.1.6 3/4. To Joseph Valentine by same 34.1.6 3/4. Total 78.3.1 ½. 26 Jun 1777 in obedience to order of York Co. Court 16 Jun 1777. By last will of said Joseph Valentine estate to be equally divided between his wife who has since intermarried with Mr. Samuel Timson and Joseph Valentine, his youngest son to whom Mr. Richard Cro: Graves is guardian ... Returned 21 Jul 1777. {YCWI 1771-1783:368}

OTHERS NAMED GRAVES

ADAM GRAVES

The Action upon the Case between John Hobday, plaintiff, and Adam Graves, defendant, on the plaintiffs' motion, is continued to amend the declaration 'till next Court. {YCWI 1722-1725:357}

In the Action of Covenant between Anne Maria Timson, plaintiff, and Joseph Frith, defendant, on the plaintiff's motion, time is granted to Consider the Defendant's Special plea–'till next Court. In the Action upon the Case between John Hobday, plaintiff, and Adam Graves, defendant, on the Defendant's Motion, a Special Imparlance is granted him 'till next Court. {YCWI 1722-1725:362}

EDWARD GRIVES

Inventory of the estate of Thos Broughton, deceased, 16 Jun 1646. Appraised by Nathaniel Warren and John Oliver. Includes: A bill from Thomas Klingwell ... by Order of Court from Edward Grives, 0700 [lbs tobacco].... {VCA:III:44}

JANE GRAVES

A power of atty from Jane Graves to Edward Barradell esqr was proved by the witnesses and order'd to be certify'd. {YCWI 1737-1740:490}

JOHN GRAVES, b. 1657, of Brucbley, Northamptonshire, father of Robert
Graves (see later entry).
On 4 Mar 1699, John Graves & Robert Graves, servants to Joseph Ring,
their petition praying order for their indentures to be committed to record the same
is accordingly granted. {YCWI 1698-1702:290}
On 19 Feb 1697, John Graves of Brucbley in Northamptonshire,
carpenter, doth bind himself an apprentice and servant to Richd Kitchiner of VA,
planter, to serve him on his [pg torn] in ye plantation of VA beyond the seas for ye
space of 4 years next ensuing arrival of the said John in said plantation and doth
hereby covenant to serve ye said Richard on his said plantation during said term,
and the said John at ye time of ye ensealing is of ye age of 40 years, a single
person & no covenant or contracted servant to any other person.... Wits: Henry
Webber, Tho Bell. {YCWI 1698-1702:301,302}
Henry Bolch, of Ratcliffe in the Parish of Stepney in the Co. of
Middlesex, cheesmonger, [assigned a] power of attorney to [allow his] friend
John Bates, of York Co., merchant ... to collect due me from John Graves and
Henry Tandy and all other persons in Virginia or Maryland or any other places
in America. Dated the last day of Mar 1707. Wits: William Cant, Griffin
Phillips, and James Randell. {YCWI 1706-1710:121}
On 8 Jul 1710, Othniel Haggatt, of the Parish of St. Michaels, Island of
Barbados, [assigned a power of attorney] to Nicholas Mcriweather, of York
River in Virginia, merchant ... to collect debts ... from any person whatsoever,
but more especially from John Graves, in the sum of £24:9 for one seat of Bills
of Exchange drawn by the said Graves of Virginia on Messrs. Michage Perry &
Lane, merchants in London, payable to Edmund Medlicutt for the proper
account of the aforesaid Haggatt. Wit: Edward Gross. {YCWI 1709-1711:30}

JOSEPH GRAVES
The suit in Chancery brought by William Cowherd, of Bristol, mariner,
against Edward Randolph, late of the City of London merchant, William
Vandridge esqr, Thomas Corbin, George Webb, John Salter, Thos Salter,
Thomas Lane, Humphry Brooks & Joseph Graves is continued. {YCWI 1732-
1737:6}

JOSHUA GRAVES
The Ac[ti]on upon the Case between Thomas Nelson, plaintiff, and
Joshua Graves, defendant, is dismist. {YCWI 1722-1725:303}

ROBERT GRAVES, son of John Graves (see earlier entry).
On 19 Feb 1697, Robert Graves, of Brucbley, Northamptonshire,

66

carpenter, with the consent of his father, hath put himself an apprentice & servant to Richard Kitchiner of VA, to serve him in ye plantation of VA beyond the seas ... [pg torn] .... Wits: John Graves, Tho Bell. {YCWI 1698-1702:301}
These are to certify that ye above named Robt Graves came before me, Tho Bell, and declared himself to be a single person & no covenant or contracted servant to any person to be of ye age of 19 years and to be desirous to serve ye above named Richd Kitchiner according to ye term of ye indenture above written which is registered in ye office for that purpose appointed by letters patents. Richd Cornwell, deputy registrar. The within indenture on ye petition of ye within bound Robert Graves is ordered to record. {YCWI 1698-1702:304}
In the action of debt between Richard Cheshire, Assignee of Samuel Fletcher plaintiff, and Robert Graves, defendant, for £4, due by note under the defendant's hand, the defendant being called but failing to answer, on the plaintiff's mocion, judgment is granted him against the said defendant and Charles Cox, security, returned for him, for the said sum and costs unless the defendant appears at the next Court and answers the plaintiff's action. {YCWI 1711-1714:173,185}

THOMAS GRAVES
Thomas Graves arrested John Chiles in an account of debt for 663 1/2 lbs of sweet scented tobacco & cask due by balance of a bill dated 18 Apr 1699 for 1300 lbs of tobacco & cask & ye def confessing judgment is ordered forthwith to pay to ye plaintiff the afsd sum. {YCWI 1702-1704:91}
Thomas Adcock arrested Thomas Graves in a case & not further prosecuting ye suite is dismist. {YCWI 1702-1704:145}
Thomas Greves obtained judgment against Rebecca Pinkethman, administrator of Timothy Pinkethman, deceased, for 1 pd 11 sl due by account proved in court & is ordered to be payd with cost. {YCWI 1705-1706:385}

THE WILLIAM & CHARLES GRYMES FAMILIES of YORK CO, VA

1. WILLIAM GRYMES, b. ca. 1594, will proved 10 Apr 1668, m. Alice (N). Alice m. 2nd John Babb. {RB 1665-1672:187}
William Grymes was granted a certificate on 24 Jan 1659 for 450 acres due for the importation of 9 persons into the Colony: Marry Lunne, John Norris, William Knowels, Michael White, Dennis Marona, Christian Herding, Edmond Mathis, John Begyll, Mary Gressam. {RB 1659-1662:75}
Edmond Mathis, servant to William Grymes, adjudged on 24 Jan 1659 to be 12 years of age and to serve till 21. {RB 1659-1662:75}
William Grymes, age c66, was deposed on 25 Feb 1660 concerning

Nathaniel Hunt, asking him to go to Capt. Holman and demand what was due him. {RB 1659-1662:112}

The land mentioned in a patent dated at James City 12 Jun 1663 was given and granted unto Wm Grimes ... and was later sold on 16 Oct 1721 by Jno Stockner, of York Hampton Parish, York Co., for £25, to Joseph Walker, of same place, merchant, all [t]his 50 acre tract of land.... {YCWI 1713-1729:372}

Katherine Frezell and William Grymes, Hampton Parish, York Co., gave bond on 3 Sep 1666 for admininstration of estate of Hugh Frezell, deceased, late husband of said Katherine. {RB 1665-1672:109}

William Fanning, servant to Mr. William Grymes, was adjudged on 18 Oct 1667 to be 17 years of age at importation, to serve to 24. {RB 1665-1672:157}

Probate of the will of William Grymes, deceased, was granted on 10 Apr 1668 to Alice Grymes, his relict. {RB 1665-1672:176}

William Grymes left a will undated that was proved 10 Apr 1668. To eldest daughter, Mary Grimes, plantation. To wife Alice, executrix, 1/3 of rest of estate, to be equally divided between my children, she to manage estate as long as she is a widow. {RB 1665-1672:179}

Upon the petition of John Babb on 24 Jun 1668, as marrying the relict of William Grymes, deceased, Grymes's estate to be appraised and divided. {RB 1665-1672:187}

The Inventory of William Grymes's estate was entered on 24 Aug 1668. Widow's third [to wife Alice], Margaret Grymes, Martha Grymes, Jane Grymes. {RB 1665-1672:303-4}

Mr. John Babb was ordered on 24 Jun 1675 to pay Mr. Thomas Wade what estate belongs to him in right of his wife, Margaret Grymes, late in guardianship of Babb. {RB 1672-1676:116}

Geffrcy Moare [Moore] left a will dated 8 Jan 1671and proved 27 Feb 1671/2. To be buried by my wife Isabell. To Thomas Overstreete, son of John Overstreete, all my land in the neck. To Jane Grimes, daughter of William Grimes, mare Bonny. To Mary Risle [Risley], daughter of John Risle, all my land ____. To Robert Jones, son of Robert Jones, all my land in the French Ordinary Field. All goods to be sold for widow Facon [Faison] and widow Morris [Morce?]. {RB 1672-1676:10}

Thomas Wade, the brother in law of Martha and Jane Grimes, orphans, was appointed on 24 Jun 1675 their guardian and to be possessed of their estate, now in hands of Mr. John Babb, their late guardian. {RB 1672-1676:116}

William was the father of MARY [also called eldest], MARGARET m. Thomas Wade, MARTHA, and JANE. William and Alice (N) were the parents of at least the latter three of the four daughters mentioned.

2. REV. CHARLES GRYMES, of Hampton Parish, York Co., VA, d. ca. 1662, m. Katherine (N).

68

In a difference in court on 29 Dec 1662 between Mr. Thomas Godlington, of London, and Mrs. Katherine Grymes, executrix, of Charles Grymes, Clerk, deceased, Godlington through his atty asked for proof she is executrix; case referred. {RB 1659-1662:180}

Second Generation

3. MARGARET GRYMES, daughter of William (1) and Alice (N) Grymes, m. Thomas Wade[20].

On 16 Aug 1695, Thomas Wade, of Merchants Hundred Parish in James City Co., VA, planter, and Margaret, his wife, for £50, sold to Anthony Sebrell, of Hampton Parish, York Co., VA, planter, a messuage and 50 acre tract of land in Hampton Parish bounded by Underhill's line & Capt Barbar's line, being part of the land formerly belonging to William Grimes.... Wits: Willm Sedgwick, Thomas Graves, Elizabeth Graves. {YCDB 1694-1701:24}

4. JOHN GRYMES, b. ca 1660, m. Alice (Townley), was a son of Rev. Charles (2) and Katherine (N) Grymes.

John and Alice (Townley) Grymes were the parents of JOHN and CHARLES.

Charles m. Frances Jennings, daughter of Hon. Edmund Jennings. {EVB:249}

Third Generation

5. JOHN GRYMES, ESQR., b. 1692, will 1747, d. 2 Nov 1748 {WMCQ 1:12:171}, proved 1748, m. Lucy Ludwell ca. 1717, was a son of John (4) and Alice (Townley) Grimes. {EVB:249; CVR}

Lucy (Ludwell) Grymes, d. 3 Mar 1749, daughter of Philip Ludwell, Esqr., was buried near her husband in Christ Church Cemetery, Urbanna, Middlesex Co., VA. {WMCQ 1:12:174}

John was Receiver General of VA from 1725 to 1748. He was succeeded by his son Philip in 1748. {CVR}

William Robertson Esqr. in open Court presented & Acknowledged his deed for land lying in Williamsburgh in this County to John Grymes Esqr. at whose [motion] ye same is admitted to Record. {YCWI 1722-1725:241}

On 12 Dec 1723, William Robertson, of York Co., gent, for £200, sold to John Grymes, of Middlesex Co., esqr, all that dwelling house with the out houses thereunto belonging wherein the said William Robertson lately dwelt in the City of Wmsburgh & being part of two lots of ground denoted in the place of the said city by the figures 26 & 27 & bounded by Francis Street, the Capitol

---

[20] See Thomas Wade Family, this volume.

Square & part of the said lots formerly sold to Doctor John Brown, the other part of the said lots sold to John Marot, deceased, and the lot late of the said John Marot and now in the tenure & occupacon of Anne Sullivan.... Wits: Wil Toplis, Jno Randolph, Graves Pack[21]. {YCDB 1713-1729:411}

On 1 Jul 1732, Henry Willis, of Spotsylvania Co., gent, and Mildred, his wife, and John Holloway, of Williamsburgh esqr, surviving executors of the will of John Brown, late of said city, deceased, for £100, sold to Alexander Kerr, of said city gent, a lott of land in Williamsburgh on Duke of Gloucester Street adjacent Capitol Square, John Grymes esqr, and a piece of ground lately sold by the said executors to John Holt, of said city, watchmaker.... {YCLRD 1729-1740:150}

In a Court session held on 17 Dec 1744, in the action of trespass between John Grymes esqr, plaintiff, and Edwin Thacker & Carter Burwell gent, acting executors of James Bray gent, deceased, defendants, the defendants say that the said deceased in his lifetime did not promise etc. and that they have fully administered his estate. {YCWI 1743-1746:318,331}

On 21 Jan 1744[/5], in the action of trespass between John Grymes esqr, plaintiff, and Edwin Thacker & Carter Burwell, gent, acting executors of James Bray gent, deceased, defendants, the defendants by leave of the court withdraw their plea & say that they cannot say but that the said deceased in his lifetime did promise & assume as in the declaration set forth, that they owe to the plaintiff 15 pd 15 sl 2 pn as he hath alledged, the plaintiff to recover against the defendants the afsd sum and his costs out of the estate of the said deceased. {YCWI 1743-1746:338}

The gent subscribers for the *Play House* in the City of Williamsburg, The Corporation of said city, have no publick building within the city wherein to hold their Common Halls & Courts of Hustings, but have hitherto used the Court House of James City Co. That the *Play House* stands in a convenient place for such uses, and has not been put to any use for several years, and is now going to decay. That the whole money which has been gathering since the Corporation was first made proves deficient to erect a prison for the city nor have they any way to raise publick money to build a town house, wherefore they shall esteem and always acknowledge it as a singular mark of your good will and favour, if you will be pleased to bestow your present useless house on this corporation for the use afsd.... Subscribers' Names: ... Francis Willis ... Philip Ludwell, Benja. Harrison, Lewis Burwell Junr, John Grymes, Henry Armistead, John Robinson, Phi Lightfoot.... Ackn 16 Dec 1745. {YCLRD 1741-1754:154}

Philip Lightfoot, of the Town of York esqr., left a will dated 31 Jul 1747 and proved 20 Jun 1748, in which he appointed the Honble John Grymes, Thomas Lee & William Nelson esqrs, Col. Anthony Walke & William Lightfoot

---

[21] This gentleman's name was Pack or Packe and not to be interpreted as Parke.

executors. {YCWI 1745-1759:103}

John and Lucy (Ludwell) Grimes were the parents of JOHN, b. 1 Jan 1718, bap. 15 Jan 1718; LUCY, b. 18 Apr 1720, bap. 24 Apr 1720, m. Carter Burwell; PHILIP, b. 11 Mar 1721, bap 18 Mar 1721; CHARLES, b. 31 May 1723, bap. 7 Jun 1723, d. 27 Dec 1727; ALICE, b. 10 Aug 1724, bap 16 Aug 1724, m. Mann Page on 29 Dec 1741 in Middlesex Co.; BENJAMIN, b. 19 Jan 1724, bapt 6 Feb 1725, m. Elizabeth "Betty" Fitzhugh 12 Feb 1747; SARAH, b. 29 Jan 1729, bap 6 Feb 1729, d. 25 Oct 1731; CHARLES, b. 11 Mar 1730, bap 18 Mar 1730, LUDWELL, b. 26 Apr 1733, bap 6 May 1733. {CCPR}

6. CHARLES GRYMES, b. ca 1690, d. 1743, m. Frances Jennings, and was a son of John (4) and Alice (Townley) Grymes. {EVB:249}

Fourth Generation

7. PHILIP GRYMES, ESQ., b. 11 Mar 1721, d. ca 1762 {CVR}, m. Mary (Randolph) ca. 1742, was a son of John (5) and Lucy (Ludwell) Grimes. {EVB:249; CCPR}

On 20 Dec 1751, Kenneth Mackenzie, of the City of Williamsburgh, doctor of physick, and Joanna, his wife, for £537.10, sold to the Honourable Philip Grymes esqr, his Majesty's Receiver General of VA, a messuage and four lotts of land on Palace Street in said city (Nos. 333, 334, 335 & 336) and are the messuage and four lots of land which the said Kenneth Mackenzie purchased of Robert Cary, of the City of London esqr, 7 Oct 1747 (except one house being the shop of said Kenneth Mackenzie which he is to remove off the premises within 6 months).... {YCLRD 1741-1754:468}

On 19 Dec 1753, the Honble Philip Grymes esqr, his Majesty's Receiver General of VA, in consequence of the trust reposed in him and by the orders of the Honble Robert Dinwiddie esqr, Governor and Commander in Chief of VA, with the advice of his Majesty's council, for £450, sold to Robert Carter Nicholas, of the City of Williamsburgh, atty at law, four lots of land ... whereas Kenneth McKenzie and Joanna, his wife, on 20 Dec 1751 sold to the said Philip Grymnes [sic] in trust and for the purposes in the indenture mentioned houses and four lotts of land on Palace Street in the said city (Nos. 333, 334, 335 & 336) which the said Kenneth McKenzie purchased of Robert Cary, of the City of London esqr, on 7 Oct 1747 ... in trust and for the use of his Majesty's Lieutenant Governor or Commander in Chief of VA.... Wit: Wm Nelson, Robert Burwell, Pet. Hay, Alexr Finnie. {YCLRD 1741-1754:585}

On 7 May 1761, Robert Carter Nicholas, of the City of Williamsburgh, and Anne, his wife, for £650, sold to the Honourable Robert Carter esqr four lotts of land on Palace Street in the City of Williamsburgh which were conveyed to the said Robert Carter Nicholas by the Honorable Philip Grymes esqr his Majesty's Receiver General and are described in the plan of said city by Nos.

333, 334, 335 & 336.... Wit: Nathl Crawley, Thomas Everard, Geo Davenport, Ben Waller.... {YCLRD 1755-1763: 356}
Philip and Mary (Randolph) Grymes were the parents of LUCY, b. 24 Aug 1743, bap 26 Aug 1743; JOHN, b. 28 Mar 1745, bap 5 Apr 1745, d. 2 Jun 1746 {WMCQ 1:12:173}; PHILIP LUDWELL, b. 5 Apr 1746, bap 9 May 1746; and CHARLES. {CCPR}

8. BENJAMIN GRYMES, b. 19 Jan 1725, bap 6 Feb 1725, m. 1st Elizabeth "Betty" Fitzhugh in King George Co. and 2nd (N) Roots. {EVB:249; CCPR}, Benjamin was a son of John (5) and Lucy (Ludwell) Grymes.

Fifth Generation

9. PHILIP LUDWELL GRYMES, b. 5 Apr 1746, bap 9 May 1746, d. 18 May 1805, m. Judith (N). {WMCQ 1:12:171}, was a son of Philip (7) and Mary (Randolph) Grymes. {EVB:249}
On 28 Jun 1770, Philip L. Grymes, Augine Smith, Will Churchhill, and Churchhill Jones witnessed the sale by Hugh Walker & Catharine, his wife, for £200, to William Acrill, of Charles City Co. gent, of ½ of the large cellar under the brickhouse called Doctor William Carter's on the S side of Duke of Gloucester Street in the City of Williamsburg, denoted in the plan of the said house by No. 3, the two rooms on the lower floor of the said house No. 4, and the two rooms on the second floor above No. 6 being over the two rooms below No. 6 as denoted in the said plan being the rooms conveye.... {YCLRD 1769-1777:62,63}
15 Aug 1770, Philip L. Grymes, Augine Smith, Will Churchhill, Churchhill Jones, John Tazewell et al. witnessed the sale by Hugh Walker, of Middlesex Co., merchant, and Catharine, his wife, for £400, sold to Andrew Anderson, of the City of Williamsburg, surgeon, all that messuage and lot of land in the City of Williamsburg denoted in the plan thereof by the figure 62 and bounded by Nicholson Street, Market Square, Duke of Gloucester Street & the lot of James Geddy.... {YCLRD 1769-1777:73}
To Philip Ludwell Grymes and Augine Smith, justices of the peace in Middlesex Co., greeting, whereas Hugh Walker & Catharine, his wife, by their indenture of sale [see above] have sold unto Andrew Anderson the fee simple estate of one lot of land in the City of Williamsburg.... {YCLRD 1769-1777:74}
Philip Ludwell and Judith (N) Grymes were the parents of PHILIP, b. 19 Sep 1775, d, 9 Nov 1801; JANE, b. 1782, d. 1 Jan 1806, m. Samuel Wm. Sayre.
Jane's tombstone reads, "Beneath this stone are deposited the remains of MRS. JANE SAYRE, Wife of Samuel Wm. Sayre, and daughter of the late Philip Ludwell Grymes, who departed this life Jan 1, 1806, Aged 24. Rest here, oppressed by pale disease no more; Here find that calm thou sought so oft before;

Rest undisturbed within this Humble Shrine, Till Angels wake thee with a voice like thine." {WMCQ 1:12:171}

10. CHARLES GRYMES, GENT, of Gloucester Co., VA, m. 1st Anne (N) Lightfoot in 1773 (who was widow of Armistead Lightfoot) and m. 2nd in 1777/8 Mary Hubard in Gloucester Co., VA. {GCM} Charles was a son of Philip (7) and Mary (Randolph) Grymes.

Thos Archer, Charles Grymes, William Mitchell, and John Chisman ackn on 18 May 1772 the sale by Thomas Powell, of York Co., surgeon, for £250, to William Prentis, of the City of Williamsburg, merchant, all that lot or parcel of ground in the said City of Williamsburg on Page Street being part of the land purch'd by Benjamin Waller from Mann Page & lately added to the said city and denoted in the plan of the sd addition by the figure 30.... {YCLRD 1769-1777:219}

On 15 Nov 1773, Articles of Agreement were created among Charles Grymes, of Gloucester Co. gent, of the one part and Anne Lightfoot, widow of Armistead, deceased, of the second part, and Jaquelin Ambler, of York Town & Co., of the third part, whereas there is a marriage shortly intended to be had & solemnized between the said Charles Grymes & Ann Lightfoot, and whereas the said Anne Lightfoot is intitled to two Negro slaves, Johnny & Jenny, and the household furniture hereunto annexed, and is also intitled to dower in the lands of her late husband the said Armistead Lightfoot, deceased, and is entitled to sundry slaves for her life purchased by the trustees appointed by Act of Assembly, all which the said Charles hath consented shall remain to her for her own separate use in case the said marriage shall take affect. Now these presents wit that the said Charles Grymes doth hereby covenant & agree to & with the said Jaquelin Ambler that in case the sd intended marriage shall take effect he the said Jaquelin Ambler shall stand seized & possessed of all the lands to which the said Ann Lightfoot is entitled for dower & of all the slaves afsd to & for the sole & separate use of the sd Ann Lightfoot & no wise subject to the debts of him the said Charles Grymes & also of the household furniture afsd.... {YCLRD 1769-1777:376}

THE EDWARD GRIMES FAMILY of LANCASTER CO, VA

EDWARD GRIMES, of Lancaster Co., VA, m. Margaret (N) Attawell (b. ca. 1600), relict of Thomas Attawell. {VCA:I:221, citing Lancaster Co records}

It is ordered with the consent of Edward Grimes that the stocke of Catle belonging to Mary Attowell, Francis Attowell, Ann Wotten and Wm Wotten with all there [sic] female increase shall be by him kept for the said orphants without any future charge for keep and Educacon of the said orphants and there

[sic] catle one cow calfe in the said acco't was given by the said Edw Grimes to Wm Wotten." {VCA:III:60, citing YorkCo records}

"The deposition of Margaret Grimes, age about 46 yeares, taken this 25 Sep 1646" regarding Ann Owle. {VCA:III:56 citing YorkCo records}

Edward Grimes left bequest to William Wraton[22] on 1 Aug 1653. {VCA:I:233, citing LancCo records}

Edward Grime and Wm White "have Causelessly bene Arested" by Robt Mascall who is ordered to pay them damages. 8 Aug 1653. {VCA:I:196, citing LancCo records}

Margaret Grime, "late relict of Tho Adawell [Attawell]" 16 Mar 1652/3." {VCA:I:196, citing LancCo records}

Edward Grime left a will dated 1 Aug 1653, probated 9 Dec 1653. To wife Margaret, personal property if she remain single for life, otherwise to be divided equally between Wm Wraton, Ann White, and Mary [Attawell] Gooch [wife of Samuel]. To daughter in law, Fra Attawell, all land, 430 acres in Rappa River. She failing in heirs, to Wm Wraton, he failing in heirs, to Ann White and she failing, to Mary Gooch. Wife executor. Supervisors: Wm Newsam and Wm Wraton. Wits: Davey Fox, John Phillips. {VCA:I:196, citing LancCo records}

Pd. 30 lb tobo for hire of men to guard the house of Marga: Grimes "on the Death of the Indian." 6 Oct 1654. {VCA:I:180, citing LancCo records}

Fra: Attawell, daughter-in-law [step daughter] of Edw Grime, m. Tho Roots, chirurgeon, on 14 Oct 1653. {VCA:I:172,221, citing LancCo records}

Mary Attwell, daughter of Thomas and Margaret (N) Attawell, m. Samuell Gooch of Lancaster Co., VA. In a pre-nuptial agreement dated 16 Mar 1652, prior to the intended marriage of Mary, daughter of Tho Adawell deceased, regarding certain cattle left her by her father ... were mentioned Edw Grimes and Marg: [Margaret], his wife, late relict of said Attawell. {VCA:I:196, citing LancCo records}

On 8 Dec 1653, Thomas Roots assigned 300 acres to Marg Grimes widow of Edw Grimes for life. {VCA:I:221, citing LancCo records}

Mary Attawell Gooch d. prior to 1 Jan 1657/8. {VCA:I:122, citing LancCo records}

OTHERS NAMED GRIMES / GRYMES

MARY GRIMES

In the will of Simon Whitaker, York Co., Bruton Parish, 24 Feb 1765, he willed parts of his estate to various family members. Also mentioned was a bequest of £5 to Mrs. Mary Grimes's children. {YCWI 1760-1771:292}

---

[22] Wraton is also spelled Wroughton, Roughton, Wratton in Lancaster Co., VA records.

RICHARD GRIMES, d. 1716, no will, m. Elizabeth (N).
Richd. Grimes, Jno. Andrews and Jno. Doswell Senr., all of the Co. of York, to the Queen, in the sum of 10,000 lbs. of tobacco. 16 Nov 1713. Sureties for said Grimes to obtain a lycence to keep an Ordinary at his now dwelling house in York Town the ensuing year. {YCWI 1711-1714:286,294}
On 19 Nov 1716, Eliza Grimes made oath that her husband Richd Grimes dyed without making any will, she having together with Charles Cox and Nathl Hooke, her securitys, enter'd into bond & ackn ye same, which bond is admitted to record & certificate if granted her for obtaining Letters of Administration. {YCWI 1716-1718:35}
In obedience to an order of court, Jno Doswell Junr, Jno Chisman, and Jno Right being first sworn before Tho Nelson, justice, did meet at ye house of Eliza Grymes on 5 Dec and did inventory and appraise ye estate of Richard Grimes, deceased. 3 old beds, bedsteds, hide and cords, rug, bolsters, pillows, blankets, sheets, 1 Indea calaco quilt, 3 ould sifs, 2 punch bowls, 3 candlesticks, 1 pr money scales, 1 pr shears, 1 pr belos, 11 chares, parcel of tubs, 3 chests, 1 table and forme, 1 pistol, holster, sword and belt, etc. 1 Negro man & 1 Negro woman. 118 pd 6 sl. Presented by Eliz Grimes, administrator, on 21 Jan 1716.... {YCWI 1716-1718:36,47,60,66,70}
In ye action of debt between Charles Lucas, plaintiff, and Eliza Grimes, administrator of Richd Grimes, deceased, defendant, for 1042 lbs of tobacco by bill under ye decendant's hand dated 10 Dec 1715 ye defendant confessed judgment to ye plaintiff for 842 lbs of tobacco being ye balance due by said bill, ordered that she pay said 842 lbs of tobacco out of deceased's estate to plaintiff with costs. {YCWI 1716-1718:92}

WALTER GRIMES
On 15 Apr 1653, Walter Grimes assigned land to Jno Piper and Robert Bowers.... {VCA:III:449 citing Lower NorfCo records}

WILLIAM GRIMES, of York Co., Virginia, m. (N).
The Court ordered that John Holloway be paid 400 lbs of tobacco from the estate of Wm Stephens, Richard Hauser, and Roger Williamson "for the cure ofe their man Wm Grymes." [Entry is undated but appears in section labeled 1637-1640.] {VCA:I:63, citing AccomacCo records}
Wm. Grimes witnessed Power of Atty on 17 Dec 1645 from Joseph Hillis to Jno Perrin for Perrin to represent Hillis in Court. In source document, this entry was headed "Dme Ro Bouth." {VCA:III:21 citing YorkCo records}
To daughter Ann Grimes 2 calves, 3 cows, a feather bed, 4 Pewter dishes, 1 trunk and 3 Guns to be delivered at day of marriage "with my now dwelling Plantation" and land, being 280 acres as by patent doth apprear. To

Ann Harden, a heifer. Residue of estate to wife, she executrix, (her name not shown). Wits: Ralph Graves, John Oliver, Richard Fenn, Joseph Croshaw. [In source document, this entry is undated but other entries on same page are dated 1655/6.] {VCA:III:129 citing YorkCo records}

THE ANTHONY LAMB FAMILY

1. ANTHONY LAMB, d. 29 Dec 1700 {CPR}, m. 1st Mary (N) (d. 3 Jan 1677) {CPR}, m. 2nd Hannah (N).

On 3 Jun Anthony Lambe appointed James Calthorp as his atty in a cause between him and Richard Moore, attorney of Capt. John Martin. {RB 1672-1678:120}

Mr. Anthony Lambe was granted a certificate on 10 Oct 1691 for importing 4 persons into this Collony: Thomas Poore, Elizabeth Ashmore, Edward Benins and Fleetwood Wright. {DW 1691-1694:71}

Sarah Love recorded on 25 Nov 1695 the cattle mark of Mary Lamb on cattle given Lamb by Silus Love. {DW 1694-1697:231}

24 Feb 1700. Hanna Lamb on her petition hath order granted for a commission of administration of her deceased husband Anthony Lamb's estate as he dyed without will, James Sclater and James Calthorpe in court entered themselves securities for the said Hannah Lamb's due performance of the said administration, and it is further ordered that Arminger Wade, James Calthorpe, William Wise & John Hunt inventory and appraise the deceased's estate and that a due return thereof be made to next court. {YCWI 1698-1702:380}

An inventory & appraisement of the estate of Anthony Lamb, deceased, taken by Willm Wise, James Calthorp & Arminger Wade on 7th this instant Mar being first sworn before Capt Daniell Taylor: 3 feather beds, bolsters, rugs, sheets, blanketts, 1 flock bed, 2 tables, 1 form, 2 chests, parcell of bottles & a case, parcell of fishing lines, some linen yarn & two flatt irons, 2 books, 1 brass kettle, 1 warming pan & other brass, etc. 22 pd 3 sl. Hannah Lamb. Presented in court 24 Mar 1700.... {YCWI 1698-1702:453}

Anthony and Hannah were parents of JOHN, b. 22 Aug 1679; ANTHONY, b. 12 Feb 1681; WILLIAM, b. 12 Feb 1681, d. 30 Sep 1698; URSULA, b. 11 Mar 1683; MARY, b. 5 Feb 1686; HANNAH, b. 25 Sep 1690; DANIEL, b. 12 Feb 1692. {CPR}

Second Generation

2. JOHN LAMB, b. 22 Aug 1679, d. 28 Mar 1733, m. Frances (N), was a son of Anthony (1) and Hannah (N) Lamb.

On 7 Nov 1718, John Lamb proferred a claim for taking up George, a runaway Negro man belonging to Saml Pond, of James City Co., upon the said Lamb's producing a certificate & making oath that he took the said Negro up at the Old Church in Poquoson (which appears to be more than 10 miles from his master's place of residence) as also that he never has received any satisfaction for that service, ordered to be certifyed to the Assembly for allowance. {YCWI 1716-1718:328}

16 Dec 1734. Upon the motion of Adam Russell praying that the estate of John Lamb, deceased, now in his possession unadministered may be delivered up, whereupon it is ordered that the same be delivered to Walter Taylor, who Anthony Lamb, one of the orphans of the said John Lamb, this day made choice of for his guardian and also appointed guardian by the court to Hannah Lamb, the other orphan of the said John Lamb, upon his giving bond and sufficient security for the care of their said estate. {YCWI 1732-1737:160}

In obedience to an order of court dated 16 Jun 1735 Bennet Tompkins, Thomas Hawkins & Thomas Phillips appraised the estate of John Lamb, deceased: 1 bedstead, bed & furniture, 3 chests, 2 iron potts, 1 brass kettle, 1 spitt, hatchet, pestle and spade, axe, a parcel of stone and earthen ware, 1 mare, 1 colt, 1 lame horse, 23 lb of pewter, 1 table and 6 chair frames, 1 yarn box, sword, catonch? box and looking glass, 12 old barrels and casks, 2 trays and 1 old spinning wheel, 1 Negro man George. £9.12.1 … recorded 21 Jul 1735. It was further ordered that they give the widow of the said John Lamb her third part of the said estate. {YCWI 1732-1737:197, 213}

John and Frances were parents of <u>ANTHONY</u>, b. 7 Oct, bapt. 27 Nov 1720; HANNAH, b. 30 Jul, bapt. 28 Sep 1723. {CPR}

3. ANTHONY LAMB, b. 12 Feb 1681, d. 15 Nov 1734 {CPR}, m. Sarah (N) (d. 18 Apr 1736) {CPR}, son of Anthony (1) and Hannah Lamb.

On 17 Jan 1736, upon the complaint of Francis Hayward gent, one of the church wardens of Charles Parish, it was order'd that the children of Anthony Lamb, deceased, be bound out by the church wardens of the said parish. {YWCI 1732-1737:336}

On 17 Mar 1743, the court ordered that the church wardens of Charles Parish bind out Anthony Lamb, an orphan, to some handycraft trade. {YCWI 1743-1746:279}

Anthony and Sarah (N) Lamb were parents of MARTHA, b. 24 Jul, bapt. 28 Aug 1720; JOHN, b. 19 Jul, bapt. 23 Aug 1723; DANIEL, b. 2 Sep, bapt. 6 Oct 1728; ANTHONY, b. 21 Dec, bapt. 23 Jan 1731. {CPR}

4. DANIEL LAMB, a son of Anthony (1) and Harriet (N) Lamb, was b. 12 Feb 1692, will 27 Jun 1744, d. 4 Jul 1744 {CPR}, will proved 19 Nov 1744, and m. Abigal (N).

On 17 Jun 1734, the Court judged Esther, a Negro girl belonging to Daniel Lamb, to be 9 years old. {YCWI 1732-37:120}

On 21 Jul 1735, Bristol, a Negro boy belonging to Daniel Lamb, was adjudged to be 9 years of age. {YCWI 1732-1737:207}

On 17 Jul 1738, Armourer & Hannah, a Negro boy & girl belonging to Daniel Lamb, were adjudged tithables. {YCWI 1737-1740:433}

On 20 Jun 1743, Will, a Negro boy belonging to Daniel Lamb, was adjudged to be 12 years old. {YCWI 1740-1743:193}

Daniel Lamb, of Charles Parish, York Co., planter, left a will dated 27 Jun 1744. To wife, Abigal Lamb, the use & fruition of my whole estate during her natural life. To son John Lamb, the Negro boy called Joe which he hath now in possession. Also to my said son John, a Negro girl called Sarah. To son William Lamb, two Negroes, my Negro man Bristol and a Negro girl Phillis. To daughter Anne Lamb, two Negroes Esther & Jimmy. To daughter Elizabeth Lamb, two Negroes Amborough & his wife Hannah. To son Danl Lamb, three Negroes Will, Lucy & Jone. To nephew Anthony Lamb, son of Anthony Lamb, deceased, 6 pd 1 sl 3 pn when he arrives to age 21. After wife's decease all the residue of my estate to be divided amongst my afsd children. I appoint my two sons, John Lamb & Wm Lamb, executors. Wits: Thos Roberts, John Hunt, John Barnes. Proved 19 Nov 1744. {YCWI 1743-1746:324}

In obedience to an order of court the subscribers appraised the estate of Daniel Lamb, deceased: Books, wicker chairs & table, case of bottles, trunk, etc. Negroes: Bustor, Embrough & Will. £36.9.6. Peter Goodwin, Merrit Moore, Bennet Tompkins ... recorded 18 Feb 1744. {YCWI 1743-1746:354}

Daniel and Abigal (N) were parents of SARAH, b. 5 Sep 1713, d. 10 Sep 1713; JOHN, b. 11 Jun, bapt. 7 Jul 1717; WILLIAM, b. 26 Mar, bapt. 1 May 1722; ANN, b. 3 Oct, bapt. 9 Nov 1724; ELIZABETH, b. 18 Feb, bapt. 19 Mar 1726; HANNAH, b. 10 Jul, bapt. 17 Aug 1729; DANIEL, b. 2 Sep, bapt. 6 Oct 1728. {CPR}

Third Generation

5. ANTHONY LAMB, b. 7 Oct 1720, d. Mar 1758 {CPR}, son of John (2) and Frances (N) Lamb, m. 1st Rachel Hay (d. 31 May 1751) {CPR}, daughter of John and Mary Hay, and m. 2nd Elizabeth Presson (d. 25 Feb 1757) {CPR}, daughter of John Presson.

On 20 Aug 1744, in an action of detinue between Anthony Lamb and Rachel, his wife, plaintiffs, and John Hay, defendant, the defendant being arrested and failing to appear, the court ordered that judgment be entr'd for the plaintiffs against the defendant for the Negro girl mentioned in the declaration of the value of £30 and costs, unless the defendant shall appear and plead at the next court. {YCWI 1743-1746:304}

John Hay left a will dated 1 May 1751, in which he left to John Lamb, son of Anthony Lamb, one young Negro boy named Jack and also six head of young cattle and as many head of sheep and one young horse or mare to the value of 3 pd and not to be paid until the said John Lamb attains the age of 21. To my brother James Hay, my whole estate of land, Negroes, stock and all other things which now belongeth to me. The land which I have given to the said James Hay be to him and his heirs, but in default of such issue then to fall to my brother Robert Hay and his heirs, and for default of such heirs to fall to my cousin John Lamb, son of Anthony Lamb, and his heirs but in default of such issue then to fall to Anthony Lamb, brother to the said John Lamb, and his heirs, but in default of such issue then to fall to the next heir at law. My will is that James Hay, my brother, who I appoint my executor have not my estate appraised. At a court held 15 Dec 1755, the writing purporting the will of John Hay, deceased, was produced in court by James Hay, the heir at law and the executor therein named, and no witnesses being subscribed thereto, Robert Wise, Thomas Toner & Anthony Lamb severally made oath that they are well acquainted with the handwriting of the deceased and verily believe the said will and the name John Hay subscribed thereto to be all of the proper handwriting of the said John Hay, deceased, and thereupon the said executor made oath thereto and the will was ordered to be recorded. The said executor together with the said Robert Wise, Thomas Tomer & Anthony Lamb, his securities, acknowledged a bond, and a certificate was granted him for obtaining a probate. Sarah Hay, widow and relict of the said deceased, absolutely refused to abide by the said will, and renounced all benefit she might claim by the same. {YCWI 1745-1759:386}

Anthony Lamb, of Charles Parish, York Co.: To son John Lamb, one Negro man named George. After my debts and funeral charges are paid to son Anthony Lamb, one Negro woman named Patt and one Negro boy named Frank. To dau Elizabeth Lamb, 30 pd.... The overplus to be divided among my three children before named. I appoint John Presson, of Elizabeth City Co., executor. Wits: Thos Tomer, Hannah Williams. Proved 20 Mar 1758. John Presson, the executor, together with Edward Tabb and James Dixon, his securities, acknowledge a bond, and a certificate was granted him for obtaining a probate. {YCWI 1745-1759:473}

In obedience to a court order dated 20 Mar 1758, Samuel Tompkins, Thos Tomer, Edward Armistead & John Richardson, being first sworn before Robert Sheild gent, justice of the peace, appraised the estate of Anthony Lamb, deceased: 1 gun and cartorch [cartouche] box, 2 pr of cotton cards, a parcel of books, a parcel of pewter, box iron and heaters, teapot, looking glass, 1 jugg, firetongs & skillet, 2 pots of lard, 1 grindstone & searce, fallow & bees was[x], spun cotton, 930 10p nails, pickt cotton, impickt [unpicked] cotton, 3 beds & furniture, 1 pr old sheets, table linnen, 1 spinning wheel, 5 chairs, 1 cupboard, 2 tables, 1 chest, a set of wedges, old hoes, 1 saddle & housings, 1 fluke hoe &

brake, 2 pots & a pr of pothooks, a parcel of lumber, 3 barrels corn, 4 sows, 3 shoats, 10 pigs, 3 turkeys, 6 hens, 2 ducks, 2 axes, etc. Negro Man named George, Negro woman named Patt & Negro boy named Frank. £71.6.2 ... recorded 15 May 1758. {YCWI 1745-1759:479}

By court order on 15 Dec 1762, settlement of estate of Anthony Lamb, deceased, was made and the balance due to the estate was £21.1.8 ½. Examined by Edward Tabb, John Kerby, Thos. Tomer and returned 21 Jun 1762. {YCWI 1760-1771:102}

John Presson, York Co., left in which he gave to son William Presson the tract of land whereon he now lives, my gun and all my shop tools and £5. To daughter Marrow, three slaves: Moll, Grace and Taffy. To daughter Martha Calbert, negro boy Harry. To granddaughter Elizabeth Lamb, negro boy Jo ... and £10 ... daughter Anne Presson my ... [rest of page obliterated] ... Execs: son, William Presson, and William Marrow, son in law, William Marrow. 22 Oct 1767. Wits: C. Clausel, William Minson, William Baley. Proved 21 Dec 1767. William Marrow was granted probate together with Young Morland, his security. William Presson, the other executor, to join in probate when he shall think fit. {YCWI 1760-1771:378}

Daniel Presson, of Charles Parish, York Co., left a will. To daughter Frances Hay, my land whereon I live during her natural life, and after her decease, to her children and grandchildren she shall think fit. But provided she leaves no issue and dies before her husband, John Hay, then I give the said land to Elizabeth Lamb, granddaughter of my brother, John Presson, deceased. If my son in law, John Hay, cut or destroy more timber off my land than may be necessary for the use of the plantation, or if he shall fail or neglect finishing my house and to keep it in repair, then my executor may rent the said house and plantation for the use of my grandchildren. To daughter Frances Hay, my young slave now at Back River. Negro woman Judith to be hired out. To daughter Frances Hay, my lot in York Town. Exec.: Friend John Robinson. 1 Nov 1782. Wits.: Cole Robinson, Thomas Robinson. Proved 20 Jan 1783. Thomas Robinson refused executorship. John Hay made oath with Robert(?) Manson and William Patrick, securities, entered into and acknowledge bond and was granted letters of administration. {YCWI 1772-1783:572}

Settlement of estate of John Presson, deceased, in account with William Marrow, acting executor, includes payment to William Brown as a legacy in right of his wife £15; William Presson £5, Anne Presson £15, Elizabeth Lamb £10. Total: £76.10.5 plus balance due to the estate £43.2.1½. By court order 15 May 1769 ... returned 17 Jul 1769. {YCWI 1760-1771:461}

Anthony and Rachel (Hay) were parents of JOHN, b. 8 Nov, bapt. 26 Dec 1742; ANTHONY, b. 18 Dec 1744, bapt. 31 Mar 1745. {CPR}

Anthony and Elizabeth (Presson) were parents of ELIZABETH, b. 25 Jan, bapt. 27 Feb 1757. {CPR}

Fourth Generation

6. JOHN LAMB, b. 11 Jun 1717, son of Daniel (4) and Abigail (N) Lamb, m. Mary (N).

John and Mary (N) Lamb were parents of WILLIAM, b. 1 Jan, bapt. 12 Feb 1743; THOMAS, b. 27 May, bapt. 22 Jun 1746, d. 6 Oct 1746; JOHN, b. 12 Oct, bapt. 8 Nov1747. {CPR}

7. ANTHONY LAMB, a son of Anthony (5) and Rachel (Hay) Lamb, was b. 18 Dec 1744, m. Betty Emory (b. 9 May 1751, d. 18 Dec 1808). {CD186:293}

Anthony and Betty (Emory) Lamb were the parents of SALLY, b. 13 Aug 1772; RACHEL, b. 8 Nov, d. 25 Nov 1773; RACHEL BETSY, b. 31 Oct 1774, d. 12 Jun 1845; ROBERT, b. 30 Oct 1777, d. 16 May 1810, unm.; JOHN, b. 8 May 1780, d. 5 Dec 1844; ANTHONY, b. 5 Aug 1782, d. 3 Aug 1784; FANHY MAYO, b. 24 May 1785, d. 27 Jul 1795; WILLIAM, b. 27 Sep, d. 11 Oct 1789; ANTHONY HAY, b. 16 Jan 1790, d. 7 Oct 1865. {CD186:293}

Fifth Generation

8. SALLY LAMB, b. 13 Aug 1772, daughter of Anthony (7) and Betty (Emory) Lamb, m. Henry Edloe.

Sally and Henry (Edloe) Lamb were parents of ANN COCKE EDLOE, b. 10 Sep 1794; and HENRY EDLOW, b. 7 Mar 1796, d. Mar 1838. {CD186:293}

9. RACHEL BETSY LAMB, b. 31 Oct 1774, d. 12 Jun 1845, daughter of Anthony (7) and Betty (Emory) Lamb, m. Thomas Spencer Hall of Accomac Co., VA.

Rachel and Thomas were parents of ROBERT LAMB HALL, b. 11 Aug 1809, d. 2 Jun 1890; MARY H. HALL, b. 8 Apr 1811; THOMAS HALL, b. 23 Oct, d. 23 Jun 1885; ANTHONY LAMB HALL, b. 7 Sep 1817. {CD186:293}

10. JOHN LAMB, of Charles City Co., VA, was b. 8 May 1780, d. 5 Dec 1844, son of Anthony (7) and Betty (Emory) Lamb, m. 1st Mary Emory Burton, widow, of Prince George Co., VA, and m. 2nd Martha Christian. {CD186:293}

John and Mary were parents of LYCURGUS ANTHONY, b. 27 Apr 1814, d. 12 Oct 1855; Rev. JOHN MOODY, b. 5 Jun 1821; and JUNIUS, b. 19 Nov 1825, d. 14 Jan 1887. {CD186:293}

11. ANTHONY HAY LAMB, b. 16 Jan 1790, d. 7 Oct 1865, son of Anthony (7) and Betty (Emory) Lamb, m. 1st 21 Feb 1822, Ann Stott Morecock (d. Oct 1832) and m. 2nd in Dec 1834, Mary Henry Hill (d. 6 Dec 1868). {CD186:293}

John and Ann (Morecock) Lamb were parents of WILLIAM B., b. 17 Feb 1823, d. 10 Oct 1824; ANN ELIZABETH, b. 23 Jun 1828, d. 20 Nov 1873. {CD186:293}

John and Mary (Hill) Lamb were parents of FANNIE CLAYTON, b. 8 Jan 1836, d. 28 Apr 1896; JAMES ANTHONY, b. 11 Dec 1813, d. 4 Mar 1870, unm. {CD186:293}

OTHERS NAMED LAMB

DANIEL LAMB

In his will dated 5 Jul 1734, Peter Robinson devises to his godson, Daniel Lamb, son of Anthony Lamb, 8pd for schooling. {YCWI 1732-37:144}

DANIEL LAMB m. Elizabeth (N).

Elizabeth Lamb, wife of Daniel, d. 15 May 1756. {CPR}

JAMES LAMB

24 Jul 1700. Danll Mackentosh arresting James Lamb in an action of debt for 226 lbs of tobacco by bill dated 6 Jul 1700 made payable upon demand and now demand being proved [pg torn] action brought ye suite is dismist. {YCWI 1700-1702:357}

JOHN LAMB

Division of the estate of William Finch, deceased. To John Lamb, *inter alia*, Negroes Jenny and Patt. 5 May 1773. {CCC:51, citing orig. p. 451}

MARTHA LAMB

In the matter of the estate of Mrs. Hannah William, deceased, in account with Martha Lamb, administratrix, balance due to the estate is £4.3.11.... Recorded 17 Jun 1765. {YCWI 1760-1771:238}

Will of Martha Lamb of York Co. To my friend Merritt Moore, my Negro woman Rachel and her three children, Jenny, Sall and Jupiter. To cousin Elizabeth Williams, my negro girl Sukey. To above named Merritt Moore, my best feather bed with bed quilt and furniture. To said Cousin Elizabeth Williams, my other bed and furniture belonging thereto and one young heifer. Wearing apparell to my friend Mrs. Ann Moore. To my friend Merritt Moore, all the remainder of my estate. 17 Feb 1776. Wits: John Kerby, Martha Dixon. Proved 19 Feb 1776. Exec.: Merritt Moore. Security: John Selator. {YCWI 1772-1783:435}

RUTH LAMB

In the May Court 1739, the churchwardens bind John Lamb, son of Ruth Lamb, to James Jackson. {CCC:52, citing orginal p. 82}

THOMAS LAMB m. Diana (N).

Thomas and Diana were parents of ELIZABETH, b. 23 Nov 1759, bapt. 13 Jan 1760; THOMAS, b. 7 Mar, bapt. 11 Apr 1762. {CPR}

THOMAS LAMB

On 24 Oct 1702, Edward Fuller, late surveyor of the highways for the lower precinque of Hampton Parish, made information to this court that divers persons notwithstanding they have been warned to meet him in order for clearing the roads in his precinque refused to performe the same, viz, Charles Collier, Roger Boult, John Hansford, Thomas Lamb, ordered that the sherriff summon them to the next court to show cause why they misperformed their duty. {YCWI 1702-1704:48}

The GABRIEL MAUPIN FAMILY

1. GABRIEL MAUPIN, m. Mary (N). After Gabriel died between 16 Feb 1718 and 15 Feb 1719, Mary m. 2nd Thomas Creas. {YCDB 1713-1729:440}

Peter Mallovill & Elizabeth his wife, having brought their suit to this court against Gabriel Mompien in a case, and not further prosecuting, ye suit is dismist. {YCWI 1702-1704:95}

Peter Mallavill arresting Gabrill Mompien in a case declared to ye plts damage of 10 pd, & ye def not appearing, order is granted against Henry Tyler, high sheriff, & the next court to be confirmed, if he causeth not the defendants then personally to appear & answer ye same. {YCWI 1702-1704:96}

In a suit between Peter Mallovill, plaintiff, and Gabriell Mompien, defendant, in a plea of trespass for 44 sl which ye plaintiff lent to ye defendant, & also 50 sl 10 pn 1/2 penny which ye defendant of other persons received for ye use of ye plaintiff & not making payment thereof according to his assumptions to ye plaintiff, to which ye def by Joseph Chermison his atty, pleaded not guilty, upon which both parties by their attys, viz., Richard Wharton for ye plaintiff & said Chermison for ye defendant agreed to refer the matter to ye court for a final determination & desition thereof & ye evidence being examined & pleas made on both sides, ye court doth conclude ye def forthwith pay to the plaintiff ye said sums with cost. {YCWI 1702-1704:124}

John Sergeton, being by ye sherrif returned summoned an evidence for Peter Mallovill, plaintiff against Gabriell Monpien, defendant, in an action of trespass, tis ordered he be paid 320 lbs of tobacco for 8 days attendance at court with cost. {YCWI 1702-1704:124}

On 25 Jun 1707, Gabriel Mompain arresting Ralph Hubbard to this Court in an acion of case for the sum of £3:10:7 ½, and he not appearing, order is granted against Wm. Barbar, Sheriff, and the next Court to be confirmed if he causeth not the defendant then personally to appear and answer of the same. {YCWI 1706-1708:78}

On 25 Mar 1708, the action of debt between Gabl. Maupin, plaintiff, and Tho. Haly, defendant, was dismist, neither party appearing. {YCWI 1706-1710:129}

On 24 Aug 1708, the Grand Jury having formerly presented Gabriel Maupin for retailing liquors contrary to Law, who this day appeared and confessed the same, therefore ordered that he be fined 50 lbs. of tobacco or 5 shillings to Charles Parish to be paid at the next Levy *alies* execution. {YCWI 1706-1710:153,158}

Gabriel Maupin being presented by the Grand Jury on 24 Sep 1708, for retailing liquors without lycence contrary to an Act of Assembly in that case made, the said Maupin having pleaded not guilty, wherefore a jury was this day impannelled and sworn to try the issue, joined whose names are James Parsons, William Wise, William Hansford, Thomas Edmonds, Edward Powers, Adduston Rogers, John Eaton, John Doswell, John Moore, Thomas Whitby, Henry Dyer and John Gibbins, who having heard the evidence and received their charge were sent out, and after some time came again into Court and Wm. Hansford, Foreman delivered their verdict of guilty, which on her Majesty's behalf, is recorded ... the Court ... ordered ..., Gabriel Maupin be fined the sum of 2,000 lbs. of tobacco according to Law. {YCWI 1706-1710:169}

Robert Hunt, being summoned, an evidence for our Sovereign Lady the Queen against Gabriel Maupin for retailing liquors without lycence, and coming into Court drunk and refusing to swear as an evidence against the said Maupin ... the Sheriff of this County take him into custody and convey him to prison till further order. {YCWI 1706-1710:169}

On 24 Sep 1708, Thomas Harrison, who as well for our Sovereign Lady the Queen as himself, exhibited an Information against Gabriel Maupin for retailing liquors in his house without lycence and he failing to prosecute, it is ordered that the said Information be dismist and that the said Harrison pay costs. {YCWI 1706-1710:169}

In the Information brought by Thomas Harrison on 24 Nov 1708, who sues as well for our Sovereign Lady the Queen as for himself, against Gabriel Maupin for retailing liquors contrary to Law, it is ordered that the Sheriff summon him to appear at the next Court to answer the said Information. {YCWI 1706-1710:179,198}

In court on 24 Mar 1708, the Information brought by Thomas Harrison, plaintiff, against Gabriel Maupin, defendant, for 2,000 lbs. of tobacco for retailing liquors in his house contrary to Law is continued till the next Court. {YCWI 1706-1710:207}

On Jun 24 1709, Francis Meloy, being summoned an evidence for Gabriel Maupin in the Information brought by Thos. Harrison and having attended two days, it is ordered that the said Maupin pay him 80 lbs. of tobacco for the same with costs *alies* execution. {YCWI 1706-1710:228}

The will of William Hansford of Bruton Parish was dated 28 Oct 1708 and recorded 24 Jul 1709. My now dwelling plantation and the land thereto belonging, to be equally divided between my two sons, William and Thomas Hansford ... when they shall accomplish the age of 21 years.... The rents of that plantation where Gabriel Maupin now lives to be equally divided between my daughter Elizabeth and my son David.... {YCWI 1706-1710:238}

On 24 Aug 1709, in the acion of debt between Gabriel Maupin, plaintiff, and Edward Foulkes, defendant, for £1:15 and one barrel of Indian corn due by two notes or bills under the defendant's hand, Francis Tyler Sub Sheriff, having made oath that he left a true copy of the action in this cause at the defendant's common place of residence and he not appearing, at the plaintiff's mocion an attachment is granted him against the defendant's Estate for the aforesaid sum with costs returnable to the next Court for judgment. {YCWI 1706-1710:245}

On 24 Jan 1709, the acion of debt between Gabriel Maupin, plaintiff, and Edward Foulkes, defendant, was discontinued, the plaintiff not prosecuting. {YCWI 1706-1710:265}

The action of debt between Gabriel Maupin, plaintiff, and Thomas Harrison, defendant, was dismist, neither party appearing on 24 Feb 1709. {YCWI 1709-1711:2}

The petition of Gabriel Maupin for lycence to keep an ordinary in this County being contrary to Law was rejected on 24 May 1710. {YCWI 1709-1711:10}

James Hubberd, Constable of the Lower Precincts of Bruton Parish, on his petition on 28 Mar 1710, is discharged from his said office, and Gabl. Maupin is appointed in his stead, and it is ordered that the said Gabl. ... immediately repair to some Justice of the Peace and take the usual oath. {YCWI 1709-1711:83}

On 16 Jul 1711, on petition of Gabriel Maupin, an order for a lycence to keep an ordinary at his dwelling house in this County is granted him, Joseph Chermeson and Robt. Jackson having offered themselves his security, who are approved of, and it is ordered that they enter into bond accordingly. {YCWI 1709-1711:97}

In the action upon the case on 20 Aug 1711 between Gabl. Maupin, plaintiff, and Willm. Coman, defendant, for £25:3:10 by account, at the plaintiff's mocion the suit is continued until the next Court. {YCWI 1711-1714:25}

On 21 Jul 1712, Gabl. Maupin, Jno. Bates and Robt. Jackson, all of the Co. of York, created a bond with the Queen, in the sum of 10,000 lbs. of tobacco. Sureties for said Maupin to obtain lycence to keep an Ordinary at his now dwelling house in this County the ensuing year. {YCWI 1711-1714:183}

On 20 Jul 1713, Gabl. Maupin, Phi. Moody and Robert Jackson, all of the Co. of York, created a bond with the Queen, in the sum of 10,000 lbs. of tobacco. Sureties for said Maupin to obtain a lycence to keep an Ordinary at his now dwelling house in this County the ensuing year. {1711-1714:266,271}

In the action of debt between Gabl. Maupin, plaintiff, and George Gilbert, defendant, the defendant came personally into Court and confessed judgment to the plaintiff for the sum of £8:3:6. Ordered that the defendant pay the same to the plaintiff with costs *alies* execution. 16 Feb 1713. {YCWI 1711-1714:307}

The action of trespass in the case on 15 Mar 1713 between Hugh Norvell, plaintiff, and Gabl. Maupin, defendant, issue being joined, is referred for tryall until the next Court. {YCWI 1711-1714:315}

On 16 Jul 1716, the action of debt between Gabriel Maupin, plaintiff & Henry Bocock, defendant, was dismist, neither party appearing. {YCWI 1716-1718:15}

In pursuance of an order of court, Benjamin Weldon & James Hubard met, and having heard & considered ye arguments of both parties, have audited & stated ye acct refer'd to us hereto annexed 13 Jul 1716. Sums paid to James Morris, Gabr Maupine, Jno Pasteur, Fran Tyler, Jno Hubard, Jos Davenport et al. Sum received of Col Byrd. Recorded 20 Aug 1716.... {YCWI 1716-1718:25}

Gabriel Maupine, plaintiff, and Jno Pasteur, defendant, on 18 Mar 1716, ye plaintiff failing to prosecute on defendant's motion, he is nonsuited & ordered that he pay defendant damage with cost. {YCWI 1716-1718:93}

Judgment being this day, 16 Dec 1718, passed unto Gabl Maupin for 2 pd & costs against Henry Hayward gent, sheriff, by means of the nonappearance of Charles Holdsworth at the said Maupin's suit, at the sheriffs motion an attachment is granted him for the said sum & costs returnable to next court for judgment. {YCWI 1718-1720:360}

Gabl Maupin on his petition hath order granted him for a lycence to keep an ordinary in Williamsburgh, he having given bond & security for that purpose, which bond being ackn is admitted to record. {YCWI 1718-1720:374}

Gabl Maupin, Saml Hyde & Patrick Ogilby, of York Co., were firmly bound unto our Sovereign Lord King George for 10,000 lbs of tobacco on 19 Jan 1718 ... the condition of this obligation is such that whereas the afsd Gabriel Maupin hath an order granted him for a lycence to keep an ordinary at his now dwelling house in Williamsburgh for the year next ensuing, if the said Gabriel Maupin doth constantly find & provide in his said ordinary good wholesome & cleanly diet & lodging for travelers & stableage, fodder & provender or pasturage & provender for their horses during the term of 1 year, & shall not suffer & permit any unlawful gaming in his house nor on the Sabbath day suffer any person to tipple or drink more than is necessary, then this obligation to be void.... {YCWI 1718-1720:384}

On 16 Feb 1718, Edward Ripping, on his petition, was discharged from the office of constable in the City of Williamsburgh, and Gabl Maupin was appointed in his stead. {YCWI 1718-1720:388}

Henry Hayward gent, sheriff, his attachment against the estate of Charles Holdsworth, by means of his nonappearance at the suit of Gabl Maupin, was discontinued. {YCWI 1718-1720:391}

On 15 Feb 1719, Mary (Marie) Maupin, John (Jean) Pasteur & Richard Harris, of York Co., were firmly bound to our Sovereign Lord King George for 10,000 lbs of tobacco ... the condition of this obligation is such that, whereas the afsd Mary Maupin hath an order granted her for a lycence to keep an ordinary at her now dwelling house in Williamsburgh for the year next ensuing, and if the said Mary Maupin doth constantly find & provide in her sd ordinary good wholesome & cleanly lodging & dyet for travelers & stableage, fodder & provender or pasturage & provender for their horses during the term of 1 year, and shall not suffer any unlawful gaming in his (sic) said house nor on the Sabbath day, suffer any person to tipple or drink more than is necessary, then this obligation to be void.... {YCWI 1718-1720:543,550}

Know all men by these presents ... Patrick Ogleby, of ye County of York ... on 16 Apr 1722, Lord ye King in ye Sum of ten ... Ye said County to which ... Lord ye King his heirs and Success... Our and every of us our heirs Excrs and .... By these presents sealed with our seals . . . The condition of this obligation is such that whereas ye above ... Mary Mompain hath an order this day granted her for a lycence to keep an ordinary at her now dwelling house in WmsBurgh in this County for ye year next.... {YCWI 1720-1722:137}

Thomas Creas, of the City of Wmsburgh, gardiner, and Mary, his wife, on 16 Dec 1724, for 5 shillings, released unto Wm Keith & Patrick Ferguson of the said city, all that messuage & dwelling house wherein the said Thomas Creas & Mary, his wife, now live, and all that lot or ½ acre of land described in the plot of the sd city by the figure 352 ... forever upon the trust & confidence & to the uses & purposes herein after menconed & declared & to & for no other use, trust or purpose whatsoever, that is to say, in trust & for the only use & behoof of the said Thomas Creas & Mary, his wife, during the term of their natural lives & the life of the longest liver of them without impeachment, and after the death of the said Thomas Creas & the said Mary, his wife, to the use & behoof of Daniel Maupin & Gabriel Maupin, sons of the sd Mary Creas by Gabriel Maupin, late her husband, deceased and of their heirs ... the said William Keith & Patrick Ferguson & their survivors shall, after the respective death of the said Thomas Creas & the said Mary, his wife, make sale & dispose of the said messuage lot of land & premises & shall be paid ½ thereof to the said Daniel Maupin & the other ½ to the said Gabriel Maupin, brother of the said Daniel

Maupin upon the proviso & condition that at & upon the death of the said Mary Creas they the sd Danl Maupin & Gabriel Maupin shall & do release & discharge the executors & adminrs of the said Mary Creas of & from all the right, claim & demand which they shall or may have claim of into or out of a certain legacy of £55 given & bequeathed to Mary Maupin, deceased, sister of the said Daniel Maupin & Gabriel Maupin in & by the will of the said Gabriel Maupin, deceased, or to any part thereof or any part or share of the personal estate of the sd Mary Maupin deceased.... {YCDB 1713-1729:440}

Thomas Creas, of the College of William & Mary, gardener ... 21 Jun 1745.... {YCLRD 1741-1754:113}

Thomas Crease, of the City of Williamsburgh gardener, left a will dated 26 Feb 1756 and proved 17 Jan 1757: To brother, Thomas Hornsby, of the City of Williamsburgh, and Margaret, his wife.... {YCWI 1745-1759:414}

Gabriel and Mary (N) Maupin were the parents of MARY, d. by 16 Dec 1724; GABRIEL; and DANIEL. {YCDB 1713-1729:440}

In 1758, Daniel Maupin, John Maupin, William Maupin were paid small fees by State of Virginia, Albemarle County, for military support. {Hening:VII:203} Daniel of Albemarle and Daniel, son of Gabriel (1) and Mary Maupin, may have been the same person.

Second Generation

2. GABRIEL MAUPIN m. Judith, prob. Pasteur, daughter of John (Jean) and Mary (N) Pasteur.

On 20 Jan 1738, John Pasteur, of the City of Williamsburg, peruke maker, for £40, sold to Gabriel Maupin and Mark Cosby, of York Co., a lot of ground on the north side of the main street in said city (No. 55) which said lot was purch by the said John Pasteur of John White and Jane, his wife, on 21 Nov 1737.... Wits: Wm Taylor, John Gibbons, John Dupree. Ackn 15 Jan 1738.... {YCLRD 1729-1740:537}

On 15 Jan 1738, a Memorandum: It is agreed between Gabriel Maupin & Mark Cosby that right of survivorship shall not take place between them, but in case of the mortality of either of them the heirs or assigns of the party so dying shall have and enjoy an equal part of the aforementioned lands.... Wits: Wm Taylor, John Gibbons, John Dupree. Ackn 15 Jan 1738.... {YCLRD 1729-1740:538}

That Gabriel Maupin and Mark Cosby refuse the right of survivorship implies strongly that they each married daughters of John Pasteur. In the transcription of the original records, the Memorandum follows directly after the Deed even though the two items have different page numbers and the date of the first item (the Deed), 20 Jan 1738 "follows" the date of the second entry (the Memorandum), 15 Jan 1738.

Samuel Wilkerson, of Williamsburgh, left a will dated 17 Feb 1739 and proved 21 May 1739. After debts & funeral expenses paid, I give to Gabriel Maupin my cloth cloaths and two pair of silk stockings, if he thinks fit to wear them, if not, to be given by my executors to some other person they think deserving of them.... {YCWI 1737-1740:494}

In the suit on 15 Sep 1740 on the petition for debt brought by Gabriel Maupin against James Barbar and Ellyson Armistead, it appearing by the return of the sherif that the defendants have been duly summon'd, and failing to appear, it is consider'd by the court that the petitioner recover against the defendant 4 pd 6 sl 6 pn with interest from 3 May last past by default, and also his costs. {YCWI 1737-1740:643}

On 15 Jun 1741, Samuel Cosby, Gabriel Maupin & James Cosby were firmly bound unto the justices for 500 pd ... the condition of this obligation is such that if the said Samuel Cosby shall well and truly pay unto John, Mary & Judith Hyde, orphans of Samuel Hyde, deceased.... {YCWI 1740-1743:34}

Gabriel (2) and Judith (prob. Pasteur) Maupin were the parents of GABRIEL.

Third Generation
3. GABRIEL MAUPIN, b. aft. 1731, m. Dorcas (N).

Mark Cosby, of York Co., left a will dated 1 Jul 1752 and proved 17 Aug 1752. To Blovet Pasteur, the shop where he now occupys to keep and to hold the shop only making repairs as shall be reasonable, but if he should leave the said shop, then to return to the freehold. To Judith Craig, daughter of Alexander & Mary, his wife, a Negro girl called Nanny. To Gabriel Maupin, son of Gabriel & Judith his wife, all my whole estate both real & personal after two legacies afsd being satisfied. But if the said Gabriel should die before he attains to the age of 21, then the whole estate shall be inherited by my friend Alexander Craig and Mary, his wife. I appoint my good friends, Hugh Orr & Alexander Craig, executors.... {YCWI 1745-1759:270}

On 14 Nov 1763, Gabriel Maupin witnessed the sale, by Matthew Sheilds & James Sheilds, both of Bruton Parish York Co., for £70, to Dudley Digges, of the City of Williamsburg, of one lott, or ½ acre of land, at the west end of the City of Williamsburg marked in the plan of the said city with the letter "H" & is the same lot which Hannah Sheilds purchased of Garrat Henrikin.... {YCDB 1763-1769:31}

On 24 Feb 1767, Thomas Craig, of the City of Williamsburg York Co., of the one part, and Alexander Craig, Edward Charlton, Gabriel Maupin & Blovet Pasteur, of the same city & co, of the other part, whereas the said Alexander Craig, Edward Charlton, Gabriel Maupin & Blovet Pasteur have become bound as securities for the said Thomas Craig for the payment of the several sums following, that is to say, the said Alexander Craig & Edward Charlton by two bonds dated 10 Nov 1761 conditioned for the payment of £175 each with lawful interest thereon unto Robert Lyon the said Alexander Craig by one bond dated [*blank*] 1764 condition for the payment of the sum of £33:16:3 unto the justices of the court of James City County as guardian of Lucy Dickeson, orphan of [*blank*] Dickenson, deceased, the said Blovet Pasteur by one bond dated 22 Aug 1764 conditioned for the payment of £100:2:3 with lawful interest thereon unto William Prentis, and the said Gabriel Maupin by one bond dated 22 Aug 1764 conditioned for the paiment of the sum of £115:17 1 penny ½ penny with lawful interest thereon unto Thomas Hornsby, now this indenture wit that in order to indemnify & save harmless the said Alexander Craig, Edward Charlton, Gabriel Maupin & Blovet Pasteur & every of them of & from all costs, charges & damages whatsoever which shall or may arise or accrue to them or either of them for or on account of their having become securities for the said Thomas Craig as afsd & also to secure the repayment of all such sums of money as the said Thomas Craig now doth or hereafter shall owe unto the said Alexander Craig, Edward Charlton, Gabriel Maupin & Blovet Pasteur or either of them & for the further consideration of 20 shillings to him paid by the said Alexander Craig, Edward Charlton, Gabriel Maupin & Blovet Pasteur, the said Thomas Craig hath sold unto them five lots of land which the said Thomas Craig lately purchased of Matthew Moody on the w side of the road leading from the Capitol in Williamsburg to Queen's Cr, one Negro man slave named Sam, 3 cows, 1 sorrel horse, 1 lot or ½ acre of land with all houses & improvements being in the Market Place in the said City of Williamsburg which the said Thomas Craig holds under a lease from the corporation of the said city together with the household furniture hereafter mentioned, that is to say, 1 Mohogany desk & book case, 3 large Mohogany tables, 1 dozen Mohogany chairs, 2 ½ dozen black walnut chairs, 1 large easy chair, 1 clock, 1 black walnut corner cupboard, 1 black walnut desk, 3 large looking glasses, 1 black walnut dressing table & glass, 3 small ditto, 5 dozen pictures & prints, 1 silver soup spoon & 6 silver table spoons, 1 dozen silver tea spoons, 15 feather beds & bedsteads, 15 pair of sheets, 15 counterpaines & rugs & the remainder rents, issues & profits of & in the said lots of land … provided & upon this express condition that if the said Thomas Craig shall well & truly indemnify & save harmless the said Alexander Craig, Edward Charlton, Gabriel Maupin & Blovet Pasteur of & from all costs, charges or damages whatsoever which shall or may arise or accrue to them or either of them for or on account of any sum of money or things whatsoever for which they or either of them now are or hereafter shall be bound as securities for the said Thomas Craig & if the said Thomas Craig shall well & truly pay unto them all such sums of money the said Thomas Craig now doth or hereafter shall owe unto them on or before 25 Jun next ensuing then this present indenture & the conveyance & everything therein contained shall … become void. Recorded 20 Jul 1767…. {YCDB 1763-1769:296}

On 28 Aug 1771, Gabriel Maupin, of the City of Williamsburg, tavern keeper, and Dorcas, his wife, for £500, sold to Alexander Craig, of the same city, sadler all that lot, or ½ acre of ground, in the City of Williamsburg in Bruton Parish bounded by Duke of Gloucester Street, Nicolson Street, the lot of Joseph Scrivener & the lot of James Southall, and is denoted in the plan of the said city by the figure 55, which said lot the said Gabriel claims under the will of Mark Cosby deceased, as heir at law of Gabriel Maupin, his father, deceased, except a small part thereof purchased by the said Alexander of William Peake & Abigal his wife.... Wits: Richard Charlton, James Galt et al.... {YCDB 1769-1777:173}

To John Randolph & Haldenby Dixon gent greeting, whereas Gabriel Maupin & Dorcas, his wife, by their indenture of sale ... have sold unto Alexander Craig the fee simple estate of ½ an acre of land ... by virtue of this writ we, John Randolph & H. Dixon, did personally go to the within named Dorcas, wife of Gabriel Maupin, and have examined her privily & apart from her husband, and before us she ackn the indenture to be her act & deed & declared that she did the same freely & voluntarily & that she was willing the same should be recorded. The [above] indenture was proved 18 Nov 1771 & 16 Dec 1771 & together with the commission & cert of the execution thereof recorded.... {YCDB 1769-1777:175}

The will of Alexander Craig, city of Williamsburg was written on 19 Dec 1772 and proved 19 Feb 1776. Execs: Friends Doctor William Pasteur, Doctor John Minson Galt and Mr. Gabriel Maupin. Wife to have her third. If she should choose that house next to Mr. Robert Nicolson's, and belonging to me, I desire it should be put in good repair with the kitchen garden and she shall have my negro wench named Judy. To grandson Alexander Dickie Galt, that half of a lot purchased of the trustees of Colonel Philip Johnson by his father, Doctor John Minson Galt, and myself adjoining the lands of Doctor William Pasteur and Mr. William Pearson. To my four daughers, Judith, Mary, Lucretia and Ann, remainder of estate. William Russell and William Mitchell depose that they were acquainted with the testator's handwriting. Probate granted to John Minson Galt and Gabriel Maupin with John Pierce and Nathaniel Burwell their securities. {YCWI 1771-1783:322}

Executors Mr. William Trebell, Mr. William Pearson and Mr. Gabriel Maupin, [who were] named in the will proved on 17 Jul 1775 of Matthew Moody, of the Capitol Landing, York Co.... refused executorship.... The sheriff ordered that he take the said estate into his hands and dispose thereof according to law, Philip Moody being the heir at law, but on 21 Aug 1775, he failed to appear. {YCWI 1771-1783:298[292]}

On 29 Apr 1777, John Minson Galt & Gabriel Maupin, executors of the will of Alexander Craig, late of the City of Williamsburg, deceased, of the one part, and William Hornsby, of the same place, merchant, of the other part, whereas the said Alexander Craig by his will dated 19 Dec 1772 duly proved & recorded in the Co Court of York did direct ... his executors to sell such part of his real estate as they should judge eligible, and whereas the said John Minson Galt & Gabriel Maupin, two of the executors named in the said will, have sold at public auction ½ of a lot of land in the City of Williamsburg to the said William Hornsby for £110 ... that lot of land on the north side of the Main Road leading from the City of Williamsburg towards York Town in Bruton Parish denoted in the plan thereof by the figure 25.... {YCDB 1769-1777:531}

Gabriel Maupin was a member of the Masonic Lodge in Williamsburg from Jul 1773 to Jun 1780. Often, the Williamsburg Lodge of Masons met at his inn. {WMCQ:1:1:23}

THE THOMAS MORGAN FAMILY

1. THOMAS MORGAN, d. 21 Jan 1691, m. 1st Elizabeth (N) and m. 2nd Elinor (N) (d. 16 Dec 1697). {CPR} [Perhaps Elizabeth and Elinor are the same.]

On 26 Sep 1698, Willm Morgan hath order granted for a commission of administration on his deceased mother's, Elliner Morgan's, estate, hee first entering into bond with good security. {YCWI 1698-1702:96}

On 14 Oct 1699, on the petition of Willm Morgan, administrator of ye estate of Ellinor, an order is granted for an appraisement of ye said deceased's estate, and John Tomer(?), Willm Wise, John Moore & Armiger Wade were ordered to appraise ye said estate. {YCWI 1698-1702:221}

An inventory of ye estate of Elinor Morgan, deceased, as it was appraised by Arminger Wade & Antho Lamb, according to order of court this 3 Feb 1699: 10 barrons, 3 breeding sows, 5 shoats, 2 cows, 2 bulls, a heifer, 5 young cows, 1 bull & cow yearling, 1 old horse, 1 small bed of flocke & feathers, rugg, 2 old blanketts, old boulster with feathers, small canvas pillow with feathers, 1 saw, tools, stirring irons, smoothin iron, etc. 30 pd 7 sl 8 pn. The mark of William Morgan. Presented in court 25 Mar 1700 and recorded.... {YCWI 1698-1702:322}

On 16 Nov 1700, John Forgason, of Charles Parish, York Co., planter, do acknowledge myselfe to owe and stand indebted unto John Tomer, of the said parish, for 31 pd 10 sl to be paid upon demand ... the condition of this obligation is such that if the afsd John Forgeson shall from time to time and at all times hereafter save, defend and keep harmless the afsd John Tomer from all manner of damage and trouble and molestation that shall happen or accrew to him by or for his being bound to the justices of York Co for William Morgan's true performance of commision of administration granted him & all & singular the estate of his mother Elinor Morgine, deceased, as by bond & likewise pay the children their just due as they come at age then this obligation to be void.... This payment is to be made to ye three youngest children of Elinor Morgine, deceased, viz.: Roger Morgin, Sarah Morgin & Elinor Morgin, to each of them 5 pd 5 sl as they come to age. Wits: William Morgine, Thomas Conner. {YCWI 1702-1704:49}

On 24 Sep 1700, John Toomer setting forth that whereas John Moore, deceased, and himselfe became security for Willm Morgan, admininstrator of his brother's estate, and since an appraisement hath been made of ye estate the said William Morgan [pg torn] to take any further care thereof and that he [pg torn] of ye same freely relinquisheth his trust therein [pg torn] it is ordered that ye said John Toomer take ye same into his possessiona and trust & be accountable for the same according to the said appraisement when thereunto called. {YCWI 1698-1702:364}

Thomas and Elizabeth [Elinor?] were parents of WILLIAM, b. 17 Nov 1677. {CPR}

Thomas and Elinor were parents of THOMAS, b. 1 Jan 1679, d. 5 Mar 1700; SARAH, b. 10 Mar 1684; ROGER, b. 2 Aug 1688, d. 17 Feb 1703; ELINOR, b. 24 Aug 1690. {CPR}

2. WILLIAM MORGAN, d. 16 May 1720, probable son of Thomas (1) Morgan, m. Ann (N). {CPR}

William and Ann were parents of THOMAS, b. 5 Mar 1706, d. 1 Sep 1710; CHARLES, b. 25 Sep 1710, d. 15 Nov 1712; JOHN, b. 24 May 1714. {CPR}

OTHERS NAMED MORGAN

HAYNES MORGAN and ELIZABETH LAWRENCE MORGAN, brother and sister of Robert Thurmer. Robert Thurmer, of the Town of York, York Co., silversmith, left a will dated Apr 1758: First, all my debts and funeral expences to be paid. I devise unto such child or children as my wife may be ensient and with child of at the time of my decease, all my estate, real and personal forever, but in case my wife should not prove ensient and with child at the time of my death, then I give unto my brother Haynes Morgan one Negro woman named Patt together with her youngest child and to my sister Elizabeth Lawrence Morgan I give two Negro girls called Sarah & Frank. All the residue of my Negroes with all my personal estate I give unto my wife Anna Catherina Thurmer during her widowhood but should she marry again, then I give unto my brother Haynes Morgan one Negro called Will and to my sister Elizabeth Lawrence Morgan one Negro called Abraham. To my wife in case she should not prove ensient and with child all my lands in Warwick County during her natural life and, after her death, I devise the said lands to my brother Haynes

Morgan, he paying thereout unto my sister Elizabeth Lawrence Morgan 25 pd. I appoint my wife, Patrick Matthews, and George Davenport executors. Wits: Mary Moir, Thos Carr. Proved 15 May 1758. Ann Catherina Thurmer & Patrick Matthews two of the executors together with Thomas Gibbs & George Davenport their securities ackn a bond, and a certificate was granted for obtaining a probate. George Davenport, the other executor, refused ... executorship.... {YCWI 1745-1759:482}

HUMPHREY MORGAN m. Anne (N).
Humphrey and Anne were parents of GERRARD, b. 15 Dec 1762, bapt. 15 Jan 1763; MARTHA, b. 15 Oct, bapt. 18 Nov 1764. {CPR}

JOHN MORGAN, b. ca. 1600.
In 1658 John Morgan, age 60, was deposed concerning a cannoe which was believed to have been brought by sd. [*sic*] Brown for the Landing place of Mr. Hawthorne and he put her in at Francis Spurrier Landing. {YCWI 1657-1659:41, abstracted by Duvall}

JOHN MORGAN
On 21 Mar 1719/20, the petition of John Morgan, servant to Ann Allen, is rejected. {YCWI 1718-1720:566}

JOHN MORGAN m. Anne Barns, daughter of Matthew Barns.
Ann Morgan, the first wife of John, d. 19 Feb 1732; and Ann Morgan, the second wife of John d. 23 Feb 1734. {CPR}
Matthew Barns, of Charles Parish, York Co, Virginia, left a will on 21 May 1732: My body to be decently buried according to the direction of my wife, Mary Barnes, whom I appoint executrix. I bequeath my worldly estate in the following manner: I lend unto my wife, Mary Barns, the use of my whole estate during her natural life and, after her decease, I give my Negro woman named Cali unto my daughter, Mary Barns. My wife may have the disposal of the value of 4 pd out of my estate to give to whom she pleases and the rest of my estate after the decease of my wife, the Negro excepted. I give, to be divided amongst my children, John, Johnson, Mary, Nathaniel, Aaron & Frances Barns and also my daughter Anne Morgan w/o John Morgan. Wits: James Calthrop, R. Hurst, Anne Moore. The will, presented in court on 19 Aug 1734 by the executrix and proved by two of the witnesses, is admitted to record.... {YCWI 1732-1737:145}
John and Ann (1st wife) were parents of THOMAS, b. 25 Oct, bapt. 26 Nov 1732, d. 9 Dec 1732.
John and Ann (2nd wife) were parents of MARY, b. 8 Dec 1734. {CPR}

94

JOHN MORGAN
On 13 Jul 1739, Martha Martin, of Charles Parish, York Co., for 5 shillings, leased to Robert Shield and John Patrick, of same parish, a 75 acre tract of land in Charles Parish, now in the occupation of John Morgan, adjacent Robert Shield, John Patrick, and John Lilburn, the said land being purchased by Lewis Burton, father to the said Martha Martin of James Broster and descended from him to the said Martha for the term of 1 year, paying one ear of Indian corn if demanded. {YCLRD 1729-1741:561}
On 15 Dec 1740, Richard Smith, of York Town, York Co., and Mary, his wife, for £2.10, sold to John Morgan, of same place, ¼ part of 1 acre being 1/2 of a lott of land lately purchased by said Richard Smith of Gwyn Reade, of Gloucester Co gent.... Wits: Henry Freeman, John Wootton, Higginson Wade. Proved 15 Dec 1740.... {YCLRD 1729-1740:622}

MARY MORGAN d. 18 Oct 1726. {CPR}
MARY MORGAN d. 15 Aug 1729. {CPR}
MARY MORGAN d. 16 Jun 1737. {CPR}

PETER MORGAN
21 Jul 1718. Peter Morgan old and infirm on his petition is by the court declared free from paying any co levy. {YCWI 1716-1718:290}

WILLIAM MORGAN m. Alice (N).
William and Alice were parents of WILLIAM, b. 12 Jul 1690. {CPR}

WILLIAM MORGAN
On 15 Jun 1719, upon the petition of William Morgan setting forth that he is by sickness rendered incapable of [pg torn] a living & praying that he may be levy free, the court are of opinion & accordingly declare him to be free from pay any publick levys. {YCWI 1718-1720:440}

THE JOHN OVERSTREET FAMILY

1. JOHN OVERSTREET, probated noncupative will 11 Sep 1671, m. Sarah (probably Moore[23]).
Before marrying John Overstreet, Sarah (prob. Moore) m. 1st (N) Seabrell and was the mother of Sarah Seabrell. Sarah (Sr.) m. 2nd Edward

[23] The basis for this assumption is Geoffry Moore's 1654 deed of gift and 1671 will giving land to Jeffry and Thomas Overstreet, likely his daughter's sons.

Jenkins and was the mother of Edward Jenkins (b. 1646), step-son of John Overstreet. {RB 1672-1676:109}

On 10 Jan 1654/5, Geoffry Moore, of the parish of Cheeskicack in Co of York, planter, gives Jeoffry Overstreet, son of John Overstreet and Sarah, his wife, 25 acres of land adjacent land and plantation of said Moore and the land of Tho Dennett. John Overstreet, the father, to have use of half the dwelling house and half the tobacco house till Jeoffry is 18. If Jeoffry die, his father to have the property. Signed Geoffry Moore. Wits: Henry Jackson, John Andrews. {VCA:III:131}

John Overstreet was granted a certificate for 250 acres on 12 Nov 1666 for the importation of five persons into this colony.... {RB 1665-1672:120}

Peter Disbary, servant to Mr. John Overstreet, was adjudged on 24 Apr 1667 to be 16 years of age. {RB 1665-1672:130}

Edward Jenkins, being 21, was discharged on 24 Apr 1667 from his father in law John Overstreet. {RB 1665-1672:130}

George Hough received, on 21 Aug 1667, from guardian and father in law, John Overstreet, all his estate. {RB 1665-1672:152}

On 7 Sep 1667, John Overstreet received, for transportation of one person, 37 acres 77 chains in Hampton Parish, Yorke Co. beginning at land of Jeoffry Moore, thence along Thomas Dennetts & Zachary Padeyes (?)[24] lyne etc to corner hickery near Edward Wade's line etc. {CP I:568}

On 24 Aug 1668, John Overstreet, became security on behalf of his son in law Nicholas Seabrell, guardian to his brother Anthony Seabrell for his estate. {RB 1665-1672:198}

Probate of the nuncupative will of Mr. John Overstreet, deceased, was granted on 11 Sep 1671 to Sarah, relict. {RB 1665-1672:458[358]}

Elizabeth Paddy, age 30, was deposed on 25 Oct 1671 concerning the nuncupative will of John Overstreet where he gave all to his wife. {RB 1665-1672:463[363]}

Geffrey Moare [Moore] left a will dated 8 Jan 1671 and proved 27 Feb 1671/2. To be buried by my wife Isabell. To Thomas Overstreete, son of John Overstreete, all my land in the neck. To Jane Grimes, daughter of William Grimes, mare Bonny. To Mary Risle [Risley], daughter of John Risle, all my land [   ]. To Robert Jones, son of Robert Jones, all my land in the French Ordinary Field. All goods to be sold for widow Facon [Faison] and widow Morris. Signed: Geffrey More. {RB 1672-1676:10}

Sarah Overstreete, relict of John Overstreete, Hampton Parish, York Co., deceased, gave, on 4 Mar 1674/5, to son Edward Jenkins, a mare. To my

---

[24] On 25 Oct 1671, Zachariah and Elizabeth Paddy, Hampton Parish, York Co., sold 50 acres of land to Richard Dobbs. {RB 1665-1672:464[364]}

son doffed[25] [Geffery?] Overstreete, filly. To my daughter, Sarah Seabrell, mare, but prohibit my son in law Nicholas Seabrell having anything to do with it. {RB 1672-1676:109}

John and Sarah (prob. Moore) Overstreet were the parents of JEFFERY {VCA:III:131} and THOMAS {RB 1672-1676:10}.

Second Generation
2. JEFFREY OVERSTREET, will 4 Nov 1702, probated 24 Mar 1702/03, m. 1st Mary (N) and 2nd Elizabeth (N), was a son of John (1) and Sarah (prob. Moore) Overstreet.

Jeffery Overstreete and wife Mary, Hampton Parish York Co., planter, sold, on 1 Mar 1675/6, to Isaac Gooding Hampton Parish Gloucester Co., planter, a 30 acre plantation plus 25 acres. {RB 1672-1676:155}

On 15 Sep 1699, Thomas Boucher hath judgment confirmed for non appearance of Edward Foulks against Jeffrey Overstreet, his security, in an action of debt for payment of 550 lbs of merchantable sweet scented tobacco due by bill under ... [illegible] ... proved by ye plaintiff's oath which said Overstreet is ordered to pay as security afsd with costs.... Thomas Boucher hath judgment confirmed for ye non appearance of Thomas Foulks against Jeffrey Overstreet, his security, in an action of debt for payment of 6 pd 11 sl due by bill dated under ye hand of sd Foulks ... [pg torn] ... and proved in court by ye plts oath which the sd Overstreet is ordered to pay as security with costs. {YCWI 1698-1702:216}

Jeffery Overstreet making suite hath order granted him for a commission of administration of Edward Jenkins & Thomas Jenkins, deceased, estates having entered into bond in court for due performance thereof. {YCWI 1698-1702:539}

On 24 Feb 1701, Jeffery Overstreet, John Saunders & Jacob Goding of York Co, Virgina, were firmly bound unto the justices of York Co. for 10,000 lbs of good sweet scented tobacco & cask ... the condition of this obligation is such that whereas the afsd Jeffery Overstreet upon his petition obtained order of administration of the whole estate of Edward & Thomas Jenkins whereby he is fully impowered to take the same into his care & custody.... {YCWI 1698-1702:559}

On 21 Jul 1701, John Morce of Hampton Parish, Yorke Co. gent, and Elizabeth, his wife, for 5 shillings, leased to Sarah Sanders, of same place, widow, a messuage and 50 acres of land in Hampton Parish bounded by Jeffery Overstreet, John Read, the Landing Road & Mrs. Sarah Sanders, which said tract of land is part of a pattent of 400 acres of land formerly belonging to John Dennitt, son & heir of Thomas Dennitt, formerly of Hampton Parish, deceased, dated 25 Aug 1642, which pattent is grounded on an elder pattent dated 14 Jan 1637 for 400 acres then granted to John Dennitt, the grandfather, this tract being

---

[25] Some experience deciphering 17th century writing and the context lead one to guess that "doffed" may actually be Geoffry.

230 acres.... {YCDB 1694-1701:331}

Jeffery Overstreet, guardian of Thomas Jenkins & Edward Jenkins, arrested William Pattison in a case and the court finding no cause of action on motion of the defendant the petitioner is nonsuited. {YCWI 1702-1704:7}

The suit between Jefery Overstreet & Silas Smith, in ye behalfe of Sarah, his wife, administrator of Thomas Jenkins & Edward Jenkins, deceased, plaintiffs against William Pattison, defendant, in an action of the case for the estate of the said deceased is dismist no further prosecution had. {YCWI 1702-1704:39}

Jeffery Overstreet left a will that was entered into the record on 4 Nov 1702. To my sone Thomas Overstreet, one cow & one heifer both with calfe, one iron pott, one featherbed, bolster, rugg, one new blanket, one sheate, one Arey mare & one horsecolt belonging to her & also all that parcell of land that my father Overstreet tooke up called ye *Carrens* binding upon this land whereon I live, land of John Mihill, & land whereon Thomas Burnane lives. To my sone Jeffery Overstreet all this plantation whereon I live & the neck of land which I purch of my brother Thomas Overstreet lying upon the Beaver Dam Swamp, and one cowe, one steere of 2 years old, one iron pot, one sowe pigg with pigg & one sett of coopers tools. I give all the rest of my estate unto my wife, Elizabeth, and my sons, Henry & Edward, and Sarah Overstreet as they shall come to age or when my daughter shall be marryed. I appoint my ... [pg torn] ... executrix. Further my will is that my sone, Thomas, have my gunne that is not fixt & to my sone Jeffery my gun that is fixt.... {YCWI 1702-1704:100}

Order for a probate of ye will of Jeffery Overstreet, deceased, was granted on 24 Mar 1702/3 to Elizabeth Overstreet, his relict, she being therein appointed executrix & proved by ye oaths of John Saunders & John Mihil, witnesses, and is ordered to be committed to record. {YCWI 1702-1704:103}

William Sedgwick arresting Elizabeth Overstreet in a case & not further prosecuting ye suite is dismist. {YCWI 1702-1704:186}

On 7 Jul 1703, Thomas Walker of Charles Parish, York Co., planter, (sone of Ralph Walker late of same co deceased) & Elizabeth, his wife, for 5 shillings, leased to Samll Dickinson, of York Parish & Co., a lott or ½ acre of Portland in York Town containing 10 poles in length & 8 in breadth bounded by the lands of Joseph Ring, Jeffery Overstreet & Col Dudley Digges, number 33 as by the grand plot on the records of York Co. doth appear.... {YCDB 1701-1708:73}

On 24 May 1706 ... the trustees of the Portland of York Town in York Co., for 180 lbs of tobacco, sold to Miles Cary Senr gent of Warwick Co., a lott, or ½ acre, of land in York Towne being part of the Port Land number 12 as by the plat on the records of said company doth appear, the said lot containing 10 poles in length & 8 in breadth & formerly taken up by Jeffery Overstreet & by him deserted ... provided that the said Miles Cary Senr shall and do in 12 months build & finish on the said lott one good house to containe at least 20'.... {YCDB 1701-1708:184a}

Jeffrey and possibly Mary (N) Overstreet were the parents of JEFFREY and THOMAS. Jeffrey and Elizabeth (N) were the parents of HENRY, EDWARD and SARAH. The assumption that Mary was the mother of Jeffrey, and not the other children, comes from Jeffrey Senior's 1702 will in which he lists Jeffrey separately from Elizabeth and the minor children.

3. THOMAS OVERSTREET, d. 9 Nov 1693, m. Mary (N) (d. by 25 Feb 1700), was a son of John (1) and Sarah (prob. Moore) Overstreet.

Samll. Padgett and Ann, his wife, made a deed of guift to John Overstreet, son of Thomas Overstreet, dec., on 9 Nov 1693, of cattle. The gift was acknowledged on 26 Mar 1694 by the Padgetts. {DW 1691-1694:314}

Ann Crosse, formerly wife of Samll. Padgett, did before her marriage with the said Abbott [sic], out of good will to John Overstreet, son of Thomas Overstreet deceased, give John a cow named Guift, with her increase, the said cattle now numbering about 7 head. Acknowledged by Samll. Padgett and Ann, his wife, on 26 Mar 1694. {DW 1691-1694:327}

Mary Overstreet, widow of Thomas Overstreet lately deceased, petitioned the Court on 25 Jun 1694 because she was in low condition and needed small necessaryes out of the estate. The petition was granted. {1694-1697:1}

On 25 Feb 1700, John Overstreet on his petition hath order given for a commission of administration of the estate of his mother, Mary Overstreet, deceased. William Hansford & Doctor Richard Stark entered security & were ordered to give bond for the same. {YCWI 1698-1702:537}

The Court ordered that John Mihill, John Roads, Robert Goodwin & John May meet at the house of John Overstreet, administrator of Mary Overstreet lately deceased, on 28 Mar then & there inventory & appraise the said deceased's estate & make return to next court. {YCWI 1698-1702:560}

On 24 Mar 1701, John Overstreet, Arthur Dickson & William Lee of York Co., Virginia, were firmly bound unto the justices of York Co. for 20,000 lbs of good sweet scented tobacco & cask ... the condition of this obligation is such that whereas the afsd John Overstreet upon his petition obtained order of administration of the whole estate of his mother Mary Overstreet whereby he is fully impowered to take the same into his care & custody.... Ackn 24 Feb 1701/2.... {YCWI 1698-1702:570}

An inventory & appraisement on 28 Mar 1702 of the estate of Mary Overstreet, deceased: 4 barrows, 2 sowes, 11 shoats, 5 cows, 1 heifer, 2 stears, 2 bulls, 1 old horse, 1 feather beds, bolsters, ruggs, blankets, 2 chests without locks, 2 tables, 1 brass spice morter & pestill, earthin ware, 2 sifters, 1 sifting tray, 33 lbs of pewter, 4 qt bottles, sword, etc. 46 pd 10 1/2 pn. John Overstreet, administrator. In obedience to a court order dated 24 Mar 1701, John Myhill, Robert Goodwin & John Rhodes appraised this estate except William Wood & ye deceased's wearing clothes. {YCWI 1698-1702:605}

Thomas and Mary (N) were the parents of <u>JOHN</u>.

Third Generation

4. JEFFREY OVERSTREET, b. ca. 1670s, was a son of Jeffrey (2) and prob. Mary (N) Overstreet.

On 21 Nov 1709, John Williams of York Hampton Parish, York Co., planter, son of John Williams late of (York) Hampton Parish, York Co., glover, deceased, for £45, sold to Philip Moody, of same place gent, a 100 acre tract of land in York Hampton Parish now in the occupation of Edward Cooper bounded by Jeffrey Overstreet, John Myhill, Thomas Barbar, the Black Swamp, John Stockdale & Arthur Dickenson.... Wit: Jno Overstreet et al.... {YCDB 1709-1713:329}

5. THOMAS OVERSTREET, b. ca. 1670s, nuncupative will, d. 1717-1719, was a son of Jeffrey (2) and prob. Mary (N) Overstreet.

On 24 Jun 1708, Thomas Chisman Senr, Robt Sheild, Thomas Tyler, Wm Rylands, Thos Walker, Benj Shepard, Benj Lovett, Charles Buds and Thomas Overstreet were presented by the Grand Jury for not coming to Church according to Law, and it was ordered that the Sheriff summon them to appear at the next Court to answer the said presentment. {YCWI 1706-1710:144}

On 26 Jul 1708, Thomas Overstreet appeared to answer the presentment of the Grand Jury against him for not coming to Church and alledged that he for a long time since hath been so deaf he could not understand what the parson said and was excused. {YCWI 1706-1710:154}

On 19 Aug 1717, Tho Overstreet petitioned and was discharged from ye office of Headborough in ye upper precincts of York Hampton Parish. {YCWI 1716-1718:152}

18 Jan 1719, on the petition of Thomas Mansfield ... being bound apprentice to Thos Overstreet, lately deceased, and his time by indenture being expired & that John Miles refuses to deliver up his indenture or to pay him according to law, the Court ordered that the sheriff summon the said John Miles to appear at next court to answer the said petition. {YCWI 1718-1720:536}

18 Jan 1719, Joseph Walker made oath that Thomas Overstreet departed this life without making any will & he, having together with Thomas Nelson, his security, entered into & acknowledge their bond ... certificate was granted him for ... administration on the said estate. {YCWI 1718-1720:537}

18 Jan 1719, Thomas Buck, Jno Lester, James Dowling & Benja Buck were appointed to appraise the estate of Thomas Overstreet, deceased. {YCWI 1718-1720:537}

Joseph Walker & Thomas Nelson, of York Co., were firmly bound unto the justices of said county for 100 pd ... the condition of this obligation is such that if the aforesd Joseph Walker, administrator of the estate of Thomas Overstreet, deceased, do make a true & perfect inventory of all & singular the goods, chattles & credits of the said Thomas Overstreet, deceased.... Ackn 18 Jan 1719. {YCWI 1718-1720:538}

On 21 Mar 1719, John Rhodes ... petitioned for his charge & trouble in taking care of the children & stock of Thomas Overstreet, deceased, from the time of his death untill administration of his estate was granted to Mr. Walk[er], the court upon regulating the account, do order that the said Joseph Walker gent, [now] administrator of the said Overstreet's estate, pay the petitioner 3 pd 2 sl out of the deceased's estate with costs. {YCWI 1718-1720:566}

The appraisement of the estate of Thos Overstreet, deceased, was presented in court 19 Dec 1720 by Jos Walker: 2 cows, 8 heifers, beds, blanketts, ruggs, boulsters, pewter, 1 gown & petticoate, 2 iron potts, 1 frying pan, brass skillet, 1 lg table & chest, 1 butter tubb, 1 sett of wedges, 1 ax, 1 saws pettle & drawing knife, 3 peche of wheat, parcell of lumber, parcell of fodder, 9 1/2 barrells corn, etc. 32 pd 17 sl.... {YCWI 1718-1720:680}

Thomas was the father of UNNAMED CHILDREN.

6. HENRY OVERSTREET, b. ca 1680s, d. aft. 1712, was a son of Jeffry (2) and prob. Elizabeth (N) Overstreet.

On 19 May 1712, the acion of case between Robert Saunders, plaintiff, and Henry Overstreet, defendant, was dismist, plaintiff not prosecuting. {YCWI 1711-1714:155}

7. JOHN OVERSTREET, b ca. 1680s, d. ca. 1708, m. Mary (N), was a son of Thomas (3) and Mary (N) Overstreet.

John Overstreet, being by ye sherrif returned summoned an evidence for Thomas Saunders, defendant, against James Morris, plaintiff, in an action of trespass, is ordered to be paid 80 lbs of tobacco for 2 days attendance with cost.... {YCWI 1705-1706:331}

John Overstreet witnessed the the will of John Roades, of Hampton Parish in York Co., that was presented to Court on 8 Jul 1708 and proved 24 Nov 1708. {YCWI 1706-1710:174}

The administration of the Estate of John Overstreet was granted to Mary Overstreet, she having together with Robt. Crawley and John Eaton entered into bond for her due administration.... {YCWI 1709-1711:18}

Inventory & Appraisement of the Estate of John Overstreet appraised on 16 Sep 1710. Itemized list of livestock and household goods, with some livestock left unappraised, and no total value of Estate given. Appraised by John Mihill, Phill. Moody, Will Babb and Robt. Jackson and presented by Mary

Overstreet, Adminstratrix {YCWI 1709-1711:65}

OTHERS NAMED OVERSTREET

JAMES OVERSTREET
James Overstreet owned 180 acres in King & Queen Co, VA in 1704.
{QRV:66}

JAMES OVERSTREET m. Elizabeth Ball
Elizabeth Ball m. James Overstreet of Brunswick Co VA, 5 Dec 1751.
{VRMM:19 citing Second Congregational (Unitarian) Church Records}

JOHN OVERSTREET
John Overstreet. By (31 Aug 1696) deed of guift given unto him, the sonn of Jeffrey Overstreet of 1 cow calfe, 10 being now the increase in possession of Jeffrey, 3 cows: Whiteback, Motley and Fordill with their increase. {DW 1694-1697:326}

THE WALTER PATRICK FAMILY

1. WALTER PATRICK, d. 3 Mar 1678, m. Elizabeth (N) (d. 27 Feb 1678), and they were the parents of JOHN, b. 2 Oct 1675; MARY, bapt. 8 Jun 1677. {CPR}

2. JOHN PATRICK m. Mary (N).
John and Mary were parents of ANN, b. 3 Dec 1686. {CPR}

Second Generation
3. JOHN PATRICK, b. 2 Oct 1675, m. Elizabeth (N).
The suit between Francis Clark, plaintiff, and John Patrick, defendant, in an action of debt is dismist by non process. {YCWI 1698-1702:547}
By court order ... Henry Hayward, Simon Stacy et al. have taken inventory of ye estate of Anthony Watts, deceased ... John Patrick, Robert Shields, Bartholomew Burcher, Sion Staley [Simon Stacey], Thomas Gibbons, Peter Manson, John Clark, Gyles Tavernor, Henry Boridell et al. for rent of Watts plantation[26], 7670 lbs of tobacco. Robt Shield. Ordered to be recorded 25 [ ] 1704.... {YCWI 1702-1704:255}
16-17 May 1712. Deed of Lease and Release. Simon Stacy of Charles Parish, York Co., planter, and Elizabeth, his wife (she being secretly examined

---

[26] On 2 Feb 1702/3, Simon Stacy purchased this land from Anthony Watts. {YCDB 1701-1708:98}

by one of the justices of the peace for sd co & consenting), for 5 shillings, leased to Jno Patrick of same place planter a 50 acre tract of land in Charles Parish, late in the occupation of Thomas Albritton & now of Edward Woodhouse ... for the term of one year.... Wits: John Moss, M. Dewick. Ackn 19 May 1712 & admitted to record.... {YCDB 1711-1713:384}

On 19 Jan 1718, John Potlin made oath that Lewis Burton, deceased, departed this life without making any will & he having together with Jno Patrick & John Welch, his securitys, entred into bond.... {YCWI 1718-1720:375}

On 21 Sep 1719, on the petition of John Welch & John Patrick, securitys, with Elizabeth Battin? for the estate of Lewis Battin?, deceased, ordered that William Potlin give them counter security or surrender the said Battin's estate to the petitioner. {YCWI 1718-1720:485}

4. JOHN PATRICK, d. 12 Oct 1732, m. 1st Sarah (N) (d. 31 Mar 1720) and 2nd Elizabeth (Curtis), daughter of Thomas Curtis. {CPR}

The petition of John Patrick against Dunn Sheilds & Susanna, his Wife, is rejected. {YCWI 1725-1727:369}

In Obedience to a Court Order bearing date 20 Nov 1727, We the Subscribers being first Sworn, have appraised as much of the Estate of Thomas Curtis, dec'd., from Dunn Sheilds as amount to the Sum of £ 59.2.1 to John Lewellin and James Dixon being the full Sum due to the Orphans. To 20 head of hogs £4.10, To 13 Sheep £ 3, To 24 head of Cattle & 1 Calf £16, To an Old Mare 22s, To 1 Steel trap, To 2 grindstones, parcel of books 8s, To 12 Chairs 1 table, To 1 old bedstead & furniture £6.5, To 2 old beds and Some furniture £3.16, Total £59.2.1. Wits: Edmund Sweny, John Chapman, Fras. Mennis At York County Court 18 Dec 1727 and admitted to record. {YCWI 1725-1727:498}

At a Court held for York County the 21st of this Instant came John Patrick and made application for an order to have two men to appraise one Negro Wench left by Thomas Curtis, deceased, to his Daughter, Elizabeth Curtis, now married to the said John Patrick ... the Gentlemen of the Court thought it proper for the said Patrick & Dun Sheild, who married the deceased Curtis Widow, to choose two men there Selves ... the Subscribers, do think the said Wench named Charge to be worth £27. At a Court held for York County 21 Mar 1725, recorded 25 Feb 1725/6. {YCWI 1725-1727:381}

13 Jan 1729. Deed of Lease. Edward Tabb gent, of Charles Parish, York Co., for 5 shillings, farm lett to Charles Wood, of same parish, a 100 acre tract of land in Charles Parish called *Piney Neck,* it being the same land devised by the will of Isabel Taplady, deceased, dated 1 Feb 1714, to Edward Tabb, the son of said Edward Tabb, adjacent Robert Sheilds, John Patrick & Sabels Creek during the term of ... [*pg torn*] ... paying one ear of Indian corn on the last day

of said year.... Wits: Plany Ward, Alexr Maver, John Hay. Ackn 16 Feb 1729.... {YCLRD 1729-1740:11}

On 20 Sep 1731, Charles Wood, of Charles Parish, York Co., for £25, sold to Robert Sheild a 100 acre tract of land in Piney Neck adjacent said Shield and John Patrick Senr.... Wits: Jones Irwin, Edward Tabb. Ackn 20 Sep 1731.... {YCLRD 1729-1740:97}

On 15 Jan 1732 the inventory & appraisement of the estate of John Patrick, deceased, was ... recorded. {YCWI 1732-1737:1}

John and Sarah (N) Patrick were parents of ELIZABETH, b. 19 Feb 1700; JOHN, b. 26 Jul 1703; MARY, b. 21 Mar 1705; SARAH, b. 4 Oct 17[08], d. 14 Oct 1709; HANNAH, b. 25 Aug 1710; FRANCES, b. 5 Oct 1711; WILLIAM, b. 16 Feb 1716; MARTHA, b. 19 Jul, bapt. 9 Aug 1719. {CPR}

John and Elizabeth (Curtis) Patrick were parents of THOMAS, b. 5 Sep, bapt. 6 Oct 1722; ALICE, b. 4 Aug, bapt. 26 Sep 1725; WALTER, b. 9 Dec, bapt. 12 Jan 1728/9, d. 20 Mar 1729; WALTER, b. 20 Jan, bapt. 21 Feb 1730. {CPR}

Third Generation
5. JOHN PATRICK, b. 26 Jul 1703, m. Elizabeth (N).

On 16 Jul 1733 John Patrick was appointed surveyor of the highways in the precinct whereof William Hauthorn was the surveyor and ordered that the said Patrick do cause the said ways to be cleared and repaired according to law. {YCWI 1732-1737:60}

18 Feb 1733. John Patrick made oath that Thomas Delany departed this life without making any will and on his motion and his giving bond and security, ordered that a Letter of Administration be granted him. {YCWI 1732-1737:93}

17 Jun 1734. Jenny a Negro girl belonging to John Patrick adjudged to be 14 years old. {YCWI 1732-1737:120}

16 May 1737. Order'd that Charles Calthrop be appointed surveyor of the highway in the room of John Patrick. {YCWI 1732-1737:364}

2-3 Dec 1738. Deed of Lease and Release. John Lilburn (Lilburne) of Charles Parish, York Co., planter, for 5 shillings, leased to John Patrick, of same parish, planter, a 50 acre tract of land in Charles Parish, called *Pinyridge,* now in the occupation of the said John Lilburn, the said land formerly taken up by William Potlin and descended from him to the said John Lilburn adjacent said John Lilburn, land of Nicholas Worley now in the occupation of Elizabeth James, Samuel Read gent, and John Hayward for the term of 1 year paying one ear of Indian corn if demanded. Wits: James Dixon, Meritt Moore, Bennet Tompkins, Thomas Roberts. Ackn 15 Jan 1738/9.... {YCLRD 1729-1740:530-531}

George Chisman, of Charles Parish, York Co., left a will dated 26 Oct 1741 in which he gave ... my Negro boy Ben I give unto my godson Wm

Patrick son of John Patrick.... Wits: John Hayward, John Patrick, R. Hurst. Proved 15 Mar 1741.... {YCWI 1740-1743:94}

On 9 Oct 1744, James Faison Junr, of York Co., and Frances, his wife, for £128, sold to John Patrick, of York Co., a 100 acre tract of land in Charles Parish, it being the plantation whereon the said James Faison now liveth except reserved out of this present deed that part of the land appropriated for a burying place, also another 15 acre tract of land bounded by the Glebe Land & Francis Cook, the said 100 acre of land being sold to the said James Faison by James Faison Senr 23 Feb 1742/3 and descended to the said James Faison by the death of his brother Elias Faison, deceased.... Ackn 18 Mar 1744.... {YCLRD 1741-1754:121}

On 13 May 1749, Thomas Roberts, of York Co., and Ann, his wife, for £101, sold to John Patrick, of York Co., two tracts of land in Charles Parish containing together 160 acres, 76 acres of the land being purchased by said Thomas Roberts of Peter Rue, the other parcel being purchaed by said Thomas Roberts and James Faison.... Ackn 17 Jul 1749.... {YCLRD 1741-1754:297}

On 16 Nov 1750, Robert Shield, of York Co., planter, for £24, sold to John Patrick, of York Co., planter, a 37 ½ acre tract of land in Charles Parish bounded by the Honourable William Nelson, said John Patrick & John Lilburn's orphans, the said land being ½ of 75 acres purchased by said Robert Shield & John Patrick of Martha Martin.... Wits: Thos Roberts, Thos Chisman, Thos Patrick. Ackn 19 Nov 1750.... {YCLRD 1741-1754:399}

John Patrick, of Charles Parish, York Co., left a will dated 14 Jan 1754. To son John Patrick, all the lands in Charles Parish which I purchased of James Faison upon condition he execute proper deeds of conveyance of all his right of the land whereon I now live and also the land at Piney Point to his brother, William Patrick, but in case he refuseth to execute such deeds then I give the said lands to William Patrick. To son Curtis Patrick those two parcels of land whereon Edward Baptist and William Britain now liveth containing 160 acres. To son Edmund Patrick, the land I purchased of John Wellons. To son William Patrick, the lands I purchased of Martha Martin. To my son Merit Patrick, the land I purchased of John Lilburn and the land that descended to me from my father. To son John Patrick, a Negro woman named Moll. To my grandchild, Mary Patrick, daughter to my son, Thomas Patrick, deceased, a Negro woman called Sarah likewise her child Jack. To son Curtis Patrick, a Negro girl called Grace. To son William Patrick, a Negro boy called Jacob. To son Merit Patrick, a Negro boy called Frank. To dau Sarah Patrick, a Negro girl named Dinah. To daughter, Mary Patrick, a Negro girl called Pegg. To daughter, Frances Patrick, a Negro girl called Nanny. To daughter, Lucy Patrick, a Negro girl called Esther. To son Edmund Patrick, a Negro boy called Paul. To son John Patrick, my pistols & holsters & sword. To son Curtis Patrick, a gun with a buccaneer stock. To son William Patrick, 1/2 doz. leather chairs & a desk. To son Curtis

Patrick, 6 head of cattle, 3 cow yearlings & 3 steer yearlings. To daughter Sarah Patrick, 6 head of cattle of the like sorts of her brother. My will is that after my debts & legacies are paid that the residue of my estate be for the use and comfort of my loving wife, Elizabeth Patrick, during the time she continues my widow, but in case she marries or should die my widow to be divided amongst my children only those children to whom I have given the cattle either by will or otherwise to be accountable to the other children for their value to be taken out of their respective parts. My desire is that my younger children continue with their mother as she continues my widow and the profits of their estates to be appropriated towards bringing them up and that my wife may continue upon the plantation whereon I now live and have the use of it during her widowhood. I order that the court have nothing to do with my estate further than to order an appraisement but in no wise for my executors to be held to give any security for the same. I appoint my wife Elizabeth, executrix, and sons John & Curtis Patrick, executors. Wits: Thos Roberts, John Hunt, Nicholas Phillips. Proved 18 Mar 1754. Elizabeth Patrick, John Patrick & Curtis Patrick, the executors, were granted a certificate for obtaining a probate.... {YCWI 1745-1759:318}

In obedience to an order of court held 18 Mar 1754 Francis Minness, Edmund Curtis & James Drewry appraised the estate of John Patrick, deceased, and have been sworn before Daniel Moore, justice of the peace. Negroes: woman named Moll, boy named Pompey, boy named Dick, girl named Grace, girl named Dinah, girl named Peg, boy named Jacob, boy named Ben, boy named Frank, girl named Nan, woman named Sarah and child Jack, man named James, girl named Rachel, woman named Bunny, boy named Paul, woman named Hagar & child Esther, boy named Casar. Yokes of steers young & old, 16 cows & calves, 8 young cattle, 26 sheep, 3 young bulls, 2 young steers, 3 young heifers, mare & colt, 2 horses, 11 hogs, 5 pigs, 8 shoats, 3 sows, case of pistols, holsters & sword, a gun, 2 tables, a desk, 6 leather chairs, 6 flag chairs, a chest, a table, bed & furniture, 2 looking glasses, parcel of butter pots, 1 jug, a saddle & housing, a side saddle, etc. 673 pd 4 sl 2 1/4 pn ... recorded 15 Jul 1754.... {YCWI 1745-1759:332}

John and Elizabeth (N) Patrick were parents of JOHN, b. 16 Oct, bapt. 20 Nov 1726; THOMAS, b. 6 Dec 1728, bapt. 12 Jan 1728/29; SARAH, b.12 Apr, bapt. 9 May 1731; CURTIS, b. 13 Jan, bapt., 10 Feb 1733, d. 1 Feb 1785; MARY, b. 26 Jul, bapt. 27 Aug 1738; WILLIAM, b. 23 Apr, bapt. 23 May 1736, d. 10 Oct 1739; WILLIAM, b. 30 Mar 1740/41, bapt. 20 Apr 1741; SUSANNA, b. 26 Jul, bapt. 9 Aug 1743, d. 26 Aug 1743; MERRIT, b. 17 Nov, bapt. 9 Dec 1744; FRANCES, b. 28 Oct 1746, bapt. 16 Nov 17[46]; LUCY; and EDMUND, bapt. 26 Apr 17[52]. {CPR}

6. WILLIAM PATRICK, b. 16 Feb 1716, son of John (4) and Sarah (N) Patrick.

10-11 May 1738. Deed of Lease, Release, and Bond. William Patrick, of Charles Parish, York Co., planter, for 5 shillings, leased to John Patrick, of same parish, planter, an 80 acre tract of land in Charles Parish, now in the occupation of said John Patrick adjacent Francis Hayward gent, John Lilburn, John Hayward, and the orphans of Edmund Chisman, the land being formerly the lands of Thomas Curtis, deceased, and by him devised to his daughter Elizabeth, wife of said John Patrick, and by them sold and conveyed to the afsd William Patrick on 25 Mar 1738 for the term of 1 year paying the rent of one ear of Indian corn if demanded. {YCLRD 1729-1740:500, 502, 504}

2 Mar 1767. Deed. William Patrick Senr, of York Co., for 5 shillings, paid by William Patrick Junr & Allen May, of the county afsd, and for indemnifying the said William & Allen from all damages & losses which they may sustain by occasion of their being bound as security for the said William to Thomas Tomer, of the said county, for the estate of John May, deceased, hath sold unto the said William Patrick Junr & Allen May one slave named Jacob together with the goods & chattels of the said William mentioned & described in a schedule hereunto annexed [*see below*] & all the estate, right, title & interest of him the said William Patrick Senr ... in trust to sell & convey the same for the best price they can get & out of the money arising from such sale to pay & discharge all such sums of money & tobacco for which the said William Patrick Junr & Allen May is or may be liable as security for the said William Patrick Senr for his keeping in hand the estate of John May, deceased, and to return the overplus if any to the said William.... Wits: John Patrick, John Toomer, Thos Hunt, Robt Manson ... [Schedule annexed:] 2 beds, 4 chests, 2 pewter dishes, 8 pewter plates, 6 pewter basons, 1 table, 6 chairs, 1 iron pot & hooks, 4 stone potts, a pair of fire tongs, 3 tubs, 1 powdering tub, 2 iron wedges & 1 spinning wheel. The indenture was proved.... {YCDB 1763-1769:314,316}

William Senr and Elizabeth (N) Patrick were the parents of JOHN, b. 23 Apr, bapt. 29 May 1757, and SARAH, b. 10 Oct 1759. {CPR}

7. THOMAS PATRICK, b. 5 Sep, bapt. 6 Oct 1722, d. ca. 1760, was a son of John and Elizabeth (Curtis) Patrick.

Settlement of Thomas Patrick's estate. In ... an order of York Court dated 21 Jul 1760, subscribers have examined the account of the administration of the estate of Thomas Patrick, deceased, and find the ballance to be £11.13.3 due from William Burt to the said estate. 22 Jul 1760. John Cry, John Jenham(?), John Chisman Junr. Returned 18 Aug 1760. {YCWI 1760-1771:14}

Fourth Generation

8. JOHN PATRICK, b. 16 Oct, bapt. 20 Nov 1726, son of John (5) and Elizabeth (N), m. Mary (N).

John Gammell, Samuel Presson & John Patrick, appraisers, made an appraisement of the estate of Mary Barnes, deceased ... recorded 20 Jan 1755.... {YCWI 1745-1759:340}

The will of John Hunt, Charles Parish, York Co. To wife, Hannah Hunt, negroes: Santy, Patty and Tom, also £70 which is in the hands of my friend, John Patrick ... 20 May 1762. Wits: John Holloway, Frances Manson.... {YCWI 1760-1771:105}

20 Jun 1774. Deed of Gift. Sarah Rogers of York Co for natural love & affection & 5 shillings have given unto her son in law, Matthew Drewry, one Negro slave named Lucy.... Wits: John Chisman Senr, John Patrick. Proved 15 Aug 1774.... {YCDB 1769-1777:431}

John and Mary (N) Patrick were parents of MARY, b. 11 Feb, bapt. 8 Mar 1755; PETER, b. 11 Feb, bapt. 13 Mar 1757; NANCY, b. 12 Apr, bapt. 9 May 1762; ELIZABETH, b. 26 Oct 1753; JOHN, b. 6 Dec 1758, bapt. 11 Jan 1759; HANNAH, b. 27 Apr, bapt. 19 May 1765. {CPR}

9. THOMAS PATRICK, b. 1726, d. 1752/3, was a son of John (5) and Elizabeth (N) Patrick.

In ... an order of court dated 20 Nov 1752, Edward Moss, Edward Moss Junr & Thomas Patrick appraised the estate of John Wright, deceased ... recorded 18 Dec 1752.... {YCWI 1745-1759:281}

In ... an order of court dated 15 Jan 1753, James Goodwin, John Goodwin & Edward Moss settled the estate of John Bond, deceased. Value of personal estate sold 69 pd 10 sl 8 pn. Paid sums to Mr. Lightfoot & Tabb ... Mary Willens, Cleaton Rogers, Charles Sheild, John Goodwin, John Tenham et al., and the estate of Thos Patrick, deceased ... recorded 19 Feb 1753.... {1745-1759:287}

In ... an order of court dated 20 Aug 1753 Edward Moss, John Tenham & William Powell appraised the estate of Thomas Patrick, deceased: 8 working steers, 4 cows & 6 young cattle, 2 cows & 2 heifers, 1 horse, 2 mares, 3 sows, 14 piggs, 3 barrows, 7 young hogs, 1 bed & furniture, 1 bed, a parcel of old chairs, 1 table, 2 chests, 12 hard metal plates, 2 old trunks, 2 old tables, 1 Bible box, iron candle mould & gun, 1 pr of money scales, 1 saw, 2 jugs, a parcel of old pots, 1 searce & glass, the 1/2 of a canoe, 1 hand mill, parcel of bottles, 2 pots, a spit & tongs, parcel of old tubs, 1 old spinning wheel, 1 mans saddle, parcel of old pewter, 3 axes, 2 cow bells, 15 barrels of corn, 1 cart, wheels & 2 chains, 1 Negro man, 11 pigs, 121 lbs tobacco, 3 calves. 110 pd 16 sl 10 pn ... recorded 17 Sep 1753.... {YCWI 1745-1759:303}

10. SARAH PATRICK

On 16 Jun 1755, John Tenham, of Yorkhampton Parish, York Co., planter, for £120, sold to Sarah Patrick, of same place, a 121 acre tract of land in

Yorkhampton Parish adjacent Ralph Wormeley esqr, Edward Moss Junr, deceased, said John Tenham and Edward Moss Senr, which is part of 136 acres purchased by the said Tenham of the said Sarah Patrick 27 Oct 1754.... Acknowledged by John Tenham and Mary, his wife.... {YCLRD 1755-1763: 24}

11. CURTIS PATRICK, b. 13 Jan 1733, d. 1 Feb 1785, son of John (5) and Elizabeth (N) Patrick, m. Martha Rogers.

   Curtis and Martha (Rogers) Patrick were parents of SARAH, b. 16 Nov 1750; SUSANNA, b. 29 Nov 1755, bapt. 18 Jan 1756; ELIZABETH, b. 12 Feb 1761; THOMAS CURTIS, b. 5 May, bapt. 1 Jun 1766; CLAYTON, b. 9 Feb, bapt. 19 Mar 1769; NANCY, b. 12 Nov 1773, bapt. 20 Feb 1774. {CPR}

   On 20 Jun 1774, Sarah Rogers, of York Co., widow, made a deed of gift for natural love .,. to my son in law, Curtis Patrick, of York Co., of one Negro man slave named, James, now in the possession of the said Curtis Patrick.... {YCDB 1769-1777:23}

   On 16 Dec 1776, James Cooke & Mary, his wife, of York Co., for £42:10, sold to Thomas Holmes, of Warwick Co., a 33 1/3 acre tract of land in the Pocoson bounded by the lands of John Gemmel, Curtis Patrick, Edmond Patrick & John Cooke.... Proved 19 May 1777 & 21 Jul 1777 & recorded. {YCDB 1769-1777:538}

   Will of Adduston Rogers, of Charles Parish, York Co.: To wife, Mary Rogers, a negro woman named Pegg with her children, namely, Sam, Dick, and Aggar(?) until my eldest son William Adduston Rogers shall come at age. When my sons shall come of age, the said negroes to be divided into three equal parts, one part I lend to my wife during her life and after her death to be equally divided between my two sons and the other two parts I give to my two sons, William Adduston Rogers and John Rogers ... partnership with William Wright ... schooling my child ... [remainder totally obliterated] ... Proved 21 Jun 1762 according to the oaths of Edmond Curtis and John Chisman the witnesses. On the motion Mary Rogers and Curtis (Curles?) Patrick, the executors therein named were granted probate with William Patrick and John Patrick, their securities. {YCWI 1760-1783:106}

   Settlement of the estate of Curtis Patrick. Payments £15.18.-. £15.5.5 due to the estate. By court order 20 May 1765. Examined by Aug. Moore, John Patrick, Thomas Tomer. Returned 21 Sep 1767. {YCWI 1760-1771:363}

   Will of Clayton Rogers, of Charles Parish, York Co. To wife Rebeckah Rogers, half my estate, and if she be with child, the other half to this child, and if she not be with child I give it to my three god children: John Rogers, son of Aduston Rogers and Sarah Patrick, daughter of Curtis Patrick, and John Patrick, son of Edmund Patrick. Executors, wife Rebeka Rogers and Curtis Patrick. 12 Dec 1772. Wits: William Patrick, William Morris, William Moore. Proved 18

Jan 1773. Probate granted to Rebecka Rogers and Curtis Patrick, with William Patrick and Benjamin Wright, their securities. {YCWI 1771-1783:138}

Sarah Rogers, of Charles Parish in York Co., left a will dated 8 Feb 1778. Whole estate to be equally divided amongst my children and grandchildren, namely, Martha Patrick, John Rogers, Anne Drewry, Mildred Patrick, William Rogers and my two grandsons, William Addirston Rogers and John Rogers, sons of my late son Adderston Rogers, deceased, which two grandsons I give one equal part with my said children to be equally divided between them, but if either of them should die without issue then to the surviving one, but if both should die then to be divided amongst my said children. Granddaughter, Patsy Patrick, should have one heifer. Negro woman Bess shall go to either of my children that she chooses. The others, namely, Tom, Phill, Hannah, Harry with the above said Bess to be equally divided as above. Executors: Curtis Patrick and John Rogers. Proved 20 May 1778. {YCWI 1771-1783:399}

12. WILLIAM PATRICK, b. 30 Mar 1740/41, bapt. 20 Apr 1741, a son of John (5) and Elizabeth (N), m. 1st Elizabeth (N) and 2nd Lucy (N). {CPR}

William and Elizabeth (N) Patrick were the parents of HANNAH, b. 30 Jun, bapt. 9 Aug 1761; MARY, b. 25 Jan, bapt. 21 Feb 1765; THOMAS, b. 14 Jan, bapt. 6 Feb 1763; FRANCES MANSON, b. 9 Nov, bapt. 11 Dec 1768; ROBERT, b. 11 Feb, bapt. 24 Mar 1767.

William and Lucy (N) Patrick were parents of ELIZABETH TOPLESS, b. 23 Dec 1772, bapt. 31 Jan 1773; WILLIAM, b. 17 Jun, bapt. 17 Jul 1774; EDMUND CURTIS, b. 29 Apr, bapt. 25 May 1777. {CPR}

13. EDMUND PATRICK, b. 26 Apr 17[52], a son of John (5) and Elizabeth (N), m. Mildred (N). {CPR}

Edmund and Elizabeth (N) Patrick were parents of JOHN, b. 22 Aug, bapt. 4 Oct 1772; SALLY CLAYTON, b. 12 Mar, bapt. 14 Apr 1775; EDMUND, b. 10 Feb, bapt. 17 Apr 1778; EDMUND CURTIS, b. 22 Oct, bapt. 5 Nov 1780; BETSY, b. 5 Oct, bapt. 27 Nov 1785. {CPR}

23 Oct 1769. Deed. Reuben Lilbon (Lilbun), of Charles Parish, York Co., taylor, for & in consideration of the rents herein after expressed, hath farm letten unto Benjamin Wright, of same place, bricklayer, and Lucy, his wife, all that parcel of land lying on the n side of the Great Landing in parish afsd bounded by the said landing, the lands of John Patrick & John Howard.... Wits: Thomas Harvey, William Patrick. Ackn [ ] Jan 1770.... {YCDB 1769-1777:34}

On 20 Jun 1774, Sarah Rogers, of York Co., for natural love & affection & 5 shillings have given unto Edmund Patrick, of same county, one Negro boy named Daniel.... Wits: John Chisman Senr, John Patrick.... {YCDB 1769-1777:432}

110

OTHERS NAMED PATRICK

ELIZABETH PATRICK
John and Elizabeth were the parents of ELIZABETH, b. 3 Jun 1689.
{CPR}

ELIZABETH PATRICK
Elizabeth Patrick was the illegitimate mother of WILLIAM LONEY, b.
19 Jun, bapt. 6 Oct 1734. {CPR}
On 18 Nov 1734, the grand jury returned into court and made the
following presentments. We present Elizabeth Patrick for having a bastard child
in Charles Parish. Elinor Hayward for having a bastard child in Charles Parish.
William Hall for absenting himself from his parish church.... {YCWI 1732-1737:155}
16 Dec 1734. The presentment of the grand jury agt Elizabeth Patrick for
having a bastard child is dismist. {YCWI 1732-1737:160}
16 Feb 1735. The action of trespass brought by Elizabeth Patrick plt agt
Philip Fisher def is dismist. {YCWI 1732-1737:267}

THE JOHN ROGERS and JOHN ADUSTON FAMILIES[27]

1. JOHN ADUSTON, b. ca. 1630, d. prob. 1674-1698, m. Joane (N) by 1659.
{RB 1659-1662:72}
On 24 Jan 1659, John Aduson was granted judgment against Obadiah
Evans, his former master, for abusing Joane Aduson, his wife. {RB 1659-1662:72}
Thomas Mitchell was assignee of John Aduston for certificate granted
Mitchell on 10 Sep 1662 for 300 acres due for the importation of 6 persons into
this Colony: William Thornton, Richard Boyne, Thomas Shuge, Lawrence
Barker, Mary Stinson, Jane Mayden. {RB 1659-1662:175}
John Aduson. Son Rogers: My (24 Sep 1672) love to you. Confess
judgment to me. I am not well and so I rest. {RB 1672-1676:24}
Dr. Mathew Slater and John Aduston, Sr. had a difference in court on
25 Nov 1672 concerning treatment cost for John Aduston, Jr. {RB 1672-1676:31}
William Hawthorne, age about 25, was deposed on 25 Jan 1674/5
concerning Mr. John Aduston and Capt. Edmund Chisman demanding to see an
ox's ears. {RB 1672-1676:100}
On 25 Jan 1674/5, John Aduston appointed "my son" John Rogers my
atty. {RB 1672-1676:100}

---

[27] Because the Rogers family uses the name Aduston frequently for many generations, a
short history of the Aduston family precedes the Rogers family presentation.

On 24 May 1700, know all men by these presents that I, Joseph Coleman, do upon payment of four beedes[28] according to obligation wholly & solely acquit & discharge John Rogers or any other party so concerned from all manner of claims whatsoever of ye estate of John Addustone, deceased, from ye beginning of ye world to this day. Witness my hand on 22 Nov 1689, Joseph Coleman. Wits: John Lawson, Robt Starke. The within discharge was presented in court by the within named John Rogers and on his request is recorded being sworn to by John Lawson…. {YCWI 1698-1702:352}

John and Joane (N) Aduston were the parents of JOHN ADUSTON, JR. b. ca. 1660s, and AGNES, m. 1st (N) Dixon, and 2nd John Rogers. {RB 1672-1676:100}

THE JOHN ROGERS FAMILY

First Generation
1. JOHN ROGERS, b. ca. 1600, d. 1676.
    A poor, ancient person, it was ordered on 20 Dec 1660 that he not pay taxes. {RB 1659-1662:100}
    John Rogers, Sr. died 1676. {WARG:135}
    John Rogers was probably the father of JOHN, b. 1630s.

Second Generation
2. JOHN ROGERS, b. ca 1630s, d. bef. 26 Sep 1698, m. Agnes (Aduston[29]) (b. 1648, d. after 9 Nov 1705). {DW 1691-1694:83-84} John (2) was probably a son of John (1) Rogers.
    Agnes married 1st (N) Dixon, and they had a son, Richard Dixon (d. 1705) {YCWI 1706-1710:1}, and Agnes m. 2nd John Rogers.
    On 24 Jun 1672, Richard Trotter empowered "my brother," John Rogers, to crave a reference in suit between me and Mrs. Amedea Stock until next Court. {RB 1672-1676:16-17}
    On 25 Jan 1674/5, John Aduston appointed "my son" John Rogers my atty. {RB 1672-1676:100}
    John Lucey, York Parish and Co., planter, left a will dated 27 Dec 1688 and proved 24 Jan 1688/9. Unto Mary Jenings, daughter of Peter Jenings of Abington Parish in Gloucester Co., 2 cows. Rest of estate unto Mary Cowley

---

[28] Beads were used as currency, just as tobacco was.

[29] Her maiden name was probably Aduston given that John Aduston named John Rogers as a "son," which designated Rogers as a stepson or his daughter's husband. Any doubt that her maiden name was Aduston lies in the fact that Richard Trotter names Agness Rogers as a "sister."

and Agnes Rogers persons I made choice to look after me in my sickness. Edward Cawley and John Rogers, exs. {DW 1687-1691:200}

Agnes Rogers witnessed the inventory of John Smyth's estate in York Parish on 5 Apr 1688, which had a total valuation of 209 pounds sterling, 12 shillings, 6 pence. Signed: Agnes Rogers. {DW 1687-1691:124-127}

Agnes Rogers, age about 43, was deposed on 21 Dec 1691 concerning the case of the hogs and Arrington's testimony. {DW 1691-1694:83-84}

On 26 Sep 1698, Major Thomas Ballard trustee to ye estate of Isaack Godding, hath order granted him for an attachment agt ye estate of John Rogers in an action of debt for 1250 lbs of tobacco & cask said Rogers being returned *non est inventus* by ye sheriff. {YCWI 1698-1702:98}

Upon trial in ye suit continued to this court between Major Thomas Ballard trustee to the estate of Isaack Godding decd plt & John Rogers def in an action of debt wherein ye plt declareth that ye def stands jointly & severally bound with Richard Dixon by a certain specialty dated 26 Mar 1688 in a sum of 1250 lbs of good sound sweet scented tobacco & cask payable to said decd Godding but ye same to him whilst living hath in no part paid nor as yet to ye plt as trustee aforesaid, and thereupon demands judgment against ye def for payment thereof to which the def pleads ye act of limitation and being therein [?] judgment granted agt him ye def for payment of 662 lbs of tobacco and cask in balance of ye afsd specialty with cost. {YCWI 1698-1702:115}

The will of Richard Trotter, gent., was registered in Charles Parish, York Co., on 8 Nov 1699 and proved on 14 Dec 1699. To sister, Agness Rogers, one mourning ring of 20 sl price. To cousin, Richard Dixon, one mourning ring of 20 sl price. To my friend Thomas Cossins one mourning ring of 20 sl price. To the above said Cossins one pair of [?]. To ye poor in Charles Parish 1000 lbs of tobacco to be paid next Oct after my decease. To cousin Agness Coleman her two youngest [pg torn] namely, Addustone & Josias, 50 pounds to be divided between them and to be paid next Jan come 12 months after my decease, but if one of them shall dye before they shall enjoy ye afsd money then all to the other, but if it shall come to pass & they both dye, than to fall to ye next female heir at law in ye same family. The Negro Peter and Negro Tom shall have their true & perfect liberty and freedom six days after my wife's decease and 15 pounds a piece for their transportation. To my wife Anne Trotter, after my debts be paid, all the rest of my estate both real & personal during her widowhood and after her decease to dispose of ye 1/2 of ye personal estate as she shall think fit, and ye other half of my personal estate, I bequeath to my cousin, Richard Dixon, Senr. I also give unto ye aforesaid Richard Dixon all my land to him & his heirs forever. If my wife shall happen to marry, then she to have 1/3 of my estate, and the other 2/3 of my estate I give to my cousin, Richard Dixon, Senr. I appoint my wife my executrix.... {YCWI 1698-1702:248}

Ann Trotter, of Charles Parish, York Co. left a will on 24 Jul 1700 which was proved on – Dec 1700. To John Figg one cow and calf. To Widow Pickett? 5 pd or 500 lbs of tobacco. To Elinor Medcalph 5 pd or 500 lbs of tobacco. To Ann Panneares widow one barrel of Indian corn to be paid every year to her during natural life. To my cozen Richard Dixon's eldest daughter Agnes Dixon one young Negro woman between 16 & 20, the said Agnes Dixon to have the said Negro woman and her offspring & her cows forever. To my cozen Richard Dixon Junr my godson one Negro girl named Elizabeth and christened in Charles Parish Church forever. To my cozen Richard Dixon Senr for ever after my legacies and other debts are paid, all my whole estate whatsoever, real or personal, land, goods, chattels, cattle, implements, household, suits?, [?] plate every thing belonging or in any wise appertaining unto Ann Trotter either in VA, England or elsewhere. I appoint my cozen Richard Dixon Senr executor.... {YCWI 1698-1702:401}

Richard Dixon left a will on 9 Nov 1705 and proved 24 Jun 1706. I give to my son, James Dixon, all my land and tenements. If he should die without heyre ... then I give all my lands in Glouster co. to my two daughters Agnes and Rebecca ... and my lands in York co., I give to my two daughters Susanah and Anne. I give to my daughter Anne my brick house ... called by the name of *Hill House*. Slaves mentioned are one negro girl commonly known by the name of Mall, in Glouster co ... one negro woman named Hannah with her child ... one mulatto man named Will and his wife Nob. To my wife, Damazinah Dixon, one negro man commonly known by the name of George. To my mother, Agnes Rogers, 20 shillings to buy her a ring, and unto Thomas Nutting 20 shillings to buy him a ring. My wife is to keep the three younger children and their Estates until they come to their respective ages or marriage ... or until she remarries.... Wits: John Hunt, Senr, Thos. Nutting.... {YCWI 1706-1710:1}

The attachment which Lawrence Smith, Sheriff, obtained on 24 May 1710 against the Estate of John Rogers by means of his nonappearance at the suit of Richard Cheshire is discontinued. {YCWI 1710-1711:13}

John and Agnes (Aduston) Rogers were the parents of JOHN, ADUSTON, and probably THOMAS.

Third Generation

3. JOHN ROGERS, b. ca. 1660, was a son of John (2) and Agnes (Aduston) Dixon Rogers.

John Rogers was executor, with Ralph Walker, of the will of John Smyth, of York Co. and Parish, planter. John Smyth left a will dated 22 Dec 1687 and proved 24 Feb 1687/8. Land in New Kent Co. purchased of Capt. Willm. Smyth of Bristol, 500 acres, to my 2 sons Henry and John Smyth. To daughter, Sarah Smyth, all my lands in Back Creek in York Parish. Property in Walton 15 miles from London to be sold for purchasing Negro slaves for my plantation in New Kent Co., for use of my sons Henry and John Smyth. My daughter in law Ann

Dixon shall have her mother's apparrell, for fulfilling the promise to her mother at the time of her death, relinquishing a deed of 50 pounds sterling at request of my wife at our marriage and made payable to Ann, her daughter, and now the wife of Richard Dixon upon the day of her marriage. My sons to have their estates at 24, my daughter, Sarah, at 16 or marriage. My brothers in law, Ralph Walker and John Rogers, execs. {DW 1687-1691:92-94}

Mr. Joseph Topping and Frances his wife were granted a judgment on 18 Dec 1689 as execs. of Jane Rabley, against John Rogers for 737 pounds tobacco. {DW 1687-1691:352}

A judgment was granted on 24 Mar 1689/90 to Sarah Squire as extx. of John Squire against John Rogers. {DW 1687-1691:408}

John Goffe, New Kent, Virginia, Gent., on 23 Sep 1685, obligated himself to give his son, William Goffe, for a marriage intended between son William Goffe and Elizabeth Dixon, daughter in law to John Rogers, 500 acres purchased of Ralph Green, Gloucester Co., planter. In case I dye, all my estate to my son William Goffe and his wife. Signed: William Gough. {DW 1691-1694:61}

Robt Sergeton petitioned in court to keep an ordinary at York Town and ye same was granted with John Rogers & John Dozwell pledging his security in court. {YCWI 1698-1702:27}

On 20 Nov 1691, Joseph Ring & Thomas Ballard, both of York Co. gent., feofees in trust appointed according to an Act of Assembly made at James City 16 Apr 1691 for the disposal of 50 acres of land in York Co. appointed for a port & town for a valuable & proportional consideration, sold to John Rogers of co afsd gent a lot or ½ acre of land containing 10 poles in length & 8 in breadth being part of the aforesaid dividend of 50 acres of land bounded by the lots of Samll Timson, Thomas Jefferson & Broad Street, as by a plat thereof under the hand of Col Lawrence Smith surveyor on the records of York Co Court ... provided that it is the true intent & meaning of these presents that the said John Rogers his heyres or assigns do begin according to the recited law & without delay proceed to finish on the said lot of land so granted a good house to contain at least 20' square wherein if he fails then this present grant to be void.... {YCDB 1694-1701:1}

On 24 May 1700, on the petition of John Rogers, Capt Danll Taylor is requested with? Willm Wise & John Trivallion to meet at ye house of said John Rogers on 6 Jun next & then & there settle ye estate of Joane Adduston, in ye hands of said John Rogers and by him to be produced before ye gentlemen aforesaid & make due return to next court. {YCWI 1698-1702:332}

On 24 May 1700, know all men by these presents that I, Joseph Coleman, do upon payment of four beedes according to obligation wholly & solely acquit & discharge John Rogers or any other party so concerned from all manner of claims whatsoever of ye estate of John Addustone, deceased, from ye beginning of ye world to this day. Witness my hand on 22 Nov 1689, Joseph Coleman. Wits:

John Lawson, Robt Starke. The within discharge was presented in court by the within named John Rogers and on his request is recorded being sworn to by John Lawson.... {YCWI 1698-1702:352}

The order of last court for John Rogers to present a settlement of ye estate of Adduston Rogers[30] is referred to 26 Aug [1700] being [?] for an overpayment? cost. {YCWI 1698-1702:355}

In Court on 24 Jul 1700, in ye suit continued to this court [pg torn] his atty Francis Nicholson esqr his Majestys Lt Governor of VA, Willm Bird, Charles [pg torn], Matthew F[?], Stiphen Fonare, [pg torn], Miles Cary, Willm Randolph ... [pg torn] ... Royal College of William & Mary in VA, plaintiffs, against Dannll Parke esqr, defendant, in an action of debt for 25 pd due to said college as a declaration by an informant ... last court pleaded *non est factines*? and ye matter being referred to this court have now upon trial the same is referred to a jury, *viz.* John Rogers foreman, Willm Browne, Thomas Edmunds, John Drewit, John Clarke, Willm Pattison, Morgan Baptist, John Connor, Robt Harris, Thomas Wootton, Adduston Rogers & James Harvey who after a hearing of ye whole matter in difference together with ye evidences and compositions of ye defs hand & seal with diverse other writings for proof and due weight & consideration the jury returned their verdict, wee find for ye plts & Dionitious Wright atty for ye plts judgment is granted agt the def for payment of ye sum of 25 pd with costs. {YCWI 1698-1702:355}

On 24 Sep 1700, John Rogers did present a settlement of ye estate of Adduston Rogers in obedience to a former order and is ordered to be recorded. {YCWI 1698-1702:366}

Whereas John Rogers obtained an attachment from one of her Majesty's justices of the peace agt the estate of Robert Wilde returned executed by the sheriff upon 1 iron pot about 4 gallons, 1 black cow, 1 parcel of tobacco quantity 79 lbs and the plt now coming to court and producing a writing betwixt him and the said def but not making appear that ever as yet he sustained any damage, wherefore the said attachment is dismist and ordered that the sheriff forthwith make restitution of the goods attached as afsd and ye complainant pay costs. {YCWI 1702-1704:13}

On 24 Mar 1706 I, John Rogers, for a valuable consideration to me in hand received by bond dated 25 Mar 1706 for my self & heyres, sell all my right, title & interest of the [*above*] deed of a lot or ½ acre of land with all housing thereunto belonging unto Capt Thomas Mountfort lying next adjacent to the Court House.... Wit: Robt P[?], Jno Addeston Rogers, Thos Edin.... {YCDB 1701-1708:174}

Capt Thomas Mountfort his deed of assignment from John Rogers dated

---

[30] An Adduston Rogers died before 24 May 1700; however, another Adduston Rogers served as a jury member on 24 Jul 1700 (see paragraph following).

116

24 Mar 1706 for his Port land lot in York Towne (No. 30) was ackn by said John Rogers to said Thomas Mountfort & ordered committed to record. {YCWI 1705-1706:403}

John Rogers his bond from Thomas Mountfort no date for payment of 50 pd per condition of three several payments was acknowledge by said Capt Thomas Mountfort to said John & recorded. {YCWI 1705-1706:404}

Lawrence Smith, gent., assignee of York Court, hath judgment granted against John Rogers in an action of debt for 16 pd 17 sl 6 pn ye balance of a conditional sum of a penal bill dated by ye hands & seals of said John Rogers & Adduston Rogers 6 Oct 1705 & is ordered to be paid with cost. {YCWI 1705-1706:416}

Charges against John Rogers for absenting himself from Church. {YCWI 1706-1710:120}

In the action on the case between William Davis and Elizabeth, his wife, Admx. of the Estate of Thomas Jefferson, plaintiffs, and John Rogers, defendant, for 30 shillings due by account, one of the plaintiff made oath that the account by him produced is just and true and that he has reserved no part in satisfaction. Judgment is granted to the plaintiff for the aforesaid sum, and it is ordered that the defendant pay the same with costs *alies* execution. {YCWI 1706-1710:245}

On 22 Sep 1710, John Rogers of York Hampton Parish, York Co., for 5 shillings, leased, for the term of one year, to John Wills of Charles Parish, county aforesaid all his lot or ½ acre of land in York Town containing 10 poles in length & 8 poles in breadth being part of the Portland & designed in the plot of the said town bounded by Broad Street, land of Edward Powers & the Court House lot, known by the number 30 and also one messuage thereon erected ... the said lot of land was purchased by me of Joseph Ring & Thos Ballard, trustees of the Port Land of York Town.... Rogers released the land to Wills for £30 the following day.... {YCDB 1709-1713:362-364}

John Rogers was the father of JOHN ADDUSTON, b. ca 1680s; ADUSTON, b. ca 1680s; and BARBARAH, m. Martin Goodwyn.

4. ADDUSTON ROGERS, d. bef. 26 Aug 1700, was probably a son of John (2) and Agnes (Aduston) Rogers.

Some information on this individual was presented in the section on John (3) Rogers.

On 5 Sep 1698, Frances Bartlett, widow of Myhill Bartlett of Charles Parish, York Co., hath bound & put her natural & well beloved daughter Elizabeth Bartlett, being aged 4 years about 2 Jan next, an apprentice to Adduston Rogers of York Parish & Co, planter, to dwell & serve him until she attains to age 21 or day of marriage.... {YCWI 1698-1702:528}

The order of last court for John Rogers to present a settlement of ye estate of Adduston Rogers is referred to 26 Aug [1700] being [?] for an overpayment? cost. {YCWI 1698-1702:355}

5. THOMAS ROGERS, b. ca. 1660, d. 1686 {WARG:135}, m. Ann (N) (she d. 1701/2, a widow). {WARG:136-137} Thomas was probably a son of John (3) and Agnes (Aduston) Rogers.
Ann m. 2ⁿᵈ John Clarke (d. 1692) and 3ʳᵈ Edmund Pynes (d. 1699) {WARG:136-137}
Ann and John Clarke were the parents of John Clarke and Robert Clarke. {DW 1694-1697:39}
Ann and Edmund Pynes were the parents of John Pynes. {YCWI 1702-1704:70}
On 24 Nov 1687, Thomas Pinchbecks [Pinktheman?] gave to Elizabeth Rogers, daughter of Thomas Rogers, deceased, one heifer in custody of her mother, Ann Rogers. Signed: Tho: [T] Pinchbecks. {DW 1687-1691:69}
On 26 Nov 1688, Ann Rogers, of Bruton Parish, York Co., gave 3 heifers to her children: Thomas Rogers, Elizabeth Rogers and Ann Rogers. {DW 1687-1691:169}
John Clarke left a noncupative will dated 4 Dec 1693 and proved 24 Aug 1694. To my wife, Ann Clarke, half my stock and personal effects. To my sons, Robert and John Clarke, the other half of my stock. To Godson, John Hubberd, a cow and calf. To Goddaughter, Ann Rogers, a heifer. To his son, Robert, a horse. To his son, John, a mare colt that the mare shall bring to his daughter in law, Eliz: Rogers. To son in law, Thomas Rogers, mare colt, and next to his Goddaughter, Ann Rogers. {DW 1694-1697:39}
Anne Pines (Pynes) of Bruton Parish, York Co, VA, left a will dated 3 Oct 1702 and proved 24 Nov 1702. To my son, Thomas Rogers, my riding horse, saddle & bridle. To my daughter, Elizabeth Rogers, one grey mare branded on the near buttock with "IC." To my son, John Pynes, my best featherbed & furniture. To my son, John Clarke, the next best feather bed, but if he should die before he comes to the age of 21, then to his brother, Robert Clarke. To my son, Robert Clark, one large brass kettle & one gun. To my daughter Anne Rogers one feather bed and furniture. To my son, Thomas Rogers, ye biggest iron pot that I have. To my daughter, Elizabeth Rogers, the next biggest iron pot. To my son, John Pynes, the next biggest iron pot & one red & white cow with her increase. To my son, John Clarke, one young mare with her increase, but if he should die before he comes to the age of 21, then to his brother Robert Clarke. All the rest of my cattle to be divided between my two sons Robert & John Clarke and the rest of my estate to be divided among my children, and I appoint my son, Thomas Rogers, executor, and likewise Thomas Pinchback & Ralph Hubbard overseers until my son shall come to the age of 21.... {YCWI 1702-1704:70}
On 19 Jun 1708, William Sharman of the City of Williamsburgh baker,

for £50, released to Joseph Chermeson of James City co, two lots number 279 & 280.... Wits: Hen Holdcraft, Stephen Furnew, Ann Rogers. Ackn 24 Aug 1708 by Benja Weldon by virtue of a power of atty from Wm Sherman.... {YCDB 1701-1708:296}

Matthew Tiplady of London merchant appointed John Goodwin of ye Parish & Co of York my atty ... [illegible].... Wits: John Rogers, Adduston Rogers, Thomas Rogers. Proved 24 May 1699 & recorded.... {YCWI 1698-1702:166}

Thomas and Ann (N) Rogers were the parents of THOMAS, b. aft. 1681{YCWI 1702-1704:70}; ELIZABETH; and ANNE. {DW 1687-1691:169; DW 1694-1697:39}

Fourth Generation
6. JOHN ADDUSTON ROGERS, b. ca. 1680s, was a son of John (3) Rogers {YCWI 1705-1706:384}, m. Jane (N), relict of Dr. Henry Andrews {YCWI 1710-1711:107}.

John Adduston Rodgers and John Rogers were mentioned in the inventory & appraisement of the estate of Capt John Goodwin, deceased, which was delivered on 15 Aug 1701.... The within inventory was presented in court by deceased's relict on 24 Sep 1701.... {YCWI 1698-1702:504}

On 29 Sep 1702, John Rogers and John Adduston Rogers witnessed the recording of the 23 Sep 1702 will of Alice Beale, widow and executrix of husband, Col Thomas Beale of York Parish, York Co. decd, for natural love and affection, give to my grandson, Peter Goodwyn, all my lands on the Back Creek in York Parish during the said Peter Goodwyn and his wife's life and after their decease to my grandson Thomas Beale of Rappahannock & his male heirs.... {YCWI 1702-1704:25}

John Adduston Rogers & Jane, his wife, relict of Doctor Henry Andrews, late of this co., decd., on petition hath order granted for a commission of administration on ye estate of said decd having entered into bond with John Rogers & Thomas Wotton, their securities. {YCWI 1705-1706:384}

In obedience to an order of court dated 29 Feb 1705, Willm Wise, Armiger Wade & Robt Kerby have appraised & inventoried ye estate of Dr. Henry Andrews decd. One Christian white servant by name John Middlebrook, 2 Negro men, 1 Negro wench. 5 feather beds, bedsteads, blankets, sheets, cords, rugs & all furniture thereto, 1 coulch[?], 3 sides upper leather, 5 sides sole leather, 1 parcel of feathers, a cask, 1 parcel nails, 5 broad hoes, 4 axes, 3 lb of powder, 3 chests, 1 box, etc. 270 pd 2 sl 9 pn. Inventory & appraisement was returned to court by John Adduston Rogers & Jane his wife, adminr, on 24 Apr 1706.... {YCWI 1705-1706:399}

On 8 Jan 1706, the suit depending to this Court between John Adduston Rogers and Jane, his wife, Admrs. of Henry Andrews, dec'd., plfs., against Damazinah Dixon, Extx. of Richard Dixon, dec'd., in an action of debt damage

£12 is referred for proof of the plf's declaration. {YCWI 1706-1710:31}
    On 25 Sep 1706, in the suite depending to this Court between John
Adduston Rogers and Jane, his wife, Admrs. of Henry Andrews, dec'd., plfs.
against Damazinah Dixon, Extx. of Richard Dixon, dec'd., in an action of debt
declared for the sum of £12 …which the said Richard in his lifetime for several
goods, wares and merchandizes by him received did assume to pay to the said
Henry in his lifetime, but never paid the same nor any parte thereof, to that the
deft. pleaded non assumpsit in manner and form, whereupon a jury, *viz.* John
Mihille, Thomas Wootton, Edmund Curtis, Charles Collier, Thomas Whitby and
John Dozwell was impaneled and sworn to try the issue, who after a full hearing
of all evidences and pleas on both sides, departed to consult their verdict and on
their return, plf. and deft. being called, returned for verdict, We find for the plf.
£9:17:4, signed John Mihill, foreman. Which on request of Stephens Thomson,
Attorney for the plf., is admitted to record and it is considered that the plf.
recover of the deft. the damage aforesaid in manner aforesaid by the inquisition
found with costs *alies* execution. {YCWI 1706-1710:41}
    On 25 Aug 1708, the case between John Adduston Rogers and Jane, his
wife, Admr. of Henry Andrews, dec'd., plfs., and Thomas Walker, deft., neither
party appearing, was dismist. {YCWI 1706-1710:162}
    On 20 Aug 1711, a power of Attorney from John Rogers of the Parish
of York Hampton, this County, planter, to John Adduston Rogers. In or about
the year 1683 did then mortgage to one Edward Jones of Bruton Parish, factor,
and Alderman Richard Booth of London, merchant, six negroes and their
increase for the payment of a debt due to the said Alderman of £35 of which
sum I have made payment of several sums of money to Edward Jones, factor
aforesaid, as per receipts under his hand doth and may appear, by the occasion
of the mortality of several Gents. therein concerned had not the opportunity of
perfecting the account this several years, now I appoint my son, John Adduston
Rogers of Charles Parish, planter, my true and lawful Attorney for me and in my
name to collect said negroes and their increase…. {YCWI 1710-1711:107}

7. ADDUSTON ROGERS was a son of John (3) Rogers.
    In the difference between John Dowzen, plaintiff, and Adduston Rogers
churchwardens at York Parish, defendants, in the case for 3 pd 7 sl due from the
said parish by an order of Vestry dated 16 May 1702, the same is referred to
auditors, *viz.* Robert Read, Lt Col Thomas Ballard & Major William Buckner to
meet at ye house of Capt Robert Snead in York Town to audit and settle ye
account betwixt the plaintiff and defendant. {YCWI 1702-1704:39}
    On 23 Jun 1703, John [3] Rogers of York Parish, York Co, VA, give
unto my grandson, John Adduston Rogers, one black cow being about 5 or years
old having a red heifer about 3 years old running with her & all their female

increase until he shall attain to ye age of 16 & after that age the increase both male & female to redound to him. To my granddaughter, Elizabeth Rogers, one red heifer about 3 years old with all her female increase until she shall attain the age of 16 years and after that age ye increase both male & female to redound to her. All ye said cattle being now in ye possession of their father, Adduston Rogers. I give to my grandson, Adduston Rogers, one red cow calf about 7 months old and all her female increase until he shall attain to ye age of 16 & after that age then ye increase both male & female to redound to him. I give unto my son, Adduston Rogers, their father, if he finds his children stock of cattle do increase so much that it prejudices his own stock of cattle then to sell or dispose of any part of the same for ye only proper use, good and benefit of ye said grandchildren & not otherwise ye said Adduston Rogers being accountable for his or her part so sold when they come to age to demand it…. {YCWI 1702-1704:120}

At a Court for York Co. on 24 May 1707, Adduston Rogers Junr., his Deed of Gift bearing date under the hand and seal of Mathew Tiplady this present Instant, for one grey mare and horse colt, was this day personally acknowledged in Court and ordered to be committed to record. {YCWI 1706-1710:62}

24 Jun 1707. Adduston Rogers being summoned to this Court to answer the Information of the Grand Jury for not keeping the roads clear in his precinque, this day made his appearance at Court and complained against Thomas Wooten for turning the roads. It is therefore ordered that the said Thomas Wooton make good and sufficient bridges in the road through his land sufficient for cart and horse betwixt this and the next Court, otherwise to be fined according to Law. {YCWI 1706-1708:74}

At a Court held for York Co. on 24 Jan 1708, Adduston Rogers, Surveyor of the Highways of the lower precinct of York Hampton Parish, on his motion is discharged from the said office, and Thomas Chisman Junr is hereby appointed in his stead, and ordered that the said Rogers give him notice of this order that he may clear the roads accordingly. {YCWI 1706-1710:183}

On 24 Feb 1708, Adduston Rogers, Surveyor of the Highways in the Lower Precinct of York Hampton Parish, being presented by the Grand Jury for not keeping the roads in repair in that precinct, the viewers appointed at the last Court to view the said roads having reported them insufficient, therefore the Court do fine and amerce the said Rogers 15 shillings according to Law for his neglect. {YCWI 1708-1710:197}

Aduston was the father of JOHN ADDUSTON, b. ca. 1680s; ELIZABETH; and ADDUSTON [JR], b. ca. 1690s. {YCWI 1702-1704:120}

8. BARBARA ROGERS, b. ca 1680s, daughter of John (3) Rogers, m. Martin Goodwin.[31]

Barbarah Rogers witnessed a deed of gift on 23 May 1701 from Thomas Edmunds of Parish & Co of York, planter, for natural love & affection I bear unto my loving goddaughter, Rebecka Wardley.... {YCWI 1698-1702:468}

Order for a probate on ye will of Mrs. Blanch Goodwyn was granted to her two sons, Robert and Martin Goodwyn, executors. It was further ordered that Edward Moss, John Rogers, Jno Wythe & Ralph Walker inventory & appraise ye testator's estate & make return to next court. {YCWI 1698-1702:517}

Martyn Goodwyn, of York Parish & Co planter, for £42, sold, on 8 Feb 1706/7, to Thomas Paynter of Abbington Parish, Gloucester Co, a tract of land on the north side of James River in Wainoake Parish, Charles City Co containing 500 acres bounded by the Cattayle Br, Jeffry Mumford, Col Daniel Clarke, Minching Br, land of James Howard formerly purchased of John Hunt & the Murrell Path.... Ackn 30 Mar 1706/7 at Charles City Co by Martin Goodwyn & recorded.... Barbar Goodwyn, wife of the said Martin Goodwin, relinquished her right of dower 24 May 1708 at York Co Court.... {YCDB 1701-1708:284}

John Rogers, of York Hampton Parish, planter, to Eliz. Goodwyn, the eldest daughter of Martin Goodwyn and Barbara, his wife, one Negro girl about 2 years of age as also the first child that the said Negro girl named Lucy shall have after she come to years of maturity. But in case the said Elizabeth shall die before she come of age and day of marriage, then the said Lucy and all her increase to be given all the rest of my grandchildren of my well beloved daughter Goodwyn's body. 1 Oct 1713. Wits: Martin Goodwyn and [Dix]on Naylor. {YCWI 1711-1714:309}

Barbara Rogers and Martin Goodwin were the parents of ELIZABETH GOODWIN. {YCWI 1711-1714:309}

9. THOMAS ROGERS, b. ca. 1685, d. bef. 24 Mar 1708 {YCWI 1706-1710:128}, m. Sarah (N), was a son of Thomas (5) and Ann (N) Rogers.

Thomas Rogers, Joseph Chermeson, and George Baskerville, of York Co., were bound to the Justices of said County in the sum of £100 on 24 Jun 1707. The three were sureties to Thomas Rogers as guardian of Robert Clark, orphan of John Clark, deceased. {YCWI 1706-1710:page B, preceding p.1}

Thomas Rogers, arresting Negro Tom, late servant to Mrs. Ann Trotter, in a case for damages for shooting the plaintiff's horse, and the defendant failing to appear, judgment is granted against Henry Tyler, high sheriff, and next court to be confirmed if he causeth not the defendant to appear and answer the same. Upon

[31] See *Colonial Families of York County, Virginia*, Vol. 2, "The Goodwin Family."

trial, for defect in plaintiff's declaration, he is nonsuited on motion of the defense and the plaintiff ordered to make payment thereof with costs. {YCWI 1698-1702:393,440}

Thomas Rogers being by ye sheriff returned summoned an evidence for John Rogers plaintiff against John Wellings & Thomas Bell [?] defendants ordered to be paid 40 lbs of tobacco for 1 day's attendance at court with costs.... {YCWI 1698-1702:119}

In the difference depending between Madam Alice Beale, plaintiff, and Thomas Rogers, defendant, in an action of case for 250 lbs of tobacco by account and ye plaintiff not proving the said debt is nonsuited with costs. {YCWI 1702-1704:3}

In ye suite between Thomas Rogers plt & Henry Hayward Junr def in a case for damages 20 pd sustained by ye plt through ye defs stopping ye plts horse on 9 Nov last past near Tiplady's Swamp ye said plt & Richard Dixon then running a race with their horses for ye sum of 10 pd by means whereof ye said plt lost ye said race to his damage as afsd which def pleaded not guilty in manner and force and for trial thereof both parties agreed at ye bar to refer ye matter to court for a determination and decision who after hearing all evidences produced and pleas made on both sides found no cause of action whereupon ye suit is dismist. {YCWI 1702-1704:206}

On 24 Jun 1707, Robert Clark, orphan of John Clark, deceased, on his petition, obtained order for the admittance of Thomas Rogers as his Guardian, who this day was entered into Bond with Joseph Chermison and George Baskerville for the due performance of his trust therein, according to Law. {YCWI 1706-1710:73}

On 24 Mar 1708, the action on the case brought by John Bates, plaintiff, against Thomas Rogers, defendant, is dismissed, the defendant being dead. {YCWI 1706-1710:128}

On 24 Nov 1708, Joseph Chermison, Francis Sharp and John Sarjanton, were bound to the Justices of York Co., in the sum of £200, as sureties for Joseph Chermison, Administrator of the whole Estate of Thomas Rogers, deceased. {YCWI 1706-1710:177}

On the petition of Sarah Rogers, widow of Thomas Rogers, deceased, it is ordered that Joseph Chermeson (who had administration on the said Estate this day granted him) deliver her out of the said Estate a bed, pot, dish & spoon for her use. {YCWI 1706-1710:179}

On 24 May 1709, in the action upon the case between John Bates, plaintiff, and Joseph Chermeson, Administrator of the Estate of Thos. Rogers, deceased, defendant, for £4:1:3 by account, the defendant appeared and alleged that there is not sufficient of the said Estate to pay the same. Therefore ordered that he state and exhibit an account thereof unto the next Court, until when the suit is continued. {YCWI 1706-1710:218}

On 24 Jun 1709, inventory & appraisement of the Estate of Thomas Rogers, late of this County, deceased, as presented by Joseph Chermeson and appraised by James Hubard, Richard Kendall and Henry Gilbert. Total value of livestock and household goods: £8:19:8. {YCWI 1706-1710:233}

Fifth Generation

10. ADUSTONE ROGERS, b. ca 1710s, was a son of Aduston (7) and Katherine (Doswell?) Rogers.

In obedience to a court order of 23 May 1716 ... a jury, together with ye county surveyor, went to survey & lay out ye line between Adduston Rogers & Peter Goodwin, both of this county, being ye dividing line of ye bay tree patent between Col Thomas Beal & John Clarkson. We ye subscribers have accordingly met together on 5 Jun on ye land in controversy ... adjacent [land of] Capt Thomas Chisman & Chew's Cr ... we have likewise allotted a certain parcel of marsh lying on ye west side of Clarkson's Creek & being contained in Mr. Goodwin's pasture ground for part of his share not contingent with his other part ... Richard Slater surveyor presented ye within report 18 Jun 1716.... {YCWI 1716-1718:10}

On 10 Sep 1723, the last Will & Testament of Thomas Curtis, deceased, was presented in Court by Susanna Curtis, one of the Executors therein, who made Oath thereto (James Dixon the other Excr. having relinquished his right to the Executorship) & being proved by the Oaths of Thomas Nixon, Adduston Rogers & Jno. Adduston Rogers.... {YCWI 1722-1725:229}

On 17 Dec 1733, by petition, in the room of Robert Ballard, of Thomas Doswell chose Adduston Rogers for his guardian, the said Ballard being called and refusing to be released of the said orphan and his estate ... was granted hereby him and ordered that the said Ballard deliver up the said estate. {YCWI 1732-1737:81}

On 17 Dec 1733, Adduston Rogers, Francis Minnis and John Patrick were firmly bound unto the justices of York Co for 200 pd ... the condition of this obligation was such that if the afsd Adduston Rogers shall well & truly pay unto Thomas Doswell, orphan of John Doswell, decd, all such estate due to the said orphan when he shall attain to lawful age then this obligation to be void.... {YCWI 1732-1737:84}

Upon the petition of Adduston Rogers on 16 Dec 1734 setting forth that William Robinson guardian to John Doswell, decd, was ordered to take care of the said John Doswell and his estate and hath failed therein, the court ordered that the said William Robinson be summoned to appear at the next court to answer the said petition. {YCWI 1732-1737:159}

Adduston Rogers, Clayton Rogers, James Rogers & John Boradell, of York Co, are firmly bound unto Lawrence Smith, Thos Nelson, Edward Digges & Jno Buckner gent, justices for York Co, for 20 pd ... the condition of this obligation is such that if the afsd Adduston Rogers, Clayton Rogers, James Rogers & John Boradell do well and truly pay all the just and lawful debts of John Powers & Susanna his wife, deceased, so far as they have assets in their hands, then this obligation to be void.... Wits: Robt Wellins, Jones Irwin ... recorded 21 Feb 1736. {YCWI 1732-1737:346}

Elizabeth Nutting, of Charles Parish, York Co, widow, left a will dated 13 Sep 1733. To my grandson Robert Armistead, son of Robert Armistead and Catherine, his wife, all the tract of land whereon I now live being in Charles Parish. To my grandson, Booth Armistead, my Negro boy, Casar, and my Negro wench, Rachel. To Elizabeth Rogers, dau of Adduston Rogers and Catherine, his wife, my Negro girl Phillis. To my grandson, William Lowry, my Negro man Paul. To my granddaughter, Angellica Armistead, my Negro child called Tom. To Robert Armistead, my grandson, aforesaid my silver tankard. All my wearing apparel to Elizabeth Goodwin, Katha Rogers and Mary Brown.... {YCWI 1732-1737:230}

Adustone and Elizabeth (N) Rogers were the parents of ADENSTONE, b. 26 Apr, bapt. 23 May 1731; JOHN ADENSTONE, b. 27 Mar, bapt. 22 Apr. 1733; and MARY, b. 19 Aug, bapt. 21 Sep 1735. {CPR}

11. JAMES ROGERS, b. ca. 1710s, will 28 Jul 1744, d. 23 Jan 1744/5, will proved 17 Jun 1745, m. Margaret (N) (d. a widow, 26 May 1781). {CPR}

The will of James Rogers of York Co. was written on 28 Jul 1744 and proved 17 Jun 1745. To wife, Margaret Rogers, all my estate both real and personal after debts & funeral expenses are paid during her widowhood to bring up my children, but if she should marry, then whole estate to be sold and divided between my wife and all my children. Wits: John Chisman, James Toomer, and Thos Pescud Junr.... {YCWI 1743-1746:373,376}

On 19 Aug 1745, Margaret Rogers was granted certification to obtain Letters of Administration on the estate of James Rogers, decd, with his will annexed. {YCWI 1743-1746:386}

In obedience to a court order dated 17 Jun 1745, John Patrick, John Gibbons & James Toomer appraised the estate of James Rogers, decd: 2 cows, 12 hogs, 1 horse, 1 feather bed & furniture, 1 gun, etc., 1 Negro named Cyrus. [Not totaled] ... recorded 15 Jul 1745.... {YCWI 1745-1759:33}

James and Margaret (N) Rogers were the parents of JOHN ROGERS, b. 1 Sep , bapt. 17 Oct 1736, d. 8 Jan 1748; ELIZABETH ROGERS, b. 17 Dec 1738; ANTHONY ROGERS, b. 17 Dec, bapt. 31 Jan 1741, d. 24 Apr 1750; and WILLIAM ROGERS, b. 9 Feb, bapt. 10 Mar 1733, d. 4 Jan 1750. {CPR}

12. THOMAS ROGERS, b. ca. 1710s, d. 17 Dec 1741 {CPR}, m. Sarah (N) Rogers.

On 15 Mar 1741/2, upon the prayer of Wm Nelson Junr gent, and his making oath that Thos Rogers, decd, departed this life without making any will, and giving bond and security, ordered that a certificate be granted him for obtaining a Letter of Administration on the said decd's estate. {YCWI 1740-43:90} Thomas and Sarah (N) Rogers were the parents of ELIZABETH ROGERS, b. May, bapt. 24 Jun 1739 and THOMAS ROGERS, b. 13 Sep, bapt. 17 Oct 1742. {CPR}

13. CLAYTON ROGERS, b. ca. 1710s, will 12 Dec 1772, proved 18 Jan 1773. Martha Martin, of York Co., left a will dated 29 Oct 1755 and proved 19 Jan 1756. To my godson, Wm Pervin, and my goddaughter, Elizabeth Rogers, all the money that William Rogers owe me (except paying Mr. Jameson what I owe him). To my goddaughter, Elizabeth Rogers, my chest with what is in it (except about 2 lbs of spun cotton which I desire Mrs. Agnes Smith to accept of) and all my wearing apparel. To Mrs. Agnes Smith, 47 sl which she is indebted to me. To Clayton Rogers, what he owes me. I leave the remainder and residue of what I possess to Mr. Francis Mannis to pay my funeral expenses, whom I do appoint executor. Wits: Thos Maning, Eliza May, John Cary.... {YCWI 1745-1759:390}

John Cox, an infant of 17 years of age or thereabouts, with the consent and approbation of the court doth voluntarily put himself an apprentice unto Clayton Rogers, of York Co, carpenter, for the term of 4 years from 17 Jul next ensuing the afsd Clayton Rogers doth oblige himself to teach his apprentice John Cox to read and write during the time of his apprenticeship. {YCLRD 1755-1763:442}

The will of Clayton Rogers of Charles Parish, York Co., was written on 12 Dec 1772 and proved 18 Jan 1773. To wife Rebeckah Rogers, half my estate, and if she be with child, the other half to this child, and if she not be with child, I give it to my three god children: John Rogers, son of Aduston Rogers and Sarah Patrick, dau. of Curtis Patrick and John Patrick, son of Edmund Patrick. Execs: wife Rebeka Rogers and Curtis Patrick. Wits: William Patrick, William Morris, William Moore. Probate granted to Rebecka Rogers and Curtis Patrick, with William Patrick and Benjamin Wright, their securities. {YCWI 1771-1783:138}

The appraisement of the estate of Clayton Rogers, decd., totaled £7.12.1, and was delivered on 18 Jan 1773 and returned on 15 Mar 1773. Appraised by James Dixon, Thomas Hunt, and William Patrick. {YCWI 1771-1783:160}

Clayton Rogers and "his wife" {CPR} [possibly Rebecca (N) {YCWI 1771-1783:138}] Rogers were the parents of THOMAS ADENSTON ROGERS, b. 18 May, bapt. 11 Jun 1738. {CPR}

Sixth Generation

14. JOHN ADUSTON ROGERS, prob. b. 27 Mar, bapt. 22 Apr. 1733, and prob. son of Aduston (10) and Katherine (N) Rogers.
John Aduston and Elizabeth Bernard Rogers were the parents of WM. ADUSTON ROGERS, b. 15 Jul, bapt. 27 Jul 1769 [Yorkhampton]; MOLLY ROGERS, b. 3 Dec 1775, bapt. 11 Feb 1776 [Yorkhampton]. {CPR}

15. ADDENSTON ROGERS, b. ca. 1730s, son of Sarah (N) Rogers, m. Mary (N).
The will of Adduston Rogers, of Charles Parish, York Co., was proved 21 Jun 1762. To wife, Mary Rogers, a negro woman named Pegg with her children, namely, Sam, Dick, and Aggar(?) until my eldest son William Adduston Rogers shall come at age. When my sons shall come of age the said negroes to be divided into three equal parts, one part, I lend to my wife during her life and after her death to be equally divided between my two sons and the other two parts I give to my two sons William Adduston Rogers and John Rogers ... partnership with William Wright ... schooling my child ... [remainder totally obliterated].... Wits: Edmond Curtis and John Chisman. On the motion, Mary Rogers and Curtis (Curles?) Patrick, the execs. therein named, were granted probate with William Patrick and John Patrick, their securities. {YCWI 1760-1783:106}
On 21 Jun 1762, the appraisement of the estate of Adueston Rogers, decd., was given in court and included negroes [2 or more ... names obliterated] ... Total: £84.13.6. Appraised by Edmund Curtis, John Chisman, Reuben Lilban (Lillian?) [Lilburn?].... {YCWI 1760-1783:133}
The will of Sarah Rogers, of Charles Parish in York Co., left her whole estate to be equally divided among her children and grandchildren namely, Martha Patrick, John Rogers, Anne Drewry, Mildred Patrick, William Rogers and my two grandsons, William Addirston Rogers and John Rogers, sons of my late son, Adderston Rogers dec'd., which two grandsons I give one equal part with my said children to be equally divided between them but if either of them should die without issue then to the surviving one but if both should die then to be divided amongst my said children. Granddaughter Patsy Patrick should have one heifer. Negro woman, Bess, shall go to either of my children that she chooses. The others, namely Tom, Phill, Hannah, Harry, with the above said Bess, to be equally divided as above. Execs. Curtis Patrick and John Rogers. 8 Feb 1778. Wit. Thos. Pescud, Giles Morris. Proved 20 May 1778. {YCWI 1771-1783:399}
The court ordered on 16 Nov 1778 that John Patrick, Nicholas Presson, Willis Wilson and Thomas Hunt appraise the estate of Sarah Rogers, deceased. Negroes: Tom, Phill, Harry, Bess, Hannah. Total: £432.11.9. John Patrick, Thomas Hunt, Nicholas Presson. Returned 17 Jul 1780. {YCWI 1771-1783:496}

Addenston and Mary (N) Rogers were the parents of <u>WILLIAM ADDENSTON</u>, b. 23 Jan 1759; JOHN, b. 9 May 1760. {CPR}

Generation 7

16. WILLIAM [ADDENSTON] ROGERS, b. 23 Jan 1759, m. Elizabeth (N), was a son of Addenston (15) and Mary (N) Rogers. William and Elizabeth (N) Rogers were the parents of SUSANNA ROGERS, b. 10 Feb, bapt. 17 Apr 1778 [Yorkhampton]. {CPR}

THE CAPT. WILLIAM ROGERS Family[32]

1. CAPT. WILLIAM ROGERS, will 16 May 1739, proved 18 Feb 1739/40, m. Theodosia (N) (will 27 Mar 1752, proved 15 Jun 1752).

On 19 May 1711, William Buckner & Lawrence Smith gent, trustees to the Portland in York Town, for 180 lbs of tobacco, sold to William Rogers, of York Town, afsd, brewer, two lots, or ½ acres, of land in York Town being part of the Portland known by the numbers 51 & 55 as by the plot on the records of the said company doth appear, the said lots each of them containing 10 poles in length & 8 poles in breadth ... provided that the said William Rogers shall & do, within 12 months, build & finish on each of the said lots one good house to contain at least 20' wherein if they fail this present grant to be void in law.... {YCDB 1709-1711:365}

On 21 Jan 1711, in the action of debt between Saml. Smith, plf. and John Martin, deft., for £5:14:2 due upon balance of Bills of Exchange protested, William Rogers, on whom an attachment was served for the Estate of the deft. in his hands, appeared and, upon examination, it was apparent that he is and has for more than 12 months past been in possession of sundry houses appertaining to the defendant's estate without paying any consideration. It is ... the opinion of the Court that he ought to pay £8 for rent and, thereupon, it is ordered that the said Rogers pay the aforesaid sum of £5:14:2 out of the said £8 with costs *alies* execution. At the plaintiff's motion, the attachment against the defendant's estate was discontinued. {YCWI 1711-1714:123}

On 20 Mar 1720, Scipio, a Negro boy belonging to Wm. Rogers, is adjudged to be twelve years old. {YCWI 1720-1722:25}

On 17 Jul 1721, JnC[?]ry, a Negro boy belonging to Wm Rogers, is adjudged to be Twelve years old; Rumford, a negro boy belonging to Wm Rogers, is adjudged to be ten years of age; and Phillis, a Negro girl belonging to Wm Rogers, is adjudged to be eight years old. {YCWI 1720-1722:59}

---

[32] This family has no apparent blood connection to the John Rogers family of this era.

128

On 19 Mar 1721/2, Wm Rogers, presented by ye grand Jury for not going to Church, on his appearance, is discharged paying fees. {YCWI 1720-1722:120}

On 17 Nov 1722, on ye petition of Wm Rogers agt his Servant Jno. Jones for running away, it appearing that ye said Jones hath been absent ... days & that ye said Rogers hath expended three hundred seventy two pounds of tobacco in retaking of him, ordered that he Serve his said Master six months for the same after his time by Indenture Custom or former order of Court is expired and that he receive ... at ye public whipping post thirty-nine lashes.... {YCWI 1720-1722:156}

On 20 Jan 1723, a Negro boy named Joe belonging to William Rogers was brought before the Court and Adjudged to be fourteen years old. {YCWI 1722-1725:248}

On 15 Jun 1724, a Negro Girl, named Betty, & A Negro Boy, named Tony, belonging to William Rogers were brought before the Court and adjudged, the Girl at fourteen & ye boy at fifteen years old. {YCWI 1722-1725:280}

To all Christian People whom these presents shall Come we, Thomas Nelson, Philip Lightfoot, Thomas Jones & John Martin, of York River in Virginia, Merchants, Arbitrators, mutually chosen between John Marriott, Citizen and Stationer of London, of the one part and William Rogers, of York River in Virginia Merchant of ye other part, and Greeting Whereas the said John Marriott and William Rogers have Submitted to our award and Arbitrament all and All manner of Actions, Causes, Suits, Bills, Bonds, Especially Judgments, Executions, Extents, Quarrels, Controversies, Trespasses, Damages, and Demands whatsoever at nay time heretofore had made moved brought, Commenced, prosecuted or depending between the said parties or either of them And to the true performance, observance and fulfilling of Such final Award order, Arbitrament and determination as should be made in Writing under our hands & Seals of and Concerning the premises, did by their respective bonds Sealed with their Seals and dated 9 Nov 1723, respectively bind themselves each to the other in the penal Sum of five hundred pounds lawful money of Great Britain as in and by the said Several bonds relation being thereunto had may more full and at large appear ... Now Know Ye that We, the said Arbitrators, having Fully Seen, heard, read, & Maturely Considered all Accounts and other matters in difference between the said parties, Do make this our final Award in manner following: First, We do adjudge, order and Award that the said William Rogers shall and do on or before 9 May 1725 Pay & Deliver to the Attorney or order of the said John Marriott in Virginia the Sum of four hundred pounds Sterling by good bills of Exchange drawn payable at Some Port or trading town in that part of Great Britain called England. Secondly, We Do adjudge, order, & Award that the Said John Marriott shall some time before the said 9 May 1725 Send or cause to be Sent to his Attorney or Attorneys in

Virginia a General Release of all Debts Dues Demands Accts & Reckonings
between him and the said Rogers from the beginning of the World which
Release shall be duly Executed under the hand & Seals of the said Marriott and
attested by three or more credible Witnesses by Whom the Same may be proved
in Virginia and contain a Clause to discharge the said William Rogers of and
from all Accounts and demands of Shopkeepers or tradesman from whom any
part of the Cargoes in partnership between the said parties were purchased and
shall be ready to be delivered to the said William Rogers on payment and
delivery of the said bills of Exchange In Testimony of this our final Award and
Arbitrament between the said parties of and Concerning the premises, We have
hereunto Set our hands and Seals this 8 May 1724 at a court held for York
County 21 Jun 1725.... {YCWI 1722-1725:345}

In Jan 1723, Wm Stark, of York Co., and Mary, his wife, for 5
shillings, leased to William Rogers of [*pg torn*] a 25 acre tract of land
purchased by the said William Stark of Joseph Mountfoot, of York Co., adjacent
the Lodge Bridge, John Read & Thomas Vines for the term of 1 year paying one
ear of Indian corn at the Feast of St. Michael.... Ackn in court 18 Jan 1730.
{YCLRD 1729-1740:71}

On 17 Jun 1734, William Rogers gent, took the oath of government and
subscribed the test as Capt of the Troop whereof Major John Buckner was lately
Captain. {YCWI 1732-1737:121}

On 18 Nov 1734, it was ordered, in the room of John Ballard gent, that
William Rogers gent be surveyor of the landings sheets & cosways [causeways]
in York Town and that he keep the same in good repair. {YCWI 1732-1737:157}

15 Sep 1735. Jack a Negro boy belonging to Capt. William Rogers
adjudged to be 13 years of age. {YCWI 1732-1737:223}

On 14 Sep 1738, Francis Moss, of York Co., and Elizabeth, his wife,
for £15, sold to Wm Rogers, of York Co. gent., a one acre lot of ground in York
Town (No. 75) which was purchased of Abram St. Leger by Benj Moss, late of
York Co., decd., and devised by his will to the said Francis Moss..... {YCLRD
1729-1740:514}

On 19 Mar 1738, it was ordered that John Ballard gent be surveyor of
the streets & landings in York Town in the room of Wm Rogers. {YCWI 1737-
1740:480}

On 17 Dec 1739, the will of Wm Rogers gent., decd., was presented by
Theodosia Rogers, the executrix, who made oath to it and being proved by the
oath of John Ballard and Wm Trotter two of the wits thereto and they also
making oath that they saw James Mitchell sign his name as a witness, ordered to
be recorded, and on the motion of the said executrix and giving bond & security,
ordered that a certificate be granted her for obtaining a probate. {YCWI 1737-
1740:525}

William Rogers, of Yorkhampton Parish, York Co., merchant, left a will dated 16 May 1739 and proved 18 Feb 1739/40. To my wife, Theodosia Rogers, one silver salver, one large silver can with a coat of arms engraved thereon, a large silver soup spoon, two silver salts, and 11 silver spoons with a crest engraved thereon and all the china ware in the house and all the glasses belonging to the b? and all the table linen & sheets and all other linens used about my house, one white bed quilt worked at the four corners and in the middle with "SH" in a cypher and also my coach and four coach horses, also my clock and all my reading books. I give unto my wife in full of her dower two lots in the City of Williamsburgh together with the dwelling house and other houses thereunto belonging, and also a lot behind Cheshise's lot number 63 in York Town that I bought of Gwyn Reade during her life and after her death to go to my two daughters, Sarah & Hannah Rogers, and in case they both should die without heir then my wife shall dispose of them among my relations to whom she shall think proper. To my said wife, the following Negro slaves, *viz.* three men by name Waterford, Adam & Blackwall and one Negro woman named Betty and her child Peggy and two Negro girls by name Lucy & Molly and their increase during her life and after her death she shall divide them between my two daughters, Sarah & Hannah Rogers, and if they both should die without heir then my wife shall dispose of them among my relations. To my wife, one tract of land adjacent to Mountfort's Mill Dam in York Co. called *Tarripen Point* during her life and after her death to go to my son, Wm Rogers. To my wife, Theodosia Rogers, the [?] land that I bought of Edmund Smith except one chain and that to be laid off at the end next the lot that I bought of Francis Moss.... To my son, William Rogers, when he shall attain to the age of 21, all my lots in York Town where I now dwell and also the warehouse by the waterside and all other my lands except the lots & land before given to my wife. But in case he should die without heir, then I give the said lands, lots & houses to be divided between my three daughters, Susanna Reynolds, Sarah Rogers & Hannah Rogers. If my said daughters should die without heirs, then I do appoint my said lands, lots & houses to be sold by my executrix and the money to be divided amongst my brother's and sister's children. To my said son, Wm Rogers, six Negro men by name Joe, Tony, Harry, George, Tom & Jack and one India man named Pritty when my said son attains to the age of 21 and not before, and also one silver tea pot, two silver cans, two silver salts, six silver spoons, my silver hilted sword, watch & spurs and a young horse colt folded 4 May 1735. To my daughter, Susanna Reynolds, two Negro men by named York & London and one Negro woman named Phillis & her three children, Chloe, Kate & Rachel, and a Negro boy named Jemmy and their increase. To my daughter, Sarah Rogers, two Negro men by name Monmouth & Ben and one Negro woman named Phoeby and her four children Sary, Nanny, Cate & Frank and all their increase when she attains lawful age of day of marriage. In case Ben should be sold then the money should be laid out in buying another Negro for her. To my daughter, Hannah Rogers, three Negro men by name Barnaby, Samson & Quarco and one Negro woman named Nany and her three children Amy, Grace & Lazarus and all their increase when she attains to lawful age or day of marriage. All the rest of my personal estate be appraised and after my debts & funeral charges are paid then the surplus to be divided between my wife and three children, that is Wm Rogers, Sarah Rogers, & Hannah Rogers, and that in lieu of my daughter Susanna Reynolds' part of said remainder of my personal estate, I give unto her the lot I bought of Francis Moss, No. 75, together with the brick house and also one chain of the land that I bought of Edmund Smith to be taken at the end next the lot.... My wife to have the care of my daughters, Sarah & Hannah Rogers.... I appoint my wife executrix. Wits: John Ballard, James Mitchell, Wm Trotter.... {YCWI 1737-1740:537}

Pursuant to an order of court dated 17 Dec 1739, John Ballard, John Trotter & Ishmael Moody, being first sworn before Wm Nelson Junr gent, appraised the estate of Capt. Wm Rogers, decd. Negroes: Waterford, Betty, Adam, Blackwall, Nanny, Lazarus son of Nanny, Amy daughter of Nanny, Grace daughter of Nanny, Barnaby, Samson, Quaqua, Tony, Jo, York, Jack, George, Tom, Monmouth, London, Ben, Pretty, Phillis, Sarah, Harry, Lucy, Little Nanny, Pheby, Phill son of Pheby, Frank daughter of Pheby, Chloe, Kate, Moll, Cato, James, Peg. 1 clock, 1 silver hilt cutting sword, 1 pr silver spurs, 1 pea pot, 5 spoons, 2 pr cans, 2 salts of [?], a parcel of china ware, a peel glasses, 1 table, a peel books, a peel sheets, table linen and quilt, 1 silver solver, 1 pr cans, 2 salts, 11 spoons & 1 soup spoon, etc. 1224 pd 5 sl 6 pn … recorded 18 Feb 1739.... {YCWI 1737-1740:553}

The estate of Capt William Rogers, decd. Cash paid Mrs. Thomson attendance, Ben Hanson, Fra Moss cryer, Mrs. Read for rent, Matthew Langston, Mr. Parks, Edmund Smith, Dr. Wharton, Richard Smith, Revd. Mr. Fontain a sermon, Edward Potter, his sons expenses going over the river to settle with Noyel, Mrs. Ann Gibbons bread, Mary Philips making cloaths, Mrs. Packe for mourning, Mrs. Matthews for schooling, Dr. Gilmer, Mr. Needler, Wm Harwood ferryman, John Worledge, Jones Irwin, Aaron Phillips, Fra Moss, Mr. Ambler, Miles Cary, Henry Walters, Wm Dudley, Wm Sherington shaving your son, James Mitchell, Benja Catton, Col. Lightfoot, John Trotter, Everard Dowsing, Law Gibbons, John Alleson, Capt Thos Reynolds, Mat Hubard, Capt Ballard, Doctor Dixon, Mr. Nelson, Mr. Parks, Mr. Hacker, Mr. Nelson, Capt Nisbet, Doctor Payras, Mr. Butterworth, Mrs. William, Mr. Hewitt, Mr. Moody, Col. Braxton, Mr. Waller, Doctor Potter, tobacco paid Moss, Ben How per note, Fred Abbott, Col Lightfoot, Henry Weatherburne, lawyers fee agt Potter, Arthur Vanner. 397 pd 7 sl 10 pn. Cash received of Mrs. Sarah Packe, Capt Harwood,

Thos Goosley, Maj. Meade, Saml Rogers, Anthony Walke, Col. Bassett, Mat Kemp, Maj. William Claiborne, Capt John Wise, John Frazer, Thomas Beven, Wm Noyell, Charles Brown, John Marshall, Samuel Rogers. 569 pd 8 sl 6 pn. Errors excepted 14 Sep 1743 per Theodocia Rogers. In pursuance of an order of court Richd Ambler, Wm Nelson Junr & John Ballard have settled the account of the estate and report 122 pd 8 pn to be due to the said estate.... {YCWI 1740-1743:226}

On 21 Nov 1743, in the action of trespass upon the case between Edmond Dobson, plaintiff, and Thomas Reynolds & Theodocia Rogers, administrators of Wm Rogers, decd, defendants, the defendants say that the said deceased did not promise & assume upon himself as the plaintiff hath declared and the cause is continued for trial. {YCWI 1740-1743:235}

Theodosia Rogers, of Yorkhampton Parish, York Co., widow, left a will dated 27 Mar 1752 and proved 15 Jun 1752. I give all my estate both real and personal and all the remainder and reversions of any estate to me, limited or descending in England or elsewhere, to my son in law, William Montgomery, of Yorkhampton Parish, York Co., merchant. I appoint my said son in law, William Montgomery, executor ... William Montgomery, the executor, together with William Stevenson & James Mitchell his securities.... {YCWI 1745-1759:264}

In obedience to an order of court dated 15 Jun 1752, John Gibbons, Robt Sheild Junr & James Pride, being first sworn before Dudley Digges Junr gent, justice of the peace, appraised the slaves and personal estate of Theodosia Rogers, decd. One small mahogany table, 1 small black walnut table, 2 looking glasses, 1 corner cupboard, 1 clock, 1 silver can, 1 salver, 11 spoons, 1 soup spoon & pap spoon, 6 tea spoons, strainer, tongs, a parcel of china & glass, 1 tea board, etc. Negroes: Waterford, Betty, Pegg & her child Betty, Lucy & her child Phillis. 303 pd 9 sl. Ordered to be recorded 17 Aug 1752.... {YCWI 1745-1759:269}

William Rogers was the father of SARAH m. Wm Montgomery; HANNAH, d.s.p., intestate; SUSANNAH m. Thomas Reynolds; WILLIAM, d.s.p. aft 1742, intestate).

2. GEORGE ROGERS, of England, older brother of Capt. William (1) Rogers.

In Feb 1742, George Rogers, of Brantridin, Essex Co., coller maker, for £20, sold to Thomas Reynolds, of London, mariner, all such houses, messuages, lands, Negro slaves, horses, cattle, goods, debts, monies, effects & estate, both real and personal, due me by the death of William Rogers, the son of my younger brother, William Rogers, of VA, decd., whereas William Rogers, late of VA, merchant, decd., was in his lifetime younger brother to the said George Rogers and at the time of his death left an estate to his only son named, William Rogers, which said son died lately intestate so that right of law in said estate is

devolved and come unto the said George Rogers. Wits: Elias Waff, James
Beliker, Cha Seabrooke, Jas Newman. {YCLRD 1741-1754:64}

3. SARAH ROGERS, daughter of Capt. William (1) and Theodosia (N) Rogers,
m. William Montgomery.
     On 30 Jun 1752, John Snelson, of Hanover Co. merchant, and
Elizabeth, his wife, for £400, sold to John Norton, of York Town, York Co.
merchant, those lots of land in the Town of York which William Rogers, decd.,
devised to his wife Theodosia Rogers, being the lots the said William purchased
of Edmund Smith and Agnes, his wife, and Gwyn Reade part of the land and
premises which the said John Snelson purchased of William Montgomery and
Sarah, his wife, 29 Jun 1752. all which lands are in the possession and
occupation of the said John Norton. Wits: Dudley Digges Junr, Robert Burwell
et al.... {YCLRD 1741-1754:519}
     On 8 Aug 1759, Power of Attorney. Sarah Montgomery, widow, relict,
executrix & devisee of William Montgomery, the younger, late of the Town of
Camberwell, Saint Mary, Lambeth Parish, Surry Co., merchant, decd., whereas a
suit in Ejectment was brought and now is or lately was depending in some court
of law in VA in America wherein Solomon Saveall on the demise of the said
William Montgomery, the younger, and of me, Sarah, his then wife, was
plaintiff and Thomas Reynolds was defendant for a messuage, garden, stable,
pothouse, warehouse and 3 acres of arable land in Yorkhampton Parish, Town of
York, and whereas 20 Oct 1758 a verdict or judgment was given for the lessors
of the plaintiff in the said Ejectment for 1/2 of the premises together with 1
shilling damages besides costs, and whereas on 27 Oct 1758 the said William
Montgomery, the younger departed this life, but before his decease made his
will dated 10 May 1758, and amongst other things gave to the said Sarah, his
then wife, all his real and personal estate in VA and appointed the said Sarah
one of his executors who duly proved the same in the prerogative Court of
Canterbury in England as by the probate of the said will by these presents that
for the more convenient recovering, converting into money, collecting and
receiving all and every of my estate both real and personal in VA which I am
any wise entitled unto either as devisee or executrix of my said late husband
William Montgomery, the younger, or as heir to my late sister, Hannah, or as I,
[Sarah (Rogers) Montgomery], being one of the daughters of William Rogers,
the elder, formerly of the Town and Co of York, by virtue of his will or as
representative of my late brother, William Rogers, decd or in my own right, the
said Sarah Montgomery have appointed John Snelson, of Hanover Co, VA,
merchant, my atty to proceed in the suit of Ejectment to execution and take
possession of the said 1/2 of said premises and to sell and dispose thereof all my
right to the best bidder for the highest and best price.... 15 Sep 1760 in a Court

134

for York Co this Letter of Attorney with the deposition of the Rev. Doctor Kemp and the certificate of the Lord Mayor of London were on the motion of John Snelson, merchant, ordered to be recorded.... {YCLRD 1755-1763:280}

4. SUSANNA ROGERS, daughter of Capt. William (1) and Theodosia (N) Rogers, m. Thomas Reynolds.

On 7 Aug 1760, Susanna Reynolds, widow and relict of Thomas Reynolds, late of the Town and Co of York, merchant, decd, and Sarah Montgomery, widow and relict of Wm Montgomery, the younger, late of the Town of Camberwell in Saint Mary, Lambeth Parish, Surry Co, Great Britain, merchant, decd., for £384, sold to James Pride, of the Town of York, esqr. two lots of land in the Town of York also a warehouse or store house at the water side at said town whereas William Rogers, formerly of the Town of York, merchant, decd., was in his lifetime and at the time of his death seized amongst other things of two one-acre lots of land in the Town of York and also a warehouse or store house at the water side under the hill at the Town of York which by his will dated 16 May 1739 he bequeathed unto his son, William Rogers, when he should attain to the age of 21 and to his heirs forever, but in case he should die without heirs then he gave the lots and houses amongst other things to be divided between his three daughters, Susanna Reynolds, Sarah Rogers & Hannah Rogers to their heirs forever, and whereas the said William & Hannah Rogers both died intestate without issue by means whereof the said Susanna Reynolds and Sarah, who afterwards intermarried with the afsd William Montgomery, the younger, decd., became entitled to 1/2 of said lots and houses as by the judgment of the General Court of VA dated 20 Oct 1758 in an Ejectment.... [*signed*] Susanna Reynolds.... {YCLRD 1755-1763:267}

John Norton and David Jameson, acting executors of the will of Thomas Reynolds, late of the Town and Co of York, merchant, decd., and Susanna Reynolds, relict of the said Thomas Reynolds, for £30.5, sold to the Honourable William Nelson, esqr, of the Town and Co of York, a 25 acre tract of land ... whereas the said Thomas Reynolds was in his life time and at the time of his death seized in a 25 acre tract of land called *Tarrapin Point* between the brs of Mountforks Mill Dam in Yorkhampton Parish which formerly belonged to Wm Starke, who by deed of lease and release dated 14 & 15 Jan 1730, conveyed the same to William Rogers, then of the Town and Co of York, merchant, now decd., who by his will dated 16 May 1739 did devise the same among other things to his son, William Rogers, and the said William Rogers, the son, afterwards died intestate without issue whereby the said land descended to George Rogers, elder brother of the said William Rogers who conveyed the same to the said Thomas Reynolds, decd., and the said Thomas Reynolds, decd., and by his will dated 19 Oct 1756 did lend unto his said wife Susanna Reynolds,

during her natural life all his whole estate, real and personal and after her decease by a subsequent clause did direct that all his personal estate, Negroes, stock, a parcel of land at Cheescake bought of Hulett and all his other lands (except his houses and lots in York Town where he then lived which he desired might be leased out until his son was of lawful age) might be sold and ... the said Susanna Reynolds hath by these presents doth consent and agree to the immediate sale of the lands and premises afsd.... Ackn 18 May 1761....
{YCLRD 1755-1763:338}

OTHERS NAMED ROGERS

ADDUSTON ROGERS, child in 1737

On 16 May 1737, upon the petition of Adduston Rogers, he made choice of John Burcher as his guardian, who together with Lawrence Gibbons and Benjamin Moss, his securities, acknowledge his bond for the care of the said orphan's estate. {YCWI 1732-1737:359}

CHARLES ROGERS, d. ca 1772.

Appraisement of the estate of Charles Rogers, deceased, showed a total: £42.11.1. Appraised by Thos. Archer, B. Brown, William Cary and returned on 17 Feb 1772. {YCWI 1771-1783:60}

ELIZABETH (ELLIOTT) ROGERS, 1782 will

The will of John Elliot, of co. and parish of York, was written on 15 Feb 1782 and proved 21 Oct 1782. To son, George Elliott, 5 shillings. To son, Barnett Elliott, 5 shillings. To son John Elliott, 5 shillings. To dau., Elizabeth Rogers, 5 shillings. To wife use of my estate during her widowhood and after her decease or marriage the estate be equally divided between surviving children of my said wife. Extx. Wife.... Extx. Chivers Elliott made oath thereto and, with Allen Chapman and Bernard Elliott, her securities, entered into and acknowledge bond. Certificate was granted her for obtaining a probate in due form. {YCWI 1771-83:552}

GILES ROGERS, d. 1676 in Bruton Parish. {WARG:134}

JAMES ADDUSTON ROGERS

On 18 Jul 1743, Cyrus, a Negro boy belonging to James Adduston Rogers, was adjudged to be 12 years of age. {YCWI 1740-1743:203}

JOHN ROGERS, a child in 1756, appears to be boarded out to the Reynolds family.

136

Thomas Reynolds, of Yorkhampton Parish, York Co, VA, left a will dated 19 Oct 1756 and probated on 19 Nov 1759. I lend unto my wife, Susanna Reynolds, during her natural life all my whole estate, real and personal, after paying my debts, and after her decease, I give it as followeth, to my daughter, Anne Reynolds, one Negro wench named Chloe and her son Emanuel and also one Negro girl named Daphne, also 500 pd to be paid her at lawful age or day of marriage by my executors provided my wife should be dead and they have my estate in possession and in case my said daughter dies before of age or married her part of my estate to be divided between my daughter, Susanna, and my son, William. I give unto my daughter, Susanna Reynolds, one Negro woman named Phaebe and her daughter, Mary, and one Negro girl named Flora also 500 pd to be paid her at lawful age or day of marriage by my executors provided my wife be then dead and they have my estate in possession and in case my daughter dies before she is of lawful age or married her part to be divided between my daughter, Ann, and my son, William. I give unto my son, William Reynolds. all the rest and residue of my estate. My will is that all my personal estate, Negroes, stock & parcel of land at Chiscake bought of Huett, and all other my lands except my houses and lots in York Town where I now live (which I desire may be leased out until my son is of lawful age) may be sold and the monies to be put out to interest for the bringing up my said son William in a plain and decent way as my executors shall see it will afford and would have him educated in writing and accounts and the most useful branches of the mathematics as geometry, trigonometry, gangeing [gauging?], dialing, surveying, gunnery, with a knowledge of the French tongue if to be got as far as time will permit until he is of proper age to put out an apprentice when I desire if it suits his inclination to have him bound to a good trading merchant such as trade to sea or not liking that to any other creditable business. If my son dies before he attains the age of 21, I desire his part of my estate may go to my daughters Ann & Susanna and their heirs and if they both die and leave no children, my executors to divide that pt/o my estate between John Rogers a child now living with me and the children of my near kinsman Humphry Hill. I appoint my friends John Norton and David Jameson of York Town and Humphry Hill of King & Queen Co executors. At a court held 20 Aug 1759 this will was produced in court by John Norton gent one of the executors.... {YCWI 1745-1759:525}

JOHN ADDUSTON ROGERS, d. ca 1743.
On 20 Jun 1743, a settlement of the estate of John Adduston Rogers, deceased, was ordered to be recorded. {YCWI 1740-1743:193}
In obedience to an order of court dated 16 May 1743, the subscribers have settled an account of the estate of John Adduston Rogers, deceased: Paid Thos Nelson, Doctor Alexr Maver, Benjamin Moss, Richard Bellamy, James

Dixon, John Johnston, Wm Robertson, Kathrine Sheldon, Mary Thomas, Thomas Powell, <u>Samuel Rogers</u>, Margaret Lyal, <u>Ann Rogers</u>, Thos Presser, John Powers, Judith Burrodale, Albrighton Wagstaff. 42 pd 2 sl 5 pn. Balance due the estate: 11 pd 7 sl 11 pn.... {YCWI 1740-1743:198}

JOHN ROGERS, buried 30 Sep 1685, was a servant to Anthony Butts. {CPR}

MARGARET (GOLDEN) ROGERS will 1776
Margret Rogers, of York Co. in Charles Parish, left a will dated 15 Jun 1776 and proved 18 Jun 1781. To grandson, Edmund Cross, all my estate when he arrives to age 21, or marries. If he dies before arriving at lawful age or married, then my estate to be divided between brother, John Golden, and my three sisters, Ann Worley, Elizabeth Golden, and Lydia Golden.... {YCWI 1760-83:573a}

MARY ROGERS m. Robert Jones, and was a sister of James Rogers.
Thomas Whitehead left a will dated 6 Apr 1669 and proved 23 May 1660. Mary Rogers, extx. and to have my plantation, all goods and mares. To my Negro man, John, my wearing clothes and set him free, 2 cows, horse and ground to plant, also, to be guardian of Mary Rogers till she be of age. If she dies, to her brother, James [Rogers], if both die, to my Negro. {RB 1659-1662:82}
Thomas Whitehead, by will, bequeathed on 26 Oct 1668, to John Wycapo, a house and grounds for life, Wycapo complaining that Robert Jones, who married Mary Rogers, extx. of deceased, refused performance of said will. {RB 1665-1672:307}
Andrew Ryder ordered on 12 Nov 1660 as guardian of Mary Rogers to deliver to Robert Jones, who married said Mary, whole estate belonging to her from the will of Thomas Whitehead, deceased. {RB 1659-1662:94}

RICE ROGERS, 1661
Mrs. Francis Bouth was granted a certificate on 26 Aug 1661 for 2000 acres due for the importation of 40 persons into this colony: Rice Rogers et al. {RB 1659-1662:126}

RICHARD ROGERS, ca 1698
An inventory of the estate of John Wooding, decd.: 1 Negro man, 1 Negro woman, 3 Negro children. 25 head of cattle, 1 gelding, 2 mares, 2 feather beds, 2 rugs, 2 blankets, 1 bolster, 2 pillows, 1 old sheet, chest, 2 tables, 2 wooden chairs, carpenters tools, etc. A list of debts belonging to ye estate: William Kerby, Willm Dorman, [pg torn], Richard Rogers, William [?]. Presented in court 24 Aug 1698 by [?] Burk & Eliz his wife.... {YCWI 1698-1702:88}
The suite between Joseph Ring plt agt Richard Rogers def in an action of

debt for 7 pd 3 sl 7 pn per bill is dismist no further prosecution had. {YCWI 1698-1702:389}

SAMUEL ROGERS

See sections on Capt. William (1) Rogers and, under "OTHERS NAMED ROGERS," John Aduston Rogers, d. 1743.

SARAH ROGERS

On 12 Oct 1750, Martha Satterwhite, of Henrico Co, VA, for natural love and affection, give unto my beloved son, Mann Satterwhite & daughter, Sarah Rogers, and to my beloved granddaughter, Martha Rogers, to the said Mann Satterwhite & Sarah Rogers 12 Negroes, to wit, Sarah, Phil, Jaban, Bess, Moll, Jimmy, Tom, Jack, Milly & Frank, also Robin & boy Phill son of Bess with all their future increase, and to my granddaughter, Martha Rogers, one Negro girl, named Sal, with all her future increase, also to the said Mann Satterwhite & Sarah Rogers all other of my personal estate (except one feather bed with the furniture which I give to my son Mann Satterwhite before any division of my estate be made). The said Mann Satterwhite, Sarah Rogers & Martha Rogers shall not be entitled to any of the afsd estate till after my decease. Wits: Samuel Reade, R. Hurst.... {YCLRD 1741-1754:408}

WILLIAM ROGERS

On 17 Aug 1741, upon the prayer of John Ballard, it's ordered that Wm Rogers be appointed surveyor of York Town in the room of the said John Ballard who now resigns that office. {YCWI 1740-1743:51}

WILLIAM ADUSTON ROGERS

John Burcher exhibited an account against the estate of Wm Adduston Rogers and ordered to be recorded. {YCWI 1737-1740:649}

On 19 Jul 1756, William Aduston Rogers, of lawful age being first sworn, deposeth that he was a witness to a will made by John Burcher, deceased, in about the year 1745, and that Walter Chapman, deceased, was also witness to the said will and that since that time he has been with him the said Burcher in several fits of illness and never heard him propose making any other will alleging that he was very well satisfied with the will that he had already made for that what he had got came by his wife and that he thought she had the best right to it as long as she lives and this deponent further saith upon reading the said will since the death of the said John Burcher remembers that his whole estate was given to his widow and after her decease to be divided among his children and that his estate was not to be appraised nor his widow who was appointed executrix to give security. Sworn to 7 Jun 1756 before Thos Reynolds & John Norton. {YCWI 1745-1759:405}

John Burcher left a will on 1 Jun 1782 and proved 17 Jun 1782. Estate to be given equally to two sons, namely John Burcher and William Burcher, and, if my sons should die before they arrive to lawful age or marriage, then I give my estate to my father in law, John Garson, and the other half to be divided amongst my brothers and sisters, namely William Adruston Rogers; Barbara Rogers and the children of Charles Shields decd; Ann Hay and the issues of James Burcher, decd; and Mary Sharlock and Clara Burcher. To give five dollars towards a meeting house, five dollars to Mr. John Dunn. Execs. friends John Garson, William Garson and Edward Moss Junr. Negroes to have the liberty of choosing their masters…. {YCWI 1771-1783:510}

Estate of John Moss, decd., to Wm. A. Rogers. Payments: £834.6.9. mount in specie brought forward: £45.16.6. To 7½ barrels of corn £4.10. Examined by Wm. Moss, Allen Chapman. Returned 21 Oct 1782. {YCWI 1771-1783:558}

WILLIAM ROGERS, 1660s-1690s

Mr. Joseph Croshaw was granted a certificate on 24 Apr 1662 for 800 acres due for the importation of 16 persons into this Colony: William Rogers et al. {RB 1659-1662:161}

William Rogers (or Royers) imported in the *Concord*, Capt. Thomas Grantham, Commander. Servant to Mr. John Duke and adjudged on 24 Jan 1675/6 to be 15 years of age, to serve to 24. {RB 1672-1676:140}

Execution against the estate of Wm Rogers on 30 Nov 1697. Six gallons cider, corn, 2 gallons mord for bills, Mr. Rogers, for Hayles. 145 lbs tobacco. On 22 Dec 1699 it was ordered that William Roberts pay to John Rogers 129 lbs of tobacco, it being the balance of all accounts the plaintiff hath made oath & that the defendant pay the same with costs…. {YCWI 1698-1702:128}

THE REVEREND JAMES SCLATER[33] FAMILY

1. REV. JAMES SCLATER, will 29 Nov 1721, d. 19 Nov 1723, will proved 17 Aug 1724, m. Mary (N) (will 27 May 1737, d. 5 Jan 1744, will proved 21 Jan 1744), and was a son of John Sclater, of Oxford, England. {CPR; Will Book, xvi:298 cited in VC:171-172; YCWI 1743-1746:342}

Rev. James Sclater, who succeeded Rev. Thomas Finney (d. 8 Dec 1686), as minister of Charles Parish in 1686, was a son of John Sclater, City of Oxford. James matriculated at Oxford, 14 Nov 1673, at age 16, and received his

---

[33] This name is also spelled Slater, Slaughter, Selator, Selater in the records examined for this volume.

B.A. degree in 1677 and M.A. in 1680. James is documented as having provided services at Mulberry Island Parish, Warwick Co., and at Bruton Parish. In 1688, he had a civil suit with Edward Thomas, a prominent Quaker, in which Thomas accused Sclater of blasphemy. Sclater prevailed and was awarded £50. {CPR}

Mr. James Slater was granted a certificate on 24 Jan 1690/1 for the transportation of 5 persons: Thomas, Maria, Bridgett, Phillip, Will and Jack. {DW 1687-1691:526}

John Eaton and Mary, his wife, Deed sold 15,722 acres purchased of Robert Calvert on 23 Jun 1690 acknowledged by them on 25 Sep 1693 to Mr. James Sclater. {DW 1691-1694:252}

On 25 Mar 1695 it was proved that Mr. James Sclater transferred power of attorney to his wife, Mary Sclater, via a letter dated 10 Jan 1694. {DW 1694-1697:119}

Judeth, Phillis and Marea, 3 Negro girls imported in the ship, *Endeavor*, servants to Mr. James Sclater, were adjudged on 24 Nov 1697 each of them to be 8 years of age. {DW 1694-1697:474}

On 23 Jun 1698, David Lewis, of Charles Parish, farmer, let to James Sclater, clerk of same parish, for 400 lbs of tobacco with cask, a 60 acre parcel of land between Quarter Field Br & Copeling Br in Charles Parish.... {YCWI 1698-1702:90}

On 27 Jul 1703, James Sclater, of York Co., clk, do appoint my wife, Mary Sclater, my atty to ask for, recover & receive from any person within this country all such sums of money, tobacco or anything else that now is or hereafter shall be due and owing unto me from any person.... Wits: Henry Hayward Junr, James Hyde, John Johnson. Proved 24 Dec 1703.... {YCWI 1702-1704:164}

Thomas Harwood, of Charles Parish York Co., gent., left a will dated Jan 1699 that was proved 24 May 1700. To Harwood Cary, eldest son to Major William Cary, of Warwick Co, 50 pd. To my friends, Major Williams & Martha, his wife, to each of them a ring of 20 sl price. To friends, James Sclater, minister of Charles Parish, and Mary, his wife, each of them a ring of 20 sl price.... {YCWI 1698-1702:345}

On 1 Jun 1702, Ralph Walker did make over all my right, title & interest in [a parcel of land] unto James Sclater & do oblige myself & wife to ackn the same to James Sclater the next court held in York Co in consideration of £38.... {YCDB 1701-1708:34}

Order for a probate of the will of William Pattison was granted unto Margret Pattison, his relict, and Margret, his daughter, they being appointed executrixes & proved by the oaths of James Sclater, William Shelldon & Elizabeth Griffin, witnesses, and is ordered to be committed to record and is further ordered that ye testator's estate be appraised by Edward Moss, John

Wythe, Bazill Wagstaff & Peter Goodwin. {YCWI 1702-1704:103}

On 24 Mar 1702, on motion of James Sclater concerning a false date by him made in writing ye will of Ralph Walker, decd, is ordered that the said Sclater amend ye date according to his true meaning. {YCWI 1702-1704:104}

On 27 Jul 1703, James Sclater, of York Co. clk., do appoint my wife, Mary Sclater, my attorney to ask for, recover & receive from any person within this country all such sums of money, tobacco or anything else that now is or hereafter shall be due and owing unto me from any person.... Wits: Henry Hayward Junr, James Hyde, John Johnson. Proved 24 Dec 1703.... {YCWI 1702-1704:164}

On 19 Apr 1705, Thomas Wheatly of Bromsly, St. Leonard in the Co. of Middlesex, Gent., gave power or attorney to James Slater, minister of Charles Parish near York River in Virginia, my true and lawful Attorney for me ... to ask demand and receive (in case of the death of my brother Soloman Wheatly in Virginia and not otherwise) debts or merchandise due unto me or to my said late brother ... and to secure his Estate unto me as I am Executor of his Will. Wits: Will Blackbourn, Francis Mackemie, Jonathan Hide, Thomas Harwar. {YCWI 1709-1711:44,50}

At court held 24 Aug 1705, James Slater, clk, bringing his servant Richard Sallaway imported in her Majesty's ship, *Faulkland,* for judgment of his age, who upon examination confessed to be 8 years old on 7 Jan last which is so adjudged by ye court. {YCWI 1705-1706:347}

Richard Browne, being ... bound with Peter Wagoner, his security, to ye Queen for 10 pd to make his personal appearance at this court to answer to such things as should be alleged against him & to stand to & abide ye award & judgment of this court against whom James Sclater appeared to inform this court against him & alleged that said Brown whilst said Slater was absent was of ill behavior towards the said Slater's wife both in word & deed miscalling and abusing of her in most scurrilory [scurrilous?] language and staring and frightening her with his unseemly action immodest to declare and likewise that he hath been of ill behavior towards the said Slater's person by hurling of billets of word over said Slater's head & that said Brown upon his bended knees at ye bar confessing himself sorry for his misdeeds ye said Slater assented that said Brown should be dismissed. {YCWI 1705-1706:353}

On 24 Mar 1706, Thomas Ballard & Willm Buckner, trustees to the Port Land of York Towne in York Co gent, for 180 lbs of tobacco, sold to James Sclater, of same place, clerk, a lot or ½ acre of land in York Towne being part of the Port Land, number 70, as by the plat on the records of the said company doth appear the said lot containing 10 poles in length & 8 in breadth ... provided the said James Sclater shall & do, within 12 months, build & finish on the said lot a house to contain at least 20' wherein if he fail this present grant to be void in law.... {YCDB 1701-1708:232}

On 25 Jun 1707, Daniel Taylor did assign over from me & my heyres to James Sclater & his heirs [a patent] forever having received a valuable consideration for the same. Wits: Hen Hayward Junr, Samll Selden, Thomas Walker ... by Danll Taylor & Mary, his wife.... {YCDB 1701-1708:241}

On 7 Jan 1707, Michael MacCormack, of York Parish & Co, for £5, sold to John Brooks, of same place, taylor, the ½ part of his lot or ½ acre of land being Portland in York Town, abutting on the now dwelling house of the said Michael MacCormack & the lot belonging to James Sclater, known by the number 31.... {YCDB 1701-1708:266}

On 22 Jul 1709, Elizabeth Varnum, of Denbeigh Parish, Warwick Co, widow, for 5 shillings, leased to William Sheldon, of York Hampton Parish, York Co, planter, a messuage & a 100 acre tract of land in Charles Parish being part of the plantation whereon the said Elizabeth Varnum did once live, bounded by the land of Capt Thomas Nutting & James Sclater ... for the term of one year.... {YCDB 1709-1713:323}

At a Court held for York Co on Jun 25 Jun 1707, James Sclater, his Deed of Assignment bearing date under the hand and seal of Capt. Daniel Taylor and Mary, his wife, this present Instant for the Portland lot in York Towne no. 25, was this day by the said Daniel and Mary personally acknowledged in Court.... {YCWI 1706-1710:76}.

John Andrews, of Great Yarmouth, in the Co. of Norfolk, merchant, eldest son and heir of John Andrews, late of Great Yarmouth aforesaid, merchant, deceased, who was the eldest brother and heir of Henry Andrews, late of these presents, to James Sclater, my true and lawful Attorney to recover lands and heridaments inherited by me from the late Henry Andrews, in Virginia ... 11 Jul 1707.... {YCWI 1706-1710:147}

On 24 Sep 1709, the difference between Henry Hayward Junr. and James Sclater, Clerk, referred to the Court by Robt. Reade and Wm. Buckner, relating to the said Sclater's maliciously scandalizing and defaming the said Hayward by publicly calling and declaring him to be a whoremaster, a ravisher and a rogue, at the said Hayward's motion is dismissed. {YCWI 1706-1710:251}

On 24 Sep 1709, the Court, on hearing the complaint of James Sclater, clerk, and Mary, his wife, against Mary Davis, Eliz. Jones and Susannah Lovell (for their reporting several scandalous and reproachful speeches), their submission and acknowledgment were of opinion that they ought to be discharged and thereupon dismissed the said difference. {YCWI 1706-1710:252}

On 24 Jun 1710, the action upon the case between Henry Hayward Junr. and Edward Tabb, Church Wardens of Charles Parish, plaintiffs, and James Sclater, defendant, is dismissed at the plaintiff's request. {YCWI 1709-1711:17}

Daniell Taylor of Charles Parish left a will dated 14 Dec 1705 and proved 17 Nov 1712. To my cousin, Eliz. Merry, a Negro boy named George.

To my two cousins, Martha and Mary Swinie and my goddaughter, Mary Sclater, 20 shillings a piece to buy them a ring. James Sclater to have 20 shillings to buy him a ring. If my cousin, Thomas Gardiner, comes into Virginia after my decease, then he to have £10 to buy him mourning, but if he comes not in person, then this legacy to be void. To my loving wife, Mary Taylor, all the remainder of my Estate whatsoever and she to be sole Extx.... Wits: John MackDaniell, James Hyde and Mary Sclater.... {YCWI 1711-1714:201}

    James Sclater, Clerk and Minister of Charles Parish, York Co., left a will dated 29 Nov 1721 and proved 17 Aug 1724. After provision for my sons, John and James, and daughters, Martha Brodie and Mary Tabb and a legacy to William Tabb [son of his deceased daughter, Elizabeth], I give to my grandson, Doyley Cary, a negro boy named Daniel. I give unto my grandson, Henry Cary, a negro boy named Jacob.... Wife Mary and sons John and James, Execs. {Will Book, xvi:298 cited in VC:171-172}

    On 7 May 1725, Joseph Stacy, of Charles Parish, York Co., planter, & Mary, his wife, for 5 shillings, leased unto James Sclater, of same place gent, all that 130 acre parcel of land which Simon Stacy father of the said Joseph Stacy purchased of Robert Sheild Senr & Mary, his wife, in the Oak Swamp in parish formerly called New Poquoson Parish, but now Charles Parish, bounded by the land of Henry Hayward, land of John Nixon & land of John Eaton, being sold out of the original patent by Robert Calvert being part of 375 acres of land granted by patent to the said Robert Calvert in 1687, 300 acres of the said land being formerly taken up & patented by William Calvert & patented 26 Jan 1663, the other 75 acres taken up by the said Robert Calvert ... for the term of one year paying the rent of one ear of Indian corn at the feast of St. Michael the Arch Angel now next ensuing if demanded.... Wits: Francis Hayward, Robert Ballard.... {YCDB 1713-1729:441}

    On 21 Jan 1744, upon the prayer of John Brodie, gent, & making oath well & truly to administer the estate of James Sclater, clk deceased, (which was not administered by Mary Sclater, his widow, now deceased), and giving bond & security, ordered that a certificate be granted him for obtaining a Letter of Administration on his estate with the will annexed. {YCWI 1743-1746:338}

    Mary Sclater, of York Co., left a will dated 27 May 1737 and proved 21 Jan 1744. To my cousin, Martha Cary, one feather bed with cover, rug, blanket & 2 sheets, etc. and some of my wearing apparel at the discretion of my daughter. To my granddaughter, Mary Sclater, my silver tankard when she comes to age 21 or married, but if she dies I give it to my grandson, William Sclater, and my desire is he have his father's picture now in my possession. All my cattle & sheep to John Tabb for my granddaughter, Mary Brodie. To my granddaughters, Mary Tabb & Mary Brodie, all my silver plate. If they die before they come of age or marry, I give the said plate to the next sister of theirs. Also to my granddaughters, Mary Tabb & Mary Brodie, 40 pd that was left to my disposal by my husband, James Sclater. But if my granddaughter, Mary Tabb, dies before she comes of age or marries, the said 20 pd to her sister Elizabeth Tabb, and if she dies, I give it to Rachel Tabb, and if my granddaughter, Mary Brodie, dies before she comes of age, then I give the 20 pd to her sister, Martha Brodie, and if she dies to Sarah Brodie. To my grandson, Richard Sclater, one Negro boy named Bob, but if he dyes before he is of age 21 and without issue, then to his brother, William Sheldon Sclater, but if both die, to return to my estate and be divided amongst the children of John Tabb & John Brodie. To my granddaughter, Mary Tabb, two young Negroes named Frank & Phillis, but if she dies then to my granddaughters, Elizabeth Tabb & Rachel Tabb. To my granddaughter, Mary Brodie, one Negro named Charles which I formerly gave her on consideration of her father's care of my family. Also to granddaughter, Mary Brodie, one Negro girl named Peg, but if she dies then to my granddaughter, Martha Brodie. To my granddaughter, Martha Brodie, one Negro girl named Rachel, but if she dies then to Sarah Brodie. All my other estate to be divided amongst the children of James Sclater & John Tabb & John Brodie. I appoint John Tabb & John Brodie, executors. I give one heifer to Martha Cary. Wits: John Tabb, John Brodie, Wm James.... {YCWI 1743-1746:342}

In obedience to an order of court dated 21 Jan 1744 and recorded on 19 Jan 1746, Peter Goodwin, Merritt Moore, Edward Tabb & Thomas Tabb appraised the estate of James and Mary Sclater, deceased, *viz.* 3 feather beds & furniture, 6 cane chairs, 2 chest draws, 1 table, a trunk, 1 brass tongs & shovel, etc. Negroes: woman Dinah, man Ned, man Jimmy, woman Beck & child, boy Bob, man Humphrey, girl Phillis, girl Peg, man Pompey, boy Fran.... {YCWI 1745-1759:52)

Mary Sclater, daughter of Rev. James Sclater of Charles Parish, m. Col. John Tabb of Elizabeth City Co. Their daughter, Mary Tabb, m. Westwood Armistead (d. leaving a will dated 9 Feb 1756). {CD186, Armistead Family:130}

James and Mary (N) Sclater were parents of ELIZABETH, b. 10 Nov 1688; JOHN, b. 10 May 1691; MARY, b. 2 Apr 1692, m. Col. John Tabb; SARAH, b. 11 Jan 1695, m. Henry Cary; JAMES, b. 6 Dec 1697; MARTHA, b. 22 Jul 1700, m. John Brody; MARY, b. 16 Oct 1702. {CPR}

2. RICHARD SCLATER, d. 7 Nov 1718 {CPR}, m. Mary (Nutting) (b. 7 Jan 1682, d. 30 Dec 1735) {CPR}

On 23 May 1704, John Heyward, of Charles Parish, York Co., schoolmaster, do appoint my beloved friend, Richard Slater, of same place, planter, to acknowledge these writings drawn betwixt William Roe, of the afsd parish, planter, and the said John Heyward to be my own proper act & deed & I do hereby grant unto my attorney Richard Slater as afsd full power & authority for me in my name to acknowledge the same .... Wits: John Chapman, William

Row.... {YCWI 1701-1708:108}

On 24 May 1704, William Roe, his deed of assignment of 125 acres of land from John Heyward, was acknowledged by Richard Sclater, attorney of said Heyward, which assignment with ye patent annexed, is ordered committed to record. {YCWI 1702-1704:203}

Richard Slater, his action of case against Damazinah Dixon, Executrix of Richard Dixon, deceased, is dismissed per non prosecution. {YCWI 1706-1710:19}

Thomas Nutting, of Charles Parish, York Co., left a will dated 11 Jul 1717 and proved 16 Sep 1717. To my daughter, Jane Nutting & her heirs, all that plantation & tract of land whereon I now dwell. But in case that there be no such heirs, then I give sd plantation to my granddaughter, Eliza Slater. To my daughter, Kath Sheldon & her heirs, all my plantation & tract of land at ye head of Charles River adjacent to Hayward's Mill. But in case my said daughter, Katherine, die without such issue, I give said plantation to my son in law, Wm Sheldon during his natural life ... To my son in law, Richard Slater, my seal ring, cane & sword. To my son in law, Jno Doswell, one gold ring marked "PS" ... To my granddaughter, Eliz Slater, two Negro children called Will & Judy being ye children of my Negro woman Frank. All ye rest of my estate (after my debts & legacies paid & my wife's due & lawful share deducted) I give unto my three daughters, Mary Slater, Katherine Sheldon & Jane Nutting, but in case my said daughter, Mary Slater, should depart this life before such division shall be made, then my will is that ye part give to her shall be divided among her three children, Elizabeth, Agnes & Mary, to remain in ye hands of my executor until they shall attain to lawful age or marriage. If it shall please God my said daughter, Mary Slater, shall live to receive & enjoy said part of my estate it is my will that it be paid & delivered to her on ye condition hereafter mentioned & not otherwise during her natural life & after her decease to be divided as afsd among her three children. My will is ye true intent & meaning of this my will that in case my said daughter, Eliz Doswell, & my said daughter, Mary Slater, shall refuse (or either of them) to give such sufficient discharge for their or either of said legacies as shall be to ye good liking & satisfaction of my executor, then in such case said legacies before given, to be void & each party so refusing to have & enjoy no more of my estate then 1 sl & said legacies before given to return to my said daughter, Jane Nutting. I appoint my son in law, Wm Sheldon, and my daughter, Jane Nutting, executors. Wits: Robert Kerby, Thomas Kerby, Robert Kerby Junr.... {YCWI 1716-1718:163}

In ... court on 16 Sep, William Row, Peter Manson & Thos Roberts Junr have inventoried & appraised the estate of Capt. Thomas Nutting, deceased, being first sworn before Thomas Roberts, justice of the peace, & at the request of the persons concerned have made a division of the said estate. To Madam Nutting ... To Willm Sheldon ... 102 pd 19 sl 6 pn. To Richard Slater's children: 4 feather beds, bolster, sheets, pillows & pillow cases, 1 quilt, 1 woolen rug, 1 blanket, 3 old curtains, 1 old vallins, 1 chest, 2 chairs, 6 head of cattle, 1 young Negro, 1 tin pan, 3 pewter pans, 1 hour glass, 1 clock, 1 iron pot, 1 iron skillet, 1 brass skillet, etc. 102 pd 19 sl 6 pn. William Sheldon executor presented in court the within inventory & appraisement on 18 Mar 1717.... {YCWI 1716-1718:239}

The will of Richard Slater, deceased, was presented by Wm Sheldon & Katherine, his wife, two of the executors who made oath to it (Eliza Nutting the other executrix having relinquished her right to the executorship) & being proved by the oaths of Robert Kirby & Wm Wise, witnesses thereto, is admitted to record together with the rough draught thereof, they having together with Wm Stark & John Gibbons, their securities entered into & ackn their bond, certificate is granted them for obtaining a probate ... 16 Nov 1718.... {YCWI 1716-1718:338}

Richard Slater's rough will: To daughter, Elizabeth Sclater, one Negro man named Isaac. To my daughter, Agness Bates, one Negro woman together with the child she now goes with. To my daughter, Mary Slater, three young Negroes named Phillis, Sarah & Jenny ... My will is that my two eldest daughters remain where they are & my youngest daughter go to her grandmother to remain with her during her grandmother's life if she will let her & the child be willing to stay & after her decease to go to her Aunt Jane to be brought up to school & maintained out of her estate. To my daughter, Elizabeth Slater, a four year old colt branded "M" as also the seal ring that was her grandfathers. To my daughter, Mary, my other seal ring. After my debts & funeral expenses be paid all the remaining part of my estate, viz. household goods, cattle, sheep, hogs, etc. with money in England I give to my three daughters, Elizabeth, Agnes & Mary. I appoint my friends, A: & B, to be sole executors. This rough draught of the will of Richard Slater, deceased, was presented in court 17 Nov 1718 by William Sheldon & Katherine, his wife, executors, who made oath to it. Elizabeth Nutting, the other executor, having relinquished her right to the executorship & being proved by the oaths of Robt Kerby & William Wise is admitted to record.... {YCWI 1716-1718:350}

Richard Slater, of Charles Parish, York Co., left a will dated 7 Nov 1718. To my daughter, Elizabeth Slater, one Negro woman aged 25 named Jaccae. To my daughter, Agnes Slater, one Negro woman named Phillis together with a Negro child to her the sd Negro belonging being her youngest child. To my daughter, Mary Slater, three (sic) young Negroes named Phillis & Jennie. My will is that what Negro children my Negro woman Hester shall bring after my daughter Agnes becomes marriageable or of age, my will is that such Negroes if any born shall properly belong to my youngest daughter, Mary Slater. My will is that my two eldest daughters, Elizabeth & Agnes, do remain the [?] with her grandmother during she comes of age or is marriagable & the next daughter to remain with her uncle & aunt William Sheldon & Katharine, his wife, until she comes of age or is marriageable. My will is that my youngest daughter, Mary Slater, do continue with her grandmother during her grandmother's life if she will let her & the child be willing to stay & after her decease to return to her uncle & aunt, John & Jane Lowry. To my daughter, Elizabeth Slater, a four year old colt branded with "M" as also the sealed ring that was her grandfather's. To my daughter, Agnes Slater, a ring that was her mother's. I give to my daughter, Mary Slater, my other seal ring which I did formerly wear. When all my debts & funeral expenses are paid out of my estate, *viz.* household goods, cattle, sheep, hogs, & what money my three daughters, Elizabeth, Agnes & Mary, have in England either in any merchant's hand in London to be divided among my afsd three daughters. I constitute & ordain William Sheldon & Elizabeth Nutting & Katharin Sheldon, my executors. Wits: Robert Kerby, Henry Wise, William Wise ... 17 Nov 1718 ... proved.... {YCWI 1718-1720:351}

In obedience to an order of court dated 17 Nov, John Sclater, Gerd Roberts & Benja Clifton hath appraised the estate of Richard Slater, deceased, so far as the executors hath brought before us. 2 steers, 8 cows, 4 heifers, 1 bull, 20 sheep, 6 shoats, 18 hogs, 1 young riding horse, 1 yoke of draft oxen, old cart & wheels, 5 weanable pigs, 12 very good Russia chairs, 1 large looking glass, 3 tables, feather beds, Flanders tick[34], pillows & cases, bolsters, rugs, surveyor's instruments, etc.... Presented in court 16 Feb 1718.... {YCWI 1718-1720:402}

..... York County Nov 19 1722
..... ith Wm Sheldon
..... Blair, Wm Stark, Edw Tabb, Gen[tlemen]
..... between James Selater and Eliza his wife [daughter of Richard Sclater]
..... and Mary Selater deft for ten
..... deft refusing to permit to be divided
..... house and three hundred acres of
..... parish of Charles in this County of
..... [Richard] Selater father of ye sd Eliza wife of Jas.
Selator ... Mary one third whereof doth appertain to ye said ... and ye heirs of her body begotten in fee and ye ... Agnes and Mary [children of Richard Sclater] by ye Curtes ye & as in ye deceased ... expressed and ye said Wm Sheldon came into Court ... any but that he holds the Mannor and ... ye declaration ... for ye said Agnes and Mary with ... that partition ought to be made ye plts ... therefore it is commanded to ye sheriff that twelve good and ... full men of his Baliwick who are not concerned or have affinity or consanguinity to ye parties or lie adjacent to any ... company with ye said Surveyor of the County he cause to ... manner and Lands aforesaid between ye ... according to ye quantity and

[34] Cotton cloth

148

value thereof ... same to ye next Court
{YCWI 1720-1722:162}

   The will of William Sheldon, of the parish of York Hampton in the
County of York, was written on 7 Apr 1727 and proved 15 May 1727 ... being
very Sick & weak ... to Wife Katherine [Nutting] Sheldon all my whole Estate
during her Natural life.... It is my desire that William Sheldon ... [*missing*]
Aunt until he comes to the Age of twenty one years ... [*missing*] then William
Sheldon ... [*missing*] & his Male ... [*missing*] heirs to the next of kin to me and
So to remain in the name of the Sheldon. To Wife, one Negro woman named
Racher. To Agnes Slater, one Negro woman named Ester. To Mary Slater, one
Negro Girl named Nelle, not to possess the negro woman until they are married.
To my Cousin, Elizabeth Conier, fifty pounds in Mr. Perry's hands to be
delivered within one year after my decease if my cousin Elizabeth Conier comes
in person to receive it, otherwise not. Item, I give unto my Cousin Mary
Lansdale fifty pounds in Mr. Perry's hands to be delivered within one year after
my decease if my Cousin Mary Lansdale comes in person to receive it,
otherwise not. Item, I give unto my Goddaughter, Anne Pamer, five pounds. To
Anne Southerland, two barrels of Indian corn yearly to be paid by my Executrix
as long as she lives she always to fetch it away yearly before Christmas. If
William Sheldon should die under age or without male issue, then the plantation
where I live I lend unto Mary Selator during her natural life, the daughter of
Richard Slater.... {YCWI 1725-1727:456-457}

   On 16 May 1729, Daniel Moore & Elizabeth, his wife, of York Co., for
5 shillings, leased to Edward Tabb, of York Co, an 85 acre tract of land being
the said Daniel Moore & Elizabeth, his wife, purparty of 327 acres now in the
occupation of the said Daniel Moore being on the narrows of Old Poquoson
River in Charles Parish it being formerly the inheritance of Booth Nutting, of
said parish, & descending from the said Booth Nutting to Mary Slater, sister &
coheir to the said Booth Nutting, deceased, and so descending to Elizabeth
Moore. wife of the said Daniel Moore and daughter of the said Mary Sclater,
deceased ... for the term of one year paying the rent of one grain of Indian corn
at the feast of St. Michael the Arch Angel if.... {YCDB 1713-1729:515}

   On 17 Aug 1739, Daniel Moore, of Charles Parish, York Co., planter,
for 5 shillings, leased to Gawton Hunt, of Abingdon Parish, Gloster Co., planter,
a 200 acre tract of land in Charles Parish adjacent Poquoson River, Thos Clifton,
land late of Wm Ferguson deceased, land late of John Hay deceased, said
Gawton Hunt & said Daniel Moor, being part of 329 acres purchased by the said
Daniel Moore from the daughters of Elizabeth Nutting, deceased, and the
daughters of Richard & Mary Selater, deceased ... for the term of 1 year paying
the rent of one ear of Indian corn on the last day of said year if demanded....
{YCLRD 1729-1740:565}

Richard and Mary (Nutting) Sclater were parents of <u>ELIZABETH</u>, b. 4 Oct 170[3?], m. James Sclater; <u>AGNES</u>, b. 26 May 1707; <u>MARY</u>, b. 9 Mar 1712, m. Samuel Reade; SARAH, b. 8 Dec, bapt. 9 Dec 1716, d. 19 Jan 1716/7. {CPR}

3. THOMAS SCLATER m. Sarah (N) (she d. 29 Dec 1709). {CPR}
 On 24 Aug 1705, Thomas Slater appeared to defend ye suit of John Cox against him for retailing of drink contrary to ye 9th Act of Assembly made at James City in 1667 & pleaded not guilty & for tryall put himself on his country, whereupon a jury was impannelled & sworn to enquire into ye fact who after a full hearing of all evidences & pleas, returned their verdict, *viz.* we find for ye def signed John Mihill foreman which is ordered to record. {YCWI 1705-1706:350}
 On 25 Jan 1708, Thomas and Sarah Slaughter, being presented by the Grand Jury for retailing liquors without lycence and it not appearing against them, are therefore discharged. {YCWI 1708-1710:187}
 Denys Hays being summoned an evidence for John Cox plt against Thomas Slater def in an information[?] is ordered to be paid 40 lbs of tobacco for 1 days attendance at court with cost.... {YCWI 1705-1706:350}
 Robt Hays being by ye sheriff returned summoned an evidence for John Cox informant agt Thomas Slater def he refusing to give evidence on oath is fined 350 lbs tobacco for his contempt. {YCWI 1705-1706:350}
 John Cox's information agt Thomas Slater & his wife for retailing drink is cont'd ye def being sick. {YCWI 1705-1706:377}
 On 9 Mar 1705, Thomas Sclater & his wife, being summoned to this court by virtue of an order of last court, to appear & answer ye information of John Cox for retailing of drink contrary to law & not appearing, ordered that ye sheriff take them into custody & them safely to keep until they enter into bond with good & sufficient security to appear & answer ye said information at next court. {YCWI 1705-1706:393}
 On 24 May 1706, the information of John Cox against Thomas Sclater & his wife, for retailing drink contrary to law, is dismist, neither party appearing. {YCWI 1705-1706:408}
 Thomas and Sarah were parents of WILLIAM, b. 5 Apr 1691; ALICE, b. 11 Feb 1697; THOMAS, b. 13 Aug 1693, d. 6 Jan 1693/4; ELIZABETH, b. 1 Feb 1694; THOMAS, b. 29 Nov 1700, d. 8 Dec 1700; MARY, b. 15 Sep 1702; JOHN, b. 12 Feb 1705. {CPR}

Second Generation
4. JOHN SCLATER, b. 1691, was a son of Rev. James (1) and Mary (N) Sclater.
 On 17 Nov 1718, John Sclater, Wm Tabb, Garret Roberts & Benja

Clifton were appointed to appraise the estate of Richard Slater, decd. {YCWI 1716-1718:340}

John Slater was appointed surveyor of this co by commission under the hand of Peter Beverly gent took the oath. {YCWI 1718-1720:375}

John Sclater, of New Kent Co., was granted 400 acres in Goochland Co. on 28 Sep 1732 on the north side of James River, then in Henrico Co., adjacent Amos Lead. 40 shillings. {CP III:419 citing Patent Book 14:468}

5. SARAH SCLATER, b. 11 Jan 1695, m. 1710 Henry Cary (will 27 May 1748, proved 2 Mar 1749/50), son of Henry Cary. {APP:603} Sarah was a daughter of Rev. James (1) and Mary (N) Sclater.

Henry Cary d. leaving a will dated 27 May 1748, proved 2 Mar 1749/50. He was a justice of Warwick Co., 1714, and of James City Co., 1726, vestryman of Bruton Parish, sheriff of Henrico Co., 1733-34. He m. 2nd 1719 Anne Edwards, daughter of John Edwards of Surry Co., and m. 3rd 1741, Elizabeth (N). {APP:603; VC:172-173 citing Chesterfield Co. *Will Book*, i:36}

Sarah Sclater and Henry Cary Junr were the parents of MARY CARY; DOYLEY CARY, b. 1712, d. bef. 1734, *d.s.p.*; HENRY CARY, b. 1714, will 8 Dec 1733, proved Mar 1734, *d.s.p.* {VC:172 citing Henrico Co. Wills}

6. JAMES SCLATER[35], b. 6 Dec 1697, d. ca 1727, estate settled 21 Dec 1741, son of Rev. James (1) and Mary (N) Sclater, m. Elizabeth (7) Sclater (d. 30 Dec 1735), daughter of Richard (2) and Mary (Nutting) Sclater. Elizabeth (7) (Sclater) Sclater m. 2nd Daniel Moore. {CPR}

7. ELIZABETH SCLATER, b. 4 Oct 1703, d. 30 Dec 1735 {CPR}, m. 1st James (4) Sclater (b. 6 Dec 1697, d. 22 Apr 1727) and 2nd Daniel Moore, son of Augine Moore. Elizabeth Sclater was a daughter of Richard (2) and Mary (Nutting) Sclater. Daniel m. 2nd Mary (N) Lewellin (d. 11 Dec 1738) {CPR}, widow of John Lewellin.

Elizabeth Sclater and Daniel Moore were the parents of MARY MOORE, b. 20 Nov., bapt., 21 Dec 1729, d. 11 Dec 1738; AUGUSTINE MOORE, b. 7 Mar 1731, bapt. 23 Apr 1732; MARTHA MOORE, b. May, bapt. 24 Aug 1734, d. 18 Jan 1734/5; and DANIEL MOORE, b. 25 Dec., bapt. 1 Feb 1735, d. 13 Oct 1739. {CPR} [See this series, Vol. II, "The Moore Family" for additional information.]

On 15 Jun 1741, upon the prayer of Daniel More, gent, it's ordered that Francis Hayward, Edwd Tabb Senr, Jones Irwin and John Chisman or any three

---

[35] James (6) Sclater m. Elizabeth (7) Sclater. The naming convention used in this series would make her Elizabeth (Sclater) Sclater.

of them do meet and settle an account of the estate of James Sclater, deceased, and that they divide the Negroes which the said deceased dyed possessed of together with the increase into three parts, and that they assigned 1/3 part to each of the children of said deceased and 1/3 part to said Daniel More.... {YCWI 1740-1743:17}

In ... court dated 15 Jun 1741, to settle an account of the estate of James Sclater, deceased, we have met and having examined the several vouchers produced to us by Capt. John Tabb executor of said Sclater's will, report the same. Paid Maj. Holloway for advice about the estate, paid Rev. James Sclater for a funeral sermon, paid the estate of Justinian Love decd, paid James Gemmil per acct, paid Capt Edwd Tabb for his note, paid Nichs Pressey, Wm Ferguson, Richd Solloway, Henry Burradell, John Hay, Capt. Edward Tabb, Thos Nelson, Capt John Tabb, Elizabeth Connier, Gerrard Roberts, Michael Markie, Saml Roberts, Thos Avery, Chas Rower, the widow & bal due to James Sclater's children.... 159 pd 16 sl 11 1/2 pn. The costs attending this petition to be paid by the widow & children.... The settlement of the estate was ... recorded 21 Dec 1741.... {YCWI 1740-1743:77}

On 17 May 1742, it was ordered that Francis Hayward gent take a list of tithables this year in the upper precinct of Charles Parish and Danl More, gent, in the lower and that John Ballard gent take the list in the lower precinct of Yorkhampton and Ellyson Armistead gent in the upper and that John Blair esqr take the list in Bruton Parish. {YCWI 1740-1743:99}

Ordered that Francis Hayward, Wm Robinson, Jones Irwin & Edward Tabb to meet & divide the Negroes of James Sclater, decd, between Richard Sclater and Wm Sheldon except Negro Judy and her children and they are to be divided into three parts, 1/3 part assigned to Daniel Moore gent and the other 2/3 between the said Richard Sclater and Wm Sheldon. {YCWI 1740-1743:155}

In ... court ... dated 21 Feb 1742, the subscribers divided the Negroes of James Sclater, decd., between Richard Sclater and Wm Sheldon (except Negro Judy & her children), and they are to be divided into three parts and 1/3 part assigned to Daniel Moore gent, and the other 2/3 between the said Richard Sclater and Wm Sheldon. Judith, Lucy, Will, Daniel & George, 116 pd 10 sl, to Richard Sclater (Mr. Moore to be paid 16 pd 8 sl. Jacob, Sarah, George, Sam & Nanny, 116 pd, to Wm Sheldon (Mr. Moore to be paid 6 pd 8 sl). Rachel & Isaac, 37 pd 10 sl, to Mr. Moore for his 1/3 part of Judith & children and an old fellow named Isaac ... 18 Jul 1743. {YCWI 1740-1743:208}

Augine Moore, of York Co. gent, & Lucy, his wife, for £906:5, sold to Richard Sclater, of same co gent, a 250 acre tract of land in Charles Parish bounded by the lands of the orphan of James Hay, Thomas Prosson, Robert Smith & the land of the afsd Sclater, which said tract of land was purchased by Daniel Moore gent, father to the said Augine Moore, of Samuel Reade & Mary, his wife, & Robert Smith & Mary, his wife, & by the will of the said Daniel

Moore devised to the said Augine Moore.... Ackn 16 Sep 1771 by Augine Moore & Lucy, his wife.... {YCDB 1769-1777:156}

James and Elizabeth (Sclater) Sclater were parents of RICHARD, b. 8 Jan, bapt. 9 Feb 1721; JAMES, b. 8 Dec, bapt. 14 Dec 1723, d. 14 Dec 1723; WILLIAM SHELLDON, b. 8 Jan, bapt. 16 Feb 1724. {CPR}

8. AGNES SCLATER, b. 26 May 1707, daughter Of Richard (2) and Mary (Nutting) Sclater, m. Edmund Smith (will 13 Dec 1750, proved 18 Mar 1750/1) {YCWI 1745-1759:212}, son of Col. Lawrence Smith (will of 11 Mar 1736/7) and Mildred (Chisman) Smith, daughter of Capt. Thomas Chisman. {APP:173; WMCQ 1:2:9-13}

On 14 Feb 1728, Agnes Sclater, of York Co., for 5 shillings, leased to Daniel Moore, of same co., an 85 acre parcel of land being the said Agnes Sclaughter's purparty [property] of 327 acres of land on the narrows of Old Poquoson in Charles Parish, late the inheritance of Richd Sclater, decd., & descended to her the said Agnes Sclaughter as one of the daughters & coheirs of the said Richard Sclaughter ... for the term of one year paying the rent of one grain of Indian corn at the feast of St. Michael the Arch Angel if demanded.... Wits: James Dixon, Benit Tompkins.... {YCDB 1713-1729:508}

Edmund Smith, of York Parish, York Co., left a will dated 13 Dec 1750 and proved 18 Mar 1750/1. To my son, Lawrence Smith, all my tract of land whereon I now live. To my son, Thomas Smith, all my land on Back Cr. To my daughter, Mildred Smith, my lot of land in York Town whereon I am now building, it is my will that the house should be finished out of my estate. Likewise to my daughter, Mildred, one Negro girl named Grace. To my daughter, Mary Smith, 300 pd and one Negro girl named Pegg. I desire that my land in Spotsylvania to be sold for the use of my estate and paying my youngest daughter's legacy. I devise that my wife have the use of my estate during her widowhood and after her decease or marriage that what part of my estate is not willed away, to be divided between my two sons, Lawrence and Thomas. I appoint my wife, William Nelson, Samuel Reade & Daniel Moore my executors ... Samuel Reade gent being appointed guardian by the court to Lawrence Smith, an infant heir at law of the decd, to contest the proof of the said will declared that he had nothing to object to, whereupon the same was proved by the oaths of the witnesses. A certificate was granted the executrix for obtaining a probate.... {YCWI 1745-1759:212}

In obedience to an order of court dated 18 Mar 1750 Philip Dedman, Edward Moss & John Tenham appraised the slaves & personal estate of Edmund Smith decd. Negroes: man named Harry, man named Jack, man named Frank, man named Tom, woman named Esther, woman called Old Esther, boy named Charles, boy named Paul, woman named Hannah, woman called Little Hannah, girl named Grace, girl named Jenny, boy named Aaron, girl named Peg, boy named Ben, boy named Phil, girl named Pleasant, man named Will, man named Pompey, man named Ben, woman named Peg, boy named Matt. 21 cows, 8 calves, 6 draught steers, 10 young cattle, 1 bull, 7 cows, 7 calves, 1 bull, 1 old bay horse, 1 young black mare, etc. 875 pd 15 sl 10 1/2 pn. Agnes Smith ... recorded 16 Sep 1751. {YCWI 1745-1759:232}

Agnes Sclater and Edmund Smith were the parents of LAWRENCE SMITH; THOMAS SMITH; MILDRED SMITH; MARY SMITH. {YCWI 1745-1759:212}

9. MARY SCLATER, b. 9 Mar 1712/13, will 21 Feb 1762, d. 7 Feb 1773, probated 15 Mar 1773, was a daughter of Richard (2) and Mary (Nutting) Sclater, m. Samuel Reade, will 10 Nov 1757, proved 20 Nov 1758, son of Robert Reade and grandson of Col. George Reade. {APP:422-423; WMCQ 1:14:120}

Samuel Reade, of Charles Parish, York Co., left a will dated 10 Nov 1757 and proved 20 Nov 1758. To wife, all this tract of land in York Co whereon I now live, during her natural life and, after her decease, then to my daughter, Frances Reade. To my two daughters, Mildred Reade and Mary Cary, all that tract of land in St. Stephens Parish, King & Queen Co whereon I now have a Qr, but in case the said land should be entailed by my father's will and my daughter Frances or any of her heirs hereafter should claim any part under the said will that then my will is that the land (where I live) given to my daughter Frances be divided among my three daughters, Mildred, Mary & Frances afsd. To daughter Mildred Reade nine Negroes namely Ned, Tom, Sawney, Grace & her child Sarah, Billy, Phill, Lewey & Kate and 15 head of cattle on the plantation in King & Queen also one good feather bed and furniture. To daughter, Mary Cary, nine Negroes namely Old Frank, Patrick, Nell, Nanny, Mary, Kate Nell's child, Little Frank, Grace Grace's child & Quash. To my daughters, Mildred Reade and Mary Cary, the remainder and residue of my stock of all kinds and all utensils of what kind so ever belonging to the plantation in King & Queen (after my daughter Mildred has her 15 head of cattle). To my daughter, Frances Reade, nine Negroes namely Hannah and her two children Bill & Harry, Mulatto Dick, Wilson, Jacob, Easter, Alse & Nell's child Sarah. To my wife, Mary Reade, four Negroes namely Paul, Patt, Arquila & Lettice to dispose of as she shall think proper at her death. I likewise give to my wife five Negroes namely York, Dick, Will, Jack, Great Sarah & Joan during her natural life and after her decease then to my three daughters, Mildred, Mary & Frances. To my wife, the remainder of my personal estate during her natural life and after her decease then to my three daughters afsd. If is my will that if I should die at any time between the 1st of Mar and the 1st of Dec that the Negroes remain on the plantation til Christmas and that they be then well clothed and have three barrels of corn each. It is my will that my executrix

154

give no security for my estate and that it be not appraised. I appoint my wife, Mary Read, executrix. Wits: Aaron Phillips, Wm Rose, Eliz Phillips, James Drewry.... {YCWI 1745-1759:505)

Inventory of the estate of Samuel Reade, decd, was taken on 8 Jan 1759 and recorded on 19 Mar 1759. 4 draft steers, 31 head of cattle, 5 yearlings, 1 calf, 18 head of hogs, 11 head of sheep, 2 horses & a mare, 1 chair & harness, 1 cart & wheels, yokes & ox chain, 40 barrels long sound corn, 1 1/2 barrels short & rotten corn, 18 bushels wheat, 1 1/2 bushels peas, 20 bushels oats, a parcel fodder, wheatstraw & oatstraw, 1 large walnut oval table, 1 larger maple table, 6 good chests, 3 old chests, 2 large trunks, 3 good feather beds, bolsters & pillows, 3 old feather beds, 5 pr good fine linen sheets, 4 1/2 pr coarser sheets, 3 pr blankets, 4 rugs, 1 suit curtains, 6 pillow cases, 2 white cotton counterpanes, 1 bed quilt, etc. Negroes: Ned, Tom, Sawney, Grace, Sarah, Betty, Phill, Lewey, Cate, Old Frank, Young Frank, Patrick, Nell, Nanny, Mary, Little Cate, Quash, Little Grace, Nanny's child Betty, Mulatto Dick, Hannah, Wilson, Alice, Little Billy, Harry, Jacob, Easter, Nell's child Sarah, Hannah's child Sarah, Paul, Patt, Arguile, Lettice, Will, York Dick, Jack, Old Sarah, Joan, Old Dick. At the King & Queen Plantation: 7 fatted hogs, 2 sows, 6 shoats, 24 head cattle, 1 large stack corn tops, a parcel corn husks, 2350 bundles blades, 2 tobacco hogsheads, 60 barrels corn, 4 axes, 7 broad hoes, 11 old hoes, 3 narrow & 1 fluke hoe, 2 grubbing hoes, 1 fat pot & iron wedges, small parcel of leather, small parcel salt, 1 bushel beans, 1 old frying pan, 1 old pot, 787 lbs. net tobacco and cask. Sums due from Robt Smith, James Longest, Richard Drewry on bond, William Rose, James Drewry, John Drewry, William Moss.... {YCWI 1745-1759:509}

The relict of Samuel Reade, Mary Reade of Charles Parish, York Co., left a will dated 9 Feb 1762 and proved 15 Mar 1773. To granddaughter, Mary Robinson, daughter of Anthony Robinson, my three negroes: Paul, Patt and Lettice and if she died in her minority and childless then to son in law, Anthony Robinson, exec.... {YCWI 1771-1783:152}

Mary Sclater and Samuel Reade were the parents of MILDRED READE; MARY READE, m. (N)[36] Cary; FRANCES READE (d. 26 Aug 1761) {CPR}, m. Anthony Robinson, son of Anthony Robinson. [See "The Robinson Family," in volume 2 of this series.]

Third Generation

10. RICHARD SCLATER, b. 8 Jan, bapt. 9 Feb 1721, will 2 Jan 1774, will Proved 21 Apr 1777 & 19 May 1777, m. Martha (N), was a son of James (6) and Elizabeth (7) (Sclater) Sclater. Richard m. 1st Elizabeth (N) and 2nd Martha (N).

---

[36] Possibly Cary's given name was John. Charles Parish register shows, "Cary, Mary, wife of John, d. 17 May 1761.

Martha m. 2nd Henry Howard. {YCWI 1771-1783:516}

Elizabeth [Booth] Nutting, of Charles Parish, York Co, widow [of Capt. Thomas Nutting], left a will dated 13 Sep 1733.... To all my orphaned children and great grandchildren which are now under the age of 14 years 20 sl each except my grandson, Richard Slate [Sclater], to whom I give my half pint silver can(?). My desire is that the several legacies above mentioned which is to be paid in money be kept in the hands of my executor until my grandchildren arrive to lawful age and then to be paid them respectively.... {YCWI 1732-1737:230}

Richd Sclater petitioned the court on 17 Aug 1741 praying that Doctor Brodie may be appointed his guardian to prosecute for him is rejected. {YCWI 1740-1743:54}

On 21 Feb 1742, Richard Sclater ackn'd his release to Daniel Moore, gent. {YCWI 1740-1743:155}

Richard Sclater, of York Co, son & heir of Elizabeth, late the wife of James Sclater, decd, and afterward the wife of Daniel Moore, of York Co. gent, for £37, and the still, quit claim unto the said Daniel Moore all manner of actions & suits which the said Richard Sclater hath by virtue of the bond entered into by the afsd Elizabeth, the late mother of said Richard Sclater, or any other matter ... concerning the discovery of a bond entered into by the afsd Elizabeth after the death of said James Sclater and before her marriage with the said Daniel Moore whereby the said Elizabeth had bound herself to give to the said Richard Sclater 1/3 part of 200 acres of land whereof she was seized together with a slave and some personal estate ... Wits: Thos Tabb, Johnson Mallory, Edmd Smith. Ackn 21 Feb 1742.... {YCLRD 1741-1754:41}

On 18 Mar 1754, Gawton Hunt and Anne, his wife, of Charles Parish, York Co., for £352, sold to Richard Sclater, of same parish, a 200 acre tract of land in said parish adjacent Poquoson River ... which land the said Gawton Hunt purchased of Daniel Moore, gent, by deeds of lease and release dated 17&18 Aug 1739, also a water grist mill on a bridge of Old Poquoson River in said parish.... {YCLRD 1741-1754:589}

On 21 Sep 1767, John Allen, the younger, Carpenter, of Charles Parish, York Co., & Frances [elsewhere Frankey], his wife. for £300, sold to Richard Sclater, of same place. gent, all the said John Allen's 125 acre tract of land in the parish afsd bounded by the lands of the said Sclater, Robert Wise, Starkey Robinson & a creek, which land the said John Allen purchased of Edward Mallory, of Elizabeth City Co, by deed dated 30 Sep 1766.... Wits: W. Mitchell, Clausel Clausell, John Cary.... {YCDB 1763-1769:324}

On 16 Sep 1771, Augine Moore, of York Co, gent, & Lucy, his wife, for £906:5, sold to Richard Sclater, of same co, gent, a 250 acre tract of land in Charles Parish bounded by the lands of the orphan of James Hay, Thomas Prosson, Robert Smith & the land of the afsd Sclater, which said tract of land was purchased by Daniel Moore, gent, father to the said Augine Moore, of Samuel Reade & Mary his wife & Robert Smith & Mary his wife & by the will of the said Daniel Moore devised to the said Augine Moore.... {YCDB 1769-1777:156}

On 17 Aug 1776, Richard Sclater, of Charles Parish, York Co, for natural love & affection, have given to my son, John Sclater, of same place, all that 300 acre tract of land whereon the said John now liveth bounded by the lands of Henry Howard, Augine Moore & John Dunn.... Wits: Robt Smith, John Kerby, John Randle.... {YCDB 1769-1777:507}

Richard Selator, of Charles Parish, York Co., left a will dated 2 Jan 1774 and proved 21 Apr 1777 & 19 May 1777. To wife, Martha Selater, all the tract of land and plantation which I purchased from Ganton(?)[Gawton] Hunt and John Allen; slaves: Ben, J ..., Sue, Alice, Harry, London and Judith; ½ of household and kitchen furniture during her natural life and, after her decease, I give the same to my son, John Selator. All other lands to son, John Selater, and 11 slaves: Paul, Will, Jack, George, Jenny, Mary, C ... Jemmy, Bristol, little Amy and Graves. To grandson, John Wells (?), 2 slaves Bob and Edy and in case of his death under age or without issue then to be equally divided between my two grandsons, Thomas Wells and William Sheldon Wells. To grandson, Thomas Wells, slaves Abel and Grace, and if he dies under age or without issue then to his brother William Sheldon Wells. To grandson, William Sheldon Wells, slaves Lewis and little Peg. To daughter, Elizabeth Kerby, during her natural life and for her support, slaves Stepney, Jacob, Lucy, Ned, Nanny, Leah and Annaka, and if she should leave a child or children by her present husband that the said child or children should first have two slaves each part of the said seven of equal value which I have given to her children she had by her former husband. To son in law, John Cary, four slaves, Great Peg, Dinah, Rachel and little Jerry. To grandson, Miles Cary, slaves Amy, Phillis and her child Jenny, Milley and her children Jenny, the daughter of Peg, Daniel and Natt. Further desire that his father John Cary have the use of the slaves until my grandson comes of age. To daughter, Elizabeth Kerby, 12 head of cattle and 12 head of sheep. To wife, my negro boy Sam and 1/4 of the remainder of my stocks of cattle, sheep and hogs; also my riding horse and riding chair. Rest of estate to my son, John Selater, Extx. Wife, and friend, David Jamison (?), my brother, Augine Moore, and my son, John Selater. Wits: Starkey Robinson, Merritt Moore, Miles Cary, Benjamin Lester.... {YCWI 1771-1783:365}

Appraisement of the estate of Richard Selater. Includes Negro man Paul, Will, Jack, Jerry, Ben, Stepney, Bob, Abel, James, Bristol, Jacob, Jerry, Sam, Lewis, Ned, David, Abram, Nat, Ben, London, Harry, Pegg, Phillis and her children Jenny and Dorinda, Mildred, Rachel, Rose, Amy, Jenny, Lucy, Leah, Pegg, Grace, Edy, Nanny, Judith, Sue, Alice and her child Mary, Grace, Jenny, Cully, Mary, Amy, and other. Total: £2859.16.0. John Patrick, Thos. Pescud,

John Chisman.... 17 Aug 1778. {YCWI 1771-1783:404}

Henry Howard, of Charles Parish, York Co., left a will dated 10 Nov 1781 and proved 17 Jun 1782. To wife, Martha Howard, one negro boy named Sam and stock of all kinds now at her sons given her by her late husband, Mr. Richard Selater [Sclater]. Also to wife during her natural life my slaves Sue and Will and these horses Fleet, Liberty and Silver Heels and after death I give the wench Sue and her increase to my son Francis Howard and will to my son Henry Howard.... Execs: wife and sons, Edward Howard and William Howard, and my friend, Jno. Selater.... Wits: John Patrick, W. Mallory, Richard Cary.... {YCWI 1771-1783:516}

James Broodie [Brodie], of York Co., left a will that was proved 17 Jun 1782. In it, he gave lands and slaves and estate in state of South Carolina to be exposed to sale and the money arising therefrom to be equally divided between my sister, Charlotte Broodie, and my relations, John Selater and his two sons, John and Richard. If sister should be dead or dies before she arrives to the age of 21 or marries, then her portion to be the property of my cousin Sally Selater. Exec., my relation, John Selater.... Wits: Merritt Moore, W. Reade, John Kirby.... {YCWI 1771-1783:520}

Richard and Elizabeth (N) were parents of ELIZABETH, b. 22 Apr, bapt. 6 May 1744, m. John Kirby. {CPR} [See this series, Vol. I for "The Kirby/Kerby Family".]

Richard and Martha (N) Sclater were parents of JOHN, b. 9 Jan, bapt. 10 Mar 1747; SALLY, b. 26 Nov, bapt. 16 Dec 1740[1750?][37], d. bef. 2 Jan 1774 (date of father's will), m. John Cary. {CPR; YCWI 1771-1783:365}

11. WILLIAM SHELDON SCLATER, b. 8 Jan., bapt. 16 Feb 1724 {CPR}, was a son of James (6) and Elizabeth (7) (Sclater) Sclater, m. Sarah Sheild, daughter of Robert Sheild.

On 20 Sep 1736, the King against Daniel Moore, guardian of Wm Sheldon Sclater, who satisfying the court concerning the said orphan's estate, ordered that the suit be dismissed.... {YCWI 1732-1737:312}

Robert Sheild, of Charles Parish, York Co., left a will dated 23 Feb 1753 and proved 21 May 1753. To my son, Robert Sheild, the plantation which I now live on.... To my son, John Sheild, all my land upon Back River.... To my daughter, Sarah Sclater, 236 pd to make up 300 pd with what she has received of me. To my daughter, Sarah Sclater, four Negroes which she has in possession.... To my daughter, Sarah Sclater, my horse and chaise and 6 head

---

[37] Sally's birth year from the *Charles Parish Register* was shown as "1740[1750?]", but, the *Register* shows Richard having a child with Elizabeth in 1744. Given that Elizabeth was not alive at the time of Richard's death, Elizabeth must have been the first wife; therefore, Sally's birth year is probably 1750.

of cattle from my Qr on Chisman's Mill Dam…. My will is that all my household goods be divided amongst my five children, Ann Howard, Robert Sheild, John Sheild, Mary Kerby & Sarah Sclater. After my debts and legacies be paid what money remains by bonds or books shall be divided among my three children Ann Howard, John Sheild & Mary Kerby. I appoint my son Robert Sheild, John Sheild & William Sheldon Sclater, executors. Wits: James Drewry, Peter Drewry, Katherine Drewry…. {YCWI 1745-1759:292}

William Sheldon Sclater, of Charles Parish, York Co., left a will dated 11 Jun 1757 and proved 18 Jul 1757. To wife, Sarah Sclater, two Negro girls namely Betty and Lucy. To nephew, Augine Tabb, son of Edmund Tabb, a Negro boy named Abram. To son, William Sheldon Sclater, all the rest of my estate except 1/3 part which I lend to my wife during her natural life and at her death to return to my said son. If my said son shall happen to die in his minority and without issue, then I give to my wife the following slaves, to wit, Fish-neck, Moll & her child, Batter, Sam, Ben, Sam, Barber, Malachi, Dan son of Sary, Bristol & Rachel. The residue of my said estate before given to my said son to be divided betwixt my two nephews, John Sclater & Augine Tabb. I appoint my brother, Richard Sclater, and my two friends, Robert Sheild & Edmund Tabb, executors … Robert Sheild & Edmund Tabb, together with Thomas Chisman, their security, acknowledge a bond, and a certificate was granted them for obtaining a probate, liberty being reserved to Richard Sclater the other executor to join in the probate when he shall think fit. On 15 Aug 1757, the said Richard Sclater took the oath of an executor and acknowledge a bond and a certificate was granted him to be joined in the said probate…. {YCWI 1745-1759:441}

In … court dated 18 Jul 1757 and recorded 19 Sep 1757, Edward Tabb, Thomas Chisman & Henry Howard appraised the estate of William Sheldon Sclater, decd. 65 hogs, 17 pigs, 39 sheep, 14 lambs, 1 yoke draft steers, 21 cows & calves, 15 young cattle, 2 steers, 1 mare & colt, 2 young mares, 1 corner cupboard, 2 doz. flat china plates, 1 dozen soup china plates, 1 salad dish, 1 dozen cups & saucers, 2 china bowls, 1 small bowl, 1 dozen silver spoons, a tea case, 1 soup spoon, 1 strainer, 1 dozen wine glasses, 3 salts, 1 tumbler, 2 cruets, 2 casters, 2 dishes & 4 plates, 1 large table, 3 mugs, 1 doz. chairs, 1 desk, 1 looking glass, 14 flag chairs, etc. Negroes: Jack a man, Will a man, Paul a man, Malichi a man, Jacob a man, Ben a man, Frank a man, Joe a man, Peter a man, Gaby a man, Sam a man, Dick a man, Sam a man, Dan a man, Bob a man, Jemmy a man, Dan a man, Bristol a boy, Titus a boy, Jerry a boy, Sam a boy, Ballow a boy, Casar a boy, Phil a boy, Will a boy, Harry a boy, Patt a girl, Cate a woman, Judy a woman, Sarah a woman, Sarah a woman, Nanny a woman, Nanny a woman, Beck a woman, Sue a woman, Aggy a woman, Betty a woman, Moll a woman, Moll a woman, Betty & child, Sarah a girl, Rachel a girl, Aggy a girl, Lucy a girl, Phillis a girl, Judy a girl, Lydia a girl, Pegg a girl, Sue a girl,

Jenny a girl, Hannah a girl, Molly a girl, Abram a boy. 1658 pd 19 sl 4 1/4 pn....
{YCWI 1745-1759:446}
Samuel Reade, Henry Howard & Edward Tabb assign unto Sarah
Sclater, widow of Wm. Sheldon Sclater, deceased, her share of the slaves of her
late husband as per order of the court dated 19 Dec 1757 and a balance of 2 pd 3
sl 4 pn is due to her. The following slaves assigned her 24 Dec 1747, *viz*. Paul,
Malachi, Peter, Sam Barber, Dan, Fish Neck Moll, Betty, Cate, Ballow, Sam,
Rachel, Agga, Jenny. 358 pd 3 sl 4 pn ... recorded 16 Jan 1758.... {YCWI 1745-
1759:460}
On 18 Aug 1760, Henry Howard and Frances, his wife, of Charles
Parish, York Co., for £76.5, sold to
William Sheldon Sclater, of same place, a 93 acre tract of land in Charles Parish
being ½ of a tract of land which the said Henry Howard purchased of Booth
Armistead bounded by Myall's Run, said Henry Howard & Howards Mill....
{YCLRD 1755-1763:274}
William Sheldon and Sarah (Sheild) Slater were parents of MARY[38], b.
3 Oct, bapt. 28 Nov 1752, and WILLIAM SHELDON, b. 17 Oct, bapt. 28 Nov
1756, d. 26 Nov 1777. {CPR}

Fourth Generation
12. JOHN SCLATER, son of Richard (10) and Martha (N) Sclater, m. Mary (N).
John Selater, Nancy Selater, Ann Selater witnessed the will of Matthew
Moody, of the Capitol Landing, York Co.... 16 Nov 1773.... {YCWI 1771-1883:292}
On 21 Nov 1774, Matthew Evans, of York Co., aged about 17 years,
doth voluntarily & of his own free will & accord put himself apprentice to John
Sclater, of York, shoemaker, to learn his art, trade & mystery & after the manner
of an apprentice to serve the said John Sclater the full term of 5 years ... & the
said master shall use the utmost of his endeavors to teach the said apprentice in
the trade or mystery of a shoemaker & to read & write.... {YCDB 1769-1777:447}
On 1 Feb 1777, John Sclater, of Charles Parish & Mary, his wife, for
£100, sold to Robert Presson, of same place, all that 50 acre tract of land in the
parish afsd bounded by the lands of Callohill Mennis, Francis Cooke, Henry
Howard & Finches Dam.... Wits: John Robinson, John Kerby, John Randle ...
21 Apr 1777 ... recorded.... {YCDB 1769-1777:530}
John and Mary (N) Sclater were the parents of SALLY, b. 27 Sep 1771,
bapt. 26 Jan 1772; MARY, b. 3 Oct, bapt. 14 Nov 1773; MARTHA, b. 17 Dec
1775, bapt. 18 Feb 1776; JOHN, b. Jun 1777, bapt. 24[?] May 1778; RICHARD,
b. 23 Feb, bapt. 13 Jun 1779; MARY, b. 11 Jul, bapt. 1 Oct 1780; ELIZABETH,
b. 11 Mar, bapt. 29 May 1782; JAMES, b. 11 Aug 1783, bapt. 5 Apr 1785;

[38] Mary is not mentioned in her father's 1757 will. She may have died by then.

160

WILLIAM SHELDON, b. 7 Feb, bapt. 5 Apr 1785; MILDRED, b. 22 Dec 1786. {CPR}

OTHERS NAMES SCLATER/SLATER/SELATER

MARY SCLATER d. 17 Apr 1701. {CPR}

MARY SLATER d. 28 Aug 1717. {CPR}

MARY SCLATER, widow of William, d. 19 Jul 1761. {CPR}

DR. MATTHEW SLATER
Dr. Mathew Slater, in difference, on 25 Nov 1672, between him and John Aduston, Sr. concerning treatment cost for John Aduston, Jr. {RB 1672-1676:31}

SACHEVEREL SELATER
Sackoverel Selater, of York Co. and Bruton Parish, left a will dated 14 Oct 1773 and proved 15 Nov 1773. To son, John Selater, his choice of cow and calf, feather bed and furniture. and other items. To daughter, Elizabeth Selater, two pewter dishes, plates, furniture, spinning wheel, etc. To daughter, Ann Selater, feather bed, furniture, dishware. To daughter, Mary Selater, feather bed, furniture, colt, saddle, £12. Rest of estate to be sold and money divided amongst daughters, Elizabeth, Anne and Mary Selater, Execs. William Graves and John Dickinson.... {YCWI 1771-1783:200}
        The appraisement of the inventory of Sacheverel Selater's estate on 15 Jan 1774 by W. Eaton, Matthew Moody Junr., William Moody Junr. totaled £92.19.11 ½ and was returned on 17 Jan 1774. {YCWI 1771-1783:210}

WILLIAM SCLATER
The action of debt between Richd Clifton plt & William Slater def is dismist neither party appearing. {YCWI 1716-1718:68}

THE NICHOLAS SEBRELL FAMILY

1. NICHOLAS SEBRELL, d. 1665, m. Darcey (N) (d. 1666).
        There being a certain quantity of corn due Nicholas Sebriell "for his servis Done at the Midle plantacon the last year 1645" to have been paid him by the then Sheriff. Order that Phillipp Thacker "then and now undersherr" collect the corn and pay Sebriell. {CD503:YkCo1648-1657:70}
        Nicholas Sebrell (Sebbrell) received 200 acres in York Co near Middle

Plantation on 30 Jan 1652, 150 acres by patent, dated 30 Jul 1638, and 50 acres for the transport of Roger Sollis. {CP I:267}

At a court for York Co on 10 May 1652, Nicholas Seav'rill informed the Court that Sir Dudley Wyatt knt dec'd, in his lifetime, cleared land belonging to [Seav'rill]. In the difference, according to the consent of Seav'rill and Mr. Wyatt in behalf of Mrs. Ann Clark extrx of said Sir Dudley Wyatt, that Nicholas Brookes Seniour and Leonard Chamberlyn, Richard Abrell and John Davies, with a lawful survey, report to the Court for the purpose of ending the difference. {CD503:YkCo1648-1657:116}

At a court for York Co on 25 Oct 1652, In dif still depending betw Mrs Hannah Clark, admrx of Sir Dudley Wyatt dec'd, and Nicholas Seabrill concerning land. Mr. Robt Booth was attorney of Mrs Clark. Mr Lewis or Lieut: Collonell John Walker to again survey said land; and four men, as before, to view the survey and report. {CD503:YkCo1648-1657:118}

Thomas Broughton received land in Northumberland Co on 23 Mar 1657, NE upon the land of Jane Perry, Widdow, and NW upon Mettonpony River, from a tract of 100 acres originally granted unto Nicholas Sebrell on 30 Jan 1652, deserted and due for transportation of 2 pers: Richard Cardy and Humphry Pester. {CP I:364}

Nicholas Seabrell received 150 acres in New Kent Co on 1 Mar 1658 on the N side of the York River and N side of a branch of Montesup Swamp for the transportation of three persons: Andrew Pclch, John Bennett, and Ralph Gandee. {CP I:387}

Nicholas Sebrell received patent for land 24 Feb 1663. A deed of Lease dated 15 Jul 1714 gave the history of the land granted to Nicholas in 1663. John Coman, son & heir at law of William Coman late of Bruton Parish, York Co decd, for 5 shillings, leased to Jacob Goddin of same place, a plantation & a 45 acre tract of land in the parish afsd being the tract of land which descended to him as being heir at law to his sd decd father Wm Coman, bounded by Maiden Swamp & land of David Stoner, being pt/o a dividend of land formerly granted to Nicho Sebrell by patent dated 24 Feb 1663 & afterward by the will of the sd Nicho he devised the sd land between his two sons Nicho & Antho Sebrell, & by the sd Nicho & Antho by a joint consent was divided between them according to the sd will as per division under their hands & seals dated 24 Jun 1672, & this part hereby mentioned to be granted belonged to Antho Sebrell & was by him sold & conveyed to Saml Eburne clerk & by him sold to Jno Eaton cordwainder by deed dated 23 Jan 1695/6 & afterwards sold & conveyed by the sd Eaton to Wm Coman father of the sd Jno by deed of sale…. {YCDB 1713-1729:21}

Adminstration of the estate of Darcey Seabrell, dec., widow, was granted to Mr. James Bray on behalf of Nicolas Seabrell, son of dec'd. Bray to be possessed (26 Feb 1666) of his estate. {RB 1665-1672:123}

The inventories of Nicholas Seabrell and of the estate belonging to Darsey, his wife, also dec, were made on 24 Apr 1667. {RB 1665-1672:136}

Robert Harrison and James Besouth divided the estate of Darcey Seabrell, widow, on 26 Sep 1667, between Nicholas and Anthony Seabrell. {RB 1665-1672:155}

On 24 Aug 1668, John Overstreet became security. The inventory made on 1 Apr 1668 of Robert Clarke, Midletowne [sic] Parish, dec., mentioned calf given by John Davis to John Clarke, son of Robert, cow given by Nicholas Seabrell to Mary Clarke, dau. of Robert.... {RB 1665-1672:186}

The petition of Anthony Seabrell to make his brother Nicholas Seabrell his guardian was granted on 24 Jun 1668. {RB 1665-1672:187,198}

Isaac Beard, servant to Nicholas Seabrell, was adjudged 14 years of age on 26 Apr 1670. {RB 1665-1672:393[293]}

On 26 Aug 1672, division of the land between Nicholas and his brother Anthony was made. {RB 1672-1676:19}

Nicholas and Darcey (N) Seabrell were the parents of NICHOLAS (b. 1646) {RB 1665-1672:325 [225]} and ANTHONY {YCDB 1713-1729:21}.

Second Generation

2. NICHOLAS SEABRILL, b. 1646 {RB 1665-1672:325 [225]}, d. 1692 {WARG:136}, m. 1st Doss (N) and 2nd Sarah, was a son of Nicholas (1) and Darsey (N) Sebrill.

Sarah Overstreete, relict of John Overstreete, Hampton Parish, York Co. dec. I give (4 Mar 1674/5) to my son Edward Jenkins, mare. To my son doffed [Jeffery?] Overstreete, filly. To my dau. Sarah Seabrell[39] a mare, but prohibit my son in law Nicholas Seabrell [probably Nicholas (2)] from having anything to do with it. {RB 1672-1676:109}

William Shepherd was imported in the *Planter's Adventure*, Capt. Ellis Els, Commander, and Shepherd was servant to Mr. Nicholas Seabrell, adjudged on 24 Jan 1675/6 to be 15 years of age, and to serve to 24 years of age. {RB 1672-1676:140}

Sarah Sebrell, relict of Nicho: Sebrell, petitioned and the order was granted on 25 Sep 1693, for admin. of estate of her husband. {DW 1691-1694:252}

On 20 Apr 1695, Nicholas Sebrell, son & heir of Nicholas Sebrell, and Sarah Sebrell, widow of said Nicholas Sebrell, late deceased, have, for £6, sold to Willm Buckner a house & lott in Yorke Town.... Ackn by the said Nich Sebrell & by Sarah, his mother, unto Willm Buckner & recorded.... {YCDB 1694-1701:16}

Whereas in obedience to an order of last court the sheriff did present on

---

[39] See the Overstreet family, this volume, for more information. Briefly, prior to her marriage to John Overstreet, Sarah Overstreet was married to Sarah Sebrell's father, (N) Sebrell, who was probably a brother or cousin of Nicholas (1) Sebrell.

his oath a panel of 24 freeholders summoned by him to serve and when called they refused ... viz., Robt Bee, Joseph Fryth, David Noner (Nener?), Nicholas Sebrell, [?], Tho Collyer, Anthony Robesson, John Pond, [?] Cooper, Jeffrey Overstreet, Robt Lawson & Willm Pattisson, they are respectively fined 100 lbs of tobacco.... {YCWI 1698-1702:477}

On 19 Nov 1702, William Harrison Junr, together with William Harrison & Nicholas Sebrell, securities, did jointly and severally confess judgment before Capt Thomas Barbar & Capt Baldwin Mathews justices to Henry Tyler trustee to the estate of Cope Doyley, late of this co, deceased, for payment of 8 pd 12 sl 6 pn with cost and stay of execution until 10 Jan 1703. {YCWI 1702-1704:52}

Samuel Sebrell, orphan of Nicholas (2) Sebrell, petitioned for his brother Nicholas Sebrell, to be admitted his guardian, he bringing good security to ye next court for due performance of his duty therein. {YCWI 1702-1704:242}

Nicholas and Doss (N) Seabrell were the parents of ANTHONY (b. 1672). {RB 1672-1676:23}

Nicholas and Sarah (N) Seabrell were the parents of NICHOLAS {YCDB 1694-1701:16}.

Nicholas was the father of EDWARD, d. 1683; THOMAS, d. 1684 {WARG:135}; and SAMUEL {YCWI 1702-1704:242}.

Third Generation
3. ANTHONY SEBRELL, b. 14 Jun 1672, bapt. 30 Jun 1672 {RB 1,672-1676:23} m. Martha, was a son of Nicholas (1) and Darsey (N) Sebrill.

On 24 Nov 1691, Joseph Ring & Thomas Ballard both of York Co gent, feoffees in trust appointed according to an act made at James City 16 Apr 1691, intitled an act for pork & for their disposal of 50 acre of land in York Co appointed for a port or town, for a valluable & proportionable consideration sold to Nicholas Sebrell of co afsd a lot—or ½ acre—of land containing 10 poles in length & 8 in breadth being pt/o ye afsd dividend of 50 acre bounded by ye lotts of Benjamin Read, Thomas Hill & York River, as by a plot thereof under the hand of Col Lawrence Smith surveyor.... {DW 1691-1694:15}

The deed of sale on 25 Mar 1695 of the 80 acre plantation of Anthony Sebrell and Martha his wife to Mr. Samll: Eborne was acknowledged to Capt. Thomas Ballard by power of attorney made by Samll: Eborne. {DW 1694-1697:119}

On 16 Aug 1695 Anthony Sebrell sold, for £50, 50 acres of land to Thomas Wade and Margrett his wife. {DW 1694-1697:188;YCDB 1694-1701:24}

Anthony Sebrell of Bruton Parish, Yorke Co planter & Martha his wife, on 8 Dec 1693, for £50, sold to Samll Eburn (Eburne) of same place clarke, a messuage, plantacon & [an] 80 acre tract of land in ye parish afsd, whereon the sd Anthony Sebrell & Martha his wife doe now inhabit being pt/o a dividend of 200 acres as a patent thereof dated 24 Feb 1663 under ye hand of Sir Willm

164

Berkley Knt then Governor which sd dividend of land was given by Nicholas
Sebrell Senr decd betwixt his two sons Nicholas & the sd Anthony Sebrells by
his will dated – Jan 1662 on record at Yorke Court, & by the sd brothers
Nicholas & Anthony since by a joynt consent divided betwixt them 24 Jun 1672
which sd tract of land of 80 acres is bounded by the Maiden Swamp & the land
of David Stoner.... {YCDB 1694-1701:49}

    Henry Duke, assignee of Dionisius Wright, arresting Robert Harrison in
a plea of debt as being bound in a bill joyntly with and for Anthony Sebrell for
320 lbs of sweet scented tobacco and caske hath judgment confessed for the said
sum by the said Harrison & is ordered to be paid with costs. {YCWI 1702-1704:5}

4. NICHOLAS SEBRELL, b. 1670s, d. 1708, m. Frances (N) (d. 1708).
{WARG:138}

    In ye suite between Joseph Chermison plt & Nicholas Sebrell def, in an
action of trespass wherein ye plt [?] that sd Nicholas on 1 Feb last past, in Bruton
Parish, with force & armes ye house of sd Joseph did then & there breake & enter
ye blades of corne & fodder & 10 barrells of corn to ye value of 10 pd then &
there found in ye custody of sd Joseph did take, carry away & spoile & other
enormitys agt ye peace & to ye plts damage 10 pd to which ye def pleaded not
guilty & put himselfe on his country & ye plt joins whereupon a jury was
impannelled & sworne to try ye issue who returned their verdict (viz) we find for
the def syned James Priest & on motion of ye def ye plt is nonsuited with cost.
{YCWI 1705-1706:335}

    Joseph Chermison his plea to arrest judgment of 9 Jun last in the
difference between himself plt & Nicho Sebrell def in an action of trespass
damages 10 pd wherein ye plt was nonsuited on request of ye def ye jury returning
for verdict wee find for ye def is overrul'd for insufficiency of his reasons and the
verdict is confirm'd from which judgment sd Joseph appeals to 6th day of next
General Court for tryall. Richd Kendall & Robt Crawley became securitys. {YCWI
1705-1706:349}

    Nicholas Sebrell his genll discharge from John Sebrell was proved by ye
oaths of Francis Meloy & Martin Megary evidences thereto & ordered committed
to record. {YCWI 1705-1706:423}

    On 24 Jun 1706, John Sebrell of King & Queen Co cooper, released &
quit claim unto Nicolas Sebrell of York Co all manner of accounts, suites, bills,
bonds, writing obligatorys, debts due, duties, sums of mony, judgments,
controversies, trespasses, damages & demands whatsoever which I ever had or
now have or may have claim or demand for since the beginning of the world. Wit:
Francis Meloy, Martin Megtray.... {YCWI 1705-1706:441}

    In the *ejection firmae* between Abell Dun, plf., against Nicho. Sebrell,
deft., the plf. declares, to wit, that when one Anthony Sebrell, on the 3rd day of
Apr in the year 1707 at the Parish of Bruton in the Co. of York, had demised to

the said Abell 20 acres of land, 10 acres of woodland and 10 acres of pastures with the appurtenances... to which the deft. this day pleaded not guilty and for tryall put himself on his country and the plf. likewise. Whereupon a jury was impannelled and sworn to try the issue, joyned by names John Drowry [Drury?], Jno. Doswell Senr., Jno. Doswell Junr., Wm. Sheldon, John Moss, Wm. Davis, Joseph Walker, Philip Moody, Jno. Adduston Rogers, Simon Stacy, John Toomer and Wm. Babb, who having received their charge, were sent out and in some time came again into Court and returned their verdict, which at the mocion of the deft. is recorded and is in these words. Wee the jury find for the deft., signed Wm. Sheldon. Therefore ordered that the plf. pay costs alies execution. {YCWI 1706-1710:92}

The verbal Will of Frances Sebrell was dated 18 Oct 1708. Wee the subscribers then being at the house of Frances Sebrell, widdow of Nicholas Sebrell, late of York Co., deceased, and the said widdow then and there being in a sick and weak condition but of perfect sence and memory ... did then and there declare that it was her will and desire that Sarah Smith, wife of Silas Smith of the County aforesaid, should have the care and tuition of two of her (Frances') children during their minority, that is to say Nathaniel and David Sebrell. Signed, Elizabeth Coman, Margrett Jepps, Sarah Goddin and Mary M. Haroson. Proved the 24 Nov 1708. {YCWI 1706-1710:175,178}

On 24 Feb 1708, Sarah Smith, Robert Crawley and William Coman presented and acknowledged their bond to the Court of York Co. for the said Smith's delivery of a negro woman, her child and their increase to the orphans of Nicholas Sebrell, dec'd., when of age, and it was admitted to record. {YCWI 1706-1710:197}

Nicholas and Frances (N) were the parents of MATTHEW (d. 1701) {WARG:137}; NATHANIEL; and DAVID.

5. SAMUEL SEBRELL, a son of Nicholas (2), m. Mary (N).

At a Court held for York County Febr. 17th 1723 ... [missing] David Cunningham
... [missing] Samuel Cobbs ... [missing] is admitted to record.
DR.   The estate of Richard Birt Junr.   CR.
To the ballance of a former acct. allowed by Burt Senr. £10.5.11 (1719)
To John Hansford ...
To Mary Lewis ...
To Mr Joseph Walker ...
To. Collo. Diggs ...
To Mr Philip Lightfoot ...
To Doctor Blair ...
To Sam Sebril.... {YCWI 1722-1725:257}

Martha Sebrell of York Hampton Parish, York Co widow [of Anthony

(3)], & Samuel Sebrell of same place planter, for 5 shillings, farm let unto Joseph Walker of same place esqr, all that messuage & 50 acre tract of land & premises in the parish afsd, bounded by Underhill's Line & Mr. Barbar's line ... for the term of one year paying the rent of one ear of Indian corn if demanded.... Wit: Godfrey Pole, Richard Parr, Thomas Colace. Ackn 16 Feb 1718 by Samuel Sebrel & Martha Sebrell, not appearing, was proved to be her act & deed, & also appeared Mary the w/o the sd Samuel & relinquished her right of dower & admitted to record.... {YCDB 1713-1729:271}

Jno Stockner of York Hampton Parish, York Co, for £25, released to Joseph Walker of same place merchant all his 50 acre tract of land in the sd parish bounded by the road, land of Arthur Dickeson, land late of Capt Phil Moody, the Black Swamp, land of William Barbar & land of the sd Joseph Walker which he lately purch of Martha & Samuel Sebrell & which two parcels of land together are the land mentioned in a patent dated at James City 12 Jun 1663 & thereby given & granted unto Wm Grimes.... Wit: Giles Moody, H. Hopkins, Godfrey Pole. Ackn 18 Oct 1721 & admitted to record.... {YCWI 1713-1729:372}

Fourth Generation
6. DAVID SEBRELL, son of Nicholas (4) and Frances (N) Sebrell.

The petition of Geo. Gilbert ... [missing] the securitys with Andrew Leprade, guardian to David Sebrell, is dismist. Leprade having given fresh Security. {YCWI 1722-1725:214}

... Andrew Laprade, at a Court held for York County held on 15 Jul 1723, became Guardian of David Sebrell, Orphan of Nicko. Sebrell deced., and hath received into his Care and Custody the whole Estate of the said Orphan if therefore the said Andrew Laprade do well & truly perform trust he hath undertaken relating to the sd. Orphan and his estate and pay or cause to be paid his full dues according to Law and custom when Shall Attain to Lawful Age or sooner if the court think fit and and also save and keep harmless the sd. Justices their heirs &c from damages that shall or may accrew to them concerning this said estate and perform all other things enjoined by Law and orders of this Court then this Obligation to be void or else remain in full force and virtue - Andrew Laprade, John Pasture [Pasteur].... {YCWI 1722-1725:214,218}

David Sebrell, taylor, for 5 shillings, leased to John Mundall of York Co [pg torn] a 160 acre tract of land in Bruton Parish adj Bruton Gleeb Road, said Sebrell's land, Thomas Hansford, land late of John Page decd, Robert Clark, Nathaniel Burwell & Jacob Goddnor ... for the term of 1 year paying one grain of Indian corn at the last day of the term.... Proved 20 Mar 1731/2 in court.... {YCLRD 1729-1740:113-115}

OTHERS NAMED SEBRELL

JOHN SEABRILL, will 1701, proved 24 May 1704.

In a Court held 25 Feb 1700 per adjournment from 24th instant, William Coman arresting John Sebrell in a case for 3 pd 4 sl 3 pn due by acct which a reference is granted to next court on the defs request. {YCWI 1698-1702:387}

John Morris his account agt John Sebrell for 3 pd 1 sl 6 pn was proved by ye oath of Thomas Adcock & ordered committed to record. {YCWI 1702-1704:205}

John Seabrill left a will dated 8 Nov 1701. To John Morris: 2 pr spurrs, a bible, 2 neckcloaths, 1 pr woosted hose, 2 pr wollen, a sadle, a pr shues, 3 yds ribin, 2 pr buckells, 12 ell dowles, 1 sl 6 pn. Errors excepted per Thomas Adcock. Proved 24 May 1704.... {YCWI 1702-1704:215}

MOSES SEBRILL

In obedience to an order of court Wil Prentis, John Holt & D. Davenport settled the accounts of the estate of John Crawley decd and made division of the same 11 Jul 1730. Paid Eliza Duffin as a nurse to Mr. Crawley, Thos Meacon, Col. John Custis for 1 barrel of corn, William Hall, Doctor Kenneth McKenzie, Wm Collins, Capt. Richard Cocke of Surry, Moses Sebrill.... {YCWI 1745-1759:184}

RICHARD SEBRELL

3 Apr 1704. Power of Attorney. Silas Smith of Bruton Parish, York Co taylor, appoint my trusty friend Richard Wharton, my atty, to appear for me in court to be held for York Co or any other following court to ackn this deed [see above].... Wit: Richd Sebrell, Claude Rouviere. Proved 24 Jun 1704.... {YCWI 1702-1704:211}

THE ARMIGER WADE FAMILY

A. ARMAGIL WAAD, b. ca 1500, d. 20 Jun 1568, bur. at the parish church, Hempstead, m. 1st Alice Paten and 2nd Anne Marbury. Armagil fathered approximately 20 children. {AB;VOL:51}

Descended from a Yorkshire family, he worked for Henry VIII, and was Clerk of King Edward VI's privy council in 1550. {AB;WJCM}

Lived in Belsize House, near Hampstead, London. {AB}

Armagil and Alice (Paten) Waad were the parents of WILLIAM and OTHERS.

B. SIR WILLIAM WAADE, b. 1546 {ACS}, d. 25 Oct 1623, bur. parish church

Hampstead, m. 1586 1ˢᵗ Anne Waller (1571-1589), m. 2ⁿᵈ (?). {AB;SL}
    In 1603, William, Lieut. of the Tower of London, was knighted,
acquiring the arms: *Quarterly:--1. Azure, a saltire between four escallops or. 2. Or, a chevron between three eagles' heads erased sable. 3. Gules, three garbs or. 4. Azure, two bars argent, on a chief of the last three maunches gules.*
{VOL:98}
    He was an ambassador for England, clerk of the King's privy concil,
and, from 1605-1613, lieutenant of the Tower of London. {AB}
    Sir William was involved with Virginia Company as early as 20 Nov
1606. {AB2} William and a Nathaniel Wade were both mentioned as members
of the second charter to the company of Virginia. {Hening:1:85,90}
    Wm and Anne (Waller) Wade had one son ARMAGIL, b ca 1589. {SL}

First Generation in America

1. ARMIGER WADE, SR., b. 1589, d. 28 Jan 1676, will pr. 24 Apr 1677, was
the son of Sir William and Anne (Waller) Waade. {CPR;EVB:348}
    Dorithy, wife of Armager, d. 25 May 1667. {CPR}
    Armiger Wade to have admr of est of Robert Halsey, decd.⁴⁰ {BF 1646-
1648:327}
    Yorke County paid Mr. Armiger Wade Burgesse 2800 lbs. of tobacco.
{BF 1648-1657:139}
    Armiger Wade member of Assembly from York County 1655-1656.
{CVR}
    William Sidwell, d. 7 Sep 1665; John Widnal, d. 22 Jul 1665; and
Thomas Draper, d. 18 Sep 1667 were servants to Armiger Wade, Sr. {CPR}
    Sarah Hemlocke, servant to Mr. Armiger Wade, was adjudged (12 Nov
1666) to be of age and free. {RB 1665-1672:111}
    Thomas Draper, servant to Mr. Armiger Wade, Sr., adjudged (24 Jul
1667) 15 years of age, to serve until 24. {RB 1665-1672:148}
    Armiger and Dorithy (N) Wade were the parents of ARMIGER, JR.;
MARY, m. Capt. John Hay (see the Hay family, this series, Vol. I); DOROTHY,
m. John Lilly. {EVB:348}

2. ARMIGER WADE, JR., d. 1708
    Armager, Jr. and Elizabeth (Plouvier?) Wade (d. 28 Jun 1696) were the
parents of ANN, b. 5 Apr 1674; DORITHY, bur. 21 May 1674 fn; DORITHY
(twin), b. 3 Jun 1679; ELIZABETH (twin), b. 3 Jun 1679; MARY, b. 16 May

---

⁴⁰ Edward Waide, b. 1611 (see "Unplaced Persons" this family), is found in the same
reference as Armiger Wade as early as 1646, a very early date. Given current evidence,
if a common ancestor exists, it would have been Armagill Waad (A), 1500-1568.

1683; and <u>FRANCES</u>, b. 31 Mar 1691, d. 13 Oct 1721. {CPR}

John Foster, d. 31 Jan 1670; John Loyd, d. 26 Apr 1671; and Joseph Burton, d. 8 Dec 1677 were servants of Armiger Wade, Jr. {CPR}

Thomas Foster, servant to Mr. Armiger Wade, Jr., adjudged (24 Jul 1667) 16 years of age. {RB 1665-1672:148}

John Foster, servant to Armager Wade, Jr., d. 31 Jan 1670. {CPR}

Thomas Sudland, servant to Mr. Armiger Wade, adjudged (20 Dec 1669) 12 years of age. {RB 1665-1672:374[274]}

Daniel Tompson, servant to Armiger Wade, Jr., adjudged (24 Apr 1670) 17 years of age. {RB 1665-1672:440[330]}

William Woodman and his wife Mary, in difference (1 Mar 1675/6) between the Woodmans and Mr. Armiger Wade, Jr., concerning service, Ordered they serve their full time. {RB 1672-1676:155}

Armiger Wade his deed of sale dated Aug 1702 from Stephen Pond for land in this co was ackn by said Stephen Pond & also his wife examined did freely ackn all her right of dower to ye land to sd Armiger Wade & is ordered committed to record. {YCWI 1702-1704:143}

Armiger Wade his deed of sale for 25 acres of land dated 15 Apr 1704 from Stepon Pond was by said Pond ackn & is ordered committed to record. {YCWI 1702-1704:202}

In the suit in Chancery depending between Henry Hayward Junr., complainant, and Armiger Wade, respondent, it is ordered that the respt. put in his answer to the compl.'s bill on oath at the next Court. {YCWI 1706-1708:159}

Will of Armiger Wade. To my son-in-law, William Trotter, my plantation at Tinker Shaws...except 40 acres of the land bounding upon Anthony Robinson's land and Mr. Kibye's [Kirby's] land, which I give to my son-in-law, John Robinson, provided his father, Anthony Robinson, gives him the same complement of land adjacent. After my son-in-law Wm. Trotter's decease, the land to be equally divided between my two grandsons, John Trotter and Wm. Trotter, and in case of their decease, the land to fall to my daughter Ann Trotter's other children successively. To my grandson, Wm. Trotter, one negro man named Tom. To my grandson, John Trotter, one negro man named Harry, living at the lower plantation. To my daughter, Anne Trotter, one negro woman named Nell. To my son-in-law, Edmund Curtis and Mary, his wife, the plantation I now live on with the land that I bought of Stephen Pond...until my grandson Armiger Trotter comes to the age of 21...unless he should dye in his minority, then to my grandson, Thomas Trotter, son of my daughter Ann Trotter. Said land to be equally divided between Armiger and Thomas Trotter when Armiger comes to the age of 21, but in case either of them should dye in their minority...then to fall to the next succeeding heir of my daughter, Anne Trotter. To my daughter, Dorothy Parsons, one negro man called Mingo and one negro gourl called Hannah. To my daughter, Mary Curtis, two negro women named

Sarah and Jenny. To my granddaughter, Frances Curtis, one negro girl called Sarah. To my daughter, Frances Robinson, one negro man called Jack and one negro gourl called Frank and the side saddle I lent her and one brake horse called Shaver. To my grandson, William Trotter, one negro boy called James. To my grandson, Armiger Parsons, one negro boy called Billy and one black mare. To my grandson, Jack[?] Parsons, one negro boy called Ausy and the other black mare. To my son-in-law, Edmond Curtis and Mary, his wife, one negro man called Great Harry and one young horse. To my daughter, Ann Trotter, one young mare about 16 months old. To my son-in-law, John Robinson, one white mare. To my daughter, Elizabeth Hayward, one young horse and as much callico as will make her a suit. To my son-in-law, Henry Hayward, the £8 which he is indebted to me and 35 shillings to buy him a ring. To my son-in-law, Humphrey Tompkins, 30 shillings to buy him a ring. To my son-in-law, James Parsons, £35 which he is indebted to me. To my friends, Capt. Thomas Nutting and Thomas Roberts Junr., each of them 30 shillings to buy them a ring. To my nephew, Robert Hay Senr., one negro woman called Abigall. The remaining part of my personall estate, that is to say, what money I have in any gentleman's hands in England with the produce of what tobacco I have already shipped, etc…be equally divided between my four daughters, Anne Trotter, Dorothy Parsons, Mary Curtis and Frances Robinson. My son-in-law, James Parsons, to be Ext. Dated this 12th day of Aug 1708. Wit. Bennet Tompkins, Jerrard Roberts and Anthony Lamb. Proved Nov the 24th 1708. {YCWI 1706-1708:172-173}

The caveat of Henry Hayward Junr. against the proving of the last Will and Tewstament of Armiger Wade is rejected. {YCWI 1706-1708:172-178}

The suit in chancery depending between Henry Hayward Junr., complainant, and Armiger Wade, respondent, is dismist, the said respt. being dead. {YCWI 1706-1708:190

An inventory of the Estate of Armiger Wade, dec'd., according to an order of Court dated the 3d day of Mar 1708/9. Total value of household goods and livestock, £283:13:8 ½. Presented and acknowledged by William Trotter, Extr. of the last Will & Testament of Armiger Wade, dec'd. {YCWI 1706-1708:213}

In the *ejection firmae* depending between Abell Dun, plf. and William Kattern and Edmund Curtis, defts. for the fifth part of 6 messuages, 6 out houses, 8 tobacco houses, 2 gardens, 2 orchards, 600 acres of land, 600 acres of wood, 300 acres of pasture, 500 acres of marsh with the appurtenances scituate, lying and being in the Parish of Charles, which one Henry Hayward the Younger and Elizabeth, his wife, devised to the plf. for a term not yet expired, and for £50 damage by means of the defts. with force and armes entring upon the possession of the plf. and him therefrom ejecting, expelling and amoving… the deft. pleaded not guilty. Whereupon a jury by name Philip Moody, Adduston Rogers, John Doswell, John Doswell Junr., John Drewry Senr., Nathaniel Hooke, John

Gibbons, Thos. Hansford, Francis Callohill, John Chapman, Richard Kendall and John Adduston Rogers were impannelled and sworn to try the issue joyned, the Attorneys having drawn up and agreed to a Speciall verdict, the jury were sent out and in short time came again into Court and returned their verdict in these words: "Wee find the Will of Armiger Wade dated the 15th day of Jan 1676 proved and recorded in York Co. Court. We find that Armiger Wade dyed seized of the lands in question and left only one son named Armiger, who dyed seized of the lands in question and left only five daughters, Ann, Elizabeth, Dorothy, Mary and Frances. Wee find that Henry Hayward the Younger, one of the Lessors of the plf., married Elizabeth, one of the daughters of Armiger, the son. Wee find the Will of Armiger Wade the son dated the 12th day of Aug 1708 proved and recorded in York Co. Court, and if upon the whole matter the plf. hath title to the lands in question, wee find for the plf. and assess damages to the value of 5 shillings. If not, wee find for the defts." The matters of Law arising from the said verdict are referred by consent of both partys untill the next Court to be argued. {YCWI 1708-1710:16}

Third Generation
3. ANN WADE, dau of Amiger and Elizabeth (Plouvier?) Wade, m. Wm. Trotter, and they were the parents of JOHN TROTTER, b. 22 Nov 1694; ELIZABETH TROTTER, bapt., 21 Mar 1697; WILLIAM TROTTER; b. 15 Jan [1698]; AMAGER TROTTER, b. 10 Dec 1701 {CPR}; MARY TROTTER; THOMAS TROTTER. {YCWI 1706-1708.172-173}
    Samuell Thomkins late constable of ye lower precinct of Charles Parrish being dead William Trotter is appointed in his stead. {YCWI 1702-1704:78}
    Wm Trotter constable of ye lower prinques of Charles Parish on his petition is discharged from his sd office and James Calthorpe is appointed in his stead. {YCWI 1702-1704:259}
    The will of William Trotter of Charles Parish, York Co., dated 16 Oct 1733, states: I lend to my wife Ann for her support and maintainance, five Negroes, to wit, Nemo, Judy, Frank, Dinah and Sary, during her natural life and my large copper stil and after her decease the stil to remain on the plantation or elsewhere. To my son John Trotter the two old Negroes Nemo and Judy. To my dutiful son Armiger Trotter one Negro named Will. To my dutiful son Thomas Trotter one Negro man named Mingo. To my dutiful dau Elizabeth Trotter one Negro man named James. To my dutiful dau Mary Trotter one Negro boy named Daniel. To my granddau Dorothy Trotter dau of my son William Trotter decd if demanded 5 sl and she is to have no more of estate whatsoever. To my granddau Gudlisbury Newby 10 pd. To my dutiful dau Ann Jordan w/o Edmd Jordan one Negro woman named Sarah and her future increase. If my Negro woman Judy should bear a child, I give the same to my little grandson Thomas Trotter son of

John Trotter. I lend to my wife 1/3 pt/o my estate when my debts and legacies are first paid during her life for her support & after her decease the three Negroes, to wit, Frank, Dinah and Sary to return and be divided among my children, as named, to wit, John, Armiger, Thomas, Elizabeth & Mary Trotter & Ann Jordan. I desire that 2/3 of my estate after my debts and legacies are paid may be divided between my children Armiger, Thomas, Elizabeth, Mary & Ann Jordan the said Ann Jordan to be accountable for what she has already received. I appoint my wife and my sons Arminger and Thomas executors. I desire the court may take no further regard of this my estate than only to grant a probate. Wit: John Robinson, Benit Tomkins, Chas Campbell. Proved 17 Dec 1733. {YCWI 1732-1737:81}

An inventory of the whole estate of William Trotter of York Co decd., 1 desk, 1 chest of draws, 1 whip saw, 1 large coal table, 12 new leather chairs, 8 old chairs, 1 small looking glass, 3 spinning wheals, 1 two armed chair, 8? beds & furniture, 8 chests, 1 pr of mony scales, 1 couch and bed, 1 pr of hand bellows, 1 warming pann, 3 brass candlesticks, 1 case and bottles, 4 flag'd chairs, 1 square table, 1 leather trunk, 1 swing looking glass, 1 potted silver tankard, 5 spoons, 1 small tumbler, etc. Negroes: Nemo, Jude, Frank, Mingo, Will, James, Daniel, Dinah, two girls named Sarah, Sarah.... Admitted to record 20 May 1734. {YCWI 1732-1737:117}

4. DOROTHY WADE, dau of Armiger and Elizabeth (Plouvier?) Wade, m. James Parsons, son of John Parsons. See Parsons Family, this volume.

16 Sep 1719. Deed of Gift. We James Parsons & Dorothy his wife of Charles Parish, York Co for natural love & effections have given unto our son James Parsons Junr all that plantacon & parsell of land which descended to us from our father Armiger Wade containing 41 acres 23 chain as by a platt of Maj Wm Buckner's.... Wit: John Robinson, Samll Hawkins, John Parsons. Ackn 21 Mar 1719/20 by James Parsons & Dorothy his wife & the sd Dorothy being also privately examined relinquished her right of dower & admitted to record.... {YCDB 1713-1729:327}

For the descendants of Dorothy Wade and James Parsons, see the Parsons family, this volume.

5. ELIZABETH WADE, dau. of Amiger and Elizabeth (Plouvier?) Wade, m. Henry Hayward, Jr.

Henry Heyward in open Court presented and acknowledged his Deed of Gift of lands lying in this County to Will Trotter. Also appeared Eliz., the wife of the said Henry, who being first privately examined relinquished her right of dower in the said lands to the said Trotter, and on his mocion the said Deed and Relinquishment are admitted to record. {YCWI 1710-1712:150}

19 May 1712. Deed of Gift. Henry Hayward of York Co gent & Elizabeth his wife one of the daus & coheirs of Armiger Wade late of York Co

decd for love & affection have given unto our well beloved brother in law William Trotter of York Co & William Trotter the younger his son (by Anne his wife, sister to the sd Elizabeth) all the land which came accrued or descended unto the sd Elizabeth as dau & one of the coheirs of the sd Armiger Wade decd being in Charles Parish now in the tenure & occupation of Edmund Curtis containing 47 acres.... Wit: Jno Robinson, Edmund Curtis. Ackn 19 May 1712 by Henry Hayward also Elizabeth his wife who being first privately examined relinquished her right of dower & admitted to record. {YCDB 1709-1713:386}

6. MARY WADE, dau. of Amiger and Elizabeth (Plouvier?) Wade, m. Edmund Curtis, son of Edmund Curtis.
    On the petition of Wm. Wise Junr., Contable of the lower precinque of Charles Parish in this County, Edmund Curtis is appointed his head borough and it is orderd that he be sworn before the next Justices to perform his office and duty therein as the Law requires. {YCWI 1706-1708:34}
    In the *ejectione firmae* depending between Abell Dun, plf. and Arthur Law, deft. for the fifth part of 6 messuages, 6 outhouses, etc. lying and being in the Parish of Charles, which one Henry Hayward and Elizabeth, his wife, demised to the plf., William Shelton made oath that he served William Trotter and Edmond Curtis, tenants in possession of the lands in question, with true copys of the conditional order made in this cause who this day by Stevens Thomson, their Attorney, appcared and were admitted defts. in the room of Arthur Law and thereupon pleaded not guilty and entred into common rule for tryall of the title at the next Court, and it is ordered that the Lessor of the plf. pay costs if cost in this acion. {YCWI 1709-1711:5}
    Pursuant to an order of court dated 15 Jan 1732 Thomas Nelson, Wil Robertson & John Ballard settled the account as well the estate of Edmund Curtis Junr the son and the balance paid to Edwd Cross his guardian in our presence by the said Trotter. Paid Frances, Elizabeth & Mary his sisters their proportion of two Negroes sold. Ballance due to him from William Trotter & paid by him to Edwd Cross guardian to afsd Edmd Curtis. His share of his father's estate. 120 pd 3 pn. A hhd of Brandy made on the plantation of the said Edmund delivered to Edward Cross. Ordered to be recorded 19 Feb 1732.... {YCWI 1732-1737:19}
    Mary Wade and Edmund Curtis were the parents of FRANCES, b. 26 Dec 1706; ROBERT, b. Dec 170[8], d. 19 Jan 1728; MARY, b. 14 May 1710, d. 21 Mar 1710[11?]; ELIZABETH, b. 21 Aug 1712; EDMUND, JR., b. 16 Sep, bap. 19 Oct 1718. {CPR}

7. FRANCES WADE, d. 13 Oct 1721, m. John Robinson (b. 25 Aug 1685, d. 7 Apr 1737, bur. 6 May 1737. {EVB:81;PNC}
    John Robinson was a son of Anthony and Mary (Starkey) Robinson.

{EVB:81}

Frances Wade and John Robinson were the parents of MARY ROBINSON, b. 24 Oct 1707; ELIZABETH ROBINSON, b. 3 Dec 17[09], d. 6 Feb 1709*[41]; ANTHONY ROBINSON, b. 9 Sep 1711, d. 7 Apr 1737, m. Mary Kirby (d. ca 1775). She m. 2nd Daniel Moore; JOHN ROBINSON, b. 4 Sep 1714, d. 5 Jun 1736; MARTHA ROBINSON, b. 12 Oct, bap. 7 Nov 1717, d. 25 Oct 1717*; STARKEY ROBINSON, b. 10 Apr, bap. 4 Jun 1720, d. 13 Jan 1720*. {CPR}

14 May 1714. Deed of Lease. Jno Robinson of Charles Parish, York Co gent & Frances his wife for 5 shillings leased to Edmund Curtis of same place gent all the third pt/o of a plantation & tract of land called Jumps in Charles Parish containing 41 acres now or late in the occupation of the sd Edmund Curtis abutting upon the river, Hickman's Cr & Robins Cr ... the land descended to Frances w/o the sd John Robinson by inheritance as one of the daus & coheirs of Armiger Wade late of the parish & co afsd decd ... for the term of one year.... {YCDB 1713-1729:15}

THE THOMAS WADE FAMILY of JAMES CITY CO.

1. THOMAS WADE, b. ca 1650s, d. 1713, m. ca 1675 Margaret Grymes. {RB 1672-1676:116}

Margaret, Martha and Jane Grymes were the daughters of William (b. 1594, d. 1668) and Alice (N) Grymes. Alice m. 2nd John Babb. {RB, 1665-1672:112,176,187,303-304}

Mr. John Babb, ordered (24 Jun 1675) to pay Mr. Thomas Wade what estate belongs to him in right of his wife, Margaret Grymes, late in guardianship of Babb. {RB 1672-1676:116}

Martha Grymes. Martha and Jane, orphans. Thomas Wade, their brother in law appointed (24 Jun 1675) their guardian and to be possessed of their estate now in hands of Mr. John Babb, their late guardian. {RB 1672-1676:116}

Anthony Sebrell. Deed of saile (26 Aug 1695) from Thomas Wade and Margrett his wife for 50 acres of the 16th instant, acknowledged. {DW 1694-1697:188}

16 Aug 1695. Deed. Thomas Wade of Merchants Hundred Parish in James City Co, VA planter & Margarett his wife for £50 sold to Anthony Sebrell of Hampton Parish, Yorke Co, VA planter a messuage & 50 acre tract of land in Hampton Parish bounded by Underhill's line & Capt Barbar's line, being pt/o the land formerly belonging to Willm Grimes.... Wit: Willm Sedgwick,

---

[41] An asterisk indicates that the inconsistent dates shown probably reflect recorder variations in calendar use rather than references to the wrong persons or errors.

Thomas Graves, Elizabeth Graves. Ackn 26 Aug 1695 by Thomas Wade &
Margarett his wife to Henry Watkins who received the same by vertue of a
power of atty to him made for the use of the within named Anthony Sebrell
being first proved in court by the oath of Willm Sedgwick one of the wits
thereunto which together with this present deed is committed to record.... {YCDB
1694-1701:24,26,27}

In the year 1697 this division of land made [*pg torn*] by us according to
ye will of George Bates of York Co in 1676 decd as herein mentioned between
Edmund Brewer & Mary his wife & his two sons John Bates & James Bates ...
[*pg torn*] ... the head of the Beaver Dam Swamp ... the manner plantation lying
s of the sd Edmund Brewer & Mary his wife, the other outside part binding on
Thomas Wade & Tindall is the sd John Bates.... Ackn 24 May 1698 by the
parties. {YCDB 1694-1701:158}

24 May 1700. Deed. Thomas Wade of James City Co sold to Robert
Green of Bruton Parish, Yorke Co a parcel of land being 30 acres in Bruton
Parish formerly the land of Matthew Hubberd & bounded by the Roade Side
coming from Queens Cr, land that was of Mr. Wylde & sd Robert Green ... in
wit whereof wee the sd Thomas Wade & Margerett his wife have sett our hands
& seals ... her right of dower & recorded. {YCDB 1694-1701:248}

23 Sep 1702. Deed. Matthew Hubbard of James City Co, VA for £7
sold to Joseph Benjafield of York Co all that 30 acre parsell of land bounded att
the lower end of the tract of land now in tenure of Thomas Wade sold by the sd
Hubbard being formerly all in one dividend but sold & parceled out to the sd
Wade & George Martin, & this 30 acre to be understood to be all the remainer
of the whole tr formerly belonging to Matthew Hubbard father of the sd
Matthew Hubbard first granted by pattent dated 13 Jan 1661 unto Col Tho
Ballard & since assigned by him unto Matthew Hubbard father of the sd
Matthew soe this 30 acre adj at the lower end of Wade's land, George Tindal's
land, the Main Swamp, Bates's Spring Br, Skimino Swamp, Martin's Spring Br,
Martin's land & Thomas Wade, lying in Bruton Parish.... {YCDB 1701-1708:56}

Robt Green his deed of sale from Thomas Wade & Margerett Wade was
ackn in court & is ordered to record. {YCWI 1698-1702:333}

19 Nov 1702. John Saunders together with Silas Smith and Thomas
Wade securitys did jointly and severally confess judgment before Capt Thomas
Barber & Capt Baldwin Mathews justices to Henry Tyler trustee to ye estate of
Cope Doyley late of this co decd for payment of 8 pd 2 sl 6 pn with cost and
stay of execution untill 10 Jan 1703. {YCWI 1702-1704:51}

19 Nov 1702. Thomas Wade together with Robert Harrison and
Nicholas Sebrell securities did jointly and severally confess judgment before
Capt Thomas Barber and Capt Baldwin Mathews justices to Henry Tyler trustee
to the estate of Cope Doyley late of this co decd for payment of 3 pd 15 sl with
cost & stay of execution untill 10 Jan 1703. {YCWI 1702-1704:55}

176

Thomas Wade bringing his negro boy, Kitt, before this Court for judgment of his age, the Court adjudgeth him of the age of 13 yeares. {YCWI 1706-1708:62}

Thomas and Margaret (Grymes) Wade were the parents of WILLIAM; JOSEPH; THOMAS.

Second Generation

2. WILLIAM, b. ca. 1680, son of Thomas and Margaret (Grymes) Wade, m. Anne (N).

15 Feb 1717. Deed. William Wade son & devisee of Thomas Wade late of York Co decd for £105 sold to James Bates of Bruton Parish, York Co merchant a 140 acre parcell of land in Bruton Parish near the place called Okn Neck being pt/o the land late of the sd Thomas Wade decd & by his will dated in 1713 the sd parcel of land was devised to the sd William Wade, bounded by the head of Wades Spring Br, Perrymans Spring Br, land of John Bates, Oken Neck Mill Road, sd Bates's line (formerly Perryman's), land of John Bates Junr & Joseph Wade's land.... William Wade & Ann the w/o the sd William relinquished her right of dower & admitted to record.... {YCDB 1713-1729:238}

16 Jul 1717. The case between Wm Wade & Anne his wife (late Anne Williams) plts & Wm Spencer def is dismist ye plts not prosecuting. {YCWI 1716-1718:145}

18 Feb 1717. William Wade presented & ackn his deed for land with livery & seizen endorsed thereon to James Bates, also appeared Ann w/o the sd Wm Wade & relinquished her right of dower to the sd Bates, admitted to record. {YCWI 1716-1718:217}

3. JOSEPH WADE, son of Thomas and Margaret (Grymes) Wade, m. Susanna (N). She m. 2nd Charles Hansford.

19 May 1718. Bond. Francis Sharp, James Dowling & Joseph Wade of York Co are firmly bound to our Sovereign Lord King George for 10,000 lbs of tobacco ... the condition of this obligation is such that whereas the afsd Francis Sharp hath an order granted him for a lycence to keep an ordinary in his now dwelling house in Williamsburgh for the year next ensuing, if the sd Francis Sharp shall constantly find & provide in his sd ordinary good wholesome & cleanly lodging & diet for travellers & stableage, fodder & provender for their horses or pasturage & provender during the term of 1 year and shall not suffer any unlawfull gaming in his house, nor on the Sabbath day suffer any person to tipple or drink more than is necessary, then this obligation to be void.... Ackn 19 May 1718 & admitted to record.... {YCWI 1718-1720:230,270}

15 Sep 1718. Bond. Elizabeth Coseby, Joseph Wade & Samuel Hyde of York Co are firmly bound unto the justices of sd co for 500 pd ... the condition of this obligation is such that if the afsd Elizabeth Coseby executrix of the will of

James Coseby decd do make a true & perfect inventory of all & singular the goods, chattles & credits of the sd James Coseby decd which have or shall come to her hands, & the same so made do exhibit into the co court, & well & truly administer according to law, & further do make a just & true acct of their actings & doings therein, & do pay & deliver all the legacys contained or specifyed in the sd will then this obligation to be void.... Ackn 15 Sep 1718 & admitted to record. {YCWI 1718-1720:315,321}

16 May 1720. On the petition of Joseph Wade praying to be released from the securityship for the estate of the orphans of James Cosbey decd, ordered that Saml Hyde who intermarryed with the widow of the sd James Cosbey & being one of the securitys for the sd orphans estate be summoned to answer the sd petition at next court. {YCWI 1718-1720:587}

1 Nov 1728. Deed of Lease. Joseph Wade of James City Co planter & Susanna his wife for 5 shillings leased unto Robert Carter of Lancaster Co esqr a tract of land at Skiminoe which was devised to the sd Joseph Wade by his father Thomas Wade by his will dated 21 Jul 1716 in these words, viz, I give unto my son Joseph Wade 170 acres of land being in York Co at Skiminoe adj the Spring Br, it is called 170 acres more or less is by general estimation supposed to contain about 200 acres & is pt/o a 365 acre tract of land formerly conveyed by Mathew Hubbard & Ellen Huberd by deed of feofment dated 18 Dec 1689 ... for the term of one year paying the rent of one pepper corn upon the feast day of St. Michael the Arch Angel now nest coming if demanded .... {YCDB 1713-1729:489, 490, 492}

17 Jun 1734. In the action of debt brought by Cole Digges & Philip Lightfoot esqr, Law Smith, Thomas Nelson, Richard Ambler, John Buckner, John Hansford, Joseph Wade, Francis Lee, Samuel Hyde vestrymen of York Hampton Parish plts agt Authur Dickenson and Ellyson Armistead defs, ordered that judgment be entr'd for the plts agt the said defs by *Nil Debit* and that a writ of inquiry of damages issue. {YCWI 1732-1737:167}

21 Feb 1736. The suit on the petition brought by Charles Hansford & Susanna his wife executrix of Joseph Wade decd agt Richd Willmott is cont'd. {YCWI 1732-1737:342}

21 Mar 1736. In the suit on the petition brought by Charles Hansford & Susanna his wife executors of Joseph Wade decd agt Richard Willmott for a gun, the parties being called and fully heard, it's considered by the court that the petitioners recover agt the def 26 sl the value of the said gun and their costs. {YCWI 1732-1737:353}

4. THOMAS WADE, son of Thomas and Margaret (Grymes) Wade.

17 Feb 1717. Florence Mecartee at last court appointed constable in the upper precinct of Bruton Parish moved that some other person might be nominated in his place by reason of his being illiterate. Thomas Wade is therefore appointed

to execute that office in sd precinct.... {YCWI 1716-1720:197}

Richard Easter is appointed constable in the upper precinct of Bruton Parish in the room of Thomas Wade. 18 May 1719. {YCWI 1718-1720:428}

16 May 1720. Bond. David Laton, Frans Sharp & Thos Wade of York Co are firmly bound unto the justices of sd co for 100 pd ... the condition of this obligation is such that if the afsd David Laton adminr of the estate of Richard Bloxom decd do make a true & perfect inventory of all & singular the goods, chattles & credits of the sd Richard Bloxom decd which have or shall come to their hands, & the same so made do exhibit into the co court, & do well & truly administer according to law, & further do make a true & just acct of their actings & doings therein, & all the rest & residue of the sd goods, chattells & credits which shall be found remaining the same being first examined by the justices & shall deliver & pay unto such persons as the sd justices by their order or judgment shall direct then this obligation to be void.... Ackn 16 May 1720 & admitted to record.... {YCWI 1718-1720:594}

THE EDWARD WADE FAMILY

1. EDWARD WADE, m. Jane (N), was a brother of William (2) Wade (see below).

An Edward Wade entered Virginia on 18 Mar 1662. {CP}

On 12 Nov 1666, Jane, wife of Edward Wade, and Anne Dickeson, wife of Arthur Dickeson, were summoned for rude carriage and deportment, to next Court. {RB 1665-1672:112}

Mr. George Rough, In difference (24 Feb 1667) between him and Mr. Edward Wade and Jane his wife, def. acknowledge they defamed pltf. {RB 1665-1672:169}

Robert Griffin, servant to Mr. Edward Wade, adjudged (7 Dec 1668) 16 years of age, to serve until 24. {RB 1665-1672:316 [216]}

Edward Wade, Sr., Hampton Parish. To (26 Jun 1671) my grandchildren Samuel and John Bond, sons of Nicholas Bond, dec., and my dau. Dori Antothea Bond, relict of said Bond, give them a mare, first mare to my dau. Jane Wade, when Samuel and John are 15. {RB 1665-1672:452[352]}

Thomas Hancocke, New Kent Co. m. on 24 Apr 1673, Dorianathea, the relict and admintx. of Mr. Nicholas Bond, dec.; and Edward Wade, Hampton Parish, York Co., gave bond as above Thomas is possessed of estates of Samuell and John Bond, sons of said Nicholas, Thomas to give them their estates at age. {RB 1672-1676:46}

Anne Elmes, servant to Mr. Edward Wade, adjudged (26 Nov 1674) 19 years of age. {RB 1672-1676:88}

Edward and Jane were the parents of DORIANATHEA, m. Nicholas

Bond; JANE and possibly EDWARD, JR.

2. WILLIAM WADE m. Elizabeth (N), was a brother of Edward (1) Wade.
Mary Pell, age c19 deposed (26 Mar 1688) about 6 Feb last past att the house of John Williams where was William Wade whoe had his horses in Williams's tobacco house, Williams' wife said shee should turne them out, words passing, Wade beat Williams' wife with many blowes. {DW 1687-1691:113}
Ann Abbott, age c24 deposed (26 Mar 1688) concerning the beating William Wade gave John Williams' wife on 6 Feb last past. {DW 1687-1691:114}
Samll. Bond, orphant. Setting forth (24 Jul 1699) by his petition that hee hath attained to 21, as does appear by certificate of the register of Hampton Parish, Ordered his estate now in the hands of William Wade be delivered unto Bond. {DW 1687-1691:141}
Samuell Bond, Discharge my unkle William Wade from all manner of debt granted by York Court 24 Jul 1688. {DW 1687-1691:168}
William Wade, York Co., and Hampton Parish and Elizabeth his wife. To (26 Nov 1688) Samuell Bond of Warwick Co., and Parish of Denby. 100 acres in Hampton Parish in the occupation of Wm. Wade. {DW 1687-1691:169-172}
Wiliam Wade posts bond (24 Sep 1696) as guardian for Willm. Lee, sonn and orphant of Henry Lee. {DW 1694-1697:335}

THE THOMAS WADE FAMILY of YORK CO.

1. THOMAS WADE, m. Jane (N).
John Parker, Thos Wade & David Layton of York Co are firmly bound unto our King for 10,000 lbs of good sweet scented tobacco ... the condition of this obligation is such that whereas the afsd John Parker hath an order this day granted him to keep an ordinary at his dwelling house in York Co for 1 year next ensuing, if the said John Parker doth constantly find & provide in his ordinary good holesom, cleanly lodging & dyet for travellers and stabliage & provender or pasturage & provender as the season shall require for their horses for 1 year and shall not suffer any unlawfull gaming nor on the Sabbath day suffer any person to tipple or drink more than is necessary, then this obligation to be void.... Admitted to record 21 May 1739. {YCWI 1737-1740:498}
Will of Thomas Wade of Bruton Parish, York Co. dated 15 Mar 1755. To son Joseph Wade 28 acres of land where he the said Joseph now lives. My will is that my son Joseph Wade shall hold and enjoy the 28 acres of land no longer than his natural life and after his death it shall return to the part I hereafter give unto my son Richard Wade. To son John Wade 40 acres of land adj said Joseph Wade. My will is that John Wade shall have free liberty of a

spring that is on a piece of ground as I shall hereafter devise to my grandson John Farthing. My will is that my son John Wade shall have and enjoy the afsd 40 acres of land during his natural life and no longer and after his death the said land shall return to the tract that I have given to my son Joseph. To my grandson John Farthing 10 acres of land adj Fleming Bates & Joseph Wade. My will is that John Farthing shall have and enjoy the afsd 10 acres of land during his natural life and no longer and after his death the said land to return to the tract I gave my son John Wade. To son Richard Wade the 1/2 of the remainder of my land that I now live on and my will is that my friend Fleming Bates shall divide the said land as I have informed him to do and further my son Richard Wade is to let his mother live with him during her life and in case Richard should marry and he and his mother should disagree my will is that the said Richard Wade shall build for his mother to live in a house. My will is that Richard Wade shall hold and enjoy the afsd land during his natural life and no longer and after his death the said land to return to the part I hereafter shall devise to my son Robert Wade. To son Robert Wade the other 1/2 of my land adj to my son Richard which Fleming Bates is to lay off during the said Robert Wade's natural life and no longer and after his death the said land is to return to the tract I gave my son Richard. My will is that what money I leave at my death may be divided amongst my wife and children heretofore mentioned. My will is that immediately after the proving of this my will that my Negroes, cattle, horses, hogs, household goods & all things that is not mentioned herein be sold and the money arising to be divided amongst my wife and children. My will is that my son Joseph Wade shall allow to this estate after my death 5 pd out of his part for a bed I lent him and what other things I lent him my desire is he may return them to be sold and my desire is there shall be no appraisement and what money falls to those that are under age shall be put out to interest and at each obtaining to lawful age shall receive his part. I appoint my wife Jane Wade and my son Joseph Wade executors. Wit: Fleming Bates (a Quaker), Ashwell Stone, Elizabeth Stone. Proved 17 Nov 1755. John Wade one of the executors together with Fleming Bates & Samuel Dyer his securities ackn a bond and a cert was granted him for obtaining a probate. Jane Wade widow and relict of the testator and the other executor named in the will renounced all benefit which she might or could claim by the said will and absolutely refused to take upon herself the executorship. {YCWI 1745-1759:382}

In obedience to an order of court ... the estate of Thomas Wade decd 3 May 1758 was divided ... 198 pd 14 sl 6 1/2 pn ... Widow's part 43 pd 18 sl 9 3/4 pn, Jos Wade's part, Jno Wade's part, Farthin's part, Richd Wade's part & Robt Wade's part, each 28 pd 19 sl 1/4 pn. Ordered to be recorded 15 May 1758. {YCWI 1745-1759:444,476}

Thomas and Jane (N) Wade were the parents of JOSEPH, RICHARD, b. 18 Apr, bap. 18 May 1739 {BP:2}, JOHN, ROBERT.

2. JOSEPH WADE, son of Thomas (1) and Jane (N) Wade, m. Elizabeth (N). On 15 Jan 1759. Thomas Cole Megary hath voluntarily put himself apprentice to Joseph Wade of York Co carpenter to learn his art, trade and mystery for the term of 4 years.... Ackn 15 Jan 1759 by the parties.... {YCLRD 1755-1763:176}

Will of Joseph Wade of Bruton Parish, York Co. To wife Elizh. Wade all my personal estate during her widowhood and after her death or marriage the estate may be equally divided between son David Bingley Wade and the child that my wife Elizabeth Wade is now with. In case of the death of said children, then to my three brothers, John Wade, Richard Wade and Robert Wade. Execs. to dispose of the tract purchased of William Norvell and William Walt ... in James City Co.... Approved 10 Feb 1762 by oath of Thomas Bowles, and Thomas Cole McGarey, witnesses thereto. Probate granted to Nathaniel Bingley, Thomas Bowles his security. {YCWI 1760-1771:89}

Elizabeth Wade, widow and relict of Joseph Wade, late of York Co., refused to abide by the will of Joseph Wade. 24 Jul 1762. Wit. James Hubbard, James ... Thos. Jones. {YCWI 1760-1771:115}

Appraisement of the estate of Joseph Wade decd. Total: £37.14.½. Appraised by Thos. Bowls, William Ratcliffe, Jonathan Barker. Returned 19 Nov 1764. {YCWI 1760-1771:219}

Settlement of the estate of Joseph Wade, administered by Nathaniel Bingley. Payments: £181.12.2 .... Balance due to the estate. £39.6.6. By court order 19 Nov 1764. Examined by John Pierce, James Shields. Returned 21 Oct ... {YCWI 1760-1771:250}

Joseph and Elizabeth (N) Wade were the parents of DAVID BINGLEY, b. 3 Dec, bap. 17 Dec 1758 {BP:6} and UNBORN CHILD.

3. RICHARD WADE, b. 18 Apr, bap. 18 May 1739 {BP:2}, son of Thomas (1) and Jane (N) Wade.

On 15 Dec 1755, Richard Wade son of Thomas Wade decd doth put himself apprentice to William Eggleston, carpenter of James City Co, to learn his art or mystery of carpenter during the term of 6 years.... 15 Dec 1755 ackn by the parties.... {YCLRD 1755-1763:43}

4. JOHN WADE, d. 1774, m. Mary (N), was a son of Thomas (1) and Jane (N) Wade.

Will of John Wade, York Co. Estate to be sold. To wife Mary Wade ½ the money after debts paid. The other half to David Bingley Wade. Execs. John Lightfoot of James City Co. and wife Mary. Wit. Fras. Lightfoot. John Wilson, James Musgrove, Sarah Barker. Proved 21 Mar 1774. Probate granted to John Lightfoot with Francis Lightfoot his security. {YCWI 1771-1783:216}

Will of Samuel Hill, York Co .... [three lines obliterated] ... dau. of
John Cosby. £3 to school William Wade the son of John Wade. £3 to school
Edmund Glanvill Hubberd, son of Matthew Hubberd ... the remainder of estate
to my mother Elizabeth Fuller. Execs. Mr. Charles Hansford in whose care I
leave my said dau. to be brought up. 30 Nov 1769. Proved 19 Feb 1770 by oaths
of Matthew Hubberd, witness thereto. Probate granted to Charles Hansford,
execs. therein named with Frederick Bryan his security. {YCWI 1760-1771:483}
John and Mary (N) Wade were the parents of WILLIAM.

5. ROBERT WADE, d. 1765, was a son of Thomas (1) and Jane (N) Wade.
Robert Wade was Burgess for Halifax co Virginia from 1758 to 1765.
In 1765, Edward Booker stood in for Wade who had died. {CVR}
By court order 17 May 1773. Appraisement of the estate of Robert
Wade decd. Total: £11.3.10. Appraised by John Kerby, John Kerby Junr.,
Merritt Moore. Returned 19 Jul 1773. {YCWI 1771-1783:187}
Robert Wade was the father of ROBERT, JOHN, STEPHEN,
EDWARD, CHARLES, SARAH STOKES, MARY HUNT; and the grandfather
of HAMPTON (son of Robert); ROBERT (son of Charles); ROBERT (son of
Robert). {EVB:348}

OTHERS NAMED WADE

ANTHONY WADE
John ... [pg torn] ... Anthony Wade arresting John H[pg torn] in an action
of debt for [pg torn] lbs of tobacco due by account ... order is granted agt Lt Col
Thomas Ballard high sheriff and next court to be confirmed if he causeth not the
def to appear and answer the same. {YCWI 1698-1702:260}

CHIDLEY WADE, d. by 1790, m. by 1778 Anne Kerby (b. 31 Aug, bap. 30 Sep
1760) {CPR}. Anne m. 2nd John Mackendree. {WMCQ 1:14:157}
Anne Kerby was a daughter of William and Margaret (Howard) Kerby.
{CPR} See this series, Vol. I, for antecedents Anne Kerby.
Will of Wm. Kerby of parish of Charles, York Co. To wife Margaret
Kerby during widowhood the plantation where I now live, all stocks of cattle
except six heifers, horses, hogs and plantation utensils, all household furniture
and negroes Phil and Judy. In case of her marriage or death my two plantations,
viz. "Sandwin" and that whereon Wm. Moore now lives.... To dau. Anne Wade
a negro girl named Hannah and to possess what I have before given her.... 21
Sep 1781.... {YCWI 1771-1783:554}
Chidley Wade paid by the estate of Samuel Hyde decd.... 16 Aug 1742.
{YCWI 1740-1743:121}

Chidley and Anne (Kerby) Wade were the parents of MARGARET JONES, b. 1778; THOMAS, b. 1781; JAMES, b. 1783; ELIZABETH HOWARD, b. 1786; and CHIDLEY, b. 1787. {WMCQ 1:14:157}.

EDWARD WADE, b. 1611.

On 17 Jul 1635, the *Paule* of London traveled from Gravesend, England to Virginia with Edward Wade, age 24. {HOT:103}

Rowland Vaughan confessed judgment to Capt. Ralph Wormeley 438 lbs tobo to be pd from debt due Vaughun from Edward Waide, etc. {BF 1646-1648:310}

EDWARD WADE, James City Co.

Edward Wade, late of the parish of Wilmington, in the county of James City, deceased, did by his certain indentures of lease and release, bearing date the fifth and sixth days of Mar, in the year of our Lord, one thousand seven hundred and eighteen, for the consideration in the said release expressed, convey to George Woodward and William Barret, then churchwardens to the parish of Wilmington, in the counties of James City and Charles City, a plantation and two hundred acres of land, or thereabouts, situate in the said county of James City.... {Hening:6:393}

EDWARD WADE, noncupative will, d. ca 1719

On 6 Jan 1714/15, Edward Wade et al. witnessed a deed of lease from Jno. Cook to Edwd Powers, both of Yorktown. {YCDB 1713-1729:49}

On 21 Sep 1719, Philip Lightfoot & Jno Roberts made oath that Edwd Wade departed this life without making any will, on their motion & giving security cert is granted them for obtaining a commission of administration on the sd estate. {YCWI 1718-1720:484}

On 21 Sep 1719, John Roberts, Phillip Lightfoot & John Gibbons of York Co [we]re firmly bound to the justices of sd co for [blank] pd ... the condition of this obligation is such that if the afsd John Roberts & Phillip Lightfoot adminrs of the estate of Edwd Wade decd do make a true & perfect inventory of all & singular the goods, chattles & credits of the sd Edward Wade decd which have or shall come to their hands, & the same so made do exhibit into the co court, & do well & truly administer according to law, & further do make a true & just acct of their actings & doings therein, & all the rest & residue of the sd goods, chattells & credits which shall be found remaining the same being first examin'd by the sd court shall deliver & pay unto such persons as the sd justices by their order or judgment shall direct then this obligation to be void.... Ackn 21 Sep 1719 & admitted to record. {YCWI 1718-1720:485,488}

21 Mar 1719[/20]. An inventory & appraisement of the estate of Edwd Wade decd taken by John Trotter & Richd Baker 12 Oct 1719. 1 horse & saddle,

1 pr saggathy & trimming, 1 parcell old cloths, 1 pott, 1 pann, 1 chest, 4 trowells, 1 coat & jacket, old bridle & bagg, 1 pr spatter dashes, 2 old rasors, 1 snuff box, 12 pd 18 sl.... {YCWI 1718-1720:573}

HENRY WADE
Maj. Joseph Croshaw was granted a cerficate (25 Aug 1662) for 1200 acres due for importing 24 persons: Henry Wade, Edward Markham, Ralph Graves et al. {RB 1659-1662:169}

HIGGINSON WADE of Warwick Co. Virginia, m. Jane (N).
Higginson Wade of Warwick Co planter maketh oath that being with William Brookes on 5th this instant Jan the said Brookes lying sick of the small pox this deponent asked him if he had made his will, Brookes answered no, upon which this deponent reply'd that no doubt but you had rather some should have what you leave in case you should dye than othersome. Brookes answered that my desire is that you meaning this deponent (there being no other person present) and John Harris should have what I have after my debts are paid and he desired then that this deponent would write down what debts were then due to him and write down the things he had left at Mr. Fountain's which this deponent did accordingly. Higginson Wade made oath before Thos Reynolds that this writing is as near as he can remember the conversation that passed between him and the decd William Brookes given his hand 14 Jan 1747/8. At a court held 18 Jan 1747 this nuncupative will was produced in court by Higginson Wade who made oath thereto and ordered to be recorded and a cert granted him for obtaining Letters of Administration of the estate of said William Brookes decd with the will annexed. Whereupon he together with Thomas Wills his security ackn a bond in the penalty of 200 pd.... {YCWI 1745-1759:77}
15 Dec 1740. Deed. Richard Smith of York Town, York Co & Mary his wife for £2.10 sold to John Morgan of same place ¼ pt/o 1 acre being ½ of a lott of land lately purch by said Richard Smith of Gwyn Reade of Gloucester Co gent.... Wit: Higginson Wade et al. Proved 15 Dec 1740.... {YCLRD 1729-1740:622}
Inventory of the estate of Lockey Miles Burnham decd. Includes negroes: man called Mordica(?), boy Frank, woman Peg, girl Sarah. Appraised 21 May 1761. Stafford Gibbs, Higginson Wade, ... Loyd. Returned ... £20. To Higginson Wade £5. To friend James Dudley, rest of my estate. Exec. friend Higginson Wade. 3 Jul 1761.... {YCWI 1760-1771:60}
14 Oct 1763. Indenture. Thomas Betsey lately from Jamaica doth voluntarily & of his own free will & accord put himself apprentice to John Parry taylor in York Town, York Co to learn his art, trade & mystery during the term of 7 years.... Wit: Matt Hubberd, Higginson Wade. Ackn 19 Dec 1763 by the parties & recorded. {YCDB 1763-1769:9}

Will of William OBrian, parish of York Hampton, York Co. To friend William Anderson Taylor of Gloster Co. £20. To Higginson Wade £5. To friend James Dudley, rest of my estate. Exec. friend Higginson Wade. 3 Jul 1764.... {YCWI 1760-1771:64}

21 Nov 1766. Deed. Edward Moody & Elizabeth his wife of Chesterfield Co for £10 sold to Higginson Wade of Warwick Co planter a 25 acre parcel of land which his father Ishmael Moody purch of Capt John Buckler in York Hampton Parish bounded on the Main Lodge Road & adj a tract of land belonging to Charles Miles.... Wit: Matt Hubberd, James Hubberd, William Hubberd. Ackn 15 Jun 1767 & recorded.... {YCDB 1763-1769:292}

20 Jan 1777. Deed. Higginson Wade & Jane his wife of Warwick Co for £14 sold to Charles Miles of York Co all their 22 acre tract of land bounded by the Public Road & the sd Miles's lands.... Wit: Thomas Charles, Henry Charles. Ackn 20 Jan 1777 by Higginson Wade & recorded.... {YCDB 1763-1769:523}

JAMES WADE

23 Oct 1733. Deed. James Wade carpenter of Bruton Parish, York Co for £19.4 sold to Thomas Wade of same parish planter a 50 acre tract of land in Bruton Parish which tract of land my father John Wade decd left by his will to my brother John Wade decd which has descended to me ...[blurred].... Wit: Philip Chesly, Giles Wade?, [?], [?] Baron, [?] Allen, [?].... {YCLRD 1729-1740:274}

James Wade ackn his deed for 50 acres of land unto Thomas Wade and also the receipt and both are admitted to record. {YCWI 1732-1737:103}

JANE WADE

The acion of case for words between Jane Wade, plf. and Thomas Toppin, deft. is dismist. {YCWI 1706-1708:238}

JOHN WADE m. Sarah Hubank

24 Oct 1701. Jno Wade & Sarah his wife one of ye daus of George Hubank decd having commenst suite agt David Stoner in a case to ye plts damage 200 lbs of tobacco and ye def being by ye sheriff returned *non est inventus* an attachment is granted agt his estate to next court. {YCWI 1698-1702:514}

24 Feb 1701. The suit between John Wade & Sarah his wife one of the daus of John Hubank decd agt David Stoner is dismist by non process. {YCWI 1698-1702:541}

6 Jun 1702. Receipt. I John Wade as marrying with Sarah ye dau of George Ubank decd do ackn to have received of David Stoner as marrying Jane ye widow, relict & adminr of sd George Ubank full value & such sumes of money, tobacco etc due to ... [pg torn] ... 6 Jun 1702. Wit: Wm Davis, Elinor?

Davis. Recorded.... {YCWI 1702-1704:291}

JOHN WADE
It is my [Daniel Cary's] will that ... My friend John Wade should have my gunn.... Proved 20 May 1751.... {YCWI 1745-1759:217}

MARTHA WADE, m. John Hewitt
William Hewitt of York Hampton Parish, York Co. 23 Nov 1730 [pg torn] ... To my son John Hewitt the remaining 100 acres of land n on the creek which divides this land from the Glebe, Mrs. Sarah Walker, Baskervil's Swamp ... To my dau Martha Wade two Negroes by name George & Hannah with their increase ... All the rest of my estate I give to my [pg torn] Hewitt, Francis Hewitt, John Hewitt, Elizabeth Hubbard, [?] Powel, Lucy Hewitt, Martha Wade and Francis Hewitt to be divided amongst them.... Wit: Arthur Dickeson, Robert Peters. Proved 19 Feb 1732. Cert was granted to the executors for obtaining probate. {YCWI 1732-1737:19}
John and Martha (Wade) Hewitt were the parents of JOHN HEWITT, b. 30 Jul, bap. 14 Aug 1743, d. 7 Oct 1743 {CPR}; WILLIAM HEWITT, d. 12 Sep 1751. {CPR}

RALPH WADE
The suit between Ralph Wade? plt & Robert Shield def in a plea of debt for 430 lbs of tobacco by bill dated 7 Jul 1699 and 144 1/2 lbs of tobacco since by acct is dismist no further prosecution had. {YCWI 1698-1702:564}

SETH WADE
18 Dec ----. To John Archer, Richard Eppes & Seth Waid gent greeting, whereas Peter Oliver & Mary his wife on 19 Jun 1758 sold unto William Barker a 66 ½ acre tract of land, and whereas the said Mary cannot conveniently travel to our court to acknowledge the conveyance, we do give unto you or any two of you the power to receive the acknowledgment which the said Mary shall be willing to make before you, and we command you to personally go to the said Mary and examine her privately and apart from her husband.... – Dec 1758 John Archer & Richard Eppes examined the said Mary and she ackn the indenture.... {YCLRD 1755-1763:177}

THOMAS WADE, m. Ann (N).
Thomas and Ann (N) Wade were the parents of PAMELA, b. 20 Nov [1746?]. {BP:6}
See John Chapman m. Ann Allin (Chapman Family, this volume) for possible information on Ann (N) Wade.

THE JOHN WELDON FAMILY

1. JOHN WELDON, GENT, of Westminster, London, will 14 Oct 1644, pr. 20 Nov 1644.

I give the mannor of Summers in Much Parendon in Essex with the advowson of the parsonage there, and all other landes in Parendon and elsewhere in the said countie, in tail successively to my eldest sonne John, my sonne George, and my daughters Elizabeth and Johanna. The lands I purchased of my brother in law George Bell in Wexham and Upton, Co. Bucks, I give to my daughter Elizabeth and her heirs, failing whom to the said Johanna and George successively ... Two shares of fower shares of land lyeinge in Pagetts tribe in the Bannuthos [Bermudas] which was purchased by my father in law George Prynne and myself of one (N) Woodhall, barber, chirurgion of London.... My land which I have by mortgage in Burnam, county Bucks by one (N) Kedge, I leave to daughter Joanna. I discharge (N) Kedge of a bond wherein he stands bound with my brother Henrie Welden for payment of £20 upon condition that, if he redeeme the said land from mortgage, he shall settle the same conveyance upon Elizabeth the eldest daughter of the said Henrie Welden and her heirs. George Prynne, executor and guardian, to provide for the education of sons until age 21 and daughters until age 21 or married. A small bequest was made to his sister in law Sarah Weldon. Wits: James Halliwell, James Heath, Jonathan Brand. {CD503:VAGleanings:459-460}

John Weldon was the father of <u>JOHN</u>; GEORGE; ELIZABETH, m. [prob Edmund] Butler; and JOHANNA, m. (N) Wright. {NAUK}

Second Generation

2. JOHN WELDON, minister, will 20 Dec 1674, probated 1 May 1675, bur. Parish of St. Mary's Newington Church, m. 1st Hannah (N), 2nd Dorothy (N). {NAUK}

In this will he names his son Samuell, executor, to whom he gave a lump sum plus shipping revenues related to business in Virginia. He provided for daughter Hannah and sons Poynes and James.

John names a brother George Weldon, sister Elizabeth Butler, "cousin" Edmund Butler, sister Joanna Wright, granddaughter Joanna Wright.

He makes a bequest to "brother" William Williams of Snowehill, Painter-stainer and, and wife Elizabeth. He bequeaths funds to clerk Herbert [Pe]ogers, sexton Nicholas Bourne.

Wits: Alies [Alice] Young, Joanna Wright, Mary Fenn. {NAUK}

In the probate, Thomas Parker, Barnabas Dunch, Eduardo Blake, and

188

Georgis Leyfeild. {NAUK}

Peter Efford[42], b. ca 1611 {RB 1659-1662:96}, in a will dated 24 Aug 1665 and proved 24 Apr 1667, left all his estate to son Nicholas Efford and dau. Sarah Efford (both under age). John Weldon, Minister of Newington and Abbertus Skinner[43], Gent., exs. {RB 1665-1672:134}

John Weldon, Parish of [St.] Mary Newington, Co. of Surry, was surviving executor (24 Apr 1667) of Peter Efford dec, and guardian to Sarah Efford, the only surviving child of said Peter. {RB 1665-1672:132}

Peter Efford, Middletown Parish, York Co. To (1 Apr 1664) my young coz. Jno. Poindexter, son of my coz. George Poindexter, Jr., a mare, and her foal to my coz. Elizabeth Poindexter. {RB 1665-1672:56}

John (2) and Hannah (N) Weldon were the parents of SAMUELL, HANNAH, and POYNES.[44]

John (2) and Dorothy (N) Weldon were the parents of JAMES.

Third Generation

3. MAJ. SAMUEL WELDON, b. ca. 1650, d. aft. 1688, m. Sarah Efford, was a son of John (2) and Hannah (N) Weldon.

Samuel Weldon was brought to Virginia in 1675 by Capt. Philip Foster. {WMCQ 1:6:121}

In 1680, Major Samuel Weldon was listed as an officer in the James City Co company commanded by Col Thomas Ballard. {CD503:VAColMil:103}

George Poindexter Senr, on 4 Oct 1688, gave 50 acres to his son John and Katherine, his [John's] wife. All my interest of the within mentioned land formerly purchased of Thomas Smyth by William Royston and by him assigned to me 24 Apr 1658. George Poindexter, York Co., had originally purchased the 50 acres in Parish of Marston upon Mill Swamp from William Bell of York Co. on 22 Dec 1671. I request my loveing cozen[45] Samll. Wolding [Weldon] to acknowledge this deed. {DW 1687-1691:303-306}

Mrs. Sarah, admintx. of Major Samuel Weldon arrested John Gardner in an action of debt on 24 Mar 1692/3. {DW 1691-1694:213}

Schedule [?] in ye letter of atty whereto it is annexed: Will Durbinfeild of Carolina, John Owens of VA, James Bray of VA in ye hands of Robt Harris of

---

[42] The Efford family previously resided on the Isle of Jersey, situated in the British Channel, where the name was spelled Effard. {EVB I:192}

[43] Albert and Martin Skinner owned shares of the ship *Neptune*. {RSES:168}

[44] The name Poynes was probably based on the surname Poynz/Poynz/Ponz, which can be traced to Co. Kent England in 1275 and, prior to that time, Norman France. {CB:619}

[45] George Poindexter was a son of Thomas Poingdestre (b. 1581) of the Isle of Jersey {CD503:Emigrants:68}. Thomas m. Elizabeth Effard. {EVB I:192}. Elizabeth and Peter Effard were probably siblings.

VA, executor of Willm Riggs of Carolina, Stephen Cocker of VA, John Bates of VA, Otho Cobbs of VA, Allexander Boneyman? of VA, Henry Gillbert of VA, Sarah Weldon of VA, et al. {YCWI 1698-1702:45}

The Quit Rent Rolls of Virginia in 1704 show that Sarah Weldon owned 100 acres in James City County. {CD503:EngDuplLostVARec:176}

Sarah Weldon of James City Co arrested Mathew Pierce for 5 pd due by account and he not appearing order is granted agt Wm Barbar high sherriff & next court to be confirmed if he causeth not ye def to appear & answer ye same. {YCWI 1702-1704:276}

James Backhurst being by ye sherrif returned summoned an evidence for Sarah Weldon plt agt Mathew Pierce def is ordered to be payd 160 lbs of tobacco for 4 days attendance at court. {YCWI 1705-1706:320,329}

In the action of Detinue between Sarah Weldon, plf. and George Gilbert, deft. for £7 damage by means of the deft. refusing to deliver the plf. one horse of said value, being her proper horse which she out of her hands and possession casually lost and by finding came into the hands and possession of the deft., the deft. by his Attorney appeared and on his mocion has an imparlance granted untill the next Court. ...[The jury] having heard the evidence produced by plf. and deft. and received their charge, went out and in short time gave their verdict in these words: "Wee find for the plf. £5 for the value of the horse and 20 shillings damage." Which verdict at the plf.'s mocion is recorded and thereupon it is considered by the Court that the aforesaid plf. recover against the deft. the horse aforesaid or the sums by the jurors assessed with costs alies execution. {YCWI 1706-1710:258,265; YCWI 1709-1711:5,11}

In the action upon the case between George Gilbert, plf. and Robert Kerle, deft. for £20 damage by means of the deft. fraudulently and deceitfully selling unto the plf. one greystoned horse known by the deft. to be the horse of one Sarah Weldon, and the deft.'s plea being overruled, the plf.'s Attorney produced a bill of sale by which the sale of the said horse appeared. It being apparent to the Court that the said Weldon did recover and obtain the value of the said horse, damages and costs of the plf. by order and judgment of this Court, it is therefore considered that the plf. recover against the deft. the sum of £6 together with all costs in the suit aforesaid had by the said Sarah Weldon against the plf. and present costs alies execution. {YCWI 1709-1711:33}

In the action of debt between Sarah Weldon, plf. and Jacob Godwin and James Morris, defts. for £40 damage by means of the defts. not rendering to the plf. the sum of £76 due by bond, the defts. being arrested and not appearing nor any security returned for them, on the plf.'s mocion judgment is granted her against the said defts. and Thomas Roberts, Sheriff, for the said sum with costs unless the defts. appear at the next Court and answer the plf.'s action. Mar 1712. {1711-1714:238}

Samuel (3) and Sarah (Efford) Weldon were probably the parents of

190

SAMUEL and BENJAMIN. They were possibly the parents of MARY[46].

4. POYNES WELDON[47], b. ca. 1665, d. by 24 Jan 1699/1700, was a son of John (2) and Hannah (N) Weldon. {NAUK}
  Daniel Parke appointed, on 9 Aug 1690, Poynes Weldon his attorney to receive all goods or money due from any person in Virginia, according to such orders as he shall receive from my brother Major Lewis Burwell or my wife. {DW 1687-1691:485}
  Thomas Hinde, by Mr. Poynes Weldon his attorney, as marrying Eliz: Dickisson [Dickenson, Dickinson], sister and a legatee of Charles Dickisson. Having summoned (24 Jan 1694/5) Mr. William Wise to answer his bill, referred. {DW 1694-1697:100}
  Elizabeth Coman, on 24 Mar 1695/6, appointed Mr. Poynes Weldon attorney for her husband, William Coman, to prosecute his suite against William Allin in an action. {DW 1694-1697:269}
  In Aug 1695, one Poynes Weldon was listed as running a tavern in the 'house lately belonging to Fra. Page and now in the possession of Captain Mathew Page' {YorkCoDeeds 6:128, 9:126-127}. The same building had been occupied before Weldon by one Thomas Taylor {YorkCoDeeds 18:189}." {CWFN:14}
  On 20 Sep 1699, Henry Smyth of ye Parish of Bridgett (als) Bridet Cottesson and ... [pg torn] London appoynt my trusty friend Joshua Cooke [pg torn] mariner my atty to aske, demand, sue for, recover & receive from ye executors of Poyns Weldon, decd, or whom else it may concern ye sume of 14 pd which is due to me Henry Smyth from sd Poynes Weldon decd by bill under his hand for ye same.... Proved 24 Jan 1699.... {YCWI 1698-1702:270}
  Poynes Weldon was probably the father of POYNES.

Fourth Generation
5. BENJAMIN WELDON, b. bef. 1690, of James City Co., d. 1732 {WMCQ 1:6:121}, was possibly a son of Samuel (3) and Sarah (Efford) Weldon.
  Benjamin Weldon, on 23 Nov 1705, witnessed the lease of land from Thomas Yateman & Anne his wife of York Parish & Co planter, for 1 shilling, to Robert Harris Senr of same place, all their right, title & interest of, in & unto a 75 acre tract of land & plantation whereon he now liveth being the last & remaining pt/o a dividend of 250 acres of land which was to the sd Thomas given & left by his decd father Thomas Yateman by his will which tract of land is bounded by Thomas Vines, John Eaton, Joseph Mounfort, Morgan Baptist,

---

[46] See William (8) Blaikley, Jr. for an explanation of this possibility.
[47] Poynes Weldon is a qualifying ancestor for descendants to enter the Jamestowne Society. {See http://www.jamestowne.org}

Willm Davis & land the sd Harris bought of the sd Yateman.... {YCDB 1701-1708:143-144,146}

William Sherman of the City of Williamsburgh, appointed Benjamin Weldon of the Co. of James City, my true and lawfull Attorney, to acknowledge in my behalf a Deed ... for my two Lots, or one acre of land, in the City of Williamsburgh with all the houses and appurtenances thereunto belonging, sold and conveyed to Joseph Chermeson. ... 19 Jun 1708.... {YCWI 1706-1710:148}

In the acion of debt between Benjamin Weldon, plf. and Thomas Pinket, deft. for 433 lbs. of good merchantable sweet scented tobacco due by bill under the deft.'s hand and seal dated 7 Sep 1708, the deft. came personally into Court and confessed judgement to the plf. for the said sum. Whereupon it is ordered that the deft. pay unto the plf. the aforesaid sum with costs alies execution. {YCWI 1706-1710:210}

Benjamin Weldon having obtained an attachment under the hand of Wm. Buckner, Gent, against the Estate of John Redwood for £18 which being returned executed on £11:10 in Mr. Ring's hands on the said Weldon's producing a bill under the deft's hand as also making oath that there is still remaining due on the said bill £2:4:11 and 3 farthings, judgment is granted him for the aforesaid sum of £11:10 in the hands of Mr. Joseph Ring. {YCWI 1706-1710:211}

On 22 Jul 1709, Benjamin Weldon witnessed the lease of land by Elizabeth Varnum to William Sheldon of York Hampton Parish, York Co planter a messuage & 100 acre tract of land in Charles Parish being pt/o the plantation whereon the sd Elizabeth Varnum did once live bounded by the land of Capt Thomas Nutting & James Sclater, which tr whereof this 100 acre is part did formerly belong to George Hadderill as by his conveyance to Humphrey Hanmer dated 12 Mar 1639 & likewise by a conveyance of [?] Hanmer being brother & heir to Humphrey Hanmer sold to Thomas Lucas on 16 Oct 1652 & then by assignment of the same conveyance from the sd Lucas assigned to Margery Griggs & so descended by inheritance to Elizabeth Varnum as being the only dau & heiress of John Griggs the only sonne & heir of Margery Griggs ... for the term of one year.... {YCDB 1709-1713:323}

Benjamin Weldon, Richard Bland et al. witnessed, on 17 Mar 1711, the lease of land by Mary Whaley of the City of Wmsburgh VA widow, for £106, to David Bray of Bruton Parish, James City Co, VA gent all those lands & plantacons in Bruton Parish, York Co.... {YCDB 1709-1713:382}

Benjamin Weldon, an evidence for Sarah Weldon, plf. against George Gilbert, deft. being summoned and having attended 6 days on the said suit, it is ordered that the said Sarah pay him 240 lbs. of tobacco for the same with costs alies execution. {YCWI 1709-1711:11}

In the acion of debt between Benjamin Weldon, Assignee of William Forbar plf, and James Biorect deft, for £4:5 in ready silver, to liking due by bill dated 8 Nov, the deft. having had time given at the last Court to plead and being now called and failing to doe the same, and the plf. having made oath that he knows of no satisfaccion made by the deft. for any part of the said sum, the judgment of the last Court against the said deft. and John Pasteur, his security, is confirmed and it is ordered that they pay the aforesaid sum in silver to liking to the plf. with costs alies execution. {YCWI 1709-1711:21,27}

Benjamin Weldon was listed as a member of the Grand Jury presented to the Honorable Alexander Spotswood, His Majesty's Lieutenant Governor and Commander in Chief of the Colony and Dominion of Virginia. {CD503:EngDupsLostRecs:273}

Benj Weldon, Jno Blair, Jno Brodnax & James Hubard are appointed to meet at ye house late of Jno Marot decd & inventory & appraise all such of decds estate as shall be produced to them by Anne Marot executrix & make report to next court & further ordered that sd Anne appear at ye same time & give security for sd estate. {YCWI 1716-1718:171}

Henry Boccock on his petition hath order granted him for a lycence to keep an ordinary at his dwelling house in Williamsburgh he having together with Thos Jones & Benja Weldon his securitys entred into bond for that purpose which bond being ackn is admitted to record. {YCWI 1716-1718:217}

In the action is the Case between Benj Weldon plt & Wm Blaikley deft for Eleven pounds Seven Shillings & & Six pence half penny Current money due by Acct. the deft. Failing to appear judgement is granted the plt. Agt the deft & Francis Tyler his Security for the Sd Sum & Costs unless the deft. Appear at the next Court & answer the plt action. {YCWI 1720-1722:26}

Know all men by these presents that we, Matt. Pierce, Benj. Weldon, and Robt Cobbs of ye County of York, are bound and firmly bound unto ye worshipfull ye Justices of ye County aforesaid in ye Sum of three hundred pounds Sterling payable to ye Justices their heirs and Successors or some of them to which payment well and truly be made We bind ourselves and every of us our and every of us our and every of our heirs Execrs Adms Joyntly and Severally firmly by these presents Sealed with our Seals 19 Feb 1721. {YCWI 1720-1722:107}

By virtue of An Order of York County hereunto annexed I, Francis Tyler under Sherrif of the said County, on 6 Feb 1723 in the tenth year of the Reign of Our Sovereign Lord George by the grace of God of Great Britain France & Ireland Defender of the Faith &c, taking with me John Blair, Benjamin Weldon, Samuel Cobbs, Richard Rickman, James Holland, Joseph Davenport, Matthew Peirce, Ralph Graves, James Backhurst, Richard King, Edward Ripping, and John Pasteur twelve good and lawfull men of York County and of the Vicinage in the said order men[tioned] in my proper person did go upon the Messuage and tenements in the said order men[tioned] and the same by their oaths (having respect to the true value of the same messuage Tenements &

appurtenances) In ye presence of Patrick Ferguson and Francis his Wife Richard Steward & Elizabeth his Wife and Anne Kendall Spinster, by John Randolph Esqr. her Guardian, have causes partition of the same messuage and tenemts. with the appurtenances to be made and the same into three equal parts to be parted and one part of the said three parts (to witt) Seventy Acres of Arrable land lying next to the main road from Wmsburgh to York Town bounded as followeth. {YCWI 1722-1725:254}

6. POYNES WELDON, b. ca 1680s, d. aft. 1713, was probably a son of Poynes (4) Weldon.

In the acion upon the case between Poynes Weldon, plf. and Robert Crawly, deft. for £9:3:2[?] and 1,995 lbs. of tobacco on ballance of accounts, the deft. failing to appear and no security being returned for him, judgment is granted the plf. for the said sums and costs against the deft. and Thomas Roberts, Sheriff, unless the deft. appears at the next Court and answers the plf.'s action. {1711-1714:315}

In the action of debt between Poyers [Poynes] Weldon plt & Robt Saunders def for 500 lbs of tobacco due by bill dated 4 Dec 1713 ye court on hearing ye evidence is of opinion that ye plt ought to recover sd sum & ye def is ordered to pay ye same to ye plt with cost. {YCWI 1716-1718:5}

7. SAMUEL WELDON, b. ca 1680s, will pr. Jul 1748 in Henrico Co VA, was probably a son of Samuel (3) and Sarah (Efford) Weldon, m. 1st Elizabeth (N) {WARG:140} and 2nd aft. 1725, Elizabeth Allen, widow of Robert Cobbs (d. 1725)[48].

In 1723, the death of John Weldon, son of Samuel and Elizabeth, was recorded in the Bruton Parish Register. {WARG:140}

In the *seire facias* brought by Saml. Weldon against Robt. Crawly for renewing two judgments of James City Co. Court for £13:9:8 ¼ and 1,065 ½ lbs. of tobacco, on the deft's mocion the suit is continued until the next Court. {1711-1714:315}

John Ballard Foreman, Robert Ballard, Samuel Weldon, Thomas Cobbs, William Prentis, Richard King, Richard Steward, Samuel Hyde, William Keith, Giles Moody, William Stone, Henry Bowcock, William Freyser, Arthur Dickerson, Joseph Mountfort, Robert Harris, Edward Cross, John Gomer, William Gordon, James Mackindo, Thomas Hauskins, Joseph Nisbitt & Thos. Powell were Impannelled and Sworn a Grand Jury.... {YCWI 1725-1727:489}

At a Court held for York County 16 Nov 1724, this bond was presented ... and admitted to record:
To Robert Tucker   £47.11.6

---

[48] See "The Cobbs Family," this volume for documentation.

To Sundry debts pd. by Jno. Williams
as [per] his Acct.   £98.4.10 ½
To Samuel Weldon
To Capt. Geor. Winter
To Robert Blaws   £60.
To Thomas Morcock Junr.   60.2.. 9
...

Poined [Poynes] Mallard.... {YCWI 1722-1725:310}
   Samuel Weldon in 1736, 4 Levys. 1000 acres. Last year account which
I paid. Sheriff's fees for arresting Martin. For summoning Howlet. Paid by
cash rec'd at Mr. Blair's store for 2 yrs Quit Rents. Tobacco account to next
book. {CD503:HenricoCo:386}
   On 5 Apr 1736, Henry Cary sold two tracts of land, the second adjacent
Winter's Branch, line of Mr. Saml Welldon, of Jno Easly, James River ... Hon.
Wm. Byrd's land, Powhite Creek, etc. {CD503:HenricoCo:411}
   Samuel Weldon, of Dale Parish Henrico Co VA, left a will proved Jul
1748 "and names children (who were under age) Daniel, Benjamin (who
received lands in Goochland), Samuel, Elizabeth and Priscilla; son-in-law
Roderick Easly; wife's daughters Sarah Jones and Martha Richardson, and her
grandson, Allen Jones, and Willie and Charlotte Jones." {WMCQ 1:6:121}
   Samuel and Elizabeth (N) Weldon were the parents of JOHN (d. 1723).
{WARG:140}
   Samuel and Elizabeth (Allen) Weldon were the parents of DANIEL;
BENJAMIN; SAMUEL, ELIZABETH; and PRISCILLA. {WMCQ 1:6:121}

Fifth Generation
8. WILLIAM BLAIKLEY, JR., grandson of Samuel (3) and Sarah (Efford)
Weldon.
   William Blaikely, Jr. was the son of William Blaikely, Sr. (d. 1736)
and Mary (N—perhaps Weldon) Blaikley. William Blaikley, Sr. m. 2nd
Catherine Kaidyee. {YCWI 1740-1743:168}
   Wm. Blaikley Jr's father, William, Sr., left a will dated 10 Feb 1733/4
and proved 21 Jun 1736. {WMCQ 1:6:121}
   William Blaikley [Sr.], of James City Co., left a will dated 10 Feb 1733/4.
My will is that all my debts to be paid. To son Will Blaikley that 100 acres of land
in Pohaten left to me by his grandmother Sarah Weldon. To my son William 1 sl.
To my dear children James, Mary & Jannet Carson Blaikley 1 sl to each of them &
my dau Elizabeth. To my wife Catherine Blaikley all my whole estate of lands,
houses, Negroes, goods & chattels or whatsoever to me doth belong meaning my
house and lott in Williamsburgh and 50 acres of land I had of George Hewgh's
lying in Pohattan and all my lands with a mill and other houses lying upon Waqua
Cr in Brunswick Co and further appoint my wife Catherine Blaikley executrix. I

desire that my wife may not give security to any court it being the true trust & confidence I have in her. I give unto my son William a legacy of 1 guiney. I give to my dau Mary a legacy of 1 guiney. I give unto my dau Jannat Carson a legacy of 1 guiney. I give unto my dau Elizabeth a legacy of 1 guiney. Wit: James Shields, Matthew Shields, Hannah Shields. The will was presented in court 21 Jun 1736 by the executrix.... {YCWI 1732-1737:291,297}

An inventory of the estate of William Blaikley, decd, of what's lying on this side of James River 30 Jun 1736. 3 beds with all furniture, 1 large black trunk, 1 white table, 10 rush bottom chairs, 2 pr old white window curtains, 2 stone chamber pots, 1 small Japan box, 1 Japan tea table, etc. Negroes: Nanny, Lucy & Hannah. This inventory sent by Catherine Blaikley 20 Aug 1736 & ordered to be recorded 20 Sep 1736.... {YCWI 1732-1737:313}

An account of what things upon the plantation in Brunswick belonging to Wm Blaikley decd.: 2 Negroes, 1 horse, 10 head of cattle, 1 sow, 4 shotes, 1 whip saw, 1 cross cat saw, a parcel of carpenters tools, 10 pd in cash. Cath Blaikley. This further inventory ordered to be recorded 15 Nov 1736.... {YCWI 1732-1737:329}

On 15 May 1738, the action of trespass brought by Thomas Nelson & William Nelson Junr gent agt Wm Blaikley is dismist. {YCWI 1737-1740:412}

John Kaidyee, of Queen Mary's Port, York Co., left a will dated 6 Jan 1742 and proved 21 Feb 1742. After debts and funeral charges are paid, to William Bryan son of my unckle Frederick Bryan my Negro wench Doll and her youngest son Tom, my desk, wearing apparell, gun, sword, pistols, saddle & bridle. To John Bryan, son of my said unckle Frederick Bryan, my watch. My house where I now dwell and the four lotts thereto belonging brought of Mr. Randolph in the lifetime of my mother to my kinsman Charles Rudder on condition of his paying 10 pd to my kinsman John Whitehead at his coming of age to help him build a home on my other four lotts hereafter left to him. To said John Whitehead the said 10 pd charged on the said Rudders legacy and also my four lotts behind Moody's purchased of Lewis Holland's executors. To my cousin Mary Blaikley my Negro wench Patt. To her sister Casson Blaikley my Negro boy Will. To her sister, Elizabeth Blaikley, my Negro girl Betty. To each of the three last legatees Mary, Casson & Elizabeth a ring to be provided for them by my executrix. To my sister, Cathrine Blaikley, my legacy of money from my father's estate. I appoint my sister Cathrine Blaikley executrix. Wits: John Blair, Matt Moody, Anne Moody.... {YCWI 1740-1743:168}

9. DANIEL WELDON, b. 1720s, who settled in North Carolina, was a son of Samuel (7) and Elizabeth (Allen) Weldon, m. Elizabeth Eaton. Elizabeth was a daughter of William Eaton of Granville Co., NC. {CD509:NCWills:108}

In 1749 Daniel Weldon was a member of the commission that set North Carolina boundaries. {WMCQ 1:6:121}

The city of Weldon, North Carolina, was named after the family. Although the North Carolina General Assembly passed a bill on 6 Jan 1843 incorporating the Town of Weldon, the settlement of the town began earlier. In 1752, Daniel Weldon purchased 1,273 acres of land, and upon his death, this tract was bequeathed to his son, Maj. William Weldon, became known as "Weldon's Orchard." Other names were given to the settlement that grew up around it including "Weldon's Place" and "Weldon's Landing," the latter referring to its location on the river. {WMCQ 1:6:121}

10. BENJAMIN WELDON, b. ca 1730, was a son of Samuel (7) and Elizabeth (Allen) Weldon.
    Benjamin left a will dated 5 Aug 1755, proved 9 Feb 1756, in which he named sisters, Elizabeth and Priscilla, and brothers, Daniel and Samuel, as well as his Jones cousins: Allen, Willie, and Martha. {WMCQ 1:6:121}

OTHER WELDONS

ANTHO. WELDEN
Mr. Francis Spike received 700 acres of land in Up. Parish Nancimond Co. on 11 Mar 1664 for the transport of Antho. Welden and 13 others to Virginia. {CP I:479}

ROBERT WELDON
Robert Weldon preferred [proffered] a claim for his taking up Jno Baram a runaway servant belonging to Nicho Aldersey of New Kent Co the sd Robert Weldon having produced a cert that he apprehended the sd runaway above 10 miles from his residence & he having also made oath that he never received any satisfaction for that service, ordered to be certifyed to the Assembly for allowance. {YCWI 1716-1718:224}

ROBERT/PRUDENCE/REBECCA WELDON
Robert and Prudence (N) Weldon were the parents of REBECCA, b. 9 Jul, bapt. 10 Aug 1723. {CPR:192}

SAMUEL WELDING
Richard Turney received 2109 acres in Northumberland Co on 8 Jul 1651 for transporting 42 persons including Samll. Welding. {CP I:218}

WILLIAM WELDING
On 9 Dec 1654, Wm Umfries to Rich Browne to represent him in 2 suits depending in this Court vs. Wm Hardich ... Wm. Welding, his mark.

Recorded 12 Jan 1654/5. {CD503:WestmorCo:657}

WILLIAM WELDON
    Arrived in Virginia on the *Bona Nova* in 1619. {HOT:201}

WILLIAM WELLDON
    William Welldon and 19 others were transported to Virginia by Mrs. Mary Fortson who received 2000 acres on the west side of Paspetanke River on 25 Sep 1663. {CP I:428}

INDEX

Abbington Parish, 121
Abbott, Ann, 179; Fred, 131
Abingdon Parish, 148
Abington Parish, 111
Abrell, Richard, 161
Accomac County, VA, 80
Acrill, William, 71
Adawell, Mary, 73; Thomas, 73
Adcock, Thomas, 66, 167
Adderly, Dorothy, 1; Ralph, 1
Adduston, Joane, 114
Addustone, John, 111, 114
Aduston, Agnes, 111, 113, 116, 117;
    Joane, 110, 111; John, 110, 111,
    160
Albemarle County, 87
Albritton, Thomas, 102
Aldersey, Nicholas, 196
Allen, Ann, 93; Daniel, 27, 28;
    Elizabeth, 27, 28, 193, 196;
    Frances, 155; Frankey, 155;
    John, 155, 156; William, 20, 26,
    51
Alleson, John, 131
Allgroe, Roger, 5
Allin, Ann, 186; Charles, 48;
    William, 190
Allman, John, 20
Ambler, Jaquelin, 72; Mr., 20, 131;
    Richard, 20, 31, 34, 132, 177
Amelia County, 36, 37, 40
America, 65, 133
Anderson, Andrew, 15, 71; Hannah,
    33; James, 33, 34; Mary, 15;
    William, 185
Andrews, Henry, 118, 119, 142; John,
    74, 95, 142
Appamattuck River, 22
Archer, Captain, 58; John, 186;

Thomas, 72, 135
Archer's Road, 58
Armistead, Angellica, 124; Booth,
    124, 159; Catherine, 124;
    Edward, 78; Ellyson, 31, 32, 33,
    35, 88, 151, 177; Henry, 69;
    Robert, 31, 124; Westwood, 144
Armore, Jerome, 20
Armstrong, Letitia, 13
Ashbe, Jack, 33
Ashmore, Elizabeth, 75
Attawell, Frances, 73; Margaret, 72,
    73; Mary, 73; Thomas, 72, 73
Attowell, Francis, 72; Mary, 72
Attwell, Mary, 73
Augine, The, 4
Avery, Thomas, 20, 151
Aylette, Mr., 22
Babb, John, 66, 67, 174; William,
    100, 165
Back Creek, 113, 118, 152
Back River, 79, 157
Backhurst, James, 189, 192
Baker, Richard, 183
Baldry, Robert, 2
Baley, William, 79
Ball, Elizabeth, 101
Ballard, Captain, 131; John, 19, 20,
    31, 33, 129, 131, 132, 138, 151,
    173, 193; Robert, 123, 143, 193;
    Thomas, 6, 112, 114, 116, 119,
    141, 163, 175, 182, 188
Banadall, Elizabeth, 20
Banister, John, 6
Bannuthos, 187
Baptist, Edward, 19, 104; Elizabeth,
    53; Morgan, 115, 190
Baram, John, 196
Barbados, 65

Barbar, Captain, 68, 174; Elizabeth, 60; James, 31, 32, 88; Mary, 1, 10, 12; Mr., 166; Thomas, 10, 48, 99, 163; William, 1, 13, 83, 166, 189
Barber, Elizabeth, 35; Mary, 2, 3, 4; Matthew, 2; Thomas, 2, 3, 12, 26, 29, 175; William, 2
Barfoot, Judith, 39
Barker, Hugh, 22; Jonathan, 181; Lawrence, 110; Richard, 22; Sarah, 181; William, 186
Barnes, John, 77; Mary, 49, 107; Richard, 55, 56
Barns, Aaron, 93; Anne, 93; Frances, 93; John, 93; Johnson, 93; Mary, 93; Matthew, 93; Nathaniel, 93
Barradale, Henry, 18; Judith, 18
Barradall, Elizabeth, 21
Barradell, Blumfield, 21; Edward, 20, 21, 31, 64; Elizabeth, 20; Sarah, 21
Barret, William, 183
Bartlett, Elizabeth, 116; Frances, 116; Myhill, 116
Baskerfield, Hugh, 16
Baskervil, George, 10
Baskervile, George, 6, 7, 11, 12, 26, 27; John, 14
Baskervill, George, 13
Baskerville, George, 4, 121, 122
Baskerville Family, 1
Baskervil's Swamp, 186
Baskervyle, Dorothy, 1; Elizabeth, 1, 2, 3, 12, 14, 15; George, 1, 3, 5, 8, 11, 12, 13, 14, 15, 57; Henry, 1; Hugh, 14, 15, 16; John, 1, 2, 3, 4, 12, 13, 14, 15, 57; Katherine, 1; Lawrence, 1; Magdalen, 1, 2, 3, 4; Magdalene, 10; Mary, 1, 2, 3, 4, 10, 12; Norvil, 14; Norvile, 16; Nowel, 14, 16; Randall, 1;

Rebecca, 1, 2, 3, 10, 12; Rebecka, 3; Sarah, 3, 15; Thomas, 1
Baskerwyle, Hugh, 15
Baskewyle, John, 21
Bassett, Colonel, 132
Batchelor's Island, 57
Bates, Agness, 146; Fleming, 15, 59, 60, 62, 63, 180; George, 175; Hannah, 32; Henry, 16; James, 16, 32, 175, 176; John, 26, 50, 65, 84, 122, 175, 176, 189; Mary, 32; Sarah, 32; Thomas, 22
Bates Mill, 61, 62
Bates's Line, 176
Bates's Spring Branch, 175
Batten, Anne, 3; Ashaell, 3; Aswell, 3; Constant, 3; John, 3, 4; Mary, 3, 4; Sarah, 3, 11; Ursula, 3; William, 4, 11
Battin, Anne, 3; Elizabeth, 102; John, 4; Lewis, 102
Batton, William, 4
Baugh, Robert, 22
Beal, Thomas, 123
Beale, Alice, 118, 122; Thomas, 118
Beard, Isaac, 162
Beaver Dam Swamp, 97, 175
Bee, Robert, 10, 25, 40, 163
Begyll, John, 66
Beliker, James, 133
Bell, George, 187; John, 37; Robert, 30; Thomas, 65, 66, 122; William, 188
Bellamy, Richard, 136
Belsize House, 167
Benins, Edward, 75
Benjafield, Joseph, 175
Bennet, James, 53
Bennett, John, 161
Bentley, John, 25; Margrett, 25
Bently, John, 24, 26

Berkeley, William, 55
Berkley, William, 164
Bermudas, 187
Bernard, Elizabeth, 126
Besouth, James, 22, 162
Betsey, The, 48; Thomas, 184
Beven, Thomas, 132
Beverley, Robert, 20
Beverly, Peter, 150; Robert, 6
Bigges, William, 12
Bingley, David, 181; Nathaniel, 181
Biorect, James, 191
Bird, James, 20; William, 115
Birt, Richard, 165
Black, James, 19
Black Swamp, 99, 166
Blackbourn, William, 141
Blackhaugh, 1
Blaikely, Mary, 194
Blaikley, Casson, 195; Catherine,
    194, 195; Elizabeth, 194, 195;
    James, 194; Jannat Carson, 195;
    Jannet Carson, 194; Mary, 195;
    William, 192, 194, 195
Blair, Archibald, 44, 45; Doctor, 165;
    John, 16, 26, 32, 59, 60, 151,
    192, 195; Mr., 194
Blake, Eduardo, 187
Bland, Richard, 11, 191
Blaws, Robert, 194
Blisland Parish, 60
Bloxom, Richard, 178
Boar Quarter, 57
Boar Quarter Creek, 57
Bobbs, Elizabeth, 28
Boccock, Henry, 192
Bocock, Henry, 85
Bolch, Henry, 65
Bolton, Henry, 34
Bona Nova, The, 197
Bond, Ann, 20; Dori Antothea, 178;
    John, 20, 107, 178; Nicholas,

178, 179; Samuel, 178; Samuell,
    179; William, 17
Boneyman, Allexander, 189
Bonfield, Christopher, 58
Booker, Edward, 182
Booth, Alderman Richard, 119;
    Elizabeth, 155; Robert, 161
Boradell, John, 123, 124
Boridell, Henry, 101
Borodell, Ann, 18; Elizabeth, 16, 18,
    20; Henry, 16, 18, 20; Judith, 18;
    Mary, 18; Matthew, 20; Sarah,
    18; Thomas, 18
Borradell, Henry, 16
Borridell, Henry, 17
Borrodale, Elizabeth, 20; Henry, 18;
    Judith, 18
Borrodall, Henry, 17
Borrodell, Henry, 19
Borrowdill, Henry, 16, 17
Boucher, Thomas, 96
Boult, Roger, 82
Bourne, Nicholas, 187
Bournham, Thomas, 51
Boush, Samuel, 35
Bouth, Francis, 137
Bowcock, Edward, 35, 61; Henry,
    193
Bowers, Robert, 74
Bowis, Robert, 34
Bowles, Thomas, 181
Bowls, Thomas, 181
Boyne, Richard, 110
Bradley, George, 48
Brafett, Ann, 5
Brand, Jonathan, 187
Brantridin, 132
Braxton, Colonel, 131
Bray, David, 191; Elizabeth, 14;
    James, 23, 69, 161, 188; Mr., 22
Brewer, Edmund, 175; Mary, 175;
    Thomas, 20

Bridet Cottesson Parish, 190
Bridgett Parish, 190
Bristol, 65, 113
Britain, William, 104
Broad Neck Creek, 63
Broad Street, 114, 116
Broadneck Creek, 62
Brodie, Doctor, 155; John, 143, 144;
    Martha, 143, 144; Mary, 143,
    144; Sarah, 144
Brodnax, John, 192
Brodrik, Thomas, 16
Brody, John, 144
Bromfield, Thomas, 22
Bromsly, St. Leonard, 141
Broodie, Charlotte, 157; James, 157
Brooke, David, 51
Brookes, Nicholas, 161; William, 184
Brooks, Humphry, 65; John, 142
Broster, James, 94
Broughton, Thomas, 64, 161
Brown, B., 135; Charles, 132;
    Elizabeth, 6; George, 6; John, 69;
    Mary, 124; William, 79
Brown, Nance & Pond, 58
Browne, Magdalen, 6; Richard, 141;
    William, 115
Brucbley, 65
Bruce, Alice, 16
Brunswick, 195
Brunswick County, VA, 101, 194
Bruton Gleeb Road, 166
Bruton Parish, 3, 4, 5, 6, 8, 11, 13,
    14, 15, 16, 23, 25, 27, 28, 30, 31,
    32, 33, 34, 35, 38, 39, 56, 57, 58,
    60, 61, 62, 63, 73, 84, 88, 90, 91,
    117, 119, 135, 140, 150, 151,
    160, 161, 163, 164, 166, 167,
    175, 176, 177, 178, 179, 181,
    185, 191
Bruton Parish Church, 22
Bruton Parish Register, 193

Bryan, Frederick, 182, 195; John,
    195; William, 195
Buck, Benjamin, 99; Thomas, 99
Buckler, John, 185
Buckner, John, 32, 123, 129, 177;
    William, 57, 119, 127, 141, 142,
    162, 172, 191
Bucks County, 187
Buds, Charles, 99
Bullifant, Philip, 38
Burcher, Bartholomew, 101; Clara,
    139; James, 139; John, 135, 138,
    139; William, 139
Burfoot, Hannah, 34; Lawson, 39, 40;
    Mary, 34, 40; Thomas, 39
Burk, Elizabeth, 137
Burleigh, Rebecca, 57
Burnam, 187
Burnane, Thomas, 97
Burnham, Lockey Miles, 184;
    Thomas, 17
Burradell, Blumfield, 20; Edward, 20;
    Elizabeth, 20; Henry, 20, 151;
    Matthew, 20
Burrodale, Elizabeth, 19; Henry, 19;
    Judith, 137
Burt, Anne, 61; Elizabeth, 18, 19;
    Harwood, 49; Henry, 25; John,
    20; Matthew, 20; Moody, 18, 19,
    20; Philip, 20, 61; William, 20,
    106
Burton, Joseph, 169; Lewis, 94, 102;
    Mary Emory, 80
Burwell, Carter, 69, 70; James, 42;
    Lewis, 69, 190; Nathaniel, 51,
    90, 166; Nathaniel Bacon, 33;
    Robert, 70, 133
Bushrod, Letitia, 2; Thomas, 2
Butler, Edmund, 187; Elizabeth, 187
Butterworth, Mr., 131
Buttin, Anne, 3
Butts, Anthony, 137

Byrd, Colonel, 85; William, 194
Calbert, Martha, 79
Callohill, Francis, 171
Calthorp, James, 75
Calthorpe, James, 171
Calthrop, Charles, 103; James, 93
Calvert, Robert, 140, 143; William, 143
Camberwell, Saint Mary, 133, 134
Camm, John, 20
Campbell, Charles, 172; William, 7, 8
Candray, Peter, 37
Cant, William, 65
Capahosick Ferry, 61
Capitol, The, 36, 89
Capitol Landing, 32, 33, 90, 159
Capitol Landing Road, 38
Capitol Landing Warehouse, 32
Capitol Square, 69
Cardy, Richard, 161
Carolina, 188, 189
Caroline County, 20
Carr, Thomas, 93
Carren, ye, 97
Carrson, Benjamin, 21
Carter, Hannah, 16; John, 16, 39; Landon, 60; Robert, 63, 177; William, 71
Carter's Grove, 51
Cary, Daniel, 186; Doyley, 143, 150; Harwood, 140; Henry, 11, 26, 33, 143, 144, 150, 194; John, 125, 155, 156, 157; Martha, 143, 144; Mary, 150, 153, 154; Miles, 97, 115, 131, 156; Richard, 157; Robert, 70; William, 135, 140
Cattayle Branch, 121
Catton, Benjamin, 131
Cawley, Edward, 112
Chamberlyn, Leonard, 161
Chapman, Allen, 135, 139; John, 20, 52, 102, 144, 171, 186; Walter,
138
Chapman Family, 186
Charles, Henry, 185; Thomas, 185; Walter, 20
Charles City County, 71, 80, 121, 183
Charles Parish, 14, 17, 31, 41, 42, 43, 45, 47, 48, 49, 50, 52, 53, 57, 76, 77, 78, 79, 83, 91, 93, 94, 97, 101, 102, 103, 104, 106, 107, 108, 109, 110, 112, 113, 116, 119, 124, 125, 126, 137, 139, 140, 141, 142, 143, 144, 145, 146, 151, 152, 153, 154, 155, 156, 157, 158, 159, 170, 171, 172, 173, 174, 182, 191
Charles River, 41, 42, 145, 148
Charlton, Edward, 88, 89; Lydia, 15; Richard, 90
Cheescake, 135
Cheeskicack Parish, 95
Chermeson, Joseph, 84, 118, 121, 122, 123, 191
Chermison, Joseph, 82, 122, 164
Cheshire, Richard, 66, 113
Cheshise's Lot, 130
Chesley, Captain, 22; Phillipp, 55
Chesly, Philip, 185
Chessman, Thomas, 26
Chesterfield County, 185
Chew's Creek, 123
Chickahominy River, 58
Chiles, John, 66
Chiscake, 136
Chisman, Edmund, 106, 110; George, 103; John, 49, 50, 72, 74, 106, 107, 108, 109, 124, 126, 150, 157; Mildred, 152; Thomas, 50, 99, 104, 120, 123, 152, 158
Chisman's Mill Dam, 158
Chiswell, Charles, 42, 46
Christ Church Cemetery, 68
Christian, Martha, 80

Churchhill, William, 71
Claiborne, William, 132
Clark, Ann, 161; Francis, 101;
    Hannah, 161; Henry, 42; John,
    20, 101, 121, 122; Mrs., 161;
    Robert, 121, 122, 166
Clarke, Ann, 117; Daniel, 121; John,
    115, 117, 162; Mary, 162;
    Robert, 117, 162
Clarkson, John, 123
Clarkson's Creek, 123
Clausel, C., 79; Clausel, 48
Clausell, Clausel, 155
Clayton, John, 26, 35; Mr., 42
Clifton, Benjamin, 18, 46, 53, 147,
    150; Richard, 160; Thomas, 148
Cobb, Ambrose, 11, 23, 24, 25, 26,
    29; Benjamin, 40; Edmund, 25,
    29; Elizabeth, 29, 40; Frances,
    29; Joseph, 40; Margaret, 29;
    Mary, 29, 30; Otho, 29; Robert,
    22, 23, 29; Samuel, 24, 25, 30;
    Thomas, 25, 38; Vinckler, 37;
    William, 24, 29; Winfield, 41
Cobb Family, 22
Cobbs, Ambrose, 7, 11, 22, 23, 24,
    25, 26, 27, 31, 33, 34, 35, 39, 40;
    Ambross, 30; Ann, 22; Anne, 22,
    37; Edith, 35, 36, 37, 40; Edith
    Marot, 37; Edmond, 35;
    Edmund, 23, 25, 27, 28, 33, 35;
    Elizabeth, 22, 25, 26, 27, 28, 29,
    30, 31, 34, 35, 39, 40; Frances,
    23, 25, 26; Hannah, 33, 34;
    James, 29, 40; Jane, 40; John, 27,
    31, 34, 35, 36, 37, 40; John
    Catlin, 37; Joseph, 40; Judith, 37,
    40; Lydia, 28; Margaret, 29;
    Margarett, 22; Martha, 28, 29,
    34, 39; Mary, 23, 24, 29, 30, 33,
    34, 35, 37; Matthew, 33, 34;
    Otho, 23, 25, 29, 189; Rebecca,

27, 28, 40, 41; Richard, 40;
    Robert, 9, 22, 23, 24, 25, 26, 27,
    28, 29, 30, 31, 34, 37, 40, 192,
    193; Samuel, 28, 31, 35, 36, 37,
    40, 165, 192; Sarah, 28, 29, 37,
    41; Theodocia, 37; Thomas, 23,
    27, 31, 32, 33, 34, 37, 38, 39, 40,
    193; Vinkler, 31, 34, 37;
    William, 23, 24, 29, 30, 35, 40
Cobs, Ambrose, 26; Thomas, 26;
    William, 30
Cocke, Isabella, 21; John C., 61;
    Richard, 167
Cocker, Stephen, 189
Coke, John, 16, 33, 38
Colace, Thomas, 166
Coleman, Agness, 112; Joseph, 111,
    114
Collier, Charles, 82, 119; Isaac, 1, 19
Collins, Judeth, 48; Martha, 2; Mary,
    2; Matthew, 48; Sarah, 2;
    William, 167
Collyer, Charles, 26; Thomas, 163
Coman, Elizabeth, 165, 190; John,
    161; William, 11, 84, 161, 165,
    167, 190
Concord, The, 139
Conier, Elizabeth, 148
Conner, Thomas, 92
Connier, Elizabeth, 151
Connor, John, 115
Cook, Francis, 104; John, 183
Cooke, Francis, 159; James, 108;
    John, 108; Joshua, 190; Mary,
    108
Cooper, Edward, 99; Joseph, 25;
    Thomas, 1
Copeling Branch, 140
Corbin, Thomas, 65
Cordell, John, 21
Cornwell, Richard, 66
Cosby, James, 88; John, 52, 182;

Mark, 14, 15, 87, 88, 90; Samuel, 88
Coseby, Elizabeth, 176; James, 177
Cossins, Thomas, 112
Coton, Staffordshire, 1
Coulthard, John, 33; Rebecca, 33
Court House, 115, 116
Court of Canterbury, 133
Cowherd, William, 65
Cowley, Mary, 111
Cowman, William, 6
Cowper, Thomas, 1
Cox, Charles, 66, 74; John, 48, 125, 149
Coxon, Bryon, 55
Craig, Alexander, 88, 89, 90, 91; Ann, 90; Judith, 88, 90; Lucretia, 90; Mary, 88, 90; Thomas, 88, 89
Crawley, John, 33, 167; Mathew, 25; Mr., 167; Nat, 26; Nathaniel, 7, 8, 25, 51, 71; Robert, 8, 9, 25, 32, 100, 164, 165, 193
Crawly, Robert, 193
Creas, Mary, 86, 87; Thomas, 15, 82, 86, 87
Crease, Thomas, 87
Cripps, Thomas, 11, 12, 27, 57
Cripps Spring Bridge, 57
Crips, Thomas, 5, 12, 56, 57
Croshaw, Joseph, 4, 5, 54, 75, 139, 184; Mary, 4, 5, 56; Richard, 55
Cross, Edmund, 137; Edward, 173, 193; Henry, 12
Crosse, Ann, 98
Cry, John, 106
Culley, Jane, 18
Cuningham, David, 26, 36, 165
Curtis, Edmond, 108, 126, 170; Edmund, 105, 119, 126, 169, 170, 173, 174; Elizabeth, 102, 103, 106, 173; Frances, 170, 173; Mary, 169, 170; Robert, 173;

Susanna, 123; Thomas, 102, 106, 123
Custis, Colonel, 39; John, 14, 32, 34, 37, 167; Major, 28, 58
Dailey, John, 19
Dale Parish, 194
Daniel, John, 35, 54
Daniell, John, 57
Davenport, D., 167; George, 71, 93; Joseph, 85, 192
David, Elinor, 186
Davies, John, 161
Davis, Anne, 38; Elizabeth, 38, 60, 116; John, 1, 3, 12, 36, 162; Lewis, 39; Mary, 5, 38, 56, 142; Thomas, 38; William, 5, 26, 56, 58, 116, 165, 185, 191
Dawson, Anthony, 56
Dedman, Philip, 152
Degraffenried, Christopher, 36
Delany, Thomas, 103
Denbeigh, 142
Denby Parish, 179
Dennett, Anne, 2; Mary, 2; Sarah, 2; Thomas, 95
Dennitt, John, 96; Thomas, 96
Deuit, Jonathan, 36
Dewick, M., 102
Dickenson, Arthur, 99; Authur, 177; Elizabeth, 190
Dickerson, Arthur, 193
Dickeson, Anne, 178; Arthur, 31, 32, 33, 35, 166, 178, 186; Lucy, 89
Dickinson, Elizabeth, 190; John, 160; Samuell, 97
Dickisson, Charles, 190; Elizabeth, 190
Dickson, Arthur, 98; Thomas, 37
Digges, Cole, 177; Dudley, 88, 97, 132, 133; Edward, 32, 123
Diggs, Colonel, 165
Dinwiddie, Robert, 70

206

Disbary, Peter, 95
Dixon, Agnes, 111, 113; Ann, 114;
 Anne, 113; Damazinah, 113, 118,
 119, 145; Doctor, 131; Elizabeth,
 114; H., 90; Haldenby, 90;
 James, 78, 102, 103, 113, 123,
 125, 137, 152; John, 60; Martha,
 81; Rebecca, 113; Richard, 111,
 112, 113, 114, 118, 119, 122,
 145; Susanah, 113
Dobson, Edmond, 132
Dodleston, Cheshire, 1
Dorman, William, 137
Doswell, Elizabeth, 145; John, 74, 83,
 123, 145, 165, 170; Katherine,
 123; Thomas, 123
Dowling, James, 99, 176
Dowsing, Everard, 131
Dowzen, John, 119
Doyley, Cope, 12, 26, 29, 163, 175
Dozwell, John, 114, 119
Draper, Thomas, 168
Dreuit, Martha, 36
Drewery, John, 49
Drewit, John, 115; Martha, 36
Drewry, Agnis, 45; Ann, 44, 45, 48,
 52; Anne, 48, 109, 126;
 Catherine, 44; Daniel, 52;
 Debach, 42; Deborah, 41, 42, 43,
 44, 45, 46; Diana, 52, 53;
 Dianna, 53; Elinor, 44; Elizabeth,
 43, 44, 45, 52; Henry, 45, 52;
 Hope, 45; James, 43, 45, 48, 49,
 52, 105, 154, 158; Jamrs, 50;
 Jane, 43, 47; John, 41, 42, 43,
 44, 45, 46, 47, 48, 49, 50, 52, 53,
 154, 170; Katherine, 49, 158;
 Margaret, 46; Martha, 51, 52;
 Mary, 43, 44, 45, 47, 48, 51, 52,
 53; Matthew, 107; Morgan, 44;
 Peter, 49, 50, 158; Richard, 50,
 154; Robert, 43, 44, 45, 47, 50,

51, 52; Robert Nicholson, 52;
 Samuel, 42, 43, 46, 52, 53;
 Sarah, 44, 47, 53, 54; Thomas,
 43, 44, 45, 52, 53; William, 41,
 44, 52, 53, 54
Drowry, Agnes, 47; John, 165
Druery, Samuell, 46
Drurey, Robert, 51
Drury, Edward, 53; John, 41, 42, 48,
 49, 53, 165; Mary, 41; Peter, 49;
 Rachell, 41; Robert, 41; Samuel,
 53; Sarah, 53; Thomas, 45, 53;
 William, 53
Dudley, James, 184, 185; William,
 20, 131
Duffin, Elizabeth, 167
Duke, Henry, 164; John, 139
Duke of Gloucester Street, 21, 37, 69,
 71, 90
Dun, Abel, 13; Abell, 164, 170, 173
Dunch, Barnabas, 187
Dunford, Wells, 51
Dunn, John, 139, 156
Dupree, John, 87
Durbinfeild, William, 188
Dyer, Henry, 83; Samuel, 180
Easly, John, 194; Roderick, 194
Easter, Mary, 57; Richard, 57, 178
Easterd, Ambrose Jackson, 60
Easton, Mr., 61
Eaton, Elizabeth, 63, 195; John, 83,
 100, 140, 143, 161, 190; Mary,
 60, 61, 63, 140; May, 63; Mr.,
 61; Pen, 16; Penkethman, 60;
 Pinkethman, 15, 16, 35, 59;
 Sarah, 27
, W., 160; William, 27, 39, 60, 61,
 63, 195
Eborne, Samuell, 163
Eburn, Samuell, 163
Eburne, Samuel, 161; Samuell, 163
Edin, Thomas, 115

Edloe, Ann Cocke, 80; Henry, 80
Edmonds, Thomas, 83
Edmunds, Thomas, 115, 121
Edwards, Anne, 150; Elizabeth, 150;
    John, 150
Efford, Nicholas, 188; Peter, 188;
    Sarah, 188, 189, 190, 193, 194
Eggleston, Benjamin, 33; William,
    181
Eggleton, Benjamin, 60
Elizabeth City County, 48, 78, 144,
    155
Elliot, John, 135
Elliott, Barnett, 135; Bernard, 135;
    Chivers, 135; Elizabeth, 135;
    George, 135; John, 135
Elmes, Anne, 178
Els, Ellis, 162
Emory, Betty, 80
Endeavor, The, 140
England, 1, 3, 8, 22, 48, 113, 132,
    133, 146, 147, 168, 170, 183
Eppes, Richard, 186
Essex, 187
Essex County, 132
Evans, Matthew, 159; Obadiah, 110
Everard, Thomas, 71
Facon, Widow, 67, 95
Faison, Elias, 104; Frances, 104;
    James, 50, 104; Widow, 67, 95
Fanning, William, 67
Farthing, John, 180
Faulkland, The, 141
Feare, Thomas, 26
Fenn, Mary, 187; Richard, 75
Fergason, John, 48
Ferguson, Elizabeth, 39; Francis, 193;
    John, 38, 39; Patrick, 86, 193;
    William, 148, 151
Ferry Road, 58
Figg, John, 113
Finch, William, 81

Finches Dam, 159
Finney, Thomas, 139
Finnie, Alexander, 70
Fips, Mary, 23
Fisher, Philip, 110
Fitzhugh, Betty, 70, 71; Elizabeth, 70,
    71
Flax Hole Swamp, 58
Fleman, Henry, 30
Fletcher, Samuel, 66
Flint County, 1
Fonare, Stiphen, 115
Fontain, Reverend Mr., 131
Forbar, William, 191
Forgason, John, 91
Fortson, Mary, 197
Foster, John, 169; Philip, 188;
    Thomas, 169
Foulkes, E., 13; Edward, 84
Foulks, Edward, 96; Thomas, 96
Fountain, Mr., 184
Fox, Davey, 73
France, 192
Francis Street, 68
Frayser, John, 27
Frazer, John, 132
Freeman, Elinor, 44; Henry, 44, 94;
    Joseph, 51; Martha, 51; Matthew,
    44
French Ordinary Field, 67, 95
Freyser, William, 193
Frezell, Hugh, 67; Katherine, 67
Friend, Elizabeth, 2
Frith, Joseph, 64
Froman, John, 21
Fryth, Joseph, 163
Fuller, Edward, 82; Elizabeth, 182
Furnew, Stephen, 118
Galt, Alexander Dickie, 90; James,
    90; John Minson, 90, 91
Gammell, John, 107
Gandee, Ralph, 161

Gantlett, William, 35
Gardiner, Thomas, 143
Gardner, John, 188
Garson, John, 139; William, 139
Gauntlet, William, 55
Geddy, James, 71
Gemmel, John, 108
Gemmil, James, 151
Gemmill, James, 32
George, The, 56
Gibbins, John, 83
Gibbons, Ann, 131; John, 13, 87, 124,
    132, 146, 171, 183; Lawrence,
    131, 135; Thomas, 101; Widow,
    37
Gibbons Spring Bridge, 34
Gibbs, Stafford, 184; Thomas, 93
Gibson, Widdow, 28
Gilbert, George, 85, 166, 189, 191;
    Henry, 123
Gillbert, Henry, 189
Gilmer, Doctor, 16, 131; George, 32,
    33
Glanister, Peter, 22
Glascock, George, 23, 24
Glebe, The, 186
Glebe Land, 104
Glenister, Peter, 23; Sarah, 23
Gloucester (Gloster) County, 6, 72,
    94, 96, 111, 113, 114, 121, 148,
    184, 185
Goddin, Jacob, 161; Sarah, 165
Godding, Isaack, 112
Goddnor, Jacob, 166
Goding, Jacob, 96
Godlington, Thomas, 68
Godwin, Jacob, 12, 189
Goffe, John, 114; William, 114
Golden, Elizabeth, 137; John, 137;
    Lydia, 137; Margaret, 137
Gomer, John, 193
Gooch, Mary, 73; Mary Attawell, 73;

Samuel, 73; William, 32
Goochland, 194
Goochland County, 150
Gooding, Isaac, 96
Goodwin, Elizabeth, 121, 124; James,
    107; John, 18, 19, 31, 32, 33, 35,
    107, 118; Martin, 121; Mr., 123;
    Peter, 51, 77, 123, 141, 144;
    Robert, 98, 99
Goodwyn, Barbar, 121; Barbara, 121;
    Blanch, 121; Elizabeth, 121;
    Martin, 116, 121; Peter, 118;
    Robert, 121
Goosetry, 1
Goosley, Thomas, 132
Gordon, William, 42, 48, 49, 53, 193
Governor's Land, 39
Grame, John, 32
Grancher, William, 55
Grantham, Thomas, 56, 139
Granville County, NC, 195
Graves, Adam, 64; Anne, 55, 56;
    Dionysia, 60, 63; Elizabeth, 59,
    60, 62, 63, 64, 68, 175; Henry,
    58, 59, 60, 62, 63; Henry Brown,
    61, 62; Jane, 64; John, 61, 62,
    65, 66; Joseph, 65; Joshua, 65;
    Mary, 27, 55, 57, 58, 59, 62; Mr.,
    16; Rachaell, 54; Rachel, 55, 56;
    Ralph, 5, 13, 27, 32, 35, 54, 55,
    56, 57, 58, 59, 60, 61, 62, 63, 75,
    184, 192; Richard, 58, 59, 60,
    62, 63; Richard Croshaw, 60, 64;
    Richard Crosher, 58, 59, 62, 63;
    Robert, 65, 66; Sally, 61, 62;
    Sarah, 60, 62, 63; Susannah, 59,
    62; Thomas, 66, 68, 175; Unity,
    5, 56, 57, 60; William, 33, 39,
    55, 57, 58, 59, 60, 61, 62, 63, 64,
    160
Gravesend, 183
Great Britain, 128, 134, 192

Great Landing, 109
Great Quarter Gut, 39
Great Yarmouth, 142
Green, Abigail, 11; Ralph, 114;
   Robert, 11, 175; Sarah, 51;
   William, 51
Gremtew, John, 49
Gressam, Mary, 66
Greves, Thomas, 66
Griffin, Elizabeth, 140; Robert, 178
Griggs, John, 191; Margery, 191
Grime, Edward, 73; Margaret, 73
Grimes, Alice, 70; Ann, 74;
   Benjamin, 70; Charles, 70;
   Edward, 72, 73; Elizabeth, 74;
   Jane, 67, 95; John, 70; Lucy, 70;
   Ludwell, 70; Margaret, 73; Mary,
   67, 73; Philip, 70; Richard, 74;
   Sarah, 70; Walter, 74; William,
   67, 68, 74, 95, 166, 174
Grives, Edward, 64
Grome, John, 39
Gross, Edward, 65
Grymes, Alice, 66, 67, 68, 70, 174;
   Benjamin, 71; Charles, 66, 67,
   68, 71, 72; Elizabeth, 74; Jane,
   67, 71, 174; John, 68, 69, 70, 71;
   Judith, 71; Katherine, 67, 68;
   Lucy, 68, 71; Margaret, 67, 68,
   174, 176, 177; Martha, 67, 174;
   Mary, 67, 71, 72; Philip, 68, 70,
   71, 72; Philip L., 71; Philip
   Ludwell, 71; William, 66, 67, 68,
   74, 174
Hacker, Henry, 16; Mr., 131
Hackers, 62
Hadderill, George, 191
Haggatt, Othniel, 65
Hales, Henry, 11
Haley, Elizabeth, 51
Halifax County, VA, 182
Hall, Anthony Lamb, 80; Mary H.,

80; Robert Lamb, 80; Thomas,
   80; Thomas Spencer, 80;
   William, 110, 167
Halliwell, James, 187
Halsey, Robert, 168
Haly, Thomas, 83
Hamners Path, 5
Hampstead, 167, 168
Hampton Parish, 2, 67, 68, 82, 95, 96,
   100, 162, 174, 178, 179
Hancocke, Dorianathea, 178;
   Thomas, 178
Hand, Thomas, 1
Handy, Elizabeth, 7, 8, 27; Robert, 4,
   7; William, 7, 8
Hanmer, Humphrey, 191
Hanover County, 60
Hanover County, VA, 133
Hansford, Charles, 2, 176, 177, 182;
   David, 84; Elizabeth, 2, 84; John,
   21, 82, 165, 177; Matthew, 21;
   Susanna, 177; Thomas, 2, 84,
   166, 171; William, 2, 6, 83, 84,
   98
Hanson, Benjamin, 131
Harden, Ann, 75
Harding, Thomas, 22
Harmer, John, 31, 36, 37
Haroson, Mary M., 165
Harris, John, 9, 20, 184; Richard, 86;
   Robert, 115, 188, 190, 193
Harrison, Benjamin, 69; Robert, 162,
   164, 175; Thomas, 83, 84;
   William, 163
Hartwell, William, 55
Harvey, James, 115; Thomas, 109
Harwar, Thomas, 141
Harwood, Captain, 131; Thomas,
   140; William, 131
Haswell & Hung, 20
Hauser, Richard, 74
Hauskins, Thomas, 193

Hauthorn, William, 103
Havewell, Robert, 45
Hawkins, Samuel, 172; Thomas, 32, 46, 76
Hawthorne, Mr., 93; William, 110
Hay, Ann, 139; Frances, 79; James, 78, 151, 155; John, 44, 47, 77, 78, 79, 103, 148, 151, 168; Mary, 77; Peter, 70; Rachel, 77, 79, 80; Robert, 78, 170; Sarah, 78
Hay Family, 168
Hays, Calthorp, 47; Denys, 149; Robert, 149
Hayward, Elinor, 110; Elizabeth, 170, 171, 172, 173; Francis, 45, 53, 76, 106, 143, 150, 151; Henry, 16, 26, 42, 46, 85, 86, 101, 122, 140, 141, 142, 143, 169, 170, 171, 172, 173; John, 103, 104, 106; William, 53
Hayward Mill, 47
Hayward's Mill, 145
Headborough, 99
Heath, James, 187
Hemlocke, Sarah, 168
Hempstead, 167
Henrico, 37
Henrico County, 33, 138, 150, 193, 194
Henrikin, Garrat, 88
Herding, Christian, 66
Hewgh, George, 194
Hewitt, Francis, 186; John, 186; Lucy, 186; Mr., 131; William, 186
Heyward, Henry, 17; John, 144, 145
Hickman's Creek, 174
Hicks, 32, Thomas, 30
Hide, Jonathan, 141
Hill, Andrew, 3; Humphry, 136; James, 16, 17; Martha, 42; Mary, 52, 81; Mary Henry, 80; Samuel, 182; Thomas, 163
Hill House, 113
Hilliard, Thomas, 58; Unity, 59, 60; William, 58, 59, 60
Hillis, Joseph, 74
Hillyard, Frances, 7, 58; John, 7, 10, 58
Hinde, Thomas, 190
Hobday, John, 64
Holdcraft, Henry, 13, 26, 118
Holder, Thomas, 1
Holdsworth, Charles, 85, 86
Holland, James, 192; Lewis, 36, 195
Hollier, Simon, 14
Holloway, John, 28, 69, 74, 107; Major, 151
Holman, Captain, 67
Holmes, Thomas, 108
Holt, John, 69, 167; Mr., 16; William, 60, 61
Hooke, Nathaniel, 51, 74, 170
Hope, George, 1; Magdalen, 1
Hopkins, H., 166; Joseph, 45; William, 25
Hornebrooke, 42
Hornsby, Joseph, 60, 61, 62, 63; Margaret, 87; Mr., 16; Thomas, 38, 87, 89; William, 90, 91
Horrinton Swamp, 62
Horse Brooke, 41
Horsington, John, 13, 57
Horsington Swamp, 60, 61
Hough, George, 95
How, Benjamin, 131
Howard, Ann, 49, 158; Frances, 159; Francis, 31, 32, 157; Henry, 155, 156, 157, 158, 159; James, 121; John, 109; Margaret, 182; Martha, 155, 157; William, 157
Howards Mill, 159
Howells, Barrantine, 30

Howels, Barrintine, 50
Hubank, George, 185; John, 185;
  Sarah, 185
Hubard, Ann, 52; James, 85, 123,
  192; John, 14, 85; Mary, 72;
  Mathew, 131; Matthew, 19
Hubbard, Elizabeth, 186; James, 181;
  Mathew, 177; Matthew, 175;
  Ralph, 26, 83, 117
Hubberd, Edmund Glanvill, 182;
  James, 84, 185; John, 117;
  Matthew, 175, 182, 184, 185;
  William, 185
Huberd, Ellen, 177
Hudson, Edmund, 47
Hughes, George, 29
Hulett, Armistant, 34; Hannah, 34;
  Sally Cobbs, 34
Hund, Thomas, 1
Hunt, Anne, 155; Ganton, 156;
  Gawton, 148, 155, 156; Hannah,
  107; John, 75, 77, 105, 107, 113,
  121; Mary, 182; Nathaniel, 67;
  Robert, 83; Thomas, 52, 106,
  125, 126
Hurst, R., 93, 104, 138; Richard, 20
Hutton, Barbara, 13
Hyde, James, 140, 141, 143; John,
  88; Judith, 88; Mary, 88; Samuel,
  31, 53, 85, 176, 177, 182, 193
Hynton, Judith, 16, 18
India Man, Pritty, 130
Indian Field, 5, 8, 55, 57, 58
Ingles, Mungo, 29
Ireland, 192

Irish, William, 4
Irwin, Jones, 44, 103, 124, 131, 150,
  151
Isle of Wight County, VA, 29, 40
Jackson, Ambrose, 8, 9, 10, 16, 33,
  59, 60; Elizabeth, 7, 8, 9, 10, 56;

Fips, 16, 39, 59, 60; Hanna, 7;
  Hannah, 8; Henry, 95; James, 82;
  Mary, 7, 8, 9; Philliman, 7, 8;
  Philloman, 27; Phipps, 8, 9, 10;
  Richard, 56; Robert, 84, 85, 100;
  Tips, 38; William, 3, 4, 7, 8, 9,
  10, 57, 61
Jackson's Land, 5
Jamaica, 184
James, Elizabeth, 103; William, 144
James City, 61, 67, 114, 149, 163,
  166
James City County, 4, 14, 15, 27, 51,
  58, 61, 63, 68, 69, 76, 89, 118,
  150, 174, 175, 177, 181, 183,
  188, 189, 190, 191, 194
James City County Court, 193
James City Parish, 27
James River, 121, 150, 194, 195
Jameson, David, 134, 136; Nr., 125
Jamison, David, 156
Jaquelin, Edward, 35
Jaxon, Robert, 26; William, 8
Jefferson, Thomas, 114, 116
Jeffreys, Matthew, 27
Jegitts, Gardan, 52
Jenham, John, 106
Jenings, Colonel, 57; Edmond, 5;
  Edmund, 29, 57; Mary, 111;
  Peter, 111
Jenkins, Daniell, 43; Edward, 95, 96,
  97, 162; Henry, 43; Thomas, 96,
  97
Jennings, Edmund, 24, 68; Edward,
  24; Frances, 68, 70
Jepps, Margrett, 165
Johnson, John, 140, 141; Philip, 90
Johnston, John, 137
Jones, Allen, 194, 196; Charlotte,
  194; Churchhill, 71; Edward,
  119; Elizabeth, 10, 142;
  Humphrey, 62; Humphry, 63;

John, 128; Margaret, 183;
Martha, 196; Morris, 10; Robert,
29, 67, 95, 137; Rowland, 22;
Sarah, 194; Thomas, 128, 181,
192; William, 58; Willie, 194,
196
Jordan, Ann, 171, 172; Edmund, 171;
Hannah, 32; Samuel, 32
Jumps, 174
Juxon, Elizabeth, 2; Mary, 2
Kaidyee, Catherine, 194; John, 195
Kattern, William, 170
Keen, John, 56
Keith, Anna, 21; Colonel, 39;
William, 21, 86, 193
Kemp, Mathew, 132; Reverend
Doctor, 134
Kendall, Anne, 193; John, 21;
Richard, 26, 123, 164, 171
Kenle, Robert, 23
Kerby, Anne, 182, 183; Elizabeth,
156; John, 79, 81, 156, 159, 182;
Margaret, 182; Mary, 49, 158;
Robert, 118, 145, 146, 147;
Thomas, 145; William, 137, 182
Kerby Family, 157
Kerle, Eleanor, 29; Elizabeth, 25;
Robert, 29, 189; William, 23, 29
Kerr, Alexander, 32, 39, 69
Kilbye, Mr., 169
Kinchley, John, 25
King, Richard, 12, 192, 193; Walter,
31, 36, 37
King & Queen County, 20, 101, 136,
153, 164
King & Queen Plantation, 154
King George County, 71
King William County, VA, 58
Kirby, John, 157; Mary, 174; Mr.,
169; Robert, 146
Kirby Family, 157
Kirle, Elioner, 29; Ellinor, 29;

Robert, 29; William, 29
Kitchiner, Richard, 65, 66
Klingwell, Thomas, 64
Knowels, William, 66
Lamb, Abigail, 76, 80; Abigal, 77;
Ann, 77, 81; Ann Elizabeth, 81;
Anne, 77; Anthony, 75, 76, 77,
78, 79, 80, 81, 91, 170; Anthony
Hay, 80; Betty, 80; Daniel, 75,
76, 77, 80, 81; Diana, 82;
Elizabeth, 77, 78, 79, 81, 82;
Fanhy Mayo, 80; Fannie Clayton,
81; Frances, 75, 76; Hanna, 75;
Hannah, 75, 76, 77; Harriet, 76;
James, 81; James Anthony, 81;
John, 49, 75, 76, 77, 78, 80, 81,
82; John Moody, 80; Junius, 80;
Lycurgus Anthony, 80; Martha,
76, 81; Mary, 75, 80, 81; Rachel,
77, 80; Rachel Betsy, 80; Robert,
80; Ruth, 81, 82; Sally, 80;
Sarah, 76, 77; Thomas, 80, 82;
Ursula, 75; William, 75, 77, 80;
William B., 81
Lambe, Anthony, 75
Lambeth Parish, 133, 134
Lancaster County, 72, 73, 177
Landing Road, 96
Lane, Mr., 65; Thomas, 65
Langston, Matthew, 131
Lansdale, Mary, 148
Laton, David, 178
Law, Arthur, 173
Laws, Arthur, 13
Lawson, John, 111, 115; Robert, 163
Layton, David, 15, 35, 179
Lead, Amos, 150
Lee, Francis, 177; Henry, 54, 179;
Thomas, 69; William, 26, 98,
179
Leprade, Andrew, 166
Lester, Benjamin, 156; John, 99

Lewellin, John, 102, 150; Mary, 150; Robert, 54
Lewis, Charles, 50; David, 140; Mary, 165; Mr., 161
Leyfeild, Georgis, 188
Lidderdale, Elizabeth, 14; John, 14
Lightfoot, Anne, 72; Armistead, 72; Colonel, 131; Francis, 181; John, 181; Mary, 181; Mr., 107; Philip, 20, 42, 69, 128, 165, 177, 183; William, 31, 69
Lilban, Reuben, 126
Lilbon, Reuben, 109
Lilbun, Reuben, 109
Lilburn, John, 48, 94, 103, 104, 106; Reuben, 48, 126
Lilburne, John, 103
Lillian, Reuben, 126
Lillingston, Benjamin, 11
Lilly, John, 168
Lockey, Anne, 1; Edward, 1, 2; Elizabeth, 2; Mary, 1
Lodge Bridge, 129
Lohman, Jacob, 42
London, 2, 23, 54, 65, 68, 70, 113, 118, 119, 128, 132, 134, 147, 167, 183, 187, 190
Loney, William, 110
Longest, James, 154
Love, Justinian, 44, 151; Sarah, 75; Silus, 75
Lovell, Susnnah, 142
Lovett, Benjamin, 99
Lower Landing, 35
Lowry, Jane, 147; John, 147; William, 124
Loyd, John, 169; Thomas, 19
Loynes, John, 30
Lucas, Charles, 74; Thomas, 191
Lucey, John, 111
Luck, Francis, 19
Ludwell, Lucy, 68, 70, 71; Philip, 68, 69
Lunne, Marry, 66
Lyal, Margaret, 137
Lyall, John, 56, 57
Lyon, Robert, 89
Macarty, Elizabeth, 16
McCollock, John, 21
MacCormack, Michael, 142
McGarey, Thomas Cole, 181
MackDaniell, John, 143
Mackemie, Francis, 141
Mackendree, John, 182
McKentock, Enos, 47
Mackentosh, Daniel, 81; Daniell, 41, 42; Enus, 42
McKenzie, Doctor, 16
Mackenzie, Joanna, 70; Kenneth, 70
McKenzie, Kenneth, 167
Mackindo, James, 193
McKintoch, Enos, 47
Macklin, William, 25
Maiden Swamp, 161, 164
Main Bridge, 14, 58
Main Lodge Road, 185
Main Road, 60, 61, 91
Main Runn, 28
Main Street, 14, 35
Main Swamp, 14, 58, 175
Maine Swamp, 5
Mallard, Poined, 194; Poynes, 194
Mallavill, Peter, 82
Mallory, Edward, 155; Johnson, 155; W., 157
Mallovill, Elizabeth, 82; Peter, 82
Maning, Thomas, 125
Mannis, Francis, 125
Mansfield, Thomas, 99
Manson, Frances, 107; Peter, 42, 101, 145; Robert, 79, 106
Marbury, Anne, 167
Margaretts, John, 22
Market Place, 35, 89

Market Square, 71
Markham, Edward, 184
Markie, Michael, 151
Marona, Dennis, 66
Marot, Anne, 192; Edith, 35, 37, 40;
    Jean, 35; John, 11, 69, 192
Marote, John, 11
Marott, John, 37
Marriott, John, 128
Marrow, William, 79
Marshall, John, 132
Marston Parish, 14, 23, 54, 58, 188
Martin, Abraham, 31; George, 175;
    Jean, 31; John, 75, 127, 128;
    Martha, 94, 104, 125; William,
    31
Martin's Land, 175
Martin's Spring Branch, 175
Maryland, 65
Mascall, Robert, 73
Massey, Mildred, 5
Maston, Elizabeth, 52
Maston Parish, 5
Mathews, Baldwin, 12, 26, 29, 58,
    163, 175
Mathis, Edmond, 66
Mattaponie, 54
Mattapony, 55
Mattapony River, 54
Matthews, Mrs., 131; Patrick, 93
Matthews Schoolhouse, 14
Maupin, Daniel, 86, 87; Dorcas, 88,
    90; Gabriel, 82, 83, 84, 85, 86,
    87, 88, 89, 90, 91; John, 87;
    Judith, 87, 88; Marie, 86; Mary,
    82, 86, 87; William, 87
Maupine, Gabriel, 85
Maver, Alexander, 103, 136
May, Allen, 106; Elizabeth, 125;
    John, 98, 106
Mayden, Jane, 110
Meacon, Thomas, 167
Meade, Major, 132
Mecartee, Florence, 177
Medcalph, Elinor, 113
Medlicutt, Edmund, 65
Megary, Martin, 164; Thomas Cole,
    181
Meloy, Francis, 84, 164
Mennis, Callohill, 159; Francis, 102
Merchants Hundred Parish, 68, 174
Meriweather, Nicholas, 65
Merry, Elizabeth, 142; John, 18;
    Thomas, 18
Mettonpony River, 161
Michage, Mr., 65
Middle Plantation, 23, 161
Middlebrook, John, 118
Middlesex County, 65, 70, 71, 141
Middlesex County, VA, 68
Middletown Parish, 23, 188
Midle Plantacon, 160
Midletowne Parish, 162
Mihil, John, 97
Mihill, John, 97, 98, 100, 119, 149
Mihille, John, 119
Miles, Adam, 1, 3; Augian, 53;
    Charles, 185; Elizabeth, 2; John,
    2, 99; Mary, 2; Sarah, 2
Mill Dam, 34, 37
Mill Swamp, 27, 28, 45, 60, 188
Miller, Matthew, 4
Mills, John, 46
Minching Branch, 121
Minge, James, 57; Unity, 57
Minness, Francis, 105
Minnis, Francis, 123
Minson, William, 79
Mitchell, James, 129, 131, 132;
    Thomas, 110; W., 155; William,
    72, 90
Moare, Geffrey, 67, 95; Isabell, 67
Moir, Mary, 93
Mompain, Gabriel, 83; Mary, 86

Mompien, Gabriel, 82
Montesup Swamp, 161
Montgomery, Sarah, 133, 134;
  William, 132, 133, 134
Moody, Ann, 33; Anne, 33, 195;
  Edward, 185; Elizabeth, 13, 185;
  Giles, 12, 166, 193; Ishmael, 18,
  19, 20, 131, 185; Martha, 31;
  Matthew, 16, 32, 33, 89, 90, 159,
  160; Merrit, 33; Mr., 131; P., 49;
  Philip, 85, 90, 99, 165, 166, 170;
  Phillip, 100; William, 51, 160
Moor, Daniel, 148
Moore, Ann, 81; Anne, 93;
  Augustine, 108, 150, 151, 152,
  155, 156; Daniel, 31, 32, 33, 44,
  105, 148, 150, 151, 152, 155,
  156, 157, 174; Elizabeth, 21,
  148; Geffrey, 67, 95; Geoffry,
  95; Griggs, 43, 44; Isabell, 67,
  95; Jeoffry, 95; John, 21, 83, 91,
  92; Lucy, 151, 152, 155; Martha,
  150; Mary, 150; Meritt, 103;
  Merrit, 77; Merritt, 81, 144, 156,
  157, 182; Mr., 151; Richard, 75;
  Sarah, 94, 96, 98; William, 108,
  125, 182
Moore Family, 150
Moory, Mary, 18
Morce, Elizabeth, 96; John, 96;
  Widow, 67
Morcock, Thomas, 194
More, Daniel, 32, 150, 151; Geffrey,
  95
Morecock, Ann, 81; Ann Stott, 80
Morgan, Alice, 94; Ann, 92, 93;
  Anne, 93; Charles, 92; Elinor,
  91, 92; Elizabeth, 91, 92;
  Elizabeth Lawrence, 92, 93;
  Elliner, 91; Gerrard, 93; Haynes,
  92; Humphrey, 93; John, 92, 93,
  94, 184; Martha, 93; Mary, 94;

Peter, 94; Roger, 92; Sarah, 92;
  Thomas, 91, 92, 93; William, 91,
  92, 94
Morgin, Elinor, 92; Roger, 92; Sarah,
  92
Morgine, Elinor, 91, 92; William, 92
Morland, Young, 79
Morris, Giles, 48, 126; James, 85,
  100, 189; John, 167; Lemuel, 25;
  Widow, 67, 95; William, 108,
  125
Moss, Benjamin, 129, 135, 136;
  Edward, 19, 20, 32, 53, 107, 108,
  121, 139, 140, 152; Elizabeth,
  129; Francis, 19, 32, 129, 130,
  131; John, 26, 102, 139, 165;
  William, 19, 49, 50, 139, 154
Mounfort, Joseph, 190
Mountfoot, Joseph, 129
Mountford's Mill Dam, 130
Mountforks Mill Dam, 134
Mountfort, Joseph, 51, 193; Thomas,
  115, 116
Much Parendon, 187
Muckendre, John, 43
Muckendry, John, 41
Muckentosh, Enos, 41
Mulatto, Dick, 153, 154; Jo, 14; Will,
  113
Mulberry Island Parish, 140
Mumford, Jeffry, 121
Mundall, John, 166
Munford, Elizabeth, 40
Murphrey, John, 29
Murrell Path, 121
Musgrove, James, 181
Myall's Run, 159
Myhill, John, 99
Nance, James, 58
Nancimond County, 196
Naylor, Dixon, 121
Needler, Mr., 131

Negro, Aaron, 153; Abel, 156;
Abigall, 170; Abraham, 92;
Abram, 156, 158, 159; Adam, 14,
130, 131; Agga, 159; Aggar, 108,
126; Aggy, 158; Alice, 61, 154,
156; Alse, 153; Amborough, 77;
Amy, 131, 156; Andrew, 61;
Ann, 61; Annaka, 156; Arguile,
154; Armourer, 77; Arquila, 153;
Ausy, 170; Ballow, 158, 159;
Barber, 158; Barnaby, 131; Bash,
45; Batter, 158; Beck, 144, 158;
Ben, 8, 103, 105, 130, 131, 153,
156, 158; Bess, 15, 28, 33, 48,
109, 126, 138; Betty, 8, 34, 59,
128, 130, 131, 132, 154, 158,
159, 195; Bill, 153; Billy, 34,
153, 170; Black Betty, 2;
Blackwall, 130, 131; Bob, 60,
64, 144, 156, 158; Bristol, 77,
156, 158; Bunny, 105; Bustor,
77; Cali, 93; Carpenter Bob, 61;
Casar, 105, 124, 158; Cate, 33,
61, 130, 154, 158, 159; Cato,
131; Cazar, 20; Charge, 102;
Charles, 39, 52, 144, 152; Chloe,
130, 131, 136; Choragio, 11;
Cully, 156; Cyrus, 124, 135;
Dan, 158, 159; Daniel, 60, 109,
143, 151, 156, 171, 172; Daphne,
136; David, 60, 64, 156; Dick,
25, 105, 108, 126, 153, 158;
Dinah, 59, 104, 105, 144, 156,
171, 172; Doll, 195; Dorcus, 64;
Dorinda, 156; Easter, 153, 154;
Edy, 156; Elizabeth, 113;
Emanuel, 136; Embrough, 77;
Ester, 148; Esther, 77, 104, 105,
152; Eve, 14; Fanny, 34, 61; Fish
Neck, 159; Fish-neck, 158; Flora,
136; Fran, 144; Frank, 3, 61, 78,
79, 92, 104, 105, 130, 131, 138,

144, 145, 152, 158, 170, 171,
172, 184; Gaby, 61, 158; George,
33, 76, 78, 79, 113, 130, 131,
142, 151, 156, 186; Grace, 79,
104, 105, 131, 152, 153, 154,
156; Graves, 156; Great Harry,
170; Great Peg, 156; Great Peter,
61; Great Sarah, 153; Grump, 61;
Guy, 25; Hagar, 105; Hancock,
62; Hannah, 48, 59, 60, 77, 109,
113, 126, 152, 153, 154, 159,
169, 182, 186, 195; Harry, 8, 48,
61, 79, 109, 126, 130, 131, 152,
153, 154, 156, 158, 169; Hester,
146; Humphrey, 144; Isaac, 62,
146, 151; Isham, 59; Isom, 62;
Jaban, 138; Jaccae, 146; Jack, 8,
38, 39, 60, 62, 78, 104, 105, 129,
130, 131, 138, 152, 153, 154,
156, 158, 170; Jacob, 104, 105,
106, 143, 151, 153, 154, 156,
158; James, 105, 108, 131, 156,
170, 171, 172; Jammy, 60; Jamy,
34; Jane, 59; Jemmy, 59, 62, 130,
156, 158; Jennie, 146; Jenny, 8,
60, 61, 72, 81, 103, 146, 153,
156, 159, 170; Jerry, 156, 158;
Jimmy, 20, 46, 77, 138, 144; Jo,
79, 131; Joan, 153, 154; Joe, 34,
77, 128, 130, 158; John, 59, 61,
137; Johnny, 72; Jomoy, 11;
Jone, 77; Jossey, 61; Juda, 11;
Jude, 19, 172; Judeth, 140;
Judith, 14, 20, 59, 62, 79, 151,
156; Judy, 20, 90, 145, 151, 158,
171, 182; Jupiter, 81; Kate, 8, 64,
130, 131, 153; Kitt, 176; Knap,
23; Lazarus, 131; Leah, 156;
Lettice, 153, 154; Lewey, 153,
154; Lewis, 156; Little Amy,
156; Little Billy, 154; Little Bob,
61; Little Cate, 154; Little Frank,

153; Little Grace, 154; Little
Hannah, 152; Little Jerry, 156;
Little Nanny, 131; Little Peg,
156; Little Peter, 61; London, 60,
130, 131, 156; Lucy, 8, 59, 62,
64, 77, 107, 121, 130, 131, 132,
151, 156, 158, 195; Lydia, 158;
Malachi, 158, 159; Malichi, 158;
Mall, 113; Marea, 140; Marget,
62; Mary, 38, 39, 136, 153, 154,
156; Matt, 153; Mildred, 156;
Milla, 64; Milley, 156; Milly,
138; Mingo, 169, 171, 172; Moll,
11, 45, 59, 61, 79, 104, 105, 131,
138, 158, 159; Molly, 130, 159;
Monmouth, 130, 131; Mordica,
184; Moses, 61; Nan, 105;
Nanny, 34, 88, 104, 130, 131,
151, 153, 154, 156, 158, 195;
Nany, 131; Nat, 156; Natt, 156;
Ned, 61, 144, 153, 154, 156;
Nell, 61, 153, 154, 169; Nelle,
148; Nemo, 171, 172, Nob, 113;
Old Dick, 154; Old Esther, 152;
Old Frank, 61, 153, 154; Old
Lucy, 59; Old Sarah, 154; Old
Will, 61; Oxford, 59; Pat, 34;
Patrick, 153, 154; Patt, 78, 79,
81, 92, 153, 154, 158, 195; Patty,
46, 107; Paul, 104, 105, 124,
152, 153, 154, 156, 158, 159;
Peg, 34, 105, 131, 144, 153, 156,
184; Pegg, 59, 104, 108, 126,
132, 152, 156, 158; Peggy, 130;
Peter, 33, 53, 59, 64, 112, 158,
159; Phaebe, 136; Pheby, 131;
Phil, 138, 153, 158, 182; Phill,
48, 109, 126, 131, 138, 153, 154;
Phillis, 19, 20, 77, 124, 127, 130,
131, 132, 140, 144, 146, 156,
158; Phoeby, 130; Phota, 11;
Pleasant, 153; Pompey, 34, 39,

105, 144, 153; Pretty, 131;
Quaqua, 131; Quarco, 131;
Quash, 153, 154; Rachael, 28;
Rachel, 46, 61, 81, 105, 124,
130, 144, 151, 156, 158, 159;
Racher, 148; Reubin, 61; Robin,
60, 138; Roger, 61; Rose, 156;
Rumford, 127; Sal, 138; Sall, 81;
Sam, 59, 61, 89, 108, 126, 151,
156, 157, 158, 159; Sam Barber,
159; Sambo, 4, 8; Sampson, 59,
62; Samson, 8, 131; Santy, 107;
Sarah, 8, 33, 60, 77, 92, 104,
105, 131, 138, 146, 151, 153,
154, 158, 170, 171, 172, 184;
Sary, 28, 130, 158, 171, 172;
Sawney, 153, 154; Scipio, 127;
Sera, 61; Short Pegg, 59; Simon,
8; Stafford, 33; Stephen, 61;
Stepney, 156; Sue, 33, 156, 157,
158; Sukey, 34, 81; Susan, 28;
Taffy, 79; Temp, 62; Titus, 158;
Tom, 19, 20, 25, 48, 53, 61, 107,
109, 112, 121, 124, 126, 130,
131, 138, 152, 153, 154, 169,
195; Toney, 61; Tony, 128, 131;
Waterford, 130, 131, 132; Will,
19, 20, 60, 63, 77, 92, 145, 151,
153, 154, 156, 157, 158, 171,
172, 195; Wilson, 153, 154;
York, 130, 131, 153; York Dick,
154; Young Lucy, 59
Nelson, Edward, 11; Mr., 62, 131;
Nathaniel, 51; Thomas, 20, 32,
44, 45, 65, 74, 99, 100, 123, 128,
136, 151, 173, 177, 195;
William, 20, 33, 51, 61, 69, 70,
104, 125, 131, 132, 134, 152,
195
Nener, David, 163
New Kent County, 5, 13, 25, 54, 60,
63, 64, 113, 150, 161, 178, 196

218

New Kent, VA, 114
New Poquoson Parish, 143
Newby, Gudlisbury, 171
Newell, David, 2; Lettia, 2
Newington, 188
Newman, Alice, 23; James, 133
Newsam, William, 73
Newton, George, 36
Nicholas, Anne, 70; Robert Carter,
    63, 70
Nicholson, Francis, 115
Nicholson Street, 14, 15, 37, 71
Nicolson, Robert, 90
Nicolson Street, 90
Nisbet, Captain, 131
Nisbitt, Joseph, 193
Nixon, John, 143; Thomas, 123
Noblin, Lucy, 52; Richard, 52
Noner, David, 163
Norfolk County, 35, 36, 142
Norris, John, 66
North Carolina, 29, 195, 196
Northamptonshire, 65
Northumberland County, 161, 196
Norton, John, 51, 133, 134, 136, 138
Norvel, Hugh, 35
Norvell, Hugh, 26, 85; William, 181
Noyell, William, 132
Nutting, Booth, 148; Elizabeth, 124,
    146, 147, 148, 155; Jane, 145;
    Katherine, 148; Madam, 145;
    Mary, 144, 149, 150, 153;
    Thomas, 113, 142, 145, 155,
    170, 191
Oak Swamp, 143
Obrian, William, 185
Ogilby, Patrick, 85
Ogleby, Patrick, 86
Oken Neck Mill Road, 176
Okn Neck, 176
Old Church, 57, 76
Old Mill, 27

Old Poquoson, 152
Old Poquoson River, 148, 155
Old Road, 57
Old School House, 58
Oliver, Edward, 5; John, 64, 75;
    Mary, 186; Peter, 186
Olliver Neck, 6
Orr, Hugh, 21, 88
Oulde Withington, Cheshire, 1
Overstreet, Edward, 97, 98;
    Elizabeth, 96, 97, 98, 100;
    Henry, 97, 98, 100; James, 101;
    Jefery, 97; Jeffery, 96, 97;
    Jeffrey, 98, 99, 101, 163; Jeoffry,
    95; John, 94, 95, 96, 98, 99, 100,
    101, 162; Mary, 96, 98, 99, 100;
    Sarah, 94, 95, 97, 98; Thomas,
    96, 97, 98, 99, 100
Overstreete, Geffery, 96; Jeffery, 96,
    162; John, 67, 95, 162; Mary, 96;
    Sarah, 95, 162; Thomas, 67, 95
Owens, John, 22, 188
Owle, Ann, 73
Oxford, England, 139
Pack, Graves, 44, 69
Packe, Mrs., 131; Sarah, 51, 131
Paddy, Elizabeth, 95
Padeyes, Zachary, 95
Padgett, Ann, 98; Samuel, 98;
    Samuell, 98
Page, Francis, 190; John, 22, 166;
    Mann, 14, 38, 70, 72; Mathew,
    190
Page Street, 72
Pagetts Tribe, 187
Palace Street, 35, 70
Palmer, Leiut, 54; Samuel, 20
Pamer, Anne, 148
Panneares, Ann, 113
Parendon, 187
Parke, Daniel, 4, 22, 23, 190; Daniell,
    41; Danniell, 115; Edmund, 63;

Jane, 41
Parker, Alexander, 21; John, 16, 179;
Thomas, 21, 187
Parks, Mr., 131; William, 16
Parr, Richard, 166
Parry, John, 184
Parsons, Armiger, 18, 47, 170;
Dorothy, 169, 170, 172;
Elizabeth, 18, 47; Jack, 170;
James, 46, 83, 170, 172; John,
172
Parsons Family, 172
Paspetanke River, 197
Pasteur, Blovet, 88, 89; Jean, 86, 87;
John, 85, 86, 87, 166, 192;
Judith, 87, 88; Mary, 87;
William, 90
Pasture, John, 166
Paten, Alice, 167
Patrick, Alice, 103; Ann, 101; Betsy,
109; Clayton, 108; Curles, 108,
126; Curtis, 48, 104, 105, 108,
109, 125, 126; Edmond, 108;
Edmund, 104, 105, 108, 109,
125; Edmund Curtis, 109;
Elizabeth, 101, 102, 103, 105,
106, 107, 108, 109, 110;
Elizabeth Topless, 109; Frances,
103, 104, 105; Frances Manson,
109; Hannah, 103, 107, 109;
John, 52, 94, 101, 102, 103, 104,
105, 106, 107, 108, 109, 110,
123, 124, 125, 126, 156, 157;
Lucy, 104, 109; Martha, 48, 103,
108, 109, 126; Mary, 101, 103,
104, 105, 106, 107, 109; Merit,
104; Merrit, 105; Mildred, 48,
109, 126; Nancy, 107, 108;
Patsy, 48, 109, 126; Peter, 107;
Robert, 109; Sally Clayton, 109;
Sarah, 102, 103, 104, 105, 106,
107, 108, 125; Susanna, 105,

108; Thomas, 103, 104, 105,
106, 107, 109; Thomas Curtis,
108; Walter, 101, 103; William,
79, 103, 104, 105, 106, 108, 109,
125, 126
Pattison, Margret, 140; William, 97,
115, 140
Pattisson, William, 163
Paule, The, 183
Paulen, Elizabeth, 3
Paynter, Thomas, 121
Payras, Doctor, 131; John, 20
Peake, Abigal, 90; William, 90
Pearson, Magdalen, 38; William, 38,
90
Peirce, Mathew, 51; Matthew, 35,
192
Pelch, Andrew, 161
Pell, Mary, 179
Pencherman, Thomas, 55
Penenan, Thomas, 37
Penny, Pennel, 34
Penston, Christopher, 25
Peogers, Herbert, 187
Perrin, John, 74
Perry, Jane, 161; Mr., 42, 65, 148
Perrymans Line, 176
Perrymans Spring Branch, 176
Pervin, William, 125
Pescud, Thomas, 48, 50, 52, 124,
126, 156
Pester, Humphry, 161
Peters, Elizabeth, 51; Robert, 26, 186
Philips, Mary, 131
Phillips, Aaron, 131, 154; Anne, 17;
Elizabeth, 154; Griffin, 65; John,
73; Nicholas, 105; Thomas, 76
Phillipson, Robert, 42
Pickett, Widow, 113
Pickman, Mary, 23
Pierce, Frances, 25; John, 90, 181;
Mathew, 27, 28, 189; Matthew,

25, 33, 34, 36, 37, 192
Pierce's Spring Bridge, 28
Pinchback, Thomas, 4, 117
Pinchbecks, Thomas, 117
Pinckithman, Timothy, 10; William, 10
Pines, Anne, 117
Piney Neck, 102, 103
Piney Point, 104
Pinket, Thomas, 191
Pinkethman, Mary, 11, 12, 23; Rebecca, 8, 11, 27, 28, 66; Rebecka, 10; Sarah, 11, 12; Thomas, 11, 12, 14, 58; Timothy, 3, 8, 10, 11, 12, 66; William, 8, 11, 23, 24, 26, 27, 30
Pinkithman, Timothy, 6; William, 7
Pinktheman, Rebecca, 27; Thomas, 55, 117
Pinyridge, 103
Piper, John, 74
Planter's Adventure, The, 162
Play House, 69
Plouvier, Elizabeth, 168, 171, 172, 173
Pocoson, 108
Pocoson River, 57
Pohaten, 194
Poindexter, Elizabeth, 188; George, 188; John, 188; Katherine, 188
Pole, Godfrey, 166
Pond, John, 163; Samuel, 76; Stephen, 169; Stepon, 169
Poore, Thomas, 75
Poplar Neck, 4
Poquoson, 76
Poquoson River, 148, 155
Port Land, 97, 116, 141
Portland, 97, 127, 142
Potlin, John, 102; William, 102, 103
Potter, Doctor, 131; Edward, 19, 32, 131

Powell, Benjamin, 34, 39; Elizabeth, 34; Mary, 34; Peter, 33, 34, 39; Thomas, 19, 72, 137, 193; William, 107
Power, Susanna, 61
Powers, Edward, 51, 83, 116, 183; John, 124, 137; Sally, 61, 62; Susanna, 62, 124; Susannah, 62
Powhaten, 23
Powhite Creek, 194
Prentis, William, 16, 20, 21, 36, 41, 72, 89, 167, 193
Presser, Thomas, 137
Pressey, Nicholas, 151
Presson, Anne, 79; Daniel, 79; Elizabeth, 77, 79; John, 77, 78, 79; Marrow, 79; Nicholas, 126; Robert, 159; Samuel, 53, 107; Thomas, 44, 47; William, 79
Price, Morris, 47
Pride, James, 132, 134
Priest, James, 164
Prince George County, VA, 80
Prise, Maurise, 27; Thomas, 27
Prosson, Thomas, 151, 155
Prynne, George, 187
Public Road, 185
Pynes, Ann, 117; Edmund, 117; John, 117
Quarter Field Branch, 140
Queen Mary's Port, 14, 36, 38, 195
Queen's Creek, 4, 7, 14, 23, 27, 32, 33, 34, 39, 89
Queens Creek, 175
Queen's Hope, 1
Rabley, Jane, 114
Randell, James, 65
Randle, John, 156, 159
Randolph, Edward, 26, 65; John, 32, 69, 90, 193; Mary, 70, 71, 72; Mr., 195; William, 13, 37, 115
Ranson, Robert, 20

Rappahannock, 24, 118
Rappahannock River, 73
Ratcliff, William, 62, 63
Ratcliffe, 65, William, 181
Read, Benjamin, 163; John, 96, 129;
    Mary, 154; Mrs., 131; Robert,
    119; Samuel, 103
Reade, Frances, 153, 154; George,
    153; Gwyn, 94, 130, 133, 184;
    Mary, 151, 154, 156; Mildred,
    153, 154; Robert, 142, 153;
    Samuel, 19, 20, 31, 32, 33, 50,
    138, 149, 151, 152, 153, 154,
    156, 159; W., 157
Redwood, John, 191
Reedy Swamp, 35
Reid, Adam, 21; James, 21
Revere, John, 23
Reynolds, Ann, 136; Anne, 136;
    Susanna, 130, 131, 134, 135,
    136; Thomas, 20, 131, 132, 133,
    134, 136, 138, 184; William, 136
Reynolds Family, 135
Rhodes, John, 99, 100; Sarah, 16
Richards, John, 34
Richardson, Dudley, 29; John, 78;
    Martha, 194; Richard, 13
Rickman, Mary, 23; Richard, 192
Riggs, William, 189
Right, Edward, 55; John, 19, 55, 74
Ring, Joseph, 65, 97, 114, 116, 137,
    163, 191; Mr., 191
Ripping, Edward, 86, 192
Risle, John, 67, 95; Mary, 67, 95
Risley, Mary, 67, 95
Roade Side, 175
Roades, John, 100
Roads, John, 98
Roberts, Ann, 104; Gerald, 32;
    Gerard, 44, 147, 151; Jerrard,
    170; John, 183; Molly, 34;
    Robert, 51; Samuel, 151;

Thomas, 14, 17, 46, 50, 51, 52,
    77, 103, 104, 105, 145, 170, 189,
    193; William, 139
Robertson, William, 21, 31, 36, 68,
    137, 173
Robesson, Anthony, 163
Robins Creek, 174
Robinson, Anthony, 31, 32, 33, 154,
    169, 173, 174; Cole, 79;
    Elizabeth, 174; Frances, 170,
    174; John, 69, 79, 159, 169, 170,
    172, 173, 174; Martha, 174;
    Mary, 154, 173, 174; Peter, 52,
    81; Robert, 20; Starkey, 155,
    156, 174; Thomas, 79; William,
    32, 52, 123, 151
Robinson Family, 154
Rockahock Path, 14, 58
Rodes, Francis, 30
Roe, William, 144, 145
Roe's Warehouse, 32
Rogers, Addenston, 126, 127;
    Adderston, 48, 109; Adduston,
    83, 108, 115, 116, 118, 119, 120,
    123, 124, 125, 126, 135, 170;
    Adenstone, 124; Aduston, 108,
    113, 116, 126; Adustone, 123,
    124; Agnes, 112, 113, 116, 117;
    Ann, 117, 118, 121, 137;
    Anthony, 124; Barbara, 121, 139;
    Barbarah, 116; Catherine, 124;
    Charles, 135; Clayton, 108, 123,
    124, 125; Cleaton, 107;
    Elizabeth, 117, 118, 120, 124,
    125, 127, 135; George, 132, 133,
    134; Giles, 135; Hannah, 130,
    131, 132, 133, 134; James, 123,
    124, 137; James Adduston, 135;
    Jane, 118, 119; John, 48, 108,
    109, 110, 111, 112, 113, 114,
    115, 116, 117, 118, 119, 121,
    122, 124, 125, 126, 127, 135,

136, 137, 139; John Adduston, 18, 26, 116, 118, 119, 120, 123, 136, 165, 171; John Adenstone, 124; John Aduston, 126, 138; Katha, 124; Katherine, 123, 126; Margaret, 124, 137; Martha, 108, 138; Mary, 108, 124, 126, 127, 137; Molly, 126; Rebecka, 109; Rebeckah, 108, 125; Rebeka, 108, 125; Rice, 137; Richard, 137; Samuel, 132, 137, 138; Sarah, 48, 107, 108, 109, 121, 122, 124, 125, 126, 130, 131, 132, 133, 134, 138; Susanna, 127, 134; Susannah, 132; Theodocia, 132; Theodosia, 127, 129, 130, 133, 134; Thomas, 113, 117, 118, 121, 122, 123, 124, 125; Thomas Adenston, 125; William, 48, 109, 124, 125, 126, 127, 128, 129, 130, 131, 132, 133, 134, 138, 139; William Addenston, 127; William Addirston, 48, 109, 126; William Adduston, 108; William Adruston, 139; William Aduston, 126, 138

Roots, Thomas, 73
Rose, Robert, 20; William, 154
Rough, George, 178
Rouviere, Claude, 167
Row, William, 14, 145
Rower, Charles, 151
Roy, Mungo, 21
Royers, William, 139
Royston, Stephen, 27; William, 188
Rudder, Charles, 195
Rue, Peter, 104
Russell, Adam, 76; Hinde, 52;
    Thomas, 52; William, 90
Ryder, Andrew, 137
Rylands, William, 99

Sabels Creek, 102
St. Andrews Creek, 5, 14, 58
St. Johns Parish, 58
St. Leger, Abram, 129
St. Mary Newington Parish, 188
St. Michaels Parish, 65
St. Peter's Parish, 62
St. Stephens Parish, 153
St.Mary's Newington Church, Par, 187
Sallaway, Richard, 141
Salter, John, 65; Thomas, 65
Sanders, Sarah, 96; William, 60
Sandwin, 182
Sarjanton, John, 122
Satterwhite, Mann, 138; Martha, 138
Saunders, John, 96, 97, 175; Robert, 100, 193
Saveall, Solomon, 133
Sayre, Jane, 71; Samuel William, 71
Scandrett, Pittman, 21
Scandutt, Pittman, 21
Sclater, Agnes, 147, 149, 152, 153; Alice, 149; Elizabeth, 144, 146, 149, 150, 152, 154, 155, 157, 159; James, 42, 75, 139, 140, 141, 142, 143, 144, 149, 150, 151, 152, 154, 155, 157, 159, 191; John, 139, 143, 144, 147, 149, 150, 156, 157, 158, 159; Martha, 144, 154, 155, 157, 159; Mary, 139, 140, 141, 143, 144, 147, 149, 150, 152, 153, 154, 159, 160; Mildred, 160; Richard, 144, 145, 147, 149, 150, 151, 152, 153, 154, 155, 156, 157, 158, 159; Sally, 157, 159; Sarah, 49, 144, 149, 150, 157, 158, 159; Thomas, 149; William, 143, 149, 160; William Sheldon, 144, 157, 158, 159, 160; William Shelldon, 152

Sclatyer, Richard, 144
Sclaughter, Agnes, 152; Richard, 152
Scot, Isaac, 23
Scrivener, Joseph, 90
Seabrell, Anthony, 95, 162, 163;
  Darcey, 161, 162; Darsey, 162;
  Doss, 163; Edward, 163;
  Nicholas, 95, 96, 161, 162, 163;
  Samuel, 163; Sarah, 94, 96, 162,
  163; Thomas, 163
Seabrill, Doss, 162; John, 167;
  Nicholas, 161, 162; Sarah, 162
Seabrooke, Charles, 133
Searburgh, Edmond, 51
Sebbrell, Nicholas, 160
Sebrel, Mary, 166; Samuel, 166
Sebrell, Anthony, 68, 161, 163, 164,
  174, 175; Darcey, 160; David,
  165, 166; Frances, 164, 165, 166;
  John, 164; Martha, 163, 165,
  166; Mary, 165; Matthew, 165;
  Nathaniel, 165; Nicholas, 13,
  160, 161, 162, 163, 164, 165,
  166, 175; Richard, 167; Samuel,
  163, 165, 166; Sarah, 162
Sebril, Samuel, 165
Sebrill, Darsey, 162, 163; Moses,
  167; Nicholas, 160, 162, 163
Sedgwick, William, 68, 97, 174, 175
Selater, Ann, 159, 160; Elizabeth,
  147, 157, 160; James, 147; John,
  156, 157, 159, 160; Mary, 147,
  148, 160; Nancy, 159; Richard,
  53, 147, 148, 156, 157;
  Sacheverel, 160; Sackoverel,
  160; Sally, 157
Selator, James, 147; John, 81, 156;
  Martha, 156; Mary, 148;
  Richard, 156
Selden, Samuel, 142
Seldon, Samuel, 50
Sergeton, John, 82; Robert, 114

Sessions, Thomas, 40
Sev'rill, Nicholas, 161
Sharlock, Mary, 139
Sharman, William, 117
Sharp, Francis, 12, 36, 51, 122, 176,
  178
Sharpe, Francis, 10
Sheild, Charles, 107; Dun, 102; John,
  49, 157, 158; Mary, 143; Patrick,
  102; Robert, 45, 49, 78, 99, 101,
  103, 132, 143, 157, 158; Sarah,
  157, 159
Sheilds, Dunn, 102; Hannah, 88;
  James, 39, 40, 60, 88; Matthew,
  88; Robert, 45, 102; Susanna,
  102
Sheldon, Katharin, 147; Katherine,
  145, 146, 148; Kathrine, 137;
  William, 26, 142, 145, 146, 147,
  148, 151, 165, 191
Shelldon, William, 140
Shelton, William, 173
Shepard, Benjamin, 99
Shepheard, Peter, 25
Shepherd, William, 162
Sherington, William, 131
Sherinton, Joseph, 25
Sherman, William, 118, 191
Shield, Mary, 31, 35, 37, 39; Robert,
  44, 53, 94, 104, 186
Shields, Anne, 37; Charles, 139;
  Hannah, 31, 195; James, 31, 33,
  34, 35, 37, 181, 195; Matthew,
  15, 195; Robert, 32, 101
Shuge, Thomas, 110
Sidwell, William, 168
Singleton, Ambrose, 42
Skimenoe, 55
Skimino, 7
Skimino Swamp, 175
Skiminoe, 58, 177
Skimnor, 7

Skinner, Abbertus, 188
Slate, Richard, 155
Slater, Agnes, 145, 146, 147, 148;
    Elizabeth, 145, 146, 147; James,
    140, 141; John, 150; Mary, 145,
    146, 147, 148, 159, 160;
    Mathew, 110; Matthew, 160;
    Richard, 14, 123, 146, 147, 148,
    150; Sarah, 42, 159; Thomas, 42,
    149; William, 160; William
    Sheldon, 159
Slaughter, Sarah, 149; Thomas, 149
Smith, Agnes, 125, 133, 153; Augine,
    71; Bryan, 5; Edmund, 32, 33,
    130, 131, 133, 152, 153, 155;
    Lawrence, 42, 44, 45, 53, 113,
    114, 116, 123, 127, 152, 153,
    163, 177; Mary, 94, 151, 152,
    153, 156, 184; Mildred, 152,
    153; Richard, 94, 131, 184;
    Robert, 151, 154, 155, 156;
    Samuel, 127; Sarah, 165; Silas,
    97, 165, 167, 175; Thomas, 152
Smyth, Henry, 113, 190; John, 10,
    112, 113, 188; Sarah, 113;
    William, 113
Snead, Robert, 51, 119
Snelson, Elizabeth, 133; John, 133,
    134
Snowehill, 187
Sollis, Roger, 161
Solloway, Richard, 151
South Carolina, 157
Southall, James, 90
Southerland, Anne, 148; James, 19
Spar, Samuel, 53
Spears, Robert, 37
Spencer, William, 176
Spike, Francis, 196
Spotswood, Alexander, 192
Spotsylvania, 152
Spotsylvania County, 69

Spottswood, Alexander, 26
Spring Branch, 177
Spring Bridge, 28, 37
Spurrier, Francis, 93
Squire, John, 114; Sarah, 114
Stacey, Simon, 101
Stacy, Elizabeth, 101; Joseph, 143;
    Mary, 143; Simon, 17, 51, 101,
    143, 165
Stagg, Charles, 41
Staley, Sion, 101
Stanhope, Sarah, 60; William, 60
Stanton, Elizabeth, 31
Stanup, Elizabeth, 7; John, 7; Mr., 16;
    William, 15
Stark, Mary, 129; Richard, 98;
    William, 44, 45, 129, 146, 147
Starke, Robert, 111, 115; William,
    134
Starkey, Mary, 173
Stear, Thomas, 50
Stephens, William, 74
Stephney Parish, 65
Stevenson, William, 132
Steward, Elizabeth, 193; Frances, 25;
    John, 11, 25; Richard, 193
Stinson, Mary, 110
Stock, Amedea, 111
Stockdale, John, 99
Stockner, John, 67, 166
Stokes, Sarah, 182
Stone, Ashwell, 180; Elizabeth, 59,
    60, 62, 180; Frances, 59;
    William, 12, 35, 193
Stoner, David, 161, 164, 185
Street, Henry, 64
Stroud, Thomas, 38
Sudland, Thomas, 169
Sullivan, Anne, 69
Summers Mannor, 187
Surry, 167
Surry County, 133, 134, 150, 188

Sussex County, VA, 29
Swallow, Israell, 4
Swan, The, 36
Sweney, Edmund, 53
Sweny, Edmund, 102
Swinie, Martha, 143; Mary, 143
Tabb, Augustine, 158; Edmund, 158;
  Edward, 31, 33, 44, 45, 46, 47,
  78, 79, 102, 103, 142, 144, 147,
  148, 150, 151, 158, 159;
  Elizabeth, 143, 144; John, 49,
  143, 144, 151; Mary, 143, 144;
  Rachel, 144; Thomas, 144, 155;
  William, 143, 149
Tandy, Henry, 65
Taplady, Isabel, 102
Tarrapin Point, 134
Tarripen Point, 130
Tatnum, Silvester, 27
Tavernor, Gyles, 101; Mary, 46;
  William, 42, 45, 46
Tavernor Family, 45
Taylor, Daniel, 142; Daniell, 75, 114,
  142; Elizabeth, 43; Mary, 142,
  143; Thomas, 16, 17, 56, 190;
  Walter, 76; William, 7, 11, 23,
  24, 87
Tazewell, John, 34, 39, 71
Tenham, Elizabeth, 18, 20; John, 18,
  19, 20, 107, 108, 152; Mary,
  108; Rebecca, 19
Tenkam, John, 50
Thacker, Edwin, 69; Phillipp, 160
Thomas, Edward, 5, 140; Mary, 137
Thomkins, Samuell, 171
Thompson, James, 34; Tarpley, 38
Thomson, Charles, 39; Mrs., 131;
  Stephens, 119; Stevens, 173
Thornton, William, 110
Thorpe, Mrs., 4; Otho, 4; Richard, 23
Thurmer, Ann Catherina, 93; Anna
  Catherina, 92; Robert, 92

Tibbs Spring Bridge, 57
Timson, Anne Maria, 64; Mary, 64;
  Samuel, 3, 31, 39, 61, 64;
  Samuell, 4, 114; William, 5, 12
Tindal, George, 175
Tinker Shaws, 169
Tiplady, Mathew, 120; Matthew, 118
Tiplady's Swamp, 122
Tobacco Ridge, 57
Tobacco Swamp, 57
Tomer, John, 26, 91; Thomas, 53, 78,
  79, 106, 108
Tomkins, Benit, 172
Tompkins, Benit, 152; Bennet, 76,
  77, 103, 170; Humphrey, 170;
  Samuel, 78
Tompson, Daniel, 169
Toner, Thomas, 78
Toomer, James, 124; John, 92, 106,
  165
Toplis, William, 37, 69
Toppin, Thomas, 185
Topping, Frances, 114; Joseph, 114
Tower of London, 168
Townley, Alice, 68, 70
Townzend, Susanna, 16; Thomas, 16
Trebell, William, 90
Trivallion, John, 114
Trotter, Amager, 171; Ann, 113, 121,
  169, 170; Anne, 112, 173;
  Armiger, 169, 172; Dorothy,
  171; Elizabeth, 171, 172, 173;
  John, 20, 131, 169, 171, 172,
  183; Mary, 171, 172; Richard,
  111, 112; Thomas, 169, 171,
  172; William, 129, 131, 169,
  170, 171, 172, 173
Tucker, Robert, 193; William, 18
Turner, John, 10
Turney, Richard, 196
Tyler, Charles, 50; Francis, 8, 84, 85,
  192; Henry, 11, 12, 24, 26, 29,

30, 82, 121, 163, 175; Thomas, 99

Ubank, George, 185; Sarah, 185

Underhill's Line, 68, 166, 174

Upper Parish, 196

Upton, 187

Urbanna, 68

Valentine, Benjamim, 64; Benjamin, 34, 63; Elizabeth, 57, 60, 62, 63; John, 64; Joseph, 63, 64; Mary, 64; Sarah, 34

Vandridge, William, 65

Vanner, Arthur, 131

Varnum, Elizabeth, 16, 142, 191; Lewis, 16

Vaughan, Anne, 63, 64; James, 63; Rowland, 183; Stanhope, 63; Stanup, 64

Vernam, Elizabeth, 17; Lewis, 17

Vinckler, Abraham, 30, 31; Lydia, 31

Vines, Thomas, 129, 190

Virginia Company, 168

Vobe, Thomas, 16

Waad, Armagil, 167; William, 167

Waade, Anne, 168; William, 167, 168

Wade, Amiger, 171; Ann, 168, 171, 186; Anne, 168, 176, 182, 183; Anthony, 182; Armager, 169; Armagil, 168; Armiger, 91, 118, 167, 168, 169, 170, 171, 172, 173, 174; Arminger, 75, 91; Charles, 182; Chidley, 182, 183; David Bingley, 181; Dorianathea, 178; Dorithy, 168; Dorothy, 168, 171, 172; Edward, 95, 178, 179, 182, 183; Elizabeth, 168, 171, 172, 173, 179, 181, 183; Frances, 169, 171, 173, 174; Giles, 185; Henry, 184; Higginson, 94, 184, 185; Howard, 183; James, 183, 185; Jane, 178, 179, 180, 181, 182, 185; John, 30, 179, 180,

181, 182, 185, 186; Joseph, 176, 177, 179, 180, 181; Margaret, 68, 176, 177; Margarett, 174, 175; Margrett, 163, 174; Martha, 186; Mary, 168, 171, 173, 181, 182; Nathaniel, 168; Pamela, 186; Ralph, 186; Richard, 179, 180, 181; Robert, 180, 181, 182; Sarah, 185; Seth, 186; Stephen, 182; Susanna, 176, 177; Thomas, 30, 67, 68, 163, 174, 175, 176, 177, 178, 179, 180, 181, 183, 185, 186; William, 168, 176, 178, 179, 182

Wades Spring Branch, 176

Waff, Elias, 133

Wagoner, Peter, 141

Wagstaff, Albrighton, 137; Bazill, 141

Waid, Seth, 186

Waide, Edward, 183

Wainoake Parish, 121

Walke, Anthony, 69, 132

Walker, Alexander, 36; Catharine, 71; Elizabeth, 97; Hugh, 71; John, 161; Joseph, 41, 67, 99, 100, 165, 166; Mr., 100; Ralph, 97, 113, 114, 121, 140, 141; Sarah, 186; Thomas, 97, 99, 119, 142

Waller, Anne, 168; Benjamin, 21, 38, 46, 59, 71, 72; Mr., 131

Walt, William, 181

Walters, Henry, 131

Walthoe, Nathaniel, 15

Walton, 113, Richard, 2; True, 2

Waqua Creek, 194

Ward, Plany, 45, 103

Wardley, Rebecka, 121

Warram, 2

Warren, Nathaniel, 64

Warrington, John, 60

Warwick County, 51, 92, 97, 108,

140, 142, 150, 179, 184, 185
Washington, George, 60
Watkins, Henry, 175; William, 43, 44
Watts, Anthony, 41, 101; John, 62
Watts Plantation, 101
Weatherburn, Henry, 14
Weatherburne, Henry, 37, 131
Webb, Elizabeth, 40; George, 65;
    William, 40
Webber, Henry, 65
Weeks, Mar, 21
Welch, John, 102
Welden, Anthony, 196; Elizabeth,
    187; Henrie, 187
Welding, Samuel, 196
Weldon, Benjamin, 85, 118, 190,
    191, 192, 194, 196; Daniel, 194,
    195, 196; Dorothy, 187, 188;
    Elizabeth, 187, 193, 194, 195,
    196; George, 187; Hannah, 187,
    188, 190; James, 187, 188;
    Johanna, 187; John, 187, 188,
    190, 193, 194; Mary, 190, 194;
    Poyers, 193; Poynes, 187, 188,
    190, 193; Priscilla, 194, 196;
    Prudence, 196; Rebecca, 196;
    Robert, 196; Samuel, 27, 189,
    190, 193, 194, 195, 196;
    Samuell, 187, 188; Sarah, 187,
    188, 189, 190, 193, 194;
    William, 196, 197
Weldon, NC, 196
Weldon's Landing, 196
Weldon's Orchard, 196
Weldon's Place, 196
Welldon, Samuel, 194; William, 197
Wellings, John, 122
Wellins, Robert, 124
Wellons, John, 104
Wells, John, 54, 156; Katherine, 54;
    Thomas, 156; William Sheldon,
    156

Welsh, John, 42
West, John, 5, 54, 56
Westminster, 187
Wetherburne, Henry, 15
Wexham, 187
Whaley, James, 5, 6, 25; Mary, 14,
    191; Thomas, 3
Wharton, Doctor, 131; Richard, 82,
    167
Wheatley, Ellis, 55
Wheatly, Soloman, 141; Thomas, 141
Whisken, John, 2
Whitaker, Simon, 73; William, 25
Whitby, Thomas, 26, 83, 119
White, Ann, 73; Elizabeth, 4;
    Frances, 6, 7, 10, 58; George, 6,
    10; Henry, 4, 5, 55, 56; Jane, 87;
    John, 53, 87; Joseph, 3, 4, 5, 6, 7,
    8, 10, 24, 56, 57, 58; Magdaleen,
    3; Magdalen, 5; Mary, 3, 4, 5, 6,
    8, 10, 56; Michael, 66; Mr., 57;
    Rebecca, 5; Rebeckah, 56; Unity,
    5, 56, 57; William, 5, 10, 56, 73
Whitehead, Henry, 56; John, 195;
    Thomas, 137
Widnal, John, 168
Wigg, Edward, 6
Wilcox, John, 21
Wilde, Robert, 115
Wilkerson, Samuel, 87
Wilkinson, Frances, 13; Robert, 22,
    23; Sarah, 22; Thomas, 13
Willens, Mary, 107
Willett, Richard, 42
William, Hannah, 81; Mrs., 131
William & Mary College, 15, 32, 87
William & Mary Royal College, 115
Williams, Anne, 176; Elizabeth, 81,
    187; Hannah, 78; John, 99, 179,
    194; Major, 140; Martha, 140;
    William, 187
Williamsburg, 14, 22, 39, 60, 71, 72,

88, 89, 90, 91
Williamsburg Lodge of Masons, 91
Williamsburgh, 11, 15, 16, 20, 21, 24,
    26, 32, 33, 35, 36, 37, 38, 40, 51,
    63, 68, 69, 70, 85, 86, 87, 117,
    130, 176, 191, 192, 193, 194
Williamson, Roger, 74
Willis, Francis, 69; Henry, 69;
    Mildred, 69; Mr., 61
Willmott, Richard, 177
Wills, John, 116; Thomas, 184
Wilmington Parish, 183
Wilson, John, 181; Willis, 126
Wimfrey, Elizabeth, 61
Winfrey, Elizabeth, 62; Mary, 61, 62
Winter, George, 194; William, 25
Winter's Branch, 194
Wise, Henry, 147; John, 132; Robert,
    78, 155; William, 14, 18, 51, 75,
    83, 91, 114, 118, 146, 147, 173,
    190
Wolding, Samuell, 188
Wood, Abraham, 22; Charles, 102,
    103; Elizabeth, 6; William, 99
Woodhouse, Edward, 102
Wooding, John, 137
Woodman, Mary, 169; William, 169
Woodward, George, 183

Wooten, Thomas, 120
Wootton, John, 94; Thomas, 115, 119
Worledge, John, 131
Worley, Ann, 137; Nicholas, 45, 103
Wormeley, Ralph, 108, 183
Wotten, Ann, 72; William, 72, 73
Wotton, Thomas, 118
Wraton, William, 73
Wray, Doctor, 30
Wright, Ann, 18; Benjamin, 109, 125;
    Dionisius, 164; Dionitious, 115;
    Edward, 54, 55; Fleetwood, 75;
    Joanna, 187; Johanna, 187; John,
    19, 55, 107; Lucy, 109; Margrett,
    8; Rachel, 54, 55; William, 108,
    126
Write, Elizabeth, 52
Wyatt, Dudley, 161; Mr., 161
Wycapo, John, 137
Wyld, Daniel, 55; Daniell, 7
Wylde, Mr., 175
Wynne, Richard, 52
Wythe, John, 13, 17, 121, 141
Yateman, Anne, 190; Thomas, 190

Yates, Elizabeth, 25; Elliner, 25;
    Peter, 25; Thomas, 25
York (Yorke), 13, 25, 32, 51, 69, 72,
    74, 79, 91, 92, 94, 97, 114, 116,
    119, 127, 129, 130, 133, 134,
    135, 136, 138, 141, 142, 152,
    159, 162, 183, 184, 193
York Hampton Parish, 67, 99, 116,
    119, 120, 121, 142, 148, 165,
    166, 177, 185, 186, 191
York Parish, 1, 13, 97, 111, 112, 113,
    116, 118, 119, 121, 142, 152,
    190
York River, 2, 128, 141, 161, 163
Yorkhampton, 126, 127, 151
Yorkhampton Parish, 18, 20, 21, 31,
    51, 60, 107, 108, 130, 132, 133,
    134, 136
Yorkshire, 167
Young, Alice, 187; Alies, 187

www.ingramcontent.com/pod-product-compliance
Lightning Source LLC
Chambersburg PA
CBHW061726270326
41928CB00011B/2132